Global Formation

Dedicated to my daughters
Cori and Mae

Global Formation

Structures of the World-Economy

Christopher Chase-Dunn

Basil Blackwell

First published 1989
Reprinted 1990
First published in paperback 1991

Basil Blackwell Inc.
3 Cambridge Center
Cambridge, Massachusetts 02142, USA

Basil Blackwell Ltd
108 Cowley Road, Oxford, OX4 1JF, UK

British Library Cataloging in Publication Data

Chase-Dunn, Christopher K.
Global formation : structures of the world-economy / Christopher Chase-Dunn.
p. cm.
Includes bibliographical references and index.
ISBN 1-55786-273-7
1. Economic history—1945– 2. Capitalism. I. Title.
HC59.C51424 1991 90-27533
330.9′ 045—dc20 CIP

British Library Cataloguing in Publication Data

A CIP catalogue record for this book is available from the British Library.

Typeset in Erhardt 10 on 12 point by Columns of Reading
Printed in Great Britain by
T.J. Press, Padstow, Cornwall

Contents

Preface

The structuralist theoretical approach to world-systems analysis developed in this book owes much to my professors at Stanford University, especially John W. Meyer and Michael T. Hannan, but also Morris Zelditch, Jr and Joseph P. Berger. The ideas emerged in proximate interaction with Walter Goldfrank, Volker Bornschier, Albert Bergesen, Albert Szymanski, Joan Sokolovsky, Stephen Bunker, Alejandro Portes, Craig Murphy, Katherine Verdery, Peter Evans, Michael Timberlake, Richard Rubinson, David Harvey, Vicente Navarro, and Neil Smith. They have been presented at meetings of the American Sociological Association, the Society for the Study of Social Problems and the International Studies Association. Earlier versions of several chapters have appeared in the *International Studies Quarterly*, *Comparative Political Studies*, *Politics and Society*, the *Humboldt Journal of Social Relations*, *Anthro-Tech*, and various of the Political Economy of the World-System *Annuals*. An earlier version of chapter 8 was co-authored with Joan Sokolovsky, part of chapter 11 with Richard Rubinson and part of chapter 15 with Aaron Pallas and Jeffrey Kentor. I have also received helpful commentary and critique on various chapters from Giovanni Arrighi, Robert Wuthnow, Kathleen Schwartzman, William R. Thompson, Christian Suter, Ulrich Pfister, Pat McGowan, David A. Smith, Patrick Nolan, Terry Boswell, Patrick Bond, Michael Johns, Phil Vilardo, Linda Pinkow, Roland Robertson, Richard G. Fox, Phil McMichael, Peter Grimes, and Ken O'Reilly.

I would like to thank Immanuel Wallerstein, Terence Hopkins, Giovanni Arrighi and the other scholars and staff of the Fernand Braudel Center at SUNY-Binghamton for encouraging me to formulate a structural approach to the study of world-systems. I hope I have done justice to their work. The collective project to develop a cumulative social science is often undermined by the pressure to individualize one's theoretical stance. I have followed Kent Flannery's (1982) advice against relieving yourself while standing on the shoulders of giants.

Also I am indebted to Shirley Sult for her help in typing and retyping the manuscript. My wife, Carolyn Hock, has provided support and inspiration while prodding me to exercise the body as well as the mind.

Christopher Chase-Dunn
Baltimore, Maryland

Introduction

This book proposes and begins to implement a structural approach to the study of the modern world-system. The stress is on the systemic patterns and the deep structural logic rather than on the conjunctural situations of particular areas or periods. My approach differs from the work of most other scholars utilizing the world-system perspective in several ways. In contrast to the stated position of the Fernand Braudel Center scholars, that theories are only heuristic devices,[1] I believe that theory construction is a valuable activity in its own right, and is a necessary part of the effort to build social science. Also, I have a fondness for quantitative empirical analysis as a method for testing theoretical propositions, although this does not prevent me from asking questions which are not quantifiable. These rather old-fashioned predilections have led me to utilize the historical interpretations of other world-system scholars to formulate causal models, and to explicitly confront conceptual and operational problems. This may seem oddly Victorian in the new age of post-structuralism, but literary trends come and go and it seems folly to abandon theory to the neofunctionalists and "rational choice" merchants.

Before outlining the intent and contents of this book I provide a short summary of the intellectual history of the world-system perspective for the general reader. Those unfamiliar with world-system terms are referred to the glossary at the end of the book. The world-system perspective seeks to analyze long-run/large-scale social change by combining the study of society-level processes with the study of intersocietal and transsocietal relations. It challenges the assumption that national societies (or tribes or city states) constitute independent units whose development can be understood without taking into account the systematic ways in which societies are linked to one another in the context of a larger network of material exchanges. These intersocietal and transsocietal networks of material exchanges are termed world-systems.

World-systems themselves have boundaries. Our modern world-system is global in the sense that all, or almost all, of the human beings on earth are strongly linked to it by virtue of their participation in economic and political networks which connect every continent. But world-systems of the past were not global. There have been intersocietal material interaction networks in small regions, unconnected with other regions by any sustained material exchange. The processes by which primitive and ancient world-systems developed and merged to become the contemporary global world-system are beyond the scope of this book.[2] Suffice it to say that the myriad of smaller systems became joined into a single large network by the end of the nineteenth century.

The shift of empirical focus from single societies to the world-system as a whole constitutes the most influential aspect of the world-system perspective as it has emerged from the scholars of the Fernand Braudel Center, especially Immanuel Wallerstein. But, in addition to this shift of focus, certain theoretical assumptions are important to Wallerstein's analysis. World-systems are understood as historical in the sense that the institutions which give them their distinctive character are human inventions. The institutional patterns which regulate competition and conflict within any world-system are themselves seen as historical creations of individual and collective actors. Historical world-systems, and the modes of interaction which they exhibit, come into existence and eventually go out of existence. They are born and they die.

An important structure of the modern world-system is the core/periphery hierarchy – a historically constructed stratification system composed of dominant core states, dependent peripheral areas and intermediate semi-peripheral states. In Wallerstein's formulation the basic logic of the modern world-system is capitalism, a mode of production which is defined as a central feature of the system as a whole. The modern world-system is a capitalist "world-economy" which emerged in Europe and Spanish America in the sixteenth century, and then expanded to dominate the whole globe by the end of the nineteenth century. A "world-economy" is defined as a world-system which contains multiple societies, multiple states, and a single economic division of labor, while a "world-empire" is an economic network across multiple cultures over which a single encompassing state apparatus has formed. The modern world-system is a world-economy, while many previous world-systems, such as the Roman Empire and the Chinese Empire, were world-empires.

Wallerstein defines capitalism as commodity production in which there are different sorts of class relations – wage labor in the core and more politically coerced forms of labor control in the periphery. Commodity production is defined in the Marxist sense – the production of commodities for profitable sale in a price-setting market. Wallerstein understands all areas within the contemporary global political economy to be within the bounds of the capitalist world-economy, including the socialist states.

This perspective on social change derives from, and is a modification of, Marx's effort to understand modern society. It focuses on capitalism as a mode of production, although it denies that capitalism can be understood by looking only at the "advanced" countries. At the beginning of the twentieth century many Marxists turned their attention to imperialism. V. I. Lenin (1965) saw imperialism as a stage of capitalism. Rosa Luxemburg (1968) saw imperialism as a necessary consequence of the operation of Marx's model of capitalist development. Nikolai Bukharin's (1973) *Imperialism and World Economy* is the most important early precursor of the world-system perspective.

Mainstream American sociologists after World War II used Talcott Parsons' digestion of Durkheim, Weber, and Pareto to construct modernization theory, which was applied to the "less developed" societies. This approach saw traditional institutions as blocking the development of modern economic and political institutions in the "backward" countries. Karl Polanyi's work (1944, 1977) during the post-World War II years carried on the project of the turn-of-the-century Marxists in analyzing capitalism on a global scale. Polanyi, a Hungarian non-Marxist socialist, emphasized the historicity of modes of integration, especially the market system. This perspective, combined with the Marxist legacy, was to shape the theoretical approach of the Braudel Center scholars.

In Latin America economists, sociologists, and political scientists reacted to modernization theory by analyzing how local societal features had been produced and were sustained by hierarchical international and transnational economic and political institutions. Dependency theory evolved in many different directions, but some of the scholars who applied and synthesized this approach moved toward the formulation of a theory of global capitalism, especially Andre Gunder Frank and Samir Amin. They, and Immanuel Wallerstein, developed the world-system perspective which this book seeks to theorize, although the Wallersteinian version will be the one most intensively considered here.

The main intent of this book is to formulate a structural theory of the capitalist world-economy, and to address the major theoretical debates which have arisen in the social science literature about world-systems. As Sidney Mintz (1985) has written, an explanation should not be "just one more chorus of the bone song." We must be explicit about which are the key relationships which compose the structures of the world-economy, the mechanisms which reproduce these structures, and the contradictions which create pressures for structural change. The theory I develop extends Marx's accumulation model to the world-system as a whole. It focuses on the world class structure and the core/periphery hierarchy as the main contradictions around which conflict and competition in the global political economy turn, and it reconceptualizes capital as a relational institution of domination and exploitation which *includes* states and the interstate system as part of capitalist relations of production.

The main structures of the world-economy are:

1 the world class system;
2 the core/periphery hierarchy;
3 the interstate system, and
4 the world market.

These are defined and interrelated in the chapters that follow.

A second intent of this book is to summarize the recent empirical research which is germane to our knowledge of the modern world-system. This burgeoning corpus is already large, and any effort to be complete becomes quickly obsolete. Since I am more sympathetic with formal comparative and quantitative studies than many of the other world-system scholars, I have tried to pay special attention to these. I have also included many studies which do not explicitly use world-system concepts, but which nevertheless examine phenomena which I deem to be relevant to world-system theoretical questions.

Part I argues that we can best understand the global system in which we live by defining capitalism in a way which builds on Marx but which modifies his conceptualization to some extent. Once we have redefined capitalism, the continuities of recent centuries become more visible. The major theoretical debates about world-systems and modes of production are addressed, and a new formulation is proposed. Then I describe a set of processes which are hypothesized to operate at the level of the world-system as a whole. This is presented as a schema of world-system constants, cycles, and trends, and this schema is then compared with the idea of stages of capitalism. Finally I discuss world culture and the role of normative integration and cultural domination in the reproduction of the global system.

Part II examines the relationships between states and the capitalist world-economy. The nature of the capitalist state in the context of the world-system, and the relative internal and external strength of core and peripheral states, are considered. The multicentric interstate system of unequally powerful and competing states is analyzed as the main political structure behind the reproduction of capitalist relations of production. Geopolitics and commodity production are interdependent forms of competition which reproduce one another. Chapter 9 formulates an explanation for the hegemonic sequence – the rise and decline of hegemonic core powers – and reviews related research.

Part III focuses on the core/periphery hierarchy. The analytic definition of core production is specified as relatively capital intensive commodity production. Definitions of the semiperiphery and the idea of boundaries between core, peripheral, and semiperipheral zones are examined. The mechanisms which reproduce the core/periphery hierarchy are described and the crossnational research which examines the effects of these mechanisms on national development is reviewed. I argue that the core/periphery hierarchy is necessary to the survival of capitalism. The problems of absolute immiseration of the periphery and the growing gap between core and periphery are considered. Chapter 13 proposes a hypothetical causal model of the relationships among several world-system fluctuations and reviews research which is relevant to this model.

Part IV considers metatheoretical stance and methodological problems. I locate my own historical/structural theorizing further toward the nomothetic end of the idiographic/nomothetic continuum relative to the position of the Braudel Center scholars. I defend structural theory against the attacks made by historicists.

On method I hold that the faults of mainstream social science are mostly problems of theoretical substance rather than research methods. While I abhor raw empiricism as much as the next fellow, I see the comparative and quantitative methods developed by modern social science as important tools for studying world-systems and for evaluating world-system theories.

The last chapter examines the implications of the theoretical conclusions in this book and the gaps in existing empirical research. Though this book is only the first step toward specifying and testing theories of the world-system, I cannot refrain from making a few remarks about the possibilities for transforming the capitalist world-economy into a more humane and peaceful world society, though these statements are not entirely deduceable from the earlier chapters. This is justified by the grave implications of some of the findings, especially the apparent tendency of the capitalist world-economy to regularly produce wars among core states, a systemic feature which, in combination with the nuclear arsenal, portends worldwide tragedy.

Here is a more detailed summary of the main conclusions reached in each chapter:

Part I addresses the substantive theoretical problems raised by a structural approach to the world-system perspective. It is an effort to go beyond the use of the world-system as a new empirical frame of reference to an explicit theory of world-system structures and processes. Chapter 1 presents a reformulation of Marx's accumulation model of capitalist development which utilizes concepts produced by the Braudel Center scholars. Contrary to the popular misconception that world-system theory emphasizes exchange relations over production relations, capitalism is defined as a system in which commodity production for profit occurs in the context of differentiated forms of labor control. Production relations are understood to differ in the extent to which labor is commodified. The class structure of world capitalism is embedded in an interstate system of unequally powerful political organizations (states), and employs politically protected, wage, and coerced forms of labor control. These forms of labor control roughly correspond to the core/periphery hierarchy.

The world-system is objectively stratified into social classes (e.g. world bourgeoisie, world proletariat, intermediate strata) but the political activities of these classes tend to be oriented toward particular "national" state apparatuses. This is the reason why many Marxists argue that the relevant perspective on class struggle is a national (or "internal") one, but it is also an important structural basis for the reproduction of divisions within the world working class. The core/periphery hierarchy and nationalism crosscut and disorganize working-class solidarity, and perpetuate the reproduction of capitalist accumulation.

Chapter 1 stakes out a position on the mode of production issue which differs from both: (a) orthodox Marxists (i.e. capitalism = the wage system); and (b) Immanuel Wallerstein's assumption that a mode of production is a feature of a whole world-system (the "totality assumption"), and thus there can only be one mode of production in a world-system.

While I claim that it is advantageous to include both core and peripheral forms of capitalist exploitation within the capitalist mode of production, the identification of the mode of production with the whole world-system creates grievous problems when we try to analyze the transformation of modes of production. Therefore I introduce the distinction between the spatial boundaries of a world-system and the logical boundaries of modes of production. This enables us to study how a mode of production becomes dominant within a world-system and how modes of production may be articulated with one another within a single world-system. I employ a typology of modes of production suggested by Amin (1980a) and Wolf (1982), except that capitalism is redefined to include both core and peripheral forms of labor exploitation for profit.

Chapter 2 describes a schema of the dynamics of systemic constants, cycles, and trends which are characteristic of the whole world-system. The systemic constants are those basic features of the capitalist mode of production described in chapter 1. The systemic cycles include the long business cycle (i.e. the Kondratieff wave), the hegemonic sequence of the rise and decline of core states, the cycle of core war severity, and the cycle of core/periphery trade and control. The systemic trends include the expansion to new populations and territories, the expansion and deepening of commodity relations, state-formation, growth of firms, the transnationalization of capital, the increasing capital intensity of production, and proletarianization.

Chapter 3 compares the above schema of cycles and trends to the periodizations of capitalist development advanced by other Marxists. It is concluded that the various hypothesized stages of capitalism are more elegantly explained as periodic combinations of world-system cycles and trends.

In chapter 4 the schema outlined in chapter 2 is used to consider the significance of developments which have occurred in the world-system since World War II, such as the decolonization of almost the whole periphery, the growth of transnational corporations, industrialization in the periphery and the semiperiphery, the growth of international organizations, and the increasing number of socialist states. It is concluded that no really qualitative changes have occurred. Rather, the seemingly new institutional and organizational forms which are observed are functional equivalents of older forms which correspond to long-standing (but not ahistorical) patterns.

Chapter 5 discusses the cultural aspects of integration and domination in the contemporary world-system. It compares the contemporary capitalist world-economy with earlier world-systems in terms of the centrality of cultural consensus and ideological hegemony in maintaining cohesion and order. The particular mix of normative, economic, and coercive integration which characterizes the contemporary system relies most heavily on market interdependence and political–military domination, although cultural hegemony plays a supporting role. The cultural hegemony of the core powers is systematically undermined by the reproduction of nations and states, and by the uneven development of capitalist commodity production which sometimes raises non-Western nations (e.g. Japan) to core status. Resistance to cultural domination is relatively easy to organize even in peripheral areas, and is legitimated to some extent by the multicentric interstate system and its associated support for national identities. The world market and the interstate system themselves require a substratum of cultural consensus without which crosscultural trade is problematic. But this culturally-based "trade ecumene" is a minimal level of agreement about media of exchange, contract, and diplomatic protocol. It does not constitute a normative order in which Durkheimian processes of moral boundary maintenance operate.

Part II focuses more directly on states and the interstate system. Contrary to the popular notion that capitalism is an economic subsystem of private firms producing for markets, and contrary to the characterization of the world-system perspective as "economistic," I emphasize the importance of states in the capitalist world-system. Chapter 6 discusses the contention that core states are strong, while peripheral states are weak. A distinction is made between internal and external state strength. With regard to external strength all parties agree that core states are generally stronger. With regard to internal state strength there is considerable controversy, but empirical evidence is presented which supports the idea that peripheral states are weaker internally than are core states. I also discuss research on the relationship between regime form and the position of states in the core/periphery hierarchy. The structural processes which sustain relatively democratic states in the core and relatively authoritarian states in the periphery are examined. The oscillation between authoritarian and populist regimes in many semiperipheral states is also considered.

Chapter 7 focuses on the multicentric interstate system of unequally powerful states. This is conceptualized as the main political structure of the capitalist world-economy. It is argued that political–military competition and competition for shares of world markets are complementary and interdependent aspects of the struggle to appropriate world surplus value. These types of competition should be analyzed as composing a single systemic logic rather than as two different modes of interaction. The reproduction of a competitive world market of capitalist commodity producers is argued to be dependent on the structure of the interstate system, and conversely, the reproduction of the interstate system is dependent on the dynamics of competition among capitals. Chapter 7 also examines certain features of the interstate system which are rarely discussed in international relations theory. In addition to the rarity of attempts to impose imperium over the core and the consistent failure of those attempts which have been made, we must wonder why hegemonic core powers never even propose such a policy. It is argued that a world-system in which the capitalist mode of production is dominant is a fertile context for the success of core states which pursue a strategy combining military control of trade routes with accumulation through profit-taking, rather than geopolitical territorial conquest and tribute-gathering. Thus it is not the hegemons, but rather challenging core powers, who set off on the road of world imperium. But these challenges do not succeed because they are incapable of obtaining sufficient support in a system in which expanding and deepening commodity production and the continuation of the multicentric interstate system hold greater promise for national ruling classes than the presentiment of shares within a world imperium.

Chapter 8 further considers these same problems, arguing that it is not a matter of "economic versus political–military" power, but rather the particular institutional features of the capitalist mode of production which explain the processes of the interstate system. The centrality of markets and capitalist accumulation undercuts the tendency to empire-formation. This chapter also compares the modern interstate system with earlier world-empires and interstate systems, and discusses the functions of world wars in restructuring the distribution of international power in response to the uneven development of national economies. It is argued that world wars are a necessary, cyclical, and structural component of the expansion and deepening of capitalism.

Chapter 9 focuses on the causes of the rise and decline of hegemonic core powers. Contrary to many characterizations, the modern world-system is not a monolithic structure of domination with a single center. Not only is there continual resistance from peripheral areas, but the core itself is multicentric and is characterized by uneven development resulting in upward and downward mobility. Empirical studies of the hegemonic sequence are reviewed, including Joshua Goldstein's demonstration of a strong link between Kondratieff economic cycles and fluctuations in war severity. Goldstein's research provides the most convincing empirical demonstration of the existence of world-system processes to date, as well as chilling support for the notion that world war is a "normal" outcome of the operation of these processes. Efforts to measure the rise and decline of hegemons are reviewed, and the implications of hegemonic sequence studies for the current era of declining US hegemony are considered.

Part III examines the core/periphery hierarchy as a structural feature of the world-system. This hierarchy is understood as an institution of socially structured inequality which is reproduced rather than eliminated by "development." The whole world-system develops but the core/periphery hierarchy, despite a certain amount of upward and downward mobility, remains a structural feature of the larger system. Chapter 10 reviews different terminologies and contending analytic definitions of the core/periphery hierarchy. An argument is made in favor of the notion of core production as relatively capital intensive production. The spatial nature of the core/periphery dimension is described as a nested hierarchy of multilevel and overlapping regional and organizational boundaries. The notion that core, periphery, and semiperiphery are distinct zones with measurably distinct boundaries is described as a useful simplifying metaphor for analytic purposes. But I suggest that the empirical core/periphery hierarchy more probably corresponds to a multidimensional set of continuous distributions.

The concept of the semiperiphery is understood as a designation for two types of intermediate positions. The various efforts which have been made to measure the position of countries in the core/periphery hierarchy are described and critiqued. I review research which reveals important structural differences among peripheral areas due to differences in the nature of the indigenous societies before incorporation into the modern world-system. And I describe important long-term reorganizations of the institutional and structural nature of the core/periphery hierarchy which have occurred over the past centuries. I then dispute recent arguments by economic historians which deny that exploitation of the periphery was an important factor in the emergence of capitalist industrialization in the core.

Chapter 11 examines various mechanisms which are argued to reproduce the core/periphery hierarchy such as wage differentials, trade composition, different forms of core versus peripheral class formation, the disarticulation of economic structures in the periphery, transnational corporate exploitation, and statecentric explanations which focus on differential processes of state formation and political class struggle. My own argument is a political theory of differential outcomes of class struggle which explains why the core/periphery hierarchy is necessary for the reproduction of capitalism and how capitalism reproduces the core/periphery hierarchy. Then I review the crossnational research which has been done on the various proposed mechanisms which reproduce international inequalities.

Chapter 12 examines recent trends in characteristics of core and peripheral countries and the empirical research which documents these trends. It also discusses the idea of absolute immiseration as it is applied to the capitalist world-system. Research reveals that the magnitude of relative core/periphery inequalities has not diminished in recent decades, but there is little evidence to support the claim of periphery-wide absolute immiseration. The consequences of world-system inequalities thus stem primarily from relative differences in a world-economy in which most of the periphery is in fact "developing" relative to itself over time, but the differences between core and periphery are not diminishing.

Chapter 13 describes a hypothetical model of cyclical changes in the core/periphery hierarchy and the temporal and causal relations between this and the hegemonic sequence of the rise and decline of core powers and changes in the level of competition/conflict among core powers. The chapter describes research which is germane to this model, including evidence of the existence of cyclical international debt crises.

Part IV confronts metatheoretical and methodological problems which surround the effort to construct and test world-system theories. Chapter 14 describes a continuum of metatheoretical orientations in the social sciences which extends from completely historicist description at one end to completely ahistorical generalization at the other. Various intermediate points on this continuum are discussed, and a case is made in favor of a more structural (less historicist) approach to world-system theory. The attack on structural Marxism is reviewed and a defense of theory is proposed. My own critique of Althusser et al. is both substantive (the failure to use a world-system frame of reference) and methodological (the substitution of rationalist critique and political debate for systematic empirical research). Nevertheless I find the distinctions between mode of production and social formation, and between structural causation and conjunctural events, to be useful for world-system theory.

The ontological status of world-systems and other objects of social scientific study are compared and the frequently made erroneous assumption that there is a necessary relationship between spatial scale and level of abstraction is contested. The potential relevance of structural world-system theory for political practice is also considered.

Chapter 15 examines the question of appropriate research methods for studying world-systems. Those who have argued that comparative and quantitative methods are inappropriate are confronted with arguments about the assumptions behind formal modeling and comparative data analysis. I contend that we can make good use of the generalized logic of time series analysis to study processes which operate at the level of the whole world-system. Several problems arising from the application of time series analysis are discussed. It is also argued that the quantitative comparison of smaller units of analysis (e.g. nation states) is indeed relevant for our understanding of some world-system processes. But findings about relationships among characteristics of e.g. nation states cannot be used as evidence for relationships among analogous features of the world-system as a whole – the so-called aggregation problem. On the other hand, knowledge of the causality of processes occurring within and between nation states is indeed relevant for our understanding of some world-system processes because not all these operate at the level of the whole.

The existence of strong world-system processes implies a problem for cross-national comparisons: the non-independence of cases – Galton's problem. I propose a solution to Galton's problem which builds world-system processes and interstate relations into the causal model for cross national analysis. Several different research designs for world-system analysis are described and compared, and a new design for testing multilevel models of causality is proposed. The chapter ends with a consideration of the possibility of systematic comparative research on a large number of world-systems, a research design which has conceptual and feasibility problems but which may nevertheless be quite useful for testing propositions about the relationship between world-systems and modes of production.

Chapter 16 examines the implications of this book for future studies of world-systems and discusses the matter of contemporary political practice. The motivation behind this work is the feeling that we don't really understand the nature of the social system in which we are living, a world of our own creation and yet beyond our control. It was a similar uneasiness that motivated Marx and the other social scientists of the nineteenth century. The efforts to synthesize the theories of the classical sociologists have not produced a theory which adequately explains the social phenomena we see in the twentieth century, especially the contradictory nature of our world-system. Talcott Parsons performed such a synthesis and the outcome was modernization theory, a poor vehicle now largely discredited. And yet simply returning to Marx, as many critics of modernization theory have done, is not really adequate either. The twentieth century needs its own Marx before we can have a new Gramsci or a new Lenin.

Many Marxists (e.g. E. P. Thompson, 1978), have abandoned theory for historical studies, arguing that theory has been used badly by the Stalinists. Theory is like technology. Good theory may be used for bad ends. And yet theory is both potentially useful for humane ends, and, I would contend, an end in itself. I find no massive contradiction between scholarship and political practice, although they are certainly not the same activity. The immediate intent of this book is theoretical. The ultimate goal, however, is to help us understand the world in order to change it.

PART I

The Whole System

This section addresses some basic explanatory problems which have emerged from the effort to theorize about the capitalist world-economy. Criticisms of the world-system perspective by other Marxists are addressed, an explication of the Wallersteinian version is performed, and certain of its assumptions are critiqued and reformulated. I will outline a perspective on modes of production in general, and an argument for modifying Marx's definition of capitalism. The question of world-system boundaries will be considered, as will the relationship between classes and the core/periphery hierarchy in so far as they are related to our understanding of capitalism as a mode of production. The Wallersteinian "totality assumption," which implies that each world-system has only one mode of production, is criticized and replaced with an analysis of logical boundaries between modes of production within historical world-systems.

The intent of this section is to move our analysis of world-systems from an orienting perspective which is used to interpret history toward a new theory of the underlying tendencies of development. I do this by explicating a *strongly theoretical* interpretation of the literature produced by the scholars of the Fernand Braudel Center, and by responding to the theoretical critiques of this literature.

There is a continuum between two polar types of explanation in the social sciences: at one extreme is ideographic historicism (the claim that each event, village, country, period, etc. is unique); while at the other extreme is completely nomothetic ahistoricism (the attempt to specify one theory which explains all social systems, small and large, simple and complex). Immanuel Wallerstein's work is consciously located on this continuum at a midpoint which is more historical than that of the structural Marxists, and yet which is more generalizing than that of most historians. Wallerstein interprets the history of "historical systems," inventing theoretical concepts that seem to be helpful along the way. By a "strongly theoretical" reading of Wallerstein I mean to formulate a causal and structuralist theory out of the insights and loosely defined concepts which he has produced.

Wallerstein's usage of the term "historical systems" demonstrates his dialectical view that whole socio-economic systems are both systemic and indeterminate to a certain extent. The real question is: exactly how systemic is the world-system? Fernand Braudel (1984:70) suggests that Wallerstein's approach is "a little too systematic." My position is that it may be possible to determine just how systemic the world-system is by clearly formulating models and testing them against empirical data.

There are those who argue that a science of society is impossible; that we cannot explain and predict social change. Human beings, the objects of analysis, are ostensibly intelligent and have free will and so, it is argued, attempts to predict their behavior are doomed. In addition, sociological theorizing is reflexive – we are trying to understand ourselves and therefore objectivity is impossible. Also, once a prediction is known the object of the prediction may intentionally (and obstinately!) choose to contradict it.

The attainments of social science do not yet completely discredit these claims, although I would contend that we are not nearly as ignorant as some critics of social science seem to think. Marx and Weber provide us giant shoulders on which to stand, and we ought not underestimate their value. But no one would dispute that social science is yet young. Our paradigms seem more reactive than cumulative, and we haven't yet attained sufficient consensus to constitute "normal science" in the Kuhnian sense. This might be because human behavior is impossible to explain and predict, or simply because we haven't yet penetrated its deep structure. My effort to theorize about world-systems posits the usefulness of models of deep social structure and begins to specify one.[1]

The search for a social "genetic code" can proceed in a number of directions, as Marx pointed out in his short discussion of the "method of political economy" (Marx, 1973:100–8). The Althusserian structuralists tend to become encompassed by their own sanitized logical world of textual interpretation and rational argument. They never, or rarely, allow the messy empirical world to penetrate. Marx pointed out that political economy must alternately move from the concrete to the abstract, and then back again. Deduction and induction are both necessary operations.

Why would it be helpful if we had a formal theory of world-system development? In addition to all the usual scientific desiderata – simplicity, explanation, prediction – such a theory might help us to avoid self-destruction, and to construct a more humane, less exploitative world society.

A theory of social change, instead of implying a philosophy of fatalistic determinism, can itself be an aid in our effort to control our own collective future.

This last goal of theorizing should be an intended consequence which is kept in mind in the course of the theory-building project, although we must avoid letting political criteria determine our theoretical decisions. The right combination of progressive intent and scientific open-mindedness is difficult to specify, but it is clear that these two should interact without either dominating the other.

MODES OF PRODUCTION IN GENERAL

In this introductory section I will discuss some general theoretical questions which provide a framework for the effort to come to grips with what is unique to the logic of the modern world-system. What is the general relationship between historical world-systems and modes of production? And what is the best way to conceptualize the boundaries of world-systems? These questions are related, and some of the simplifying assumptions made by Wallerstein have caused unnecessary confusion and disputation.

By mode of production we mean the basic underlying logic which any social system exhibits. For Marx this was necessarily related to the problem of material production. He focused on the social relations and institutions that organize production and distribution of the material goods required for the reproduction of a society and its members. In class societies a very fundamental set of institutions which are the center of modes of production are those *social relations of production* which allow a class of exploiters to appropriate surplus product from a class of direct producers. These institutions – forms of labor control – vary across different modes of production.

A related but somewhat different way of conceptualizing social logics was developed by Karl Polanyi. Polanyi (1977) designated three modes of societal integration which are said to characterize exchange in very different types of societies: normative, political, and market. *Reciprocity*, the normative distribution of resources according to culturally agreed upon rules of justice, exists in all societies, but is the most important mode of integration in "communal" or kin-based classless, stateless societies. *Redistribution*, or the politically determined distribution of goods becomes more important once specialized coercive organizations (states) have emerged to monopolize legitimate violence. States and empires use political organization and formally organized coercion to extract surplus product from direct producers. State-formation proceeds in tandem with class-formation, such that privileged positions with respect to basic resources become associated with life-long (not age-based) statuses. The emergence of hereditary aristocratic lineages usually precedes primary state-formation. Reciprocity does not cease to exist within class/state societies, but it becomes articulated with, and dominated by, the logic of "redistributive" or better, *tributary* modes of production and distribution. There are many types and varieties of the tributary modes of production, some very centralized, some very decentralized (i.e. feudalism). And the institutional forms of class relations vary greatly within the tributary modes. But the logic of politically coercive organizations dominates both class struggle and intersocietal competition.

The third type of integration proposed by Polanyi is the *price-setting market*. A market is not identical with all exchange. Exchange may be regulated according to custom (reciprocity), according to law (redistribution), or by competitive buying and selling. The gathering of people in a village square to exchange goods does not necessarily constitute a market in Polanyi's sense. The rates of exchange (prices) must be determined (or greatly affected) by the buying and selling decisions of a large number of separate actors trying to maximize their individual returns. A price-setting market is, of course, an ideal type, the same one which is at the center of classical and neoclassical economic theory. But Polanyi was at pains to point out that this form of interaction is not a natural and universal way in which all people exchange with one another. Rather it is an historical creation which emerges under certain conditions and which becomes the dominant form of exchange in a certain type of society. The process of commodification, the transformation of land, labor, and wealth into commodities which are exchanged in price-setting markets, becomes the object of analysis rather than a background assumption about human nature and the propensity to truck, barter, and maximize profit.

A major theoretical problem has been how to combine Marx's modes of production with Polanyi's modes of integration. Samir Amin (1980a) and Eric Wolf (1982) have found similar solutions regarding the conceptualization of precapitalist modes of production.[2] They agree with Polanyi that stateless, classless societies have a mode of production in which normative obligations, usually defined in terms of kinship ties, regulate production and exchange. Amin terms these "communal," while Wolf calls them "kin-based" modes of production. Ethnographic studies (e.g. Sahlins, 1972) support the notion that reciprocity is the dominant form of exchange and that true market relations are rarely found in such societies.

With regard to Polanyi's redistributive mode of integration, other theorists have pointed out that the term "redistributive" is somewhat unfortunate. It was derived from the study of chiefdoms, societies which are somewhat more stratified than most stateless societies, but not so stratified as societies in which true states and social classes have emerged. Neil Smelser (1959) suggests that the kind of appropriation of resources which occurs with the emergence of states and empires should rather be termed "mobilization."

Amin and Wolf propose that social systems in which political coercion is the dominant relation of production and distribution should generally be termed "tributary modes of production." Feudalism is one such mode of production, and so are the so-called "asiatic" and "slave" modes designated by other Marxists. The tributary modes differ from one another in terms of class relations (i.e. serfdom, clientilism, slavery, tenantry, corvée, helotry, etc.)[3] and also in terms of the degree of centralization of state power – feudalism versus absolutism. But they all share the feature that political power and coercion are the main determinants of outcomes in competition among classes, states, and empires.

Robert Brenner (1977) rightly located Wallerstein's theoretical perspective on the terrain of a dispute about the transition to capitalism in Europe which took place among Marxists in the 1950s. The dispute really involved two problems. One was how to conceptualize exchange, and the importance of commodity production as a basis of capitalism. Brenner contended that Wallerstein and the "neo-Smithian" Marxists before him (e.g. Paul Sweezy, 1976) put too much emphasis on the emergence of markets. Brenner argued that the most central determinant of the logic of a mode of production is the form of class relations. Following Dobb (1963), Brenner tended to limit his notion of class relations to those institutions which regulate the immediate relations between a direct producer and his/her immediate exploiter at the "point of production."

A second issue which threaded through the Brenner critique was the matter of "internal" versus "external" determinants. The many Marxists who have accepted Brenner's critique of the world-system perspective associate the alleged emphasis on exchange with the discussion of international trade. This is thought to depreciate the importance of internal class relations and class struggle. The problem of "internal to what" is usually unexamined. Some emphasize the firm or the plantation or the village. Others are thinking about the nation state or the region.

The Wallersteinian perspective was misperceived by Brenner and the others who have adopted the "exchange versus class struggle" criticism. Wallerstein was not arguing that exchange or trade is a more important aspect of a mode of production than class relations. Rather, he was pointing to the multilevel character of systems of exploitation and emphasizing the mystifying consequences of characterizing all international trade as equal exchange. Class relations and relations of coercion and exploitation exist at several levels: within firms (as the important work of Braverman (1974), Burawoy (1979) and Edwards (1979) has recently illuminated), but also at the level of localities, regions, nation states, and the core/periphery hierarchy. These relations can all be understood broadly as class relations, or production relations in the Marxist sense. And the internal/external distinction is as mystifying as the idea that international trade (or wage labor) is always equal exchange. Wallerstein contends that it is the boundaries between organizations, and nation states, as well as the core/periphery hierarchy, which divide those oppositional forces which would challenge the logic of capitalism.

Following Polanyi, Wallerstein points out that exchange is not simply exchange. Each material exchange has an institutional underpinning which we must investigate in order to understand the logic of the system we are studying. Some exchanges are customary, some are politically determined and some are in the context of a price-setting market. And, as Marx clearly believed, much of the logic of capitalism is contained in the institution of commodity production for the market.

Commodification is the process by which formerly non-market-mediated activities come to take the commodity form. It is important to understand that commodification is not an either/or matter. There may be more or less of it in different realms or activities within a social system. We know from studying the historical development of commodity production that archaic wealth (prestige goods) was first commodified in the sense of becoming a generalized medium of exchange – money. Land slowly became something which was alienable and saleable. And the commodification of food, raw materials, services, and labor occurred in spurts, in interstitial areas, and to varying degrees within the tributary modes of production. Precapitalist empires, themselves still dominated by the logic of the tributary mode of production, became more and more commercialized. Wealth, land, and labor increasingly became commodified, but the logic of market integration still played only a subordinate role.

Labor is never a perfect commodity. Neither is wealth or land. We must speak of degrees of labor commodification. Customary work relations are the least commodified because obligations are usually personal and dependent on normative consensus and internalized values. Politically structured labor relations based on coercion may become partially commodified. Thus slave labor is more commodified than serfdom, and is more manipulable and congruent with the logic of profitable commodity production. Consideration of costs and profits, the price of slaves, and the ability to buy more slaves or sell them off, lent plantation and latifundian enterprises a rather capitalistic nature even within precapitalist world-systems.

Wage labor is the most perfectly commodified form of labor control because the price tends to be regulated by the cost of the reproduction of labor power; the capitalist can buy only the labor time he needs, and so wage labor is even more flexible for the cost-conscious capitalist commodity producer than is slave labor. Labor time, rather than the laborer, has become a commodity. And there is the additional benefit that exploitation is more opaque, because the exchange of wages for labor time is defined as an equal exchange. Slavery is less easily legitimated.

Both Marx and Wallerstein see commodity production as necessary to capitalism, but Marx argued that "fully formed" capitalism can only be based on wage labor, while Wallerstein argues that peripheral capitalism can be based on less commodified forms of labor control. Two points should be made about this definitional disagreement. The first is that it can be agreed that wage labor is important to capitalism, because it is the most commodified form of labor control. But it may be unwise to define other types of labor control as necessarily non-capitalist for two reasons. The first is that there may be different levels of capitalism. Marx acknowledges this when he discusses merchant capitalism and simple commodity production. And secondly, these allegedly less capitalist forms of capitalism may be articulated or integrated in systematic ways with "full" capitalism.

Even more importantly, as I shall argue in chapter 1, the survival of capitalism may depend on the articulation of different forms of labor control. In chapter 2 I build upon earlier work to hypothesize a schema of empirically observable cycles and trends which are thought to be characteristics of the contemporary world-system as a whole. Chapter 3 compares the stages of capitalism suggested by some Marxists with the idea of cycles of world-system development. In chapter 4 the schema developed in chapter 2 is employed in a consideration of structural changes in the world-system which have occurred since World War II. Chapter 5 examines the nature of global culture and the role it plays in the reproduction and transformation of the contemporary world-system. Let us now examine further the question of how capitalism is most usefully defined.

1

The Deep Structure: Real Capitalism

The goal of this chapter is to reformulate Marx's theory of capitalist accumulation using insights provided by the analysis of the modern world-system. We begin by exploring three approaches to theorizing about the deep structural dynamics of the world-system: (a) a purely formal approach to the specification of logical boundaries between modes of production; (b) the process of commodification and its limits; and (c) the problem of world classes. The epistemological assumptions behind this effort to theorize the world-system are described and defended in chapter 14. After reformulating Marx's theory we will critically evaluate one of Wallerstein's simplifying assumptions, the idea that the mode of production is necessarily a feature of a whole world-system, and the corollary that each world-system has only one mode of production.

My ultimate goal is to reformulate Marx's theory to take into account those systematic aspects of capitalist development which Marx neglected. This requires:

1 a clear specification of Marx's model;
2 a critique of its inadequacies in the light of our knowledge of world-system processes;
3 a reformulation of the concepts and basic axioms; and
4 a test of the new formulation against contemporary and historical social reality.

This book begins these tasks, but it certainly does not finish them.

MARX'S MODEL OF CAPITALIST ACCUMULATION

Marx began his explication of the laws of capitalist development with a dialectical analysis of a fundamental institution of capitalism – the commodity. From this institutional form, which allegedly contains the secrets of the deep structure of capitalism, he derives the law of value, the roles of capital and labor, and the accumulation of capital through the production and appropriation of surplus value. This theoretical formulation has several advantages. It is elegant. It focuses on what are indubitably essential features of the capitalist mode of production – market exchange, commodified labor, the concentration of means of production in private hands, and the accumulation of capital by means of the production of commodities and the exploitation of commodified labor.

There are two main issues which divide Marxists over the definition of the basic characteristics of the capitalist mode of production: (a) the nature of class relations in capitalism, and (b) the importance of the state and the interstate system for capitalism. Marx's most abstract model of the capitalist accumulation process, as presented in volume 1 of *Capital* (1967a), assumed a closed system in which there is a single *laissez-faire* state standing behind property relations, but not directly engaging in the accumulation process. The model also assumed only two classes: capitalists owning and controlling the major means of production, and proletarians selling their labor power for wages in a competitive labor market.

Marx defined capitalism as a system in which ownership and control of the major means of production are in the hands of private (not state) entrepreneurs who produce commodities for a competitive market. For Marx the commodification of labor is primarily through a competitive labor market – the wage system – in which proletarians who own no means of production are "free" to sell their labor power to capitalists. He developed his model on the basis of his observations of nineteenth-century British capitalism. He assumed that Britain was the highest form of capitalist development and thus that the analysis of British industry should reveal the essential characteristics of the capitalist mode of production. He expected that all national societies would develop along the same basic path that had been followed by the British (Marx 1967a: 8–9).

Thus, according to Marx, the basic characteristics of fully developed capitalism are:

1. *Generalized commodity production* The production of commodities for profitable sale on a price-setting (competitive) market.
2. *Private ownership of the major means of production* Private capitalists accumulate capital by making investment decisions within a logic of profit maximization. This implies that the capitalist state does not

directly interfere in investment decisions or in the market, but rather provides legitimation and order, using its power primarily to guarantee external defense and internal peace consistent with the institutions of private property.

3 *The wage system* Labor power is a commodity sold by proletarians (who do not own means of production) to capitalist owners of the means of production in a competitive labor market.

The problem with Marx's formulation is not so much what it includes as what it leaves out. Marx seeks to overcome the vacuities of classical political economy by conceptualizing capitalism as an historical system which came into existence through the use of force (see *Capital*, volume 1, part 8) and which will pass out of existence through the development of its own internal contradictions. But, in seeking analytical elegance in his specification, Marx abstracts from a number of processes which should be included within the specification of the capitalist mode of production. For example, in volume 1 of *Capital* Marx assumes:

1 the existence of an English-type caretaker state which does not directly interfere in the process of development;
2 no international trade – a closed system;
3 a completely competitive relationship among capitals; and
4 the complete commodification of labor power such that there exists only a class of workers with no institutional power to obtain more than the subsistence wage, and a class of capitalists who own and control all means of production.

Certainly simplifying assumptions are required in any theory which attempts to specify the essential tendencies of a mode of production. We should not include sunspots or climate change in our theory. Some processes must be designated as exogenous, while others, we hope, capture the kernel of the social system we are studying. The problem I am raising is that Marx may have distorted the kernel somewhat by his choice of simplifying assumptions.

My reading of the world-system literature leads me to question the wisdom of several of Marx's theoretical decisions. It is not a matter of the simplifying assumptions being incorrect in one or another concrete empirical situation. This is true of every theoretical abstraction. It is rather that the essential processes of capitalist development may be distorted by the particular assumptions made by Marx. Marx attributed a great deal to historical specificity, as have many Marxists since. But his theory was an abstraction from the complications of history. The approach I will outline here will do the same thing, except that it will draw the boundaries between the essential endogenous process of capitalism and the historical excrescences in a different way.

The hard task is to reformulate a new theory of the essential kernel of capitalism. Bertell Ollman (1976) has convincingly argued that Marx held to a philosophy of "internal relations" in which an essential part (termed a "monad" by Leibnitz) contains relations that express the basic nature of the whole system under analysis. This consists in identifying the crucial or kernel set of relations. Some Marxists (Dobb, 1947; Brenner, 1977) have argued that the key social relation for capitalist society is the relationship between capital and labor as it occurs within the firm, or as Marxists say, at the point of production. This is undoubtedly an important relationship and a spate of excellent studies have focused on the labor process as it has developed in contemporary core capitalism (Braverman, 1974; Edwards, 1979; Burawoy, 1979). The world-system perspective encourages us, however, to notice how control institutions (relations of production) are structured beyond the point of production, in states, and, indeed, are institutionalized in the core/periphery hierarchy.

ADDITIONS TO MARX'S MODEL

The conceptualization of the world-system as a multilayered system of competing groups has been very helpful in accounting for the historical development of capitalism. Here I would suggest that the processes of state-formation, nation-building, class-formation, and the reproduction of the core/periphery hierarchy can be theorized as fundamental to the capitalist mode of production itself. Obviously these processes are beyond the scope of a narrowly economic view of capitalism, but it is precisely the transcendence of such an economistic theory which is necessary if we are to theorize the development of capitalism as a whole system.

The disadvantage of this inclusion of processes formerly thought to be historical into the basic model of capitalist development is that it complicates the model greatly. Instead of a kernel social relation located at the point of production we have a much more complicated set of organizational, political, market, interstate, and world class relations. What is needed is a new synthesis of these processes which has the virtues of Marx's original theory: simplicity and the identification of a relational kernel.

One of the key insights into capitalist development stimulated by Wallerstein's (1979a) theoretical writings is that commodity production regularly takes place in an arena that is importantly structured by non-economic relationships. There has never been an empirically existing perfect market within the capitalist system. Instead capitalism is structured as a set of power relations, sometimes taking the form of price-setting markets, but just as often constituted as institutionalized power or authority relations among classes and states. Thus capitalism is a competitive system in which no single organization exercises monopoly control over production and consumption, but within certain organizational realms monopoly power is temporarily exercised. This organizational power is most often institutionalized within state structures or guaranteed by property laws which are backed up by states. Thus mercantilism is not a stage of capitalist development, but, with some variations in form and extent, a constant feature of capitalism. In the long run, however, these extra-economic sources of control are themselves subjected to competition in the arena of the world-system.

Thus the organizational structures of states and firms, and the structured relations among classes, are subjected to a competing-down process which occurs in the interstate system and the world market (see chapters 7 and 8). This accounts for certain regularities which can be observed in the world-economy. Not only are peripheries underdeveloped, but the uneven development of core countries results in the rise and fall of hegemonic core powers. This is because the correct combination for success in the capitalist system depends not only on efficient production for the market, but also on the right mix of state investment in infrastructure, regulation of classes, and the exercise of military power and diplomacy in the interstate system.

Marx's simplifying assumption that workers in a purely capitalist system receive only the wages necessary for the reproduction of the labor force does not accurately reflect the process of class struggle which occurs within the capitalist system. Many core workers undoubtedly receive wages beyond reproductive necessity, and many peripheral workers receive wages which are below what they need to reproduce themselves and thus must rely on other resources. Marx assumed that trade union movements would more or less automatically develop into socialist challenges to the logic of capitalism. By now it is obvious that trade unions by themselves do not challenge the basic logic of capitalism, although they do raise the wage bill paid by capital. This suggests that the process by which workers resist their perfect commodification should be seen as a normal part of capitalist development itself. Their differential success in this is known to be mediated primarily by the extent to which they are able to gain access to state power, and to utilize this access to guarantee their right to bargain collectively with capital.

While the forms of the welfare state and the political legitimation of labor unions exist not only in the core but also in the periphery, and while the real level of protection which workers are able to receive from their own unions and their states varies over time in all states, it is still the case that there is a significant differential between the core and the periphery in terms of political protection versus the use of political coercion in class relations. These systematic variations must be taken into account in any theory of accumulation, uneven development, and crisis. Erik Wright's (1978:147–54) explication of the different theories of crisis refers to one cause of the decline of the rate of profit as the "profit-squeeze" model, in which workers are effective in maintaining a wage level which discourages new capital investment. This is an example of the inclusion of the consequences of class struggle into the model of accumulation itself.

Another consequence of the systematic inclusion of extra-economic determinants of class position is that it enables us to better understand exploitation in the periphery. A great debate has emerged among Marxists about the definition of the capitalist mode of production. Many reassert Marx's claim that the fully developed capitalist mode of production can only exist in the context of the wage system. Thus the slavery and serfdom which were created in peripheral areas during the expansion of the European world-system are classified as precapitalist modes of production which were articulated with capitalism.

This debate about the articulation of modes of production has been reviewed and clarified by Aidan Foster-Carter (1978). He suggests that theorization of the capitalist mode of production at the world-system level may bring about a synthesis of the currently somewhat Balkanized discussions of particular theoretical questions by Marxists concerned with problems of development. Foster-Carter recommends that the theorization of capitalism should go beyond an economistic approach to include political dimensions. I think he is mistaken, however, as were Brenner (1977) and Frank (1979a), to suggest that world-system articulation ought to be conceptualized as "exchange." Certainly the form of exchange (commodity production versus gift-giving or tribute payments) is important, but international trade and the core/periphery hierarchy should be analyzed in terms of production relations as well. As Albert Bergesen (1983) has strongly argued, it is institutionalized power (in the form of private property, colonialism, and neocolonial geomilitary influence) which stands behind the fictively equal trade between core and periphery.

When we include non-economic dimensions of class into our definition of capitalist production relations we must abandon the assumption of a perfect price-setting labor market. Intraclass stratification into "segmented labor markets" is often structured by extra-economic institutions, e.g. nationalism, racism, sexism, ethnic solidarities, trade unions, and immigration laws.

In the periphery extra-economic coercion plays a much greater part in production relations. Even so, the cost of slave or serf labor and their relative efficiencies or inefficiencies entered into the calculation of profitability and investment decisions. The elimination of these extreme forms of labor coercion in the periphery has by no means equalized the levels of coercion exercised over core and peripheral workers. The wage differential beyond the difference in productivity analyzed by Arghiri Emmanuel (1972) is based on the exercise of coercion in the world-system. Peripheral states generally exercise more repressive controls over worker organizations. If legal protections for workers exist, they are usually not enforced. And the core/periphery division of labor itself (differences in productivity as well as wages) contributes to the great income inequalities which exist between core and peripheral workers. These differences, which may be partly conceptualized as stratification *within* the world proletariat, are produced both by the direct exercise of core power through state action and transnational corporate politics, and as the indirect consequence of the core/periphery division of labor.

The Wallersteinian world-system perspective contends that the core/periphery hierarchy and the exploitation of the periphery by the core are necessary to the reproduction of capitalism as a system. Thus, rather than a temporary stage on the road to fully developed core capitalism, the "primary accumulation" (Frank, 1979a) by which the core exploits the periphery is one of the main mechanisms which allow the continuation of expanded reproduction in the core. The relative harmony of capitalists and workers in the core (which can be observed in the interclass alliances typified by social democratic regimes or the "business unionism" form of class struggle in the United States) is possible because of the key role performed by exploitation of the periphery.

It is undeniable that the greater proportion of surplus value produced in the world-economy is, and has long been, produced in the core, but the exploitation of the periphery both creates extra amounts of surplus value which can be redistributed in many indirect forms to core workers, and also reinforces the ideologies of nationalism and "national development" which facilitate class alliances in the core. Albert Szymanski (1981: chapter 5) shows evidence against several propositions which support the "necessity of imperialism" argument. He does not, however, contradict the claim that the core/periphery hierarchy allows capitalist accumulation to proceed as a result of its effects on class peace in the core. Szymanski's critical evaluation of the "aristocracy of labor" thesis (1981: chapter 14) does not disprove that core workers benefit from the core/periphery hierarchy, and in fact Szymanski admits that the concentration of cleaner, better-paid jobs in the core is an important contributor to the depolarization of class conflict within core countries. This suggests that decreases in the exploitation of the periphery by the core may have potentially revolutionary consequences for core countries, and thus for the capitalist world-system as a whole.

LOGICAL BOUNDARIES BETWEEN MODES OF PRODUCTION

The discussion of structures often proceeds at a metatheoretical level in which great paradigms clash but little is accomplished for cumulative social science. A theoretical holism which simply asserts that the essential features of a social system (the monad or kernel) exist at the level of the whole system, is such a metatheoretical claim. As an heuristic device it has the same scientific status as the claim that the point of production is the spatial location of the systemic monad. Both of these metatheoretical points of departure try to conceptualize the deep structure spatially, and they do so in order to help us sort out the central qualities from which the more complicated world of appearances and concrete realities can be explained.

But the attempt to identify the qualities of modes of production with spatial entities may produce more confusion than clarification. If we assume that each world-system has one and only one mode of production, as Wallerstein does, how do world-systems change? It is more useful to conceptualize modes of production in terms of *logical boundaries* rather than spatial boundaries. This allows for the articulation between different modes, and for the competition between modes within a single socio-economic system. It may be the case that most spatially designated socio-economic systems have one mode of production which is dominant, but if we eliminate the possibility of the co-existence of modes, we cannot discuss situations in which modes of production may be vying with each other for domination, and thus our ability to analyze transformation is accordingly limited.

A clear specification of the underlying structural tendencies of capitalist development is necessary to distinguish institutional forms and social movements which reproduce capitalism (or allow it to intensify or to expand to a larger scale) from those forms and movements which may act to transform the capitalist system into a qualitatively different system. Here Althusser (Althusser and Balibar, 1970) has given us a useful distinction – that between the mode of production (the basic essence of capitalism as a system) and the social formation (the concretely existing set of social institutions which contain historical survivals of earlier modes of production and nascent elements of modes of production of the future). The idea of "social formation" will here apply to the whole world-system rather than to separate national societies. Accordingly the book is entitled *Global Formation*.

The above posits the existence of a systemic essence – the basic tendential laws of capitalist development. My discussion focuses on the logical "boundaries" between different modes. It is argued that these boundaries must be specified clearly in order to understand how fundamental social change – the qualitative transformation of social systems – occurs.

We must consider the possibility that two or more modes of production may co-exist within a single world-system. Foster-Carter's (1978) review of the mode of production controversy discusses several important conceptual distinctions. He points out that both articulation (in the sense of the complementary interpenetration of two modes), and contradiction (in the sense of conflict and competition among modes) are necessary in order to understand the interactions among modes of production. As Foster-Carter puts it, "Each concept needs the other: articulation without contradiction would indeed be static and anti-Marxist; but contradiction without articulation . . . fallaciously implies that the waxing and waning of modes of production are quite separate activities, each internally determined, whereas in fact they are linked as are wrestlers in a clinch" (1978:73).

AN ANALYTIC NARRATIVE

Here follows a rather abstract and brief sketch of the history of the capitalist world-system which will be helpful in sorting out the relationship between modes of production and world-systems. Wallerstein contends that the transition to capitalism occurred for the first time in the European world-economy during the "long sixteenth century" (1450–1640). This system was imperialistic from the beginning in that it was composed of a hierarchical division of labor between core and peripheral areas. It emerged from European feudalism, a somewhat unique social system which was itself a devolved combination of the Roman Empire and the Germanic tribal societies (Anderson, 1974a). European feudalism during its classic period (the ninth through eleventh centuries AD) was not a world-system in the strict Wallersteinian sense. The manorial economy was composed of economically self-sufficient units, and thus there was no territorial division of labor exchanging fundamental products. This weakly integrated system was fertile ground for the emergence of markets and capitalism.[1]

Fernand Braudel's (1984) narrative of the European world-economy differs from Wallerstein's in theoretically relevant ways. Though he avoids committing himself to formal definitions, Braudel makes a distinction between capitalism and the market economy. For him capitalism is *haute finance* and mercantile monopoly spreading over the top of market exchange like a parasite, able to influence the development of states and economies by subtle manipulations. Braudel differs from Wallerstein by conceiving of the European world-economy as a set of layered modes of production with capitalism at the top and precapitalist modes such as slavery and serfdom in the periphery. This layered approach leads him to include the city state Mediterranean world-economy of the twelfth century in his narrative of the development of the capitalist world-system. He also contends that a world-economy necessarily has a single city at its center, and he describes the seesawing hegemonies of Venice, Antwerp, and Genoa during the period before Wallerstein's European world-system allegedly experienced the transition to capitalism.

What we have here are two different notions of the transition to capitalism. For Braudel just the top layer was capitalist, and it was merchant or commercial capitalism, not industrial capitalism. For Wallerstein each world-system has only one mode of production, so the entire European world-economy (both core and periphery) experienced the transition from feudalism to capitalism during the long sixteenth century (Wallerstein, 1974: chapter 8).

Braudel's notion of a layered world-system with capitalism at the top and precapitalist modes in the periphery is similar to the formulations of many other theorists (e.g. LaClau, 1977). But unlike LaClau, Braudel implies not only that capitalism creates and sustains peripheral exploitation, but that capitalism is dependent on the existence of a periphery. In this he follows the lead of Rosa Luxemburg (1968). Here is where Wallerstein's formulation is superior. The idea of a mode of production as a self-sustaining logic of reproduction would seem to require that sectors or layers which are necessary to the reproduction of the logic be defined as part of that logic.

According to Wallerstein the period of the fifteenth and sixteenth centuries was a period of transition in which the logic of capitalism came to dominate European feudalism. The key struggle was the defeat of the Habsburg attempt to convert the nascent capitalist world-economy into a tributary world-empire.

The peripheralization of Eastern Europe was possible in part because the timing of the process of infeudation there was delayed due to the weaker influence of the Roman Empire. The so-called "second serfdom" of Eastern Europe was really its first serfdom (Anderson, 1974a). The development of serfdom out of the Slavic village communities corresponded, in Poland, with the emergence of the European world-economy such that serfdom became a form of labor control utilized for the production of commodities for export to the core areas of Western Europe.

From its base in Europe and Latin America the European-centered capitalist world-economy expanded in a series of waves to eventually dominate the whole globe by the end of the nineteenth century. But the process of expansion was also accompanied by a process of the deepening of capitalist relations in the areas where they had already become dominant, that is in Europe and Latin America. The commodification of land, labor, and wealth not only was expanded to new areas by trade and by force, but also was intensified to include more and more areas of life within the older regions of the capitalist world-economy. In the core this meant the more thorough subjugation of the labor process to the logic of efficient and profitable commodity production (Marx, 1976:1025–38) and in the periphery it meant the partial decline of the directly coercive aspects of labor control and the rise of more opaque market-mediated wage labor relations.

Capitalist slavery and serfdom were eventually replaced by less directly repressive forms of labor control. The process of proletarianization deepened in both the core and the periphery as subsistence production and home production (worker's gardens, non-monetized family labor, etc.) became commodified, making workers more and more exclusively dependent on the sale of their labor power. In the periphery at times "precapitalist" forms of labor control were either created anew or revitalized to produce commodities for export to the core. In addition, many "part-time proletarians" received low wages made possible by their partial dependence on village communities which served as labor reserves for the sector of the economy producing peripheral commodities (Murray, 1980).

Thus the expansion of capitalism during some phases reproduced "precapitalist" forms of production, while during other phases it broke these forms down and replaced them with production relations more similar to those of the core. Proletarianization and the commodification of life has therefore increased in both the core and the periphery, with a certain lag in the periphery, and the retention in the periphery of more coercive types of labor control. These are more coercive relative to the core but less coercive relative to the earlier periphery.

At the level of the core/periphery hierarchy capitalist production relations have similarly become less directly coercive and more formally organized as market relations between equals, even though the unequal power of core and peripheral states in the interstate system, and the "market advantages" of core capitalism (employing capital intensive technology and skilled highly paid labor) remain great. Nevertheless, neocolonialism is not colonialism. The sovereignty of contemporary peripheral nation states may often be in question, but it is undoubtedly greater than when colonial empires carved up Asia, Africa, and the Americas. Similarly, "peripheral industrialization" and "dependent development" (Evans, 1979) may not constitute the end of economic domination by the core, but they certainly involve more core-like capitalist relations of production than did the purely extractive peripheral industries of earlier centuries.

In this brief description of the spread and deepening of capitalist relations of production we can see the importance of specifying both the spatial and logical boundaries of capitalism. The intensification of commodified relations within both the core and the periphery of the capitalist system is an important process which has consequences for the ability of capitalism to reproduce itself. An exclusively spatial metaphor for conceptualizing production relations blurs the distinction between the logics of different modes of production. I am arguing that, though articulation of wage labor production with non-wage forms of commodified labor is an endogenous feature of capitalism, we must analyze the logical boundaries of modes of production without relying too heavily on the spatial dimension.

Socialism is a mode of production which subjects investment decisions and distribution to a logic of collective use value, and as such, socialist movements reintroduce non-commodified relations into the interstices of capitalist relations. But the complete institutionalization of a socialist mode of production awaits the day when this qualitatively different logic becomes dominant in the world-system. Thus the question of logical boundaries is important for allowing us to see how a particular organizational form may reproduce capitalist relations or contribute to the transformation of capitalism.

A particular institution may, of course, do both at the same time. Thus labor unions have forced capital to expand mechanization at the same time as they have placed constraints on capitalist control of a certain share of surplus value. Similarly, "socialist" states may reproduce the logic of commodity production on a national scale (state capitalism) while at the same time creating a more socialist logic of distribution, at least within their own political boundaries (Chase-Dunn, 1982b). Thus logical boundaries must be specified which enable us to understand the qualitative distinction between capitalism and socialism even when these are not differentiated spatially.

We can borrow a metaphor from biological systems in order to begin this task. Alker (1982) and Lenski and Lenski (1982) have argued that social systems are reproduced by "genetic" codes. These theorists share a cybernetic conception of systemic structure in which social information becomes coded in cultural and symbolic systems. Materialists may utilize the imagery of the genetic theory of deep structure and reproduction without adopting an idealist philosophy. For Marx the "genetic structure" of social systems was inherent in the institutions by which material life was reproduced. He posited a tension between the technical and social forces of production (technology, labor process) and the relations of production (those political institutions which allow exploitation to take place). Cultural institutions were thought to be reflections of the more basic struggle over material production. Thus the essential nature of a particular mode of production could be understood from an analysis of the typical institutions of production and class exploitation. A deep structure theory which follows the materialist approach will start with an analysis of class relations. These are conceptualized in various ways by different Marxists and these differences have profound effects on the understanding of modes of production and their transformation.

A PURELY FORMAL APPROACH

What is a model of deep structure? We have various formal alternatives which may be useful. A theory may be specified axiomatically as a series of propositions and derived hypotheses. Nowak (1971) has thus formalized parts of Marx's accumulation model of capitalist development. Such an axiomatic theory could employ the kind of dialectical causal logic suggested by Wright (1978:15–26). Or a theory may posit the existence of a set of basic processes in terms of causal relations among a number of variables. The equations which describe this kind of model may be written, and alternative specifications are easily posited. Let us take this second form and imagine that we have decided upon a set of key variables for representing the underlying model of capitalist development. We then have a number of equations which posit causal relations among basic variables under specified scope conditions. If we want to use dialectical logic we may model complicated non-Aristotelian relations among variables (see Alker, 1982).[2]

Let us think about what it would mean to formally specify the *logical boundaries* of such a formalization of the basic processes of the capitalist system. We can ask what would have to change to constitute a qualitatively different system. If we could somehow actually know the exact specification which corresponds to the actual capitalist mode of production at a single point in time we would likely find out that the historicists are partly right. Even ignoring those aspects of social reality which are largely conjunctural, the most appropriate structural model is likely to be *always changing* to a certain extent. Let us assume that this "background" change is fairly constant over time and that it is relatively small. If, indeed, the basic structure changes rapidly, then generalizations about modes of production are inappropriate, and the best we can do is to write history.

The problem of "stages of capitalism" might be understood in such a formalistic approach by focusing on larger changes in the parameters specifying relations among variables. Qualitative transformation in such a formalistic approach could be designated as more fundamental change in the model such that wholly different processes with different variables are created and become dominant in the overall determination of development. This would correspond to transformation of structural "constants" which are then seen as constant not relative to all socio-economic systems, but only with regard to a particular mode of production.

Many problems are raised by such a purely formal approach to system transformation. How can we distinguish between changes in the model which are unimportant for the basic structure, or which reproduce the same system logic using new organizational forms (perhaps on a greater spatial scale), from changes which truly transform the system logic? The distinctions between background, stage, and transformative change suggested above are based on formal distinctions within mathematically or logically specified models. Certainly such an approach would need to combine these formal distinctions with substantive considerations about the nature of modes of production. If we want to be able not only to say that fundamental change has occurred, but also to say in what direction change is occurring, we need to have substantive models of the various possible modes of production: kin-based, tributary, capitalist, and socialist. Here we will work mainly on the specification of the capitalist mode, although it should be remembered that the problem of logical boundaries implies the necessity of specifying the other modes as well.

We require a substantive core of assertions on which to base our theory of world-system development. It might be possible to work inductively from empirically observable cycles and trends (see chapter 2). It should be recognized that quite different deep structure theories might account for any particular set of empirical patterns, though an inductive approach would probably rule out some theories. At this point I will proceed in the other direction, from prior theorizing, although it should be emphasized that this deductive kind of theoretical development should not remain a self-contained universe. Different formulations must eventually contend with one another to account for empirical evidence. We are a long way from sufficient clarity, however, and the first task is to think through some general theoretical problems.

A question which poses nicely the problem I wish to confront is "what is capital?" Marx understood capital to be a social relationship, an institutionalization of control through property ownership of the means of production. For Marx capital contained within itself the relationship with labor, a relationship in which property-less workers must sell their labor time to capital-owners. How might we modify this definition in the light of the insights provided by viewing capitalism as a world-system? I will approach this problem from two directions. The first uses insights about the state and the interstate system to reformulate the definition of capital. This involves the analysis of the process of commodification and its limits. The second approaches the problem of domination more directly by analyzing the relationship between classes and the core/periphery hierarchy. Let us consider these in turn.

COMMODIFICATION AND ITS LIMITS

Marx began with the commodity. The commodity is a standardized product produced for exchange in a price-setting market, in which the conditions of production are subject to reorganization as a result of changes in input costs. A work of art is not a commodity because it is not (by definition) standardized or reproducible. Your mother is not a commodity because she is not replaceable in the market. There are no perfect commodities, but many social objects approximate commodities. It is uncontestably the case that the deepening of capitalist relations involves the commodification of ever more areas of human life. Production for use in the home becomes replaced by the purchase of commodities. Economists commonly project the character of commodities onto everything. Children become consumer durables. Some sociologists carry on in the same manner, although they sometimes differentiate purely economic from "social" exchange (Blau, 1964). The "market mentality" tends to analyze all interaction as commodified exchange.

All of human life is not organized in the commodity form. Some things represent collective "goods" or transcendent values which have no calculable market price. Many relationships, even in "advanced" countries, involve real transcendent solidarity which is not reducible to a business deal. Friendship, love, patriotism are often described in the language of "rational choice," but part of the nature of these relationships involves a merging of the individual interests (the constitution of a corporate entity) such that the terms of exchange among parts are undefined, and undefinable.

Marx observed that the market, especially the market for labor, while it formally represents an exchange among equals, is actually an institutional mystification of the main type of exploitation which typifies capitalist society: the appropriation of surplus value. One of his great contributions was to show how the formal equality of the market could produce socially structured inequality. I have mentioned above that Marx's model of capitalist accumulation assumes a perfectly operating system of markets for labor and other commodified objects. This assumption has led to the narrow view, held by both Marxists and non-Marxists, that capitalism is limited to a market system in which "private" owners of the means of production employ commodified labor to accumulate capital.

The public/private distinction is fundamental to Marx's definition of "independent producers," and thus also to his distinction between production for use and production for exchange. It is assumed that, in a market economy, independent producers seeking to maximize their own returns exchange commodities with one another. The production of use values, on the other hand, assumes some unity of interests, either because an individual or family is producing for itself, rather than for the market, or because the unit producing use values does it according to a calculus which includes other principles in addition to strict economic efficiency. Thus use values may be produced by a traditional division of labor in an Indian village in which "prices" are customary (Mandel, 1970), by a state within a tributary mode of production according to a logic of political domination, or by a socialist society in which investment decisions and exchange terms are democratically determined using a calculus of social need.

A historical–structural perspective on capitalism suggests that we should seek its kernel in the main specific types of competition and integration which operate in the whole terrain of interaction. Since the market principle is historically only part of the determination of success and failure in the world-system, we should incorporate the dynamics of those non-market processes which are important to successful accumulation into our conceptualization of the kernel relations. It has been argued by some critics of Wallerstein that states and the interstate system (which form the political basis of world capitalism) operate according to somewhat different principles from firms and classes struggling to survive and succeed in the arena of the world market (Skocpol, 1977; Zolberg, 1981). In chapter 7 I argue that the logic of competition and conflict in the interstate system (geopolitics) and the logic of competition in the world market should be understood as interdependent determinants of the dynamics of capitalist development. The present task is to ground this idea in an analysis of the process of commodification and its limits.[3]

The expansion of capitalism has largely consisted of a deepening and widening of commodified relations. More and more aspects of life become commercialized. More and more interactions are mediated by markets. And the spatial scale of market integration grows. But there are clearly limits to the degree of commodification which it is possible for capitalism to survive as a social system. Capitalists themselves, workers' organizations, and especially states sometimes resist market forces and act to erect institutional barriers to the commodification of certain relations. Much of politics in capitalist society is a seesawing struggle among different groups over the process of commodification and its limits. This struggle is a normal part of capitalism itself, although the resistance to commodification holds the possibility of challenging the basic logic of capitalism.

Some of the limits on commodification are erected by political groups operating explicitly in their own interests. Thus cartels, guilds, and trade unions are organizations which resist market forces in the name of "special interests." But the most extensive efforts to regulate market forces are carried out by states in the name of "society." Public health regulations, minimum wage legislation, national parks and many other institutional features of capitalist societies are legitimated in terms of state provision of "public goods" which either market forces would not provide or which must be protected from commercialization in the name of those "universal interests" represented by the state.

Karl Polanyi's (1944) sweeping portrayal of the "great transformation" outlined the growth of markets and the commodification of wealth, labor, and land in England and on the Continent. Polanyi also portrayed a societal reaction to commodification in which the negative effects of market forces were becoming subject to regulation by states. This reaction to the commercialization of society was understood by Polanyi as the basis of the emergence of socialism. The expansion of the welfare state, even though a long and uneven process, would eventually alter the logic of capitalism toward a more collective form of rationality.

Polanyi's depiction of the transition to socialism is more historical and open-ended than the functionalist notion of an equilibrium between differentiation and integration or an automatic dialectic which mechanically produces social transformation. Obviously the political tussle over the extension and limitation of commodification involves class struggles, ideological hegemony, complicated matters of consciousness formation, etc. and is anything but automatic. But Polanyi's analysis falters because he fails to consider the importance of the fact that these struggles take place within a larger terrain formed by the world economy and the interstate system. Despite his focus on many international aspects of capitalist development, Polanyi does not see that the structure of the interstate system itself poses a major difficulty for his theory of the transition to socialism. The limits on commodification, and also the limits on collective rationality, are set in a competitive struggle in which firms, classes, and most importantly *states* are the players against one another.

The myth of the nation as a transcendent solidarity is an important determinant of success or failure in this struggle. States must be able to legitimate their actions and to mobilize participation (tax-paying and warfare) in order to survive or prevail in the world-economy. Those that do this less efficiently or less effectively are likely to lose out in the competitive struggle. Thus both political mobilization and comparative advantage in the world market are important to the logic of capitalism.

The ideological mystification which holds that the state represents the "general will" or the "universal interest" is not false only because states are controlled more by capitalists than by workers. It is also false because states represent only the interests of their own citizens. Thus the state is only one more political organization in a larger arena of competing political organizations. Even if a state did represent all of its citizens these would not be universal interests from the point of view of the socio-economic system as a whole. The "society" represented by each state is a national society, a subgroup in a larger whole. And there is no world state to aggregate the interests of all participants in the world-system.

The political structure of capitalism is not the capitalist state. It is the capitalist interstate system. This fact alters Polanyi's model of commodification and its limits as a process for the transition to socialism because there is no effective organization to represent, even ideologically, the collective rationality of our species. This is why the limits which are placed on commodification do not easily add up to the transformation to socialism. As trends in the last decade have shown, austerity regimes, deregulation and the extension of commodification within the "socialist" states occur globally during certain periods, although not in the same way everywhere. The ability of any single national society to construct collective rationality is limited by its interaction within the larger system.

The expansion and deepening of commodification has always created reactions and stimulated the formation of political structures to protect people from market forces. Capitalists themselves organize political institutions which limit market forces. Contrary to much ideology, most real living capitalists usually prefer monopolistic certainty to the vagaries and risks of market competition. Thus capitalist states have always tried to protect the capitalists who control them. States act to expand markets or to destroy barriers to market competition when their own capitalists will benefit because they enjoy a competitive advantage. And workers and peasants have tried to protect themselves from market forces through guild organizations, community structures, workers' co-ops, labor unions, and political parties. Marx's (1967a) discussion of the struggle over the length of the working day shows how middle-stratum professionals sometimes become involved in welfare-oriented regulation of market forces. The abolition of child labor and slavery are additional examples of limits to commodification created by movements with complex class identities.

The constraints on market forces imposed in one region, state, or industry are often one of the most important driving forces in the expansion of commodification to new areas. Successful labor organizing causes capital to look elsewhere for labor. Monopolies organized locally or nationally encourage consumers to try to gain access to outside markets where goods may be cheaper, and cheaper production in these outside markets is also encouraged. Thus commercialization and regulation interact in a spiral which drives a number of the long-run trends visible in the world-system. Commodification causes political organizations to emerge, which then result in incentives for the further extension of commodification. This may undermine earlier, smaller-scale political organizations by pricing them out of competition or by causing them to internally impose new conditions of "market efficiency." So far the scale of market forces has always been able to escape political regulation, now even encompassing the "socialist" states and encouraging their movement toward deregulation and levels of allocation more typical in the larger world-economy.

The size of firms, the spatial scale of markets, and the depth of market integration increase partly in reaction to political efforts to regulate market forces. The "internationalization of capital" is partly explained by escape from political regulation and labor unions, and a good portion of the trend toward ever greater state-formation – the arrogation of powers over more and more areas of life – can be attributed to state action *vis-à-vis* market forces. Increasingly states not only react to market forces with regulation but they intervene to *create* market forces. As firm size and the spatial scale of markets have grown, state responsibility for economic development has increased. The state not only serves private entrepreneurs and tries to attract capital, sometimes it itself is the entrepreneur. This occurred first in several second tier core and semiperipheral countries trying to catch up with British industrialization, but now peripheral capitalists regularly use the only organization they have access to which is large enough to compete in the global economy – the state. State capitalism is thus a trend, not of socialism, but of the increasing scale of production and market integration in the capitalist world-economy.

What are the implications of the above for our effort to redefine capital in the light of the historical patterns of capitalist development in the world-system? For one thing we need to reconsider the question of forms of property and capitalism. The emphasis on commodification and the importance of markets in the context of multiple competing and unequally powerful political organizations leads us to question a narrow interpretation of "private" property as the only appropriate form of ownership for capitalism. General Motors would still be a capitalist firm competing in the world automobile market even if it were to become owned and controlled by its employees. Even state-owned firms are subject to constraints based on the ability of the state which owns them to compete in the larger global political economy. Capital is that sort of power which is able to combine the operation of profitable commodity production with the relatively efficient provision of those "public goods" which are necessary or advantageous to profitability. Thus capitalists, in this sense, are neither private owners of productive wealth nor state managers, but rather the combined operations which produce success or failure in the capitalist world-system. I am not suggesting that we should abandon the distinction between privately held capital and the state, nor am I suggesting that these do not often have contradictory interests. What I mean is that "success" in the capitalist system requires both of these and their co-operation whether or not the jobs be differentiated to separate organizations or more integrated, as when states directly control commodity-producing firms. Thus states are part of the relations of production in capitalism, and capitalism cannot be understood as separate from the logic of nation-building, state-formation, and geopolitics as they typically operate in the context of an expanding and deepening process of commodification.

In order to understand how geopolitics and the competition among states in the interstate system is integrated with capitalist commodity production we must analyze the form and content of interstate competition within the capitalist world-economy. This subject is taken up in the second part of this book.

WORLD CLASSES AND THE CORE/PERIPHERY RELATIONSHIP

Let us now turn to the way in which exploitation and domination are structured – the interaction of interclass and intraclass conflict in the world-system. Albert Bergesen (1983) has argued that the core/periphery relationship can be conceptualized as a kind of class relationship. He shows convincingly that the relationship between the core and the periphery is not simply an exchange between equal partners. Structured power has created and sustained the hierarchical division of labor between the core and the periphery, and continues to do so. Bergesen's argument is an important response to Brenner's (1977) characterization of the world-system perspective as "circulationist."

Nevertheless, rather than collapsing the categories of class and core/periphery, it may be more helpful to use them both and to study their interaction. First, what is the difference between the two? According to Marx, the capitalist/proletarian relationship is based on ownership and/or control of productive property versus a class of workers who do not own means of production and must sell their labor power. This institutional situation is understood to have come into existence through the use of extra-economic coercion, and to be largely sustained by the normal processes of capitalist economic competition. The core/periphery relationship is analytically understood as a territorial division of labor in which core areas specialize in capital intensive production using skilled highly paid labor, and peripheral areas specialize in labor intensive production using low wage (or coerced) and relatively unskilled labor.[4]

The world economy is composed of "commodity chains," forward and backward linkages of processes of production (Hopkins and Wallerstein, 1986). These commodity chains link raw materials, labor, the sustenance of labor, intermediate processing, final processing, transport, and final consumption. The great bulk of consumption in the capitalist world-economy is of products whose commodity chains cross national boundaries, and a large portion of these link the core and the periphery. Wallerstein contends that core activities take place at those "nodes" on commodity chains where capital intensive technology and skilled highly paid labor are used, and where relatively greater surplus value is appropriated (see chapter 10).

The core/periphery relationship was brought into existence by extra-economic plunder, conquest, and colonialism, and is sustained by the normal operation of political–military and economic competition in the capitalist world-economy.

The world class structure is primarily composed of capitalists (owners and controllers of means of production) and property-less workers. This class system also includes small commodity producers who control their own means of production but do not employ the labor of others,[5] and a growing middle class of skilled and/or professionally certified workers.

The territorial core/periphery hierarchy crosscuts this world class structure and interacts with it in important ways. Thus the categories of core capitalist/peripheral capitalist, and core worker/peripheral worker are useful for an analysis of the dynamics of world capitalism. Core labor is usually conceived as organized by the wage system in which competition in a labor market determines wages. But at least some core workers have long been in the category of *protected labor* in the sense that trade unions, welfare legislation, and/or other politically articulated institutions (such as immigration controls) give them some protection from competition in the world labor market and some advantages in the struggle with capital. Guilds protected workers and producers from competition within medieval cities, encouraging the development of capitalist production outside city walls. Core states, and other states as well, develop politically mediated mechanisms for protecting workers, but the uneven process of capitalist accumulation manages to find ways around many of these protections. The point is that the world class system may be best understood as *a continuum from protected labor through wage labor to coerced labor* which roughly corresponds to the core/periphery hierarchy.

It is important to realize that labor may be commodified without receiving a formal wage. The serfs and slaves who produced surplus value for peripheral capitalists in earlier centuries were treated as commodities in the sense that their labor process was directed by a logic of capital accumulation, even though they did not have the juridical freedom to sell their labor time to capital. There are many degrees and forms of the commodification of labor.

Sidney Mintz (1977) addresses the question, "was the plantation slave a proletarian?" and his answer, after examining the interconnections between industrial capitalism in England and plantation production of raw materials, is a qualified yes. Mintz (1985) also focuses on the organizational nature of sugar plantations as capitalist firms. Not only were plantations producing commodities for profit, but, Mintz points out, the combination of agriculture with the processing of sugar cane exhibited features of industrial production usually associated with the factory system in core areas. Rather than trying to lump slaves and wage workers together as proletarians in order to account for the important linkages between the two, the Wallersteinian approach sees them as two kinds of labor control which are commodified, one typical of the core, and the other, with an added dose of extra-economic coercion, most often found in peripheral capitalism.

Marx clearly distinguishes proletarian from slave labor in his model of fully developed capitalist accumulation. In volume 1 of *Capital* Marx (1967a:168) outlines his definition of commodified labor as the buying and selling of *labor power*. The proletarian is defined as one who is free to sell his labor time, but is not himself a commodity in the sense that a slave is. He is also "free" of the ownership of the means of production and so is institutionally compelled to sell his labor power because he cannot produce for subsistence. We would expect to find an argument by Marx as to why this narrow definition of commodified labor is important in his theory of capitalism, but instead we find a kind of circularity in his definition of a commodity. He declares that "the exchange of commodities of itself implies no other relations of dependence than those which result from its own nature" (Marx, 1967a:168).

It is implied by Marx that slave labor is not itself a commodity because slaves are not specifically produced for sale. Actually slave-breeding in mid-nineteenth-century Virginia did approximate production for exchange, but we may wonder about many other goods which are produced both for subsistence and for sale. Are bananas not a commodity because the peasant may eat them as well as sell them (Trouillot, 1988)? Is labor power, the ability of human effort to transform nature, produced exclusively for sale? By narrowing his definition of a commodity Marx thus limits his definition of capitalism to the wage system. He says, "Otherwise with capital, the historical conditions of its existence are by no means given with the mere circulation of money and commodities. It can spring into life only when the owner of the means of production and subsistence meets in the market with the free labourer selling his labour-power. And this one historical condition comprises a world's history" (Marx, 1967a:170). Actually it comprises the history of the core zone, which is itself not comprehensible without consideration of the accumulation carried out in the periphery through forms of labor which were partly commodified while also containing a large dose of politically mediated coercion.

Coercion beyond the operation of free labor markets remains an important condition for reproducing wage differentials in the contemporary world. After all, if there were no extra-economic barriers to labor migration, day laborers in the United States would not earn ten times more than day laborers in Mexico. It is not the operation of a perfect labor market which determines proletarian status, but the subjection of labor to the logic of profit-making, and this is accomplished by a wide variety of institutional means.

The combination of capital/labor relations and core/periphery relations produces many of the consequences which are fundamental to the capitalist development process. The dynamics of the interstate system and the process of uneven development are the result of interclass and intraclass conflict and competition as well as international competition. Class alliances or "relative harmonies" between capital and sectors of labor within core countries cause, and are caused by, the internationally strong states and internally relatively well integrated nations of the core. The more coercive and exploitative interclass relations of the periphery are partly the result of alliances between peripheral and core capitalists, as are the relatively weaker states and less integrated nations of the periphery. State socialism, the most important of the anti-capitalist movements which have emerged within the capitalist world-system, was possible because of the "combined and uneven development" which occurred in semiperipheral areas (Trotsky, 1932), where crosscutting contradictions (conflicts among capitalists and between capitalists and workers) were exacerbated by an intermediate position in the core/periphery hierarchy.

The interstate system, centered on powerful core states which contend with one another for hegemony, is an important structural basis of the continued competition within the world capitalist class. No state represents the "general" interests of the capitalist class as a whole. Rather, subgroups of the world capitalist class control particular states. This multicentric structure of the world capitalist class allows the process of competitive capitalist uneven development to continue. The rise and fall of hegemonic core states and changes in the structure of international alliances allow for flexibility in the world polity and accommodate changes in the distribution of comparative advantages in commodity production. A single world capitalist state would be much more likely to politically sustain the interests of those capitalist subgroups which controlled it, and thus to impede the shift in productive advantage from less to more "efficient" producers. Similarly such a state would become the single object of orientation of anti-capitalist movements. Thus, unlike the present interstate system, in which successful social constraints on capital often lead to the state's loss of centrality in the world market and capital flight, in a world capitalist state the aggregation of workers' interests would likely be more effective in actually transforming the logic of the political economy toward a more democratic and collectively rational system.

The world-system perspective contends that the core/periphery hierarchy, rather than being a passing phase in the transition of "backward" areas toward core-type capitalism, is a permanent, necessary, and reproduced feature of the capitalist mode of production. This contention is supported by historical studies and crossnational comparative research (see Bornschier and Chase-Dunn, 1985) which have substantiated the continuation of mechanisms that reproduce core/periphery inequalities. The periphery of the world-economy has certainly "developed" and changed greatly since the incorporation of Latin America, Asia, and Africa into the Europe-centered capitalist world-economy, but the hierarchical relationship between the core and the periphery remains.

What is the function of this territorial hierarchy for capitalism as a system? It has probably never been the case, even in the heyday of pure plunder, that more surplus value was extracted from the periphery than was produced in the core. Most of the surplus value accumulated in the core is produced by core workers using relatively more productive technology. Nevertheless, the surplus value extracted from the periphery has played a crucial role in allowing the relatively peaceful process of expanded reproduction in the core to proceed. This has occurred in three ways: (a) by reducing the level of conflict and competition among core capitalists within core states; (b) by allowing adjustments to power relations among core states to be settled without destroying the interstate system; and (c) by promoting a relative harmony between capital and important sectors of labor in the core.

This last point is politically sensitive because it is contrary to much Marxist class analysis. It also raises the admittedly difficult question of long-run versus short-term class interests. There has been much discussion about whether or not core workers exploit peripheral workers, or benefit from their exploitation (Emmanuel, 1972:271–342). It is clear that many core workers do benefit from the exploitation of the periphery in a number of different ways. They are able to buy peripheral products cheaply. The territorial division of labor between the core and the periphery enables a larger proportion of core workers to have cleaner and more skilled jobs. The profits from imperialism enable some core capitalists to respond more flexibly to worker demands for higher wages. The greater affluence of the core allows core states to devote more resources to welfare, and to maintain a relatively greater degree of pluralism and democracy.

Thus the Marxists who have maintained that lack of socialist militancy among core workers is entirely due to "false consciousness" based on nationalism and anti-socialist propaganda are wrong, although the status-based mechanisms of ideological hegemony are also important in maintaining class harmony in the core. The objective structuring of interests based on the crosscutting nature of class and core/periphery exploitation has stabilized the capitalist world-economy. This structural basis of capitalism implies that constraints on the ability of core capitalists to keep on exploiting the periphery may have revolutionary consequences for class relations within core countries. If core/periphery wage differentials were to decrease, core workers would be less subject to the "job blackmail" backed up by the threat (and reality) of capital flight.

WHAT IS REAL CAPITALISM?

Let us combine the above discussions of commodification and class–core/periphery together to postulate a new specification of the capitalist mode of production. Real capitalism can be defined as:

1 Generalized commodity production in which land, labor, and wealth are substantially commodified.
2 Private ownership and/or control of the means of production, which may be exercised by individuals or organizations, including single states, which are themselves players in the larger competitive arena of commodity production and geopolitics. This allows for "state capitalism."
3 Accumulation of capital based on a mix of both competitive production of commodities and political–military power, in which commodity production has the greater weight in the determination of outcomes in the system as a whole.
4 Exploitation of commodified labor which is, however, not always paid a wage.
5 The combination of class exploitation with core/periphery exploitation such that the former is more important quantitatively in the accumulation of capital, but the latter is nevertheless essential because of its political effects on the mobility of capital and in reducing class conflict and weakening anti-capitalist movements in the core.

This adds considerably to Marx's more elegant formulation, but the elements added allow us to account for many of the structural features of the contemporary world-system by referring to its mode of production. Samir

Amin (1974) has suggested a slightly different formulation which defines core capitalism the way Marx did, except that it is articulated with and reliant on peripheral capitalism. Core capitalism is defined by Amin as "autocentric" self-expansion of capital, while peripheral capitalism is externally determined (by the core) and uses an extra dose of coercion in its class relations. The definition suggested above is intended to analytically combine the interstate system and the core/periphery hierarchy into our definition of capitalism in order to explain certain features of the modern world-system which are quite problematic when Marx's definition is used in its unmodified form.

Now we have an explanation, based on the capitalist mode of production itself, for why socialism has not emerged in the "most developed" (core) areas. The core/periphery hierarchy operates to reduce class antagonisms or to suppress class conflict both in the core and, to some extent, in the periphery. In peripheral areas a comprador bourgeoisie often rules with core support, but when anti-imperialist movements emerge they are most often broad anti-core class alliances. But in the semiperiphery class antagonisms are not crosscut by the core/periphery hierarchy, and it is there that the strongest attempts to create socialism have been made.

The above definition also allows us to theoretically account for the general features which many different peripheral areas have in common. We do not mean to contend that all peripheral areas are the same. The original social structural characteristics and cultures of the societies which were incorporated into the expanding European world-economy undoubtedly affected the particular institutional forms which emerged in different areas (see chapter 10). Yet the process of peripheralization and exploitation, with its phases of alternately sustaining and destroying "precapitalist" institutions and forms of labor control (depending on changing opportunities in the world market) has a certain unity which the world-system definition of capitalism captures.

The processes of uneven development, the rise and fall of hegemonic core powers, and the upward and downward mobility of areas in the core/periphery hierarchy are more clearly understood when we incorporate the interstate system and the core/periphery hierarchy into our notion of capitalism. All these advantages are strong reasons to adopt the above definition of the capitalist mode of production which is suggested by Wallerstein. But some of Wallerstein's simplifying assumptions, like those of Marx, may have created more problems than they solved.

WORLD-SYSTEM BOUNDARIES AND MODES OF PRODUCTION

As has been mentioned above, Wallerstein's totality assumption holds that the mode of production is a feature of a whole world-system, and by extension that each world-system has only one mode of production. This simplifying assumption has allowed us to examine the systematic ways in which capitalism and imperialism are linked, and to reconceptualize the capitalist mode of production as including both core and peripheral types of capitalist exploitation. Now that this is accomplished we can re-examine the totality assumption in order to resolve certain problems which it causes.

Many critics of the world-system perspective have pointed out that the equation of a mode of production with a whole world-system makes problematic the understanding of the transformation of modes of production. If each world-system can have only one mode of production, how do modes change? The simplifying assumption which equates spatial boundaries with logical boundaries runs into difficulties when we try to understand how modes of production have been transformed in the past and how they might be transformed in the future.

The simplest Wallersteinian definition of a world-system focuses on a network of material exchange, the exchange of fundamental or necessary goods – food and raw materials. In order to use this definition we need not consider the question of the mode of production or the institutional forms of the exchanges. We only need to know the extent of direct and indirect material flow densities. This is a convenient and empirically useful definition which allows us to investigate the relationships between world-systems and modes of production rather than assuming that each world-system has only one mode of production. Its application to the idea of a European world-economy raises difficulties.

The idea of Europe is a civilizational idea. Wallerstein inherited a long tradition of historical interpretation which accounted for the rise of Europe to world domination in terms of differences between Europe and the "Orient." Europe was never (or only briefly) a separate world-system according to the definition of material exchange networks. Rather, there has existed for at least two millenia a multicentric Eurasian world-system.[6] The European core area and its dense network of bulk goods (food and raw materials) has been strongly linked to North Africa and West Asia since the Greeks and the Romans emerged to core status. And this Western subsystem has been in important interaction with India and China for a very long time.

Wallerstein substitutes the mode of production criterion for the network of bulk goods criterion when he analyzes the interaction between Europe and India (Wallerstein, 1986) or between Europe and the Ottoman Empire (Wallerstein, 1979c). These are alleged to be separate world-systems because Europe is capitalist while India and the Ottoman Empire are not. Wallerstein's totality assumption tends to impair the analysis of the systemic consequences of interactions between Europe and India. It also tends to interpret the emergence of capitalism and market systems within the Indian Ocean region (see Chaudhuri, 1985) and within the Ottoman Empire only in terms of interaction with Europe.

To be fair Wallerstein's (1974:59–63) analysis of why capitalism did not emerge in China can be read as a description of modes of production contending within a single world-system, as can his analysis of the transition to capitalism in sixteenth-century Europe. But he avoids the language of contending modes of production and the coming to dominance of a mode of production. His laudable intent is to stay away from the scholastic discussions of articulation which have led to the proliferation of modes of production (Hindess and Hirst, 1975; Taylor, 1979; Wolpe, 1980). The main thrust of Wallerstein's analysis has been to demonstrate the connectedness of core and peripheral kinds of exploitation. Once this is accomplished by reconceptualizing the capitalist mode of production as above we no longer need the totality assumption.

This assumption also creates difficulties when we attempt to understand the transition to socialism in the twentieth century. Although I have argued that existing socialist states have not yet developed an autonomous socialist mode of production (Chase-Dunn, 1982b), I would not want this to be true by definition. As difficult as it may be in practice for a city or a nation state to develop an autonomous and self-sustaining socialist mode of production in the context of the contemporary capitalist world-system, I would not argue that it is impossible in principle.

In conclusion let me summarize. I have redefined the capitalist mode of production to allow the explanation of systemic features which are not easily explained using Marx's definition. Incorporating the interstate system and the core/periphery hierarchy as central features of capitalism allows us to understand the general patterns of development in the global political economy and the general features of class struggle and international uneven development. It also allows us to understand the general features of development in peripheral areas. By redefining capitalism as I have, it becomes possible to drop Wallerstein's totality assumption while retaining the above explanatory advantages. It also allows us to separately analyze the logical boundaries of modes of production and the spatial boundaries of world-systems.

Does this suggest that the articulation of modes of production is "moved out" to the boundary between peripheral capitalism and other modes of production? This spatial analogy is improper if it implies that other modes of production can exist only on the perimeter of the world-system. It is possible that elements of socialism, or the tributary mode of production, exist in the core or the semiperiphery as well as in the periphery and beyond. Ernest Mandel (1977) has contended that street lights, which are free, non-commodified "public" goods produced for the use of everyone, are socialist institutions even within the heart of capitalism.

As has been mentioned, however, the general analytic framework which allows us to have more than one mode of production within a concrete social system does not by itself tell us how these may be in interaction, or in contradiction, with each other. For this we must have a substantive theory of the nature of each, and knowledge of their compatibilities and contradictions. I have surmised elsewhere that socialism, a holistic mode of production in its very nature, may have a more difficult time emerging and growing in the interstices of capitalism than capitalism did within the terrain of the tributary mode of production. This is because capitalism thrives on competition and conflict, and only grudgingly constructs collective rationality, whereas socialism requires co-operation, and has difficulty sustaining it in the context of a still strong and fiercely competitive capitalist arena.

Let us now turn to a consideration of certain observable cycles and secular trends which are characteristics of the whole capitalist world-system.

2

Constants, Cycles, and Trends

This chapter describes a number of features of the capitalist world-system as a whole which are, in principle, more directly observable than its deep structural essence. In fact, however, much of the operationalization and evidence-gathering which needs to be done in order to verify these hypothesized surface level patterns has not been done. I will discuss those studies which have been carried out, and their implications for the schema I am proposing in later sections, especially chapter 13.

I will argue in chapter 4 that a proper understanding of the structural features, systemic logic, and normal cycles of the capitalist world-economy reveals that the global system has not undergone any important transformative change in the period since World War II. The rapid changes of scale and apparently new institutional forms are interpreted as continuations of processes long in operation. This argument requires that we have a fairly clear idea of the deep structural logic of capitalism, and an accurate specification of the processes which maintain the systemic features of the modern world-system and drive forward its cycles and trends.

What follows is a list of structural constants, cycles, and trends which are asserted to be features of the whole world-system. The constants are those deep structural features of the capitalist mode of production adduced from our discussion in chapter 1. The cycles and trends are suggested by our empirical knowledge of the modern world-system, although only some of these have been quantitatively studied over long periods of time. The present list is a revised version of that presented in Chase-Dunn and Rubinson (1977), modified by consideration of the similar discussions contained in Hopkins and Wallerstein (1982: chapters 2 and 5) and the empirical studies cited below.

The term "cycle" as utilized in world-system studies does not imply a perfect sine wave with unvarying amplitude, symmetry, and period. Joshua Goldstein (1988: chapter 8) contends that social cycles typically involve processes which are sufficiently indeterminate to preclude exact mathematical specification, and thus we analyze sequential changes with only approximately specified periods. Robert Philip Weber (1987) maintains that sequences with "quite irregular" periodicity should rather be termed "fluctuations" and the word "cycle" should be saved for more rigorous occasions. I will not worry about these matters for now since most of the "cycles" discussed in this chapter are hypothetical.[1]

SYSTEMIC CONSTANTS, CYCLES, AND TRENDS

In order to study change we must have a clear idea of the structural constants, cycles, and trends operating in the capitalist world-economy. For the moment particular historical contingencies will be ignored.

Structural Constants

As explained in chapter 1, the capitalist world-economy is a world-system in which the capitalist mode of production has become dominant. Thus this historical system has a deep structural logic of capitalist capital accumulation which drives it to expand and which contains systemic contradictions which will provoke its transformation to a different logic once expansion and deepening of capitalist social relations have approached their limits.

The constant structural features of the capitalist world-system are:

1 The interstate system – a system of unequally powerful nation states which compete for resources by supporting profitable commodity production and by engaging in geopolitical and military competition.

2 A core/periphery hierarchy in which the countries which occupy a core position specialize in *core production* – relatively capital intensive production utilizing skilled, high wage labor. Peripheral areas contain mostly *peripheral production* – labor intensive, low wage, unskilled labor which has historically been subjected to extra-economic coercion.

3 Production relations in the capitalist world-economy are more complex than Marx (1967a) assumed in his basic model of capitalist accumulation. The direct producers differ in their access to political organizations, most importantly, states. Thus there is a reproduced differentiation between core labor and peripheral labor. Labor is commodified, but it is not a perfect commodity. Direct producers (workers) vary in terms of the degree to which their interests are protected or coerced by political organizations. Core workers often enjoy the protection of state-legalized labor unions and welfare laws, although many remain in the condition of "free" laborers more subject to the vicissitudes of the labor market. At the other extreme are those

peripheral workers who are directly subjected to extra-economic coercion – historically, serfs, slaves, and contract laborers as well as workers in countries where independent trade unions and labor parties are suppressed by the state. Thus the continuum from protected to coerced labor is a constant differentiation within the world work force although, as we shall see below, the trend toward proletarianization moves a greater proportion of the work force toward full-time dependence on capitalist commodity production.

4 Commodity production for the world market (which includes both national and international markets) is the central form of competition and source of surplus value in the capitalist mode of production. This form of competition is fundamentally interwoven with the competitive political processes of state-formation, nation-building, and geopolitics in the context of the interstate system. The world market is not a perfect price-setting market, although it has long been, and remains, a very competitive arena. Monopolies are politically guaranteed *within subunits* (single states or the colonial empires of individual core states), and super-profits deriving from these monopolies are subjected to a long-run competition as the political conditions for maintenance of monopolies are themselves subjected to the forces of economic and geopolitical competition.

Systemic Cycles

1 The long business cycle (K-wave). This is a *worldwide* economic cycle (see Van Duijn, 1983) in which the relative rate of capital accumulation and overall economic activity increases and then decreases toward stagnation in a 40- to 60 year period. This cycle was first discovered through the analysis of price series by N. D. Kondratieff (1979). The causes of the K-wave are explained within a Marxist framework by Mandel (1980). Goldstein (1988) shows how the long wave is composed of two cycles, a price cycle of inflation and deflation, and a production cycle of growth and stagnation. According to Goldstein (1988: chapter 10) the price cycle lags behind the production cycle by about 10–15 years. Suter (1987) has recently presented an analysis of world-system debt cycles which integrates the K-wave with the shorter (15–25 year) Kuznets cycle as they have interacted in the nineteenth and twentieth centuries.

2 The hegemonic sequence. This refers to a fluctuation of hegemony versus multicentricity in the distribution of military power and economic competitive advantage in production among core states. Hegemonic periods are those in which power and competitive advantage are relatively concentrated in a single hegemonic core state. Multicentric periods are those in which there is a more equal distribution of power and competitive advantage among core states. In only a very rough sense is this a cycle because its periodicity is very uneven. It should rather be termed a sequence or

fluctuation. There have been three hegemonic core states since the sixteenth century: the United Provinces of the Netherlands, the United Kingdom of Great Britain, and the United States of America. The national-level conditions and system-level processes which cause the rise and decline of hegemonic core states are explicated in chapter 9.[2]

3 The cycle of core war severity. Recent research by Goldstein (1988) confirms that the severity of world wars – wars among core states contending for dominance in the world-system – is periodic in a 40- to 60-year cycle which is strongly related in time to the Kondratieff wave. There have been several peaks of severity (in terms of battle deaths per year) of core war since 1500, but the three most severe periods of world war – the Thirty Years War, the Napoleonic Wars, and World Wars I and II – were each followed by the emergence of a new hegemonic core power. These processes are discussed in more detail in part II of this book.

Samir Amin (1980a) has suggested that world wars represent normal forms of competition within capitalism as a system. The political structure within which peaceful capitalist accumulation proceeds becomes unable to provide stable support after a period of uneven economic growth, and world wars establish a new power framework for continued capitalist accumulation. Albert Bergesen (1985a) discusses this idea in an analysis of the relations among several world-system cycles.

4 The structure of core/periphery trade and control. A periodic change in the pattern of control and exchange between the core and the periphery has characterized the world-system since 1450. Periods of relatively free market multilateral exchange have been followed by periods in which trade was more politically controlled and tended to be contained within colonial empires (Krasner, 1976). Bergesen and Schoenberg (1980) have also demonstrated that waves of expansion of colonial empires are correlated in time with the existence of warfare among core states. Models of the relationships between these cycles are formulated in chapter 13.

Systemic Trends

A number of systemic trends increase in waves which roughly correspond in time with some of the cycles described above.

1 Expansion to new populations and territories. The capitalist world-system has expanded to incorporate and (usually) peripheralize formerly external arenas in a series of waves since the sixteenth century. These waves have been documented in terms of the expansion of formal colonial administration by Bergesen and Schoenberg (1980). The limits of this type of expansion were reached at the end of the nineteenth century when nearly the whole globe became integrated into a single hierarchical division of labor.

2 The expansion and deepening of commodity relations. Land, labor, and

wealth have been increasingly commodified in both the core and the periphery. More spheres of life have become mediated by markets in the core than in the periphery, but all areas have experienced a secular increase in every epoch of the modern world-system. This trend, like others, is somewhat cyclical in that during periods of economic stagnation commodification slows down, or even reverses as some people fall back on subsistence production and/or re-invent mutual aid forms of support.

3 State-formation. The power of states over their populations has increased in every period in both the core and the periphery (Boli, 1980). States have increasingly expropriated the authority and resources of other societal actors and organizations, although this trend has been uneven, and there have been periods when state control temporarily decreased or became more decentralized in particular areas.

4 Increased size of economic enterprises. The average size in terms of assets and employees controlled by economic enterprises has increased in every epoch. Agricultural enterprises and industrial enterprises have gone through periods when this trend has slowed down or even temporarily reversed. The causes of this concentration of capital are different in upward and downward phases of the K-wave (Bergesen, 1981).

5 The transnationalization of capital. Much contemporary literature discusses the "internationalization" of capital (Lapple, 1985; Hymer, 1979). This usage is incorrect, because the agents of exchange are never nations, and neither are they usually states. Rather, capital flows across the borders of states, and is thus transnational (or transstate). Capital has been transnational at least since the long sixteenth century, when substantial direct investments by productive and merchant capital were made across core states (Barbour, 1963) and by core capitalists in peripheral areas (Frank, 1979b). Since then capital has become increasingly transnational in the sense that the proportion of total world investment which crosses state boundaries has risen. The most recent expansion of transnational corporations is thus a continuation of a trend long in operation (Bornschier and Chase-Dunn, 1985: chapter 3).

6 Increasing capital intensity of production and mechanization. Several "industrial revolutions" in both agriculture and manufacturing since the long sixteenth century have increased the productivity of labor in both the core and the periphery, although the core retains its relatively higher level of productivity. Capitalist relations of production have deepened across the system, subjecting the labor process to greater amounts of direct control, although decentralization in the form of small commodity production, subcontracting (putting-out), or bureaucratization of labor control (Edwards, 1979) reproduces a "competitive sector" of independent producers and forms of autonomy. The long-run trend among transnational firms has been toward more direct control over production and the expansion of the scale of co-ordination of production, but some industries and sectors remain decentral-

ized, and in certain periods centralization slows down or even reverses in some regions.

7 Proletarianization. The process of class-formation has increased the dependence of the world work force on participation in labor markets. Subsistence redoubts, urban informal sectors, and domestic economies have functioned to sustain a substantial semiproletarianized sector of the world work force,[3] but the long-run trend has been to move a greater and greater proportion of direct producers into full-time dependence on commodity production. This has been true of both the core and the periphery, with a greater lag in the periphery. Similarly, the extent of extra-economic coercion used to compel labor in the periphery has decreased somewhat over time, as the alternatives to labor market participation have been reduced. Capitalist slavery, serfdom, and contract labor have been largely eliminated, although the relative degree to which political coercion is applied in class relations remains greater in the periphery than in the core. This includes the suppression of trade unions and peasant and/or labor parties by authoritarian peripheral states, often supported by core states.

8 The growing gap. There has long been a trend toward a growing gap in average incomes between core and peripheral areas. Within core areas the middle strata of cadres necessary to capitalist core production has expanded its relative size as a proportion of the labor force, and the wages of important sectors of the working class have increased relative to incomes and levels of living in peripheral areas. Mandel (1975) and Amin (1975) contend that both core and peripheral workers received only subsistence wages until the 1880s when, they allege, the gap between these incomes first emerged. But if we are sensitive to smaller differences and include middle strata in our estimates of average income, we are likely to find that the trend toward a growing gap has been in operation since the sixteenth century.

The above schema of structural cycles and trends has been combined into a "descriptive model" which depicts relations in time among the different features (see Chase-Dunn, 1978:170). A causal model of the relationship between the hegemonic sequence and the core/periphery hierarchy is specified in chapter 13 (see figure 13.2). In chapter 4 we use the above schema to examine claims that fundamental changes have occurred in the world-system since World War II. Now let us compare the idea of stages of capitalism with the above schema of world-system cycles.

3

Stages of Capitalism or World-system Cycles?

The periodization of capitalist development has proven to be a controversial topic in both classical and contemporary theories. The conceptualization of stages of development is important because whatever position one adopts has implications for our understanding of both the past and the possible futures of systemic transformation. Most stage theories, including those of some Marxists and the modernization school, focus on national societies as the unit of analysis. National societies are thought to evolve through historical stages, being relatively "advanced" or "underdeveloped." Other Marxists and dependency theorists have focused our attention on the fact that national societies interact with one another in systematic ways and form together a larger system which itself evolves. This reconceptualization solves many of the problems created by the assumption that national societies are independent, but it raises a number of new issues. How are we to conceptualize this larger system and what is the best way to periodize its development? When has it simply adjusted to its own contradictions and when has it become a fundamentally different type of system?

I would like to dismiss outright the notions which entertain a unilinear development of national societies and discuss different approaches to stages of world-system development. Here I will contrast two contemporary views. The first focuses on a series of stages in which the relations between the core and the periphery are thought to be qualitatively different, based on the predominance of different kinds of capital in the core. The second acknowledges these differences but focuses instead on characteristics of the system as a whole which vary over time. It argues that some system characteristics are cyclical in nature, while others are secular trends, and thereby our attention is focused on the similarities of the different periods rather than their differences. Neither of these approaches is "historicist" in the sense of emphasizing what is entirely unique about a particular period. Rather, they both focus on the way in which systematic laws of motion of capital accumulation produce different institutional forms in different periods.

STAGES OF CAPITALISM AND DEPENDENCY

A number of recent Marxist works focusing on the world-system argue a periodization of capitalist development which distinguishes between three (or four) stages in which the characteristics of core capital and its relationship to peripheral areas vary. I will review and compare these periodizations, and then outline a different approach.

Albert Szymanski (1981:95) summarizes his version of periodization as follows:

> Imperialism has gone through four qualitatively distinct stages: first, noncapitalist mercantile imperialism from around 1500 to around 1800; second, competitive capitalist imperialism from around 1840 to around 1880; third, early monopoly capitalist imperialism from around 1890 to around 1960; and fourth, late monopoly capitalist imperialism since the 1960s.

In another version Andre Gunder Frank (1979a:9) approvingly quotes Samir Amin as follows:

> I distinguish 3 periods: (1) mercantilist, (2) developed (*achevé*) capitalist (post industrial revolution, pre-monopolist) and (3) imperialism. To each of these periods there correspond specific functions of the periphery at the service of the essential needs of accumulation at the center. In stage (1) the essential function of the periphery (principally American, supplementarily African which supplied the former with slaves) is to permit the accumulation of money wealth by the Atlantic merchant bourgeoisie, wealth which transforms itself in real (*achevé*) capitalism after the industrial revolution. Hence the system of plantations (after the pillage of mines) around which all of America turns from the XVI to the XVIII centuries. This function loses its importance with the industrial revolution when the centre of gravity of capital moves from commerce to industry. The new function of the periphery thus becomes to lower (a) the value of labor power (through the provision of agricultural products of mass consumption) and (b) the value of the constituent elements of constant capital (by providing raw materials). In other words the periphery permits fighting against the tendential decline in the rate of profit (as Marx as well observed – AGF). To achieve this during period (2) capital has only one means at its disposal: commerce. During period (3) on the other hand, capital also has the very efficient means of the export of capital.

Amin's position on periodization is further explained in his *Imperialism and Unequal Development* (1977:229–35).

Let us focus on the characteristics attributed to each stage and the differences which are alleged to exist between stages. The first transition is that between mercantile (or merchant) capitalism and industrial (competitive, developed) capitalism. The distinctions made here involve assertions about class relations, exchange relations, and the relationship between the state and the economy. Much of this follows from Marx's discussion of merchant capitalism in volume 3 of *Capital* (1967b:323–37) and his distinction between merchant capitalism and the fully developed capitalist mode of production – industrial capitalism. Marx's abstract model of capitalist dynamics as presented in volume 1 of *Capital* assumes a system in which there is competition between capitals, sale of commodities at their labor value, non-interference by the state in the economy, and a closed system in which there is no international trade. Of course Marx did not claim that this model directly represented any concrete society. It is rather an abstraction employing simplifying assumptions which is intended to explicate the underlying developmental tendencies of the capitalist mode of production. British national society in the nineteenth century was Marx's inspiration and is probably the case which approximates most closely to the abstract model. Marx believed that he had teased out the underlying nature of capitalism by examining what he considered to be its purest and most highly developed concrete case, and that other countries would follow Britain's path of development.[1] It was argued in chapter 1 that some of his simplifying assumptions were mistaken, not because they were empirically inaccurate, but because they missed much of that which is fundamental to capitalism as a system.

Marx's model of capitalist accumulation was not intended to apply to the stage of mercantile capitalism. In this stage commercial capital (involving the buying and selling of commodities produced by independent producers) is the most prevalent and important form of enterprise. Merchant capital does not directly co-ordinate production and sales. Production is left to independent producers. Thus merchant capital does not directly subject production to the logic of capitalism. Merchants make profit by buying cheap and selling dear, often by exploiting price differentials between areas which are not integrated into a single market economy. Production capital, on the other hand, directly combines raw materials and labor purchased from proletarians to produce commodities for sale. This integrates the value relations between different types of production such that "abstract labor" comes to exist. This means that market integration is complete and the division of labor is subjected to a single price system. Qualitatively different types of work come to be related to one another in a single quantitative dimension, that of labor value. The commodification of labor is necessary for this to occur, and most Marxists believe that this is only accomplished under the wage system.

Thus merchant capital (before the existence of integrated markets) exchanges "unequals" in the sense that goods are produced in economies in which a single standard of value has not been formed. Merchants make profit by moving commodities from areas in which they have low prices to areas in which they have high prices. It is only within fully developed industrial capitalism that commercial capital (operating *within* a single price system) makes profit by receiving part of the surplus value produced in the production process, not by exchanging unequals. Merchant capital operates solely in the "sphere of circulation," although Marx asserted that it acted as a solvent on precapitalist relations of production under some conditions.

It is similarly asserted that proletarianization is only rudimentary during the period of mercantile capitalism, that is, the wage-earning class is small and there are many extra-market constraints which prevent labor (and other "factors of production") from taking the commodity form. Marx's (1967a:717–33) discussion of primitive accumulation describes how English and Scottish peasants were forcibly separated from the means of production and turned into sellers of labor power from the last part of the fifteenth century on.

The stage of mercantile capitalism is also characterized as a period in which political relations were much more determinant of the terms of exchange and the conditions of production than in later industrial capitalism. The guilds, municipal monopolies, noble privileges, and state policies of mercantilist "armed" trade (Parry, 1966) are understood as proof that market mechanisms were as yet only weakly operating. States operated as "violence-controlling" organizations providing protection for economic operations, enabling their benefactors to realize what Frederic Lane (1979) has called "protection rent." As we will see in part II, this involvement of state power and geopolitical military competition in the accumulation process can be understood as a normal part of capitalism in all periods.

Primitive accumulation in the periphery (plunder, forced labor, monopoly trade) is understood by many Marxists, including Marx himself, as one of the main processes which created the capitalist mode of production, but which is not in itself part of that mode of production.

In the emergence of industrial capitalism a number of important changes are alleged to have occurred. For one thing the "bourgeois revolutions" in Europe destroyed many of the local political encumbrances on trade and production. The formation of national markets was accomplished by the elimination of many of the prerogatives of merchant capital and landed nobilities. Commodity production became much more competitive, at least within the national markets of the core countries. And in the middle of the nineteenth century there was a temporary reduction of political constraints on international trade with the lowering of European and American tariff barriers.

According to many histories of capitalist development this is the period when industrial (or productive) capital came to dominate the economy for the first time. The wage system and the process of expanded accumulation became self-reproducing. Industry became organized as a competitive interaction of small firms, and the rate of technological change increased dramatically. The factory system in which labor was brought together with machinery was created in the English Midlands.

The core/periphery relationship is alleged to have been predominantly a matter of commodity trade during this period, and Ernest Mandel (quoted in Frank, 1979a:8) asserts that this constituted the "equal exchange of equals." A single measure of world value was constituted by the integration of the world division of labor into a single interactive market. It is alleged that trade between the core and the periphery contained equal amounts of labor value in the period of competitive capitalism. And Mandel (1975:49–61) argues that competitive industrial capitalism encouraged indigenous capital-formation in the periphery.

There is some disagreement about the effects of core/periphery trade on the periphery during the period of competitive capitalism. Some Marxist scholars argue that merchant capital tended to dissolve precapitalist relations of production by drawing people into commodity production for the world market. On the other hand, Geoffrey Kay (1975) argues that merchant capital tended to underdevelop the periphery by perpetuating precapitalist forms of production, shoring up traditional rulers, and extracting surplus product. He contrasts this to what he sees as the developmental effects of industrial capital, which directly subjects labor in the periphery to capitalist production, creating the potential for autonomous capitalist growth in the periphery. A similar argument is made by Bill Warren (1980).

Most stage theories envision an important new period of capitalism emerging in the late nineteenth century with the formation of the "monopolies." Since Lenin (1965) this allegedly new development in the core has been causally linked with "imperialism," i.e. the exploitation of peripheral areas by the monopoly capitals of the core. Amin (1977) reserves the term imperialism for this kind of exploitation, and calls earlier capitalist exploitation of the periphery "expansionism." The emergence of "monopoly capitalism" is thought to involve a change in the operation of the process of accumulation. Monopoly pricing within national markets and the extraction of surplus profits by large firms has been understood as a new departure in which the distribution of surplus value is distorted. The so-called "monopoly sector," the sector in which the largest firms dominate the most profitable types of production, is thought to obtain a larger share of the total surplus value by draining surplus value from the "competitive sector."

In addition, the growth of state expenditures and increases in the social wage are understood as subsidizing the costs of reproducing labor power, and thus lowering the wage bill of "monopoly capital." State spending, especially on military forces, is thought to provide a necessary outlet for "economic surplus" (Baran and Sweezy, 1966) and to help resolve the irrationalities of capitalist production by providing employment and investment opportunities not generated in the private sector. The domination of "finance capital" (a coalition of banking and industrial capital) (Hilferding, 1981) in combination with the much more direct involvement of states in sponsoring economic development (Poulantzas, 1973) is alleged to have had important effects on the tendencies of the accumulation process. Arguing the directly opposite position from that of Kay (1975) discussed above, Mandel contends that the emergence of monopoly capitalist imperialism and the export of investment capital to the periphery put a brake on the indigenous capitalist development of the periphery which had begun during the period of competitive capitalism. The declining rate of profit in the core led to the massive export of investment capital to the periphery, but the monopoly nature of this capital and the use of state power in formal colonialism led to the exploitation and underdevelopment of the periphery, according to Mandel.

Mandel, Amin, and Arghiri Emmanuel (1972) contend that the core/periphery relationship altered during the late nineteenth century due to the emergence in the 1880s of a wage differential between core workers and peripheral workers. Previous to that, workers in both the core and the periphery had received subsistence wages, but in the late nineteenth century, due to the diminishing reserve army of labor in England and because of the partial success of labor struggles there, wages for English workers began to rise above subsistence. This brought about the "unequal exchange" analyzed by Emmanuel (1972) in which core/periphery trade came to be the "unequal exchange of equals." When there is a wage differential beyond differences in productivity, market exchange conceals a transfer of surplus value from low wage to high wage regions. This occurs when there is an equalization of the profit rates due to capital flows, but no equalization of wage rates due to labor migration. While both labor and capital have flowed from the core to the periphery and vice versa throughout the history of the capitalist world-system, it is alleged by Emmanuel that the frictions preventing wage equalization are greater than the frictions encountered by exports of investment capital.

Many Marxists argue that the middle of the twentieth century brought the emergence of yet another stage of capitalist development. This has been termed "late capitalism" by Mandel and is thought to be characterized by the increased importance of "technological rents" and the further institutionalization of science in the profit-making process (see also Habermas, 1970). This period is also characterized by the great expansion of the transnational corporations that co-ordinate production and profit-making on a global scale.

The alleged consequences of this new stage for core/periphery relations are described in chapter 4. Whereas Kay (1975) argued that production capital of any kind involving direct investment and control of peripheral production caused autonomous capitalist accumulation in the periphery, Warren (1980) argued that it is the export of *industrial* capital which causes capitalist growth in the periphery. Following Warren, Szymanski (1981) made a distinction between "early" and "late" monopoly capitalist imperialism, with only the latter having positive growth effects on the periphery.

The thesis that the latest stage of capitalism is less detrimental to the economic growth of the periphery is shared to a certain extent by some dependency theorists (e.g. Dos Santos, 1963; Cardoso and Faletto, 1979). Peter Evans (1979) discusses the emergence of "dependent development" in the Latin American periphery based on the production of manufactured goods for the home markets of Latin American countries by transnational corporations. While these authors agree that the "new dependency" (or "associated-dependent development") perpetuates the core/periphery structure of power in many ways, they also believe that overall economic growth is increased by this new form of core penetration. This contention is disputed by Frank, Amin, and Mandel, who believe that real economic development in the periphery is only possible in the context of a socialist revolution.

As discussed in chapter 4, Folker Fröbel, Jürgen Heinrichs and Otto Kreye (1980) have argued that a "new international division of labor" has been created by transnational corporations using free production zones in the periphery to employ cheap labor to produce manufactured goods for the world market. John Borrego (1982) contends that the core/periphery hierarchy itself is disappearing with the emergence of a new stage of "metanational" capitalism. This kind of emerging stage of global capitalism is also described by Robert Ross and Kent Trachte (forthcoming).

CYCLES OF WORLD-SYSTEM DEVELOPMENT

Another view of the stages of development of the capitalist world-system is that proposed in chapter 2. This view periodizes development in terms of characteristics of the system as a whole: constant features, cyclical processes, and secular trends. It suggests a modified model of the capitalist mode of production which is true to the spirit, but not the letter, of Marx's accumulation model. The capitalist mode of production is understood as commodity production for profit on the world market in which labor is a commodity but is not always paid a wage. Capitalist production relations are understood as the articulation between wage labor in the core and coerced labor in the periphery. The interaction between core and periphery is understood as fundamental to capitalism as a system. Thus imperialism (generally understood, including colonialism, direct investment, core/periphery trade, and neocolonialism) is conceived to be integral to the functioning of the capitalist mode of production. Capitalism thus includes both expanded reproduction in the core and primary accumulation in the periphery. Primary accumulation is not merely a process of creating capitalist production relations, but is rather a permanent and necessary feature of capitalism as a mode of production. The state and the interstate system are not separate from capitalism, but are rather the main institutional supports of capitalist production relations. The system of unequally powerful and competing nation states is part of the competitive struggle of capitalism, and thus wars and geopolitics are a systematic part of capitalist dynamics, not exogenous forces.

According to Wallerstein (1974), the first epoch of capitalist development, from 1450 to 1640, was the period of the transition from feudalism and the somewhat precarious emergence of the institutions and class relations of the capitalist mode of production in Europe. The crisis of feudalism, fundamentally a class struggle between lords and peasants, was resolved by a reorganization of accumulation on the basis of primarily agrarian capitalism and a territorial expansion. Marx's (1967a:713–50) analysis of "primitive accumulation" as the process of creating the institutional bases of capitalism clearly applies to this epoch. The direct plunder of Africa and the New World which brought money-capital to Europe was followed by the forcible creation of a proletariat in the core and the extension of serfdom and slavery in the periphery. The reorganization of agriculture on an increasingly capitalist basis, albeit quite differently in the core and in the periphery, was accompanied by the further development of capitalist production in the towns of the core. The process of capitalist accumulation, involving both uneven development and successive periods of expansion to new areas, became the main determinant of development in the European world-economy during the long sixteenth century.

The second epoch, from 1640 to 1815, is understood as one in which the European capitalist world-economy stagnated somewhat and then was stabilized (Wallerstein, 1980a). This was the period of Dutch hegemony and the fierce competition among the Dutch, English, and French for the colonial profits of the older Portuguese and Spanish empires. The competition between the English and the French for hegemony was finally resolved after the failure of Napoleon's bid for world empire (or earlier; see Braudel, 1977:102).

The third epoch, from 1815 to 1917, is understood as the period of the final expansion of the capitalist system to the whole globe and its consolidation. This period saw another economic reorganization known as the "industrial" revolution, which was actually just another expansion of capital intensity in industrial and agriculture production. The "factory system" further extended the trend toward rapid urbanization of the work force in the core. The *Pax Britannica* was followed by the "new imperialism" in which the newly rising core and semiperipheral powers – the USA, Germany, Italy, and

Belgium, Japan, and Russia – scrambled for peripheral territory in competition with the older core powers. This period of disorganization and intense competition led eventually to what is conventionally called World War I.

The fourth epoch, from 1917 to the present, is understood as the final consolidation of the system and the beginning of the period of its crisis and transformation to a fundamentally different kind of system. This is the period of the *Pax Americana*, the decolonization of almost all of the periphery, the increased integration of global production by capitalist firms (public and private), and the emergence of anti-capitalist forces which increasingly limit the manuevering room for capitalist accumulation. The period since 1945 is scrutinized more closely in the next chapter.

The four epochs outlined above can be understood analytically as involving three kinds of structural elements: (1) those underlying institutional features and developmental laws that are basic to capitalism as a system; (2) cyclical processes which repeat themselves in each of the epochs; and (3) secular trends which increase at a varying rate across all of the epochs. These elements and some of their interrelations have been described in chapter 2.

The cycles and trends listed in chapter 2 must be applied to each epoch with some qualifications. The first epoch (1450–1640), due to the as yet poorly formed and unstable institutional basis of capitalist development, did not exhibit all the features characteristic of later epochs. Thus Portugal and Spain, though performing some of the functions of hegemonic core states in this period, were not centers of comparative advantage in commodity production. The attempt by the Habsburgs to impose a political empire over the whole European world-economy revealed a "precapitalist" predilection for political domination reminiscent of the tributary modes of production. It is significant that later hegemonic core powers have never attempted to create a world imperium.

During the first epoch the center of economic hegemony moved from Venice to Genoa and then to Antwerp (see Braudel, 1984). George Modelski (1978) has argued that Portugal played the role of a "great power" providing international order through geopolitical leadership during the sixteenth century. Spatial differentiation of economic and political–military hegemony was a common characteristic of tributary world-systems. Only in the fully institutionalized capitalist world-economy which emerged in Europe did these roles become merged, and this occurred first with the rise of Dutch hegemony in the seventeenth century. In the second epoch (1640–1815) the hegemony of Amsterdam was fully established during and following the Thirty Years War. Its hegemony was soon challenged by British and French rivals. The economic slowdown of the seventeenth century was followed by the expanding Atlantic economy of the eighteenth century in which Britain and France fought for supremacy. The cyclical expansion of the colonial empires occurred near the end of every epoch. Bergesen and Schoenberg (1980) show that the peaks of expansion (in terms of the number of new colonies established) were in 1640, 1785, and 1890 (see figure 13.4). Colonial expansion was accompanied by more political control by core states over core/periphery trade, whereas during periods in which a single core power attained economic hegemony there was a more market-determined trade relationship between the core and the periphery. This cycle of core/periphery trade and control structures occurred in every epoch.

The third epoch (1815–1917) may be understood as the "classic" period in terms of the trends and cycles described above. The British came into both political–military and economic hegemony after the defeat of the French in a series of wars from 1756 to 1815. Napoleon's failure to impose imperium on the world-economy allowed the British hegemony in production to expand into the markets of the continent and the newly independent Latin American states.

The fourth epoch (1917 to the present) is confusing in so far as it is a period in which the contradictions of capitalist development meet certain "ceiling effects" or obstacles which constrain readjustment of the capitalist accumulation process (Chase-Dunn and Rubinson, 1979). For example, a number of the secular trends described have run up against limits. There are no more human societies for the capitalist mode of production to invade and conquer. There is no more territory to be grabbed by colonizing core states. As Lenin pointed out, further expansion by competing core states must involve the redivision of territory already conquered. This constraint on expansion has been further exacerbated by the achievement of formal sovereignty in almost the whole periphery. Thus competing core states must often vie with one another for access to the periphery by offering better terms. This is a far cry from the 1885 Berlin Congress on Africa in which the core states divided that continent among themselves without consulting Africans at all.

These ceiling effects which limit the further expansion of the capitalist system to new populations and territories do not, of course, preclude its deepening. They do, however, tend to limit the degrees of freedom available to capital in its attempt to adjust to the contradictions created by its own development. Also, the "socialist" revolutions which have taken state power in the semiperiphery and the periphery create obstacles to the maneuverability of capital. If the present period is one of transformation we should expect a combination of the old cycles characteristic of previous epochs with newly emerging institutions and forms of struggle. One of the most important tasks is to sort out the processes of the old system from the harbingers of a new one.

For example, the schema in chapter 2 would predict that the decline of United States hegemony would be followed by a period of intense conflict between core states, colonial expansion in the periphery, and the emergence of a new hegemonic core state. A number of new features of world-system development may modify this scenario, however. The formal recolonization of the periphery by core states seems unlikely. Functional substitutes in the form of gunboat diplomacy, covert intervention, and contention about "back-yards" or imperial spheres of influence may bring a similitude of the old colonial empires, but the differences are important. The costs of empire have undoubtedly increased in this world where the peripheral states band together to demand a "new international economic order," though the success of this peripheral solidarity has been limited. The emergence of a new hegemonic core state, or block of states, in the next 40 years also seems unlikely. As likely is the emergence of some limited form of world political authority following a period of disorganization (or war) among the present core states. World-state-formation would represent a fundamental systemic change.

With the above qualifications to the cyclical schema in mind let us now compare the world-system approach to periodizing capitalist development with the "stages of capitalism" approach outlined in the first part of this chapter.

DIFFERENCES BETWEEN THE TWO TYPES OF PERIODIZATION

Broadly speaking, the world cycles approach emphasizes the continuity of the basic capitalist processes in each of the periods, while the "stages of capitalism" approach emphasizes differences of form and consequence. Wallerstein's approach implies that production capital (both agricultural and industrial) has always been the driving force of development and thus "industrial revolutions" have occurred in every epoch. In the sixteenth century it was not merchant capital but production capital in agriculture and town manufactures which, with revolutionized class relations, created the basis for increased productivity and a strengthened set of states in the core. In the seventeenth century it was Amsterdam's productive advantage in the herring industry, dairy farming, and shipbuilding which was the basis of its hegemony, not only mercantile "armed trade" (Wallerstein, 1980a: chapter 2). Similarly, investment in the periphery by the great chartered companies, the establishment of plantations worked by slaves, and the extensive export of capital from Amsterdam to other core countries as well as to peripheral areas (Barbour, 1963) cannot be understood under the rubric of "merchant capital."

Sidney Mintz's (1985) analysis of the place of sugar production and consumption in the development of the modern world-system describes sugar cane plantations in the Caribbean as "factories in the field." Mintz (1985:46–52) contends that these agricultural enterprises, which combined planting with a processing operation to produce crystallized sucrose, were an important and early instance of the factory system. Mintz's (1985:59–61) thoughtful discussion of the capitalistic nature of the plantation system qualifies to some extent his earlier contention that the sugar-producing slaves can be understood as proletarians (Mintz, 1977). He emphasizes the processual connections between New World slavery and the wage-based industrial capitalism which was expanding in England, but he also points to important differences between the two. These differences are reconciled with an understanding of capitalism once we employ the notions of core and peripheral forms of capitalism necessarily linked with one another.

Some authors have contended that the slave-based plantation system was a form of merchant capitalism, a contention which would seemingly be contradicted by the fact that plantations involved the direct investment of core capital to produce commodities. For Marx merchant capitalism was defined as the purchasing of goods which are resold for a profit. The idea of merchant capital has been extended beyond this definition, especially by Fox-Genovese and Genovese (1983). They link their idea of merchant capital with slave production and stress the anti-capitalist world view of the slave-holders as evidence that they were not capitalists. Eugene Genovese's earlier work (1971, 1974) demonstrates fascinating linkages among consciousness, ideology, resistance, and economic structures, but the contention that the aristocratic ideals of the slave-holders proves that they were not capitalists equates ideological and structural positions too simply. The critiques by slave-owners of industrial slums and the crass cash nexus of the impersonal wage system (in contrast to their own paternal concern for their slaves) may rather be interpreted as the fruit of political competition between two groups of capitalists with conflicting interests. It would not have been the first time (or the last) that a group of capitalists with investments sunk in a certain form or scale of production employed the ideology of paternalism (or nationalism) against a newer competing group.

The tendency for states to interfere with trade and to regulate production, and the establishment of guilds and associations attempting to protect the positions of certain producers, are not seen as characteristics unique to a period of "mercantilism." Rather, these attempts to use political organizations to guarantee market advantages are understood as normally recurring moments of capitalist development itself. Every capital is anxious to obtain political protection of its own markets and resources. Arguments in favor of free trade are employed by those who fear the political controls of others. In such a light the similarities of "mercantilism" with "monopoly capitalism" are most apparent. Braudel (1977:95) makes this point, but argues that the creation of a protected home market only became crucial in the nineteenth century. Prior to this, according to Braudel, it was city states rather than nation states that performed the role of hegemonic core power. It may rather be that certain processes create a fairly constant ratio between the size of the home market of the hegemonic core power and the total size of the system.

Thus Amsterdam's United Provinces may be understood as intermediate between Venice's petite "national" territory and London's Great Britain. And, of course, the giant size of the US internal market corresponds with the greater extent and density of the contemporary world market.

The argument has been made by some of the proponents of the "stages of capitalism" view of periodization that the form and consequences of the core/periphery relationship have changed from period to period. Plunder was followed by trade, and that by direct production for export, and then transnational corporate control of production for the peripheral market itself. While it is clear that the forms of labor exploitation in the periphery have changed, the basic underlying process of "primary accumulation" (in the sense of politically coercive labor control) have been a reproduced feature of the core/periphery relationship right up to the present.[2]

Clearly, the form of primary accumulation has changed from epoch to epoch, and in some sense it has become less "primitive" – that is, closer in form to the "free" labor of the core. Thus the direct plunder of treasure and slaves was replaced by the establishment of "coerced cash crop" labor (capitalist slavery and serfdom) – which was then later replaced by colonial trade economies in which labor was either paid a below-subsistence wage or else small commodity producers were exploited through a politically controlled unequal market exchange. Neocolonial forms of labor exploitation are undoubtedly closer in form to the "free" labor of the core, but they are still more determined by direct political coercion.

Giovanni Arrighi (1978) argues that the different forms of core/periphery relations are used at all times, with varying weights depending on the period and the historical situation of the particular core power. It is most probably the case that "economic" penetration of the periphery by merchants, settlers, and direct investment is more prevalent during periods of rapid growth in the world-economy, while more politically coercive forms of penetration (formal colonialism, monopoly trade, and forced labor) are employed more frequently when the world-economy is in contraction and competing producers rely more on state power to protect or extend their share of world surplus value.

It may be true that the gap between the degree of coercion of core labor and that of peripheral labor has narrowed, but it has most certainly not been eliminated. What is clear from a long-run perspective is that the juridical form of labor control, that is whether or not labor is formally paid a wage, is not the only determinant of the commodity nature of labor. Nor is it the only dimension of the core/periphery hierarchy. Even if the entire world-economy were to be composed of capitalists and wage laborers, the interstate system would tend to reproduce the core/periphery hierarchy. The size of the relative gap between the incomes of core and peripheral workers has greatly increased over the long run, while absolute levels of living have risen, albeit unevenly, in the periphery. Thus immiseration has tended to be relative rather than absolute (see chapter 12), while exploitation (in the formal Marxist sense) has everywhere increased.

The Wallersteinian world-system perspective implies that there has always been a core/periphery wage differential, contrary to the arguments of Emmanuel, Amin, and Mandel that this developed only in the late nineteenth century. This differential has certainly increased over the long-run operation of the system, but core workers and the middle strata have always had political advantages as well as an involvement in more profitable and more skilled types of production, and these factors resulted in higher average incomes for core workers from the sixteenth century on. This problem is considered further in chapter 10.

Brenner (1977) has made an important critique of Wallerstein's contention that the "second serfdom" in Eastern Europe was a capitalist response to market opportunities created by the emerging division of labor between the core and the periphery in the long sixteenth century. Brenner argues that the system in which serfs were legally bound to work on the landlord's demesne did not allow increases in productivity through the use of new techniques. Thus he claims it was not capitalist. It is of course true that coerced labor is somewhat incompatible with capital intensive processes of production. But this was hardly the issue for Polish landlords who wanted to produce something to exchange for West European products. Their class position gave them a political advantage which made the use of coercion rational from the point of view of their own profits.

Contrary to what Brenner implies, Wallerstein has never said that coerced labor is the most efficient or productive form from the point of view of the whole system. Serf labor, although not very productive, was partially commodified in the sense that it was subjected to exploitation for the purpose of profitable commodity production, and its "price" (costs of political coercion) influenced the costs of production and the profitability of the operation. Brenner claims that the juridical nature of serfdom prevented it from responding to market forces, but the enserfment of Polish peasants in the sixteenth century was driven forward in response to the West European demand for grain. And the further coercive exploitation of East European serfs in the seventeenth century was a response to declining world wheat prices (Wallerstein, 1980a:129–44).

Another point of contention between the two types of periodization is whether or not the *consequences* of core penetration of the periphery have changed with the reorganizations of dominant capital and core/periphery relations. As stated above, Kay (1975), and others (Warren, 1980; Szymanski, 1981) have argued that contemporary transnational investment in peripheral countries creates the possibility for autonomous capitalist economic development in these countries. On the other hand, many dependency theorists have argued that the consequence of transnational investment is to continue to underdevelop peripheral countries relative to those other peripheral countries which are less dependent on foreign investment. Crossnational comparative research on the post-World War II period reveals that countries with higher levels of penetration by foreign capital grow more slowly (other things being equal) than countries with lower levels of transnational corporate penetration (Bornschier and Chase-Dunn, 1985). In addition, it has been shown that, contrary to Szymanski's argument, it is transnational investment *in manufacturing* that has the largest negative effects on aggregate national economic growth. These studies reveal that foreign capital investment inflows have immediate positive effects on GNP growth, but long-run negative consequences as the effects of structural distortions and repatriation of profits spread to the national economy as a whole. The implication of these findings is that core capital continues to have the effect of recreating the gap between core and periphery. Changes in the form and structure of core/periphery relations which have occurred in the twentieth century have not operated to eliminate the development of underdevelopment.

It may be the case that, just as the terms of trade between core and periphery are known to alternate cyclically in favor of, or against, the periphery (Barrat-Brown, 1974), the wage gap also exhibits a cyclical as well as a secular increase. If this is true the increase noted by Mandel (1975) and Amin (1975) in the 1880s may have been part of a cyclical shift rather than a completely new trend in core/periphery relations as they allege. Research on recent trends in the core/periphery wage differential is reported in chapter 12.

One explanation for uneven development is the effect which class struggle has on the concentration of capital in a particular area. Successful accumulation is usually accompanied by rising wages due to demand for skilled labor, exhaustion of the reserve army of the unemployed, and the growth of trade unions which allow workers to influence access to jobs and the level of wages. This process of class struggle eventually causes capital to flow to areas where labor is cheaper to obtain a competitive advantage. This is part of the explanation for the flow of capital to the periphery. But the continued cheapening of constant capital inputs by technological development can also cause cheap labor in the periphery to lose its competitive advantage. Thus, as Mandel points out, capital intensive agricultural production within core countries in the twentieth century has replaced much labor intensive peripheral agricultural production. This "seesawing" process of uneven development, the alternating concentration and spread of capitalist production techniques and investment, creates a cycle in which the gap between core wages and peripheral wages may become alternately larger or smaller. Though the gap has definitely increased over the last hundred years (chapter 12), it remains to be empirically demonstrated whether or not this trend also contains a cycle.

In discussing differences between the twentieth century and earlier epochs it is important to distinguish that which is superficially different from that which reveals a fundamental crisis of capitalism. One reason to carefully consider the problem of periodization *within* the capitalist mode of production is so that we may be able to distinguish those new forms which reproduce capitalism from those forms which might transform it. The mere scale of phenomena in the twentieth century, the rate of change, the size of organizations, the global nature of production and consumption, are often seen as qualitative differences from earlier epochs. The world cycles approach emphasizes the continuity with the earlier epochs in terms of the underlying processes at work, but also alerts us to those key features which should be watched to detect signs of structural transformation.

The discussion of the growth of monopoly or oligopoly power, or of the emergence of a new stage of "monopoly capitalism," often assumes that the use of politically organized price distortions alters the underlying rules of capitalist development. On this basis some Marxists have argued that volume 1 of Marx's *Capital* is no longer relevant for the analysis of development because it assumes equilibrium prices and competition among capitals. I argue in chapter 4 that this is not the case. The world-economy remains a very competitive arena in which there are no *long-run* monopolies. The profit rate which equalizes over the long run is the "surplus" profit rate, that which includes profits due to the exercise of monopoly power. In this light *Capital*, with some revisions (the addition of the interstate system and class struggle) remains relevant for understanding contemporary capitalist development.

Also, in the twentieth century we have "state capitalism" in which states themselves act like firms which are competing in the world market. Here the use of political mobilization, coercion, and productive advantage are combined in a very direct way. This is *not*, however, a completely new feature. Political power has always been used to distort market processes in favor of certain groups. What remains the case in this epoch is that there is no single overarching political authority which can control the whole arena of economic competition, and so the process of capitalist accumulation continues. Let us now look more closely at the period since World War II.

4

The World-system since 1945: What has Changed?

To answer completely the question posed in the title of this chapter we would need a clear formulation of the deep structural logic of the capitalist world-economy, and a way of determining the extent to which new developments have altered its logic. The level of specification obtained regarding the nature of the capitalist mode of production in chapter 1 is somewhat crude. Yet we can employ it and the schema presented in chapter 2 to make some guesses about the extent of change. Of interest in such an exercise is the problem of when quantitative change becomes qualitative change.

A NEW STAGE OF CAPITALISM?

Several recent analysts claim that capitalism has entered a new stage since World War II. This contention utilizes the notion that capitalism goes through stages which differ from one another in systemically important ways.[1] In chapter 3 I have argued that a theory of cycles and trends can account for most of the changes across epochs which are claimed to be stages of capitalism. Here I want to focus on the changes alleged to have occurred since World War II, or to be occurring now.

Albert Szymanski (1981:95) contends that a transition from "early monopoly capitalist imperialism" to "late monopoly capitalist imperialism" occurred around 1960. John Borrego (1982) speaks of the recent transition from national to metanational capitalist accumulation. Robert Ross and Kent Trachte (forthcoming) speak of the transition from monopoly capitalism to global capitalism.

The substantive observations on which claims of a qualitative transition are based differ among the different authors. Szymanski argues that the most recent stage is based on the decolonization and industrialization of the periphery. Borrego, and Ross and Trachte, focus on the increased importance of globally operating firms. These contentions and others will be analyzed below.

My discussion of the various claims about qualitative change will be organized into the following topics:

1 the transnationalization of capital;
2 technological rents;
3 the new international division of labor;
4 world classes and world state formation; and
5 a socialist world-system.

The Transnationalization of Capital

Some social scientists, on first perceiving the reality of the world-economy, have assumed that its importance as a systemic logic which has major effects on the development of subunits is of quite recent origin (e.g. Michalet, 1976), or that it has just recently become transnational[2] (Hymer, 1979). These claims may be broken down into their constituent arguments, which involve the logic of investment decisions, monopolization, effects on states, and effects on prices and value. Arguments about the effects of the growth and reorganization of transnational firms on the peripheral countries will be discussed below in the section on the "new international division of labor."

It is undeniable that transnational firms have grown in size and importance since 1945. Their expansion and operations in particular countries have been the subject of many excellent studies (Biersteker, 1978; Evans, 1979; Gereffi, 1983; Bennett and Sharpe, 1985) as have various aspects of economic and political institutions within core states that have affected the growth of transnational investment (Krasner, 1978; Hawley, 1983; Lipson, 1985). The fact of this growth is presented by some analysts as evidence that the logic of the world-system must have changed. This connection needs to be examined.

The great chartered companies were the first transnational corporations, engaging in both merchant capitalism (buying cheap and selling dear) and productive capitalism (the direct organization of commodity production). They were joint stock companies which were allocated monopoly rights and political–military protection by the individual core states that chartered them. These "monopolies," however, were usually incomplete and often short-lived because competition among the chartered companies of different core states was rife.

Some authors have alleged that the contemporary transnational corporations are controlled by international groups of capitalists not aligned with any particular core state (e.g. M. Dixon, 1982). In terms of the ownership of stock, it has been shown that almost all of the modern transnational firms are, in fact, owned and controlled by capitalists from a single core state (Mandel,

1975). Nevertheless there is some co-participation in ownership across national boundaries. This feature, however, is not new. Barbour (1963) reports that disgruntled seventeenth-century Amsterdam merchants not able to obtain shares in the Dutch East India Company were instrumental in the formation of the English East India Company.

The fact that some capital was transnational in the seventeenth century does not contradict the contention that it is more transnational now. The question is, what difference does that make for the logic of investment decisions and capital accumulation? The great chartered companies, along with peripheral plantations and mines, were primarily operated according to the logic of productive capital rather than merely merchant capital (Barr, 1981). But it is undoubtedly the case that the direct organization of production by capital has become much more firmly entrenched since the seventeenth century. Merchant capital, buying products from independent producers, has been increasingly replaced by productive capital directly controlling the production of commodities. Transport and communications costs have declined in a geometric fashion, facilitating the expansion of the spatial extent of investment strategies. Thus the world-economy is more integrated by global investment decisions and international sourcing than ever before. But does this constitute a change in logic or merely a change in scale?

The schema presented in chapter 2 accounts rather well for most of the recent changes, especially as it designates trends toward transnationalization, capital intensity, and the increasing size of firms. It could be argued, however, that these quantitative trends have led to qualitative changes in the nature of the game.

One undeniable consequence of the greater integration of the world-economy by transnational corporations and the shift away from merchant capitalism is the increasing systemness of the system. Merchant capitalism trades commodities between regions that have not become fully integrated as systems of production. Marx (1967b) describes how merchant capital eventually creates "abstract labor" by subjecting qualitatively different kinds of production to an equivalent standard – "socially necessary labor time." Unintegrated systems have price structures which vary according to their social structural uniquenesses, differences in natural endowments, and techniques of production.

Merchant capital moves goods from areas where they are cheap to areas where they are dear in the "exchange of unequals" (Amin, 1980a). But the long-run consequence of such exchanges is to alter the allocation of labor time in both areas such that they move toward the formation of a single equilibrated system in terms of the "efficient" allocation of labor and other scarce resources.

No market system is ever in perfect equilibrium in the above sense, and indeed a certain inequality of labor values is part of the institutional nature of the capitalist world-economy – the unequal exchange between the core and the periphery (Emmanuel, 1972). The long-run consequence of the action of market exchange is to produce a single interactional set of prices which reflect the competitive rationality of a market system. Most of the remaining structural barriers to the equalization of wages and other prices are generated by the structure of capitalism itself. They are generally not "survivals" from the past, but are themselves produced by competition and conflict among classes and states in the context of the capitalist mode of production.

The trends toward the transnationalization of capital, the further integration of the world-economy, and the growing importance of production decisions on a global scale, reduce the importance of the remnants of precapitalist systems. The capitalist mode of production became dominant in the European world-economy of the long sixteenth century, but it still interacted with precapitalist modes of production which continued to have some influence on the historical development of the system. As it expanded it incorporated other socio-economic systems into itself and these too have left some institutional remnants which have influenced the particular configurations of development in different areas (Wolf, 1982; Nolan and Lenski, 1985). Some institutional aspects of these precapitalist modes of production undoubtedly remain, but their importance has certainly decreased with the growing integration of the system.

Some analysts have argued that the increasing importance of the transnational corporations has altered the logic of capitalism toward a less competitive, more monopolized and monolithic system. It is true that a large and growing component of international trade is made up of *intra*firm transfers. The effect of this, it is alleged, is to decrease the overall amount of competition in the system.

This argument is analogous to the discussion of the transition from competitive to monopoly capitalism (see chapter 3). It is alleged that there was once a stage of capitalism in which the state did not interfere in production decisions or markets, but merely provided the institutional support for the operation of free markets in land, labor, and capital. Firms were small, start-up costs were low, and thus the competitive market system forced firms to produce as cheaply as possible and to sell their products at the lowest possible prices.

This version is alleged to describe Britain in the late eighteenth and early nineteenth centuries. In fact it describes certain sectors of the British economy which have become idealized in economic myth. It is true that capitalism is a dynamic system which has always had a "competitive sector" of high-risk, small-scale entrepreneurs and that, at certain periods in certain countries, something approximating the free market model has actually operated.

Once we focus on the world-economy rather than national economies a number of things become clear. First, most states most of the time have attempted to influence production and market forces in favor of some group of capitalists. The *laissez-faire* state is merely a special case, in which one set of comparatively advantaged capitalists has succeeded in reducing the political favoritism formerly offered to another set. Second, although monopolies are granted by states and enforced within municipalities and by other political organizations, cartels, guilds, unions, etc., *there are no long-run monopolies in the capitalist world-economy*. The political organizations which grant monopolies are themselves in competition with one another, and, since no one can really escape interaction in the larger arena for long, protectionist measures and monopoly rights are themselves subjected to a logic of competition.

These observations are no less true in the 1980s than they were in previous centuries, except that the size of the largest firms has increased relative to the size of states. It is this last development which has caused some authors to argue that competitive capitalism has changed into monopoly capitalism.

Monopoly pricing allows firms to pass on costs to those consumers over whom they have some direct or indirect political influence. If the world-system had a single overarching state apparatus, true and complete monopolies could be maintained. But in a world-economy with a competitive interstate system, monopolies are partial and temporary.

At the global level there are no industries that could be described as uncompetitive, despite the growth of transnational firms. The recent glut of steel, cars, oil, ships, and other world commodities reminds us of the continuing "anarchy of production decisions" which has always been a feature of capitalism (Strange and Tooze, 1981).

Ross and Trachte (forthcoming) argue the opposite: that the emergence of global capitalism *increases* the competitiveness of the system as market shares are no longer guaranteed within national boundaries. The relevant market for leading edge, core industries has always been the world market (both national and international markets). The rise of oligopoly within national markets enabled core firms to compete in terms of product development instead of price competition within their "own" national markets, while the international markets have been and continue to be more price competitive. The product cycle, in which new products are developed in the core countries and older products move on to the price competition of second tier core and semiperipheral countries, is not new. Joint ventures between Japanese and American auto and electronics firms may be somewhat novel, but they do not constitute oligopoly at the global level.

Ross and Trachte also claim that capital flight has taken on new significance as a key lever of domination in the relationship between capital and labor. It is clearly true that the spatial scale of production location has expanded beyond the organizational capacity of contemporary trade unions, but this also happened in the late nineteenth and early twentieth centuries as textile production moved out of New England to the Southern states of the US. Truly international unionism could once again enable workers to combat capital's ability to utilize job blackmail, although few signs of a new wave of trade union internationalism are visible.

Several analysts have suggested that the increased importance of transnational corporations has diminished the power of nation states. Raymond Vernon stated this thesis most strongly in his *Sovereignty at Bay* (1971). A modified version has been discussed by Marlene Dixon (1982) in her essay on "dual power." It is clearly the case that transnational corporations have increased their power *vis-à-vis* small peripheral states. And, simply as a function of their size, the largest firms may have increased their influence over core states as well. It should be remembered, however, that states have also increased their powers. The question is, whether or not the changing relationship between the size of firms and the power of states has altered the logic of the game.

Above it was pointed out that, contrary to the contentions of some authors, most of the world's largest firms continue to be primarily controlled by capitalists from one or another of the core states. Thus there are no truly multinational firms from the point of view of ownership. Among the 50 largest transnational firms in the world only Unilever and Royal Dutch Shell could be considered "binational" in terms of ownership (Bergesen and Sahoo, 1985). The extent to which these firms may constitute an integrated world bourgeoisie is discussed below in the section on world class-formation. Here I wish to address the relationship between firms and states.

It is obvious that transnational firms do not control their own armies, nor do they have powers of taxation. The usual distinction between "private" firms and public organizations becomes very problematic when we consider the case of state capitalism. But, even considering the growth of direct state control of production, there remains an important difference between economic and political sources of power in the capitalist world-economy.

Firms continue to rely on states for the provision of "order." Frederic Lane (1979) has analyzed this interaction in terms of the notion of "protection rent," and the best state (from the capitalist point of view) is the one that provides the social conditions for profit-making at cost. Transnational corporations have contradictory interests *vis-à-vis* states. On the one hand they need *world order*, not merely order within national boundaries, and this requires a fairly stable set of alliances among the strongest core states. On the other hand, they make great profits from their ability to play off states against one another. States compete to offer the best deals to attract the capital investments of the transnationals. And transnationals desire to maintain the maneuverability which the multistate system guarantees.

The power of the transnational firms should not be overestimated, however. Their dependence on individual states is still very great. They cannot suppress strikes, political challenges, or nationalizations without being able to mobilize the police forces and armies controlled by states, and so they must maintain influence and control over states. This cannot be done solely by threat of capital flight. It must also be done by supporting friendly politicians, paying taxes, and demonstrating "good citizenship" as shown by public affairs campaigns and "social" activities. This is most true of their relations with core states, of course. But even in peripheral states they must co-opt some support, even if this only means bribing a few generals.

The "sovereignty at bay" thesis was most believable when it was first put forth in the 1960s. At that time the world economy was still growing. Stagnation had not yet raised the banner of protectionism and the use of political power to maintain access to markets and profit-making opportunities. When the pie is shrinking the world-system turns toward a much more statecentric system, which provides the basis for neomercantilist "realist" interpretations (e.g. Krasner, 1978). M. Dixon's (1982) dual power thesis is correct. The complicated game of competition in the capitalist world-economy is a combination of profitable commodity production with efficient use of geopolitical power. But this is not a new development. Rather we have experienced in recent years a shift which has occurred many times before, from capitalist profit-making in an expanding market to equally capitalist geopolitical competition involving mercantilism, austerity, and the threat of world war.

"Creative financing" and the casino quality of international financial transactions (Strange, 1986) have certainly become more salient in the current period partly because of the geometric leap in the turnover time of finance capital which is associated with faster communications and the further transnationalization of capital and commodity and money markets. But it was in the 1920s that Hilferding (1981) first proclaimed that finance capital had created a new stage of capitalism because the banks had taken control of capitalist production. The struggle between money-capital and production capital has seesawed back and forth for centuries. The seemingly magic quality of funny money has always eventually returned to some more stable relationship to use values, and I expect that the current wild period will lead to a period of "devalorization" by one means or another.

Technological Rents

Mandel (1975) and Habermas (1970) argue that post World War II capitalism is different in important ways because the largest firms compete with one another for technological rents derived from the application of science and engineering to production. Rather than competing for markets for the same product by cutting costs and prices, the largest firms compete by developing new products. A version of this argument has been used by Arrighi (1982) in his description of the important differences between the last decades and earlier periods of world-system development. Arrighi argues that the emphasis on competition through the engineering of new products is the major explanation for "stagflation," the allegedly peculiar combination of slower economic growth and higher unemployment with price inflation. The uniqueness of stagflation is in some doubt however. Goldstein (1986) argues that there has always been a lag between the long cycle of production and the long cycle of prices. This would imply a "normal" interval of stagflation within the K-wave (see Goldstein, 1988: chapter 10). Nevertheless Arrighi may be right that the operation of trends toward the larger size of firms, transnationalization, and competition through product differentiation have made stagflation a more salient feature of the most recent downturn.

The New International Division of Labor

Several versions of the "new international division of labor thesis" have been offered. The most extreme version of the thesis claims that the core/periphery territorial division of labor has been eliminated, with metanational capitalist accumulation taking place globally irrespective of territorial location. Another version contends that peripheral capitalism (based on "primary" accumulation using coerced labor to produce cheap, labor intensive raw material inputs) has been eliminated as a consequence of the industrialization of peripheral countries. Yet another version emphasizes the political autonomy of former peripheral areas following decolonization and the demise of the colonial empires. We shall examine these arguments in turn.

First let us describe the core/periphery hierarchy as it has been conceptualized in the world-system perspective. The underlying analytic basis of this territorial hierarchy is the distinction between core production and peripheral production. Core production is relatively capital intensive and employs skilled, high wage labor; peripheral production is labor intensive and employs cheap, often politically coerced labor. In core areas there is a predominance of core production, and the obverse condition exists in peripheral areas. This means that there may be backwaters of peripheral production within core states. Wallerstein defines semiperipheral states as areas containing a relatively equal mix of core and peripheral types of production.

One of the main structural features which reproduce this territorial hierarchy is the exercise of political–military power by core states. It is not simply a matter of original differences among areas in terms of wage levels and "historical" standards of living, as Emmanuel (1972) implies. The wage differential between core and peripheral workers is a dynamic and reproduced feature of the system. Core states (the most powerful political organizations in the system) are induced to provide some protection for the wages of their citizens, as well as supplemental benefits composing the social wage. The core/periphery wage differential is greater than that which would be due to differences in productivity alone, and this differential is maintained by restrictions on international labor migration from the periphery to the core. The great differences in capital intensity between the core and the periphery also account for a good portion of the wage differential.

This territorial division of labor is not static. It has expanded along with the expansion of the whole system, and there has been some upward and downward mobility within the structure. The whole system moves toward greater capital intensity, so production processes which were core activities in the past have become peripheral activities at a later time.

The international division of labor has been reorganized several times before in the history of the capitalist world-economy (Walton, 1985). The original plunder by core states of external arenas (extremely primitive accumulation) was replaced by the production of raw materials using coerced labor. Core investments in plantations and mines were followed by investments in utilities, communications, and transportation infrastructure. As domestic markets in the periphery developed, local and core capital took up profitable opportunities in manufacturing, and, in the most recent phase, industrial production for export has emerged in the periphery. Throughout these reorganizations the whole world-economy has developed more capital intensive production, but the gap between the core and the periphery has been reproduced.

Ulrich Pfister and Christian Suter (1987) have demonstrated that, despite the particular forms of reorganization which the core/periphery hierarchy experiences, there are recurring cycles in the core/periphery relationship as well. Their study, and another study by Suter (1987), demonstrate the existence of waves of capital exports from the core to the periphery followed by periods of debt crisis and default by peripheral borrowers. The experience of the 1970s and 1980s is similar in many ways to three earlier periods of massive debt crisis which have occurred in the world economy since 1800.

The core/periphery hierarchy has been reinforced by an unequal distribution of political–military power among core states and peripheral areas. Historically this was organized as a system of colonial empires in which core states exercised direct political domination over peripheral areas. Chirot (1977: map 2) and Szymanski (1981) have argued that the nearly complete decolonization of the periphery has reduced the power differential between core and peripheral states. Contrary to most discussions of neocolonialism, Chirot claims that formal sovereignty has eliminated the periphery, and that Asia, Africa, and Latin America can now be categorized as semiperipheral.[3]

Chirot's claim that decolonization has created a world-system with no periphery is undoubtedly a mistake. Was Latin America then semiperipheral immediately upon attaining independence from Spain in the early nineteenth century? Is Haiti, or Bangladesh, or Chad possibly semiperipheral now? But the underlying contention that the core/periphery power differential may have diminished should not be so easily dismissed. The phenomenon of OPEC, the Conference of Non-aligned Nations, and the heavy support in the United Nations for a New International Economic Order may indicate some truth in the hypothesis of a reduction in the magnitude of the core/periphery power differential.

Clearly some formerly peripheral countries have become semiperipheral, and the United States has lost some of its former hegemony. But core states as a whole may have gained additional power at the same time that peripheral states have attained formal sovereignty. Only carefully operationalized empirical research on changes over time in the global distribution of military power capabilities, state access to resources, and level of economic development can resolve this problem. Until this research is done we can only use partial evidence to inform us about possible changes in the magnitude of core/periphery inequality (see chapter 12).

Another contention about the new international division of labor focuses on the growth of industrial production in the Newly Industrializing Countries (NICs) (Caporaso, 1981). Sometimes this phenomenon is interpreted as the end of a core/periphery system. Deindustrialization in the core, industrialization in the periphery, and a shift toward control by global transnational corporations are portrayed as the beginning of a new era of metanational capitalism (Borrego, 1982).

The notion of upwardly mobile semiperipheral countries has been convincingly utilized to understand the recent developmental paths of Brazil, Mexico (Gereffi and Evans, 1981), and India (Vanneman, 1979), as well as the nineteenth–century United States (Chase-Dunn, 1980). The notion of "dependent development" conceptualized by Cardoso (1973) and applied by Evans (1979) has proven extremely fruitful for understanding the bargaining and competitive struggles among transnational firms, semiperipheral state managers, and national capitalists in Brazil and other countries.

Cardoso's (1973) analysis of the shift from classical dependence (production of raw materials for export to the core) to dependent development (Brazilian production of manufactured goods for the domestic market by transnational corporations) claimed that a change had occurred in the effects of dependence on overall economic development. Cardoso argued that the transnational firms would now have an interest in the expansion of the domestic market and so they would act economically and politically to foster the growth of the national economy, albeit in a way which might exacerbate inequalities among classes, and this was allegedly demonstrated by the Brazilian "miracle." Crossnational research on the effects of dependence on foreign investments in manufacturing does not support Cardoso's claim. Bornschier and Chase-Dunn (1985: chapter 7) find that dependence on manufacturing transnationals has a large long-run retardant effect on GNP growth in a crossnational comparison, although short-run effects of inflows of foreign capital are positive, accounting, at least in part, for the short-lived miracle in Brazil. This shows that one of the mechanisms which reproduced the classical core/periphery hierarchy (exploitation through foreign investment) continues to operate in the "new" international division of labor.

Fröbel, Heinrichs, and Kreye (1980) have emphasized the importance of manufacturing in the periphery for export to the core. They document the growth of so-called free production zones, areas juridically outside the tariff and labor regulations of peripheral countries which allow transnational firms to have "export platforms" for the utilization of cheap peripheral, often female, labor. The industrial exports of the Asian "Gang of Four" (South Korea, Taiwan, Singapore, and Hong Kong) are important cases of the shift toward peripheral industrial production for the world market.[4] Fröbel, Heinrichs, and Kreye emphasize that this kind of peripheral industrialization steals jobs from core nations by shifting industrial production overseas. Ross and Trachte (1983) have argued that the recent growth of sweatshops employing undocumented immigrant workers in New York City is an instance of the "peripheralization of the core."[5]

The problem is whether or not these developments are the first stages of a shift toward metanational capitalism, or are simply the continuation of uneven capitalist development in a period of economic stagnation, with upward and downward mobility occurring in a structural hierarchy which is still intact. The decline of the economic hegemony of the United States has occurred mainly *vis-à-vis* other core powers, Western Europe and Japan. This is a continuation of the sequence of core competition, with uneven development occurring within countries (the decline of the older industrial Northeast "rust bowl" and the rise of the Sunbelt) a well as internationally.

No one could seriously claim that the core/periphery hierarchy has already been eliminated. Immense differences still exist in the level of living and the capital intensity of production. The transnational corporations have their headquarters in the great world cities of the core countries. Industrial production in the periphery has certainly grown, but it remains a very small proportion of world industry (Petras et al., 1981: chapter 6). The heavy intermediate industries (e.g. steel, chemicals) which have grown in the semiperiphery are no longer the leading sectors of the world economy. In chapter 12 I review studies which estimate recent trends in the magnitude of core/periphery inequalities. There is no evidence in favor of the notion that the core/periphery hierarchy is moving toward greater equality.

Neither the industrialization of the periphery nor the deindustrialization of the core has reduced the magnitude of core/periphery inequalities. To claim that core countries have become peripheralized because some areas within the core have experienced economic decline is certainly an exaggeration.

Similarly, discussions of the arrival of "post-industrial" society in the core are certainly premature. The proportion of the work force in services and non-manual labor has undoubtedly grown in core countries. But, at least for the US (a declining hegemonic core power), this is a repetition of a pattern which can be seen in the trajectories of hegemonic predecessors – the United Provinces of the Netherlands and the United Kingdom of Great Britain. Both of these hegemons began their ascent by developing a competitive advantage in consumer goods, followed by the export of capital goods, and finally lived out the twilight or their golden ages as centers of world finance and services. The United States is, generally, following this same sequence (see chapter 9).

While it is true that industrialization has occurred in some areas of the periphery and in most of the semiperiphery, it should be remembered that industrialization is the application of greater amounts of fixed capital, machinery, and non-human energy to production. It is an increase in capital intensity. This increase has continued in the core at the same time that it has occurred in the periphery, and thus the relative distribution of capital intensity may not have changed. Indeed, much of the peripheral industrialization has been quite labor intensive. The free production zones exist primarily to exploit cheap labor. And even capital intensive production in semiperipheral areas generally uses technology which has become obsolete in the core.

Very little quantitative empirical work has been done on changes in the magnitude of inequalities in the world-system as a whole. In chapter 12 this matter is discussed in detail and new evidence is presented. Here I would like to refer to a table which calculated the distribution of world resources in 1950, 1960, and 1970 which was presented in a review of theories and trends of convergence and divergence among national societies by Meyer et al., (1975). An updated version of the table is presented in chapter 12 but it does not contain data on educational enrollments, and it is these which I wish to compare to other attributes and resources here.

Table 2 in Meyer et al. (1975:232) showed that the poorest countries did not increase their share of world GNP between 1950 and 1970, while they did increase very slightly their proportion of world electrical energy consumed. Between 1950 and 1960 they increased their share of the world's nonagricultural work force from 7.3 percent to 9.5 percent. The figures confirm the impression that the economic structure of the peripheral countries has indeed changed, but that they have not, as a result, increased their share of world output.

The largest increases for the least developed countries are in the areas of educational enrollments and urbanization. These institutional features (which are often associated with "modernization" of national societies) have grown rapidly. These changes, however, are only superficially similar to the educational expansion and urbanization processes which occurred during earlier times in core countries.

Education does not expand only as a function of the growth of domestic demand for skilled labor in industry and services. Between 1950 and 1970 educational enrollments expanded everywhere in the periphery and semiperiphery of the world-system (Meyer and Hannan, 1979) regardless of the level or rate of economic development. It is much easier for peripheral states to create the trappings of modernization than to change their relative position in the core/periphery division of labor.

Similarly, the urbanization explosion in the periphery and semiperiphery has been dubbed "overurbanization" by some observers because it has occurred in the absence of a similar growth rate of industrial employment. The gigantic cities of the periphery most often import capital intensive technology from the core, which does not create a large demand for workers in industry. Squatter settlements and the teeming "informal sector" of peddlers, domestic servants, and small commodity producers swell the urban population. This informal sector provides cheap inputs to large-scale enterprises and government by subsidizing the costs of reproducing labor power, and by producing products for sale which are cheap because of the exploitation of unpaid family labor, or subminimum wage labor (Portes, 1981). The urban informal sector, then, is the functional equivalent of rural labor reserves, village economies, and the "domestic mode of production" which cheapened the wage bill in classical dependent economies by reproducing part-life-time proletarians (semiproletarians).

In addition, the city systems which have grown up in Latin America are much more centralized around a single large city than those in core countries. This "urban primacy" emerged, not during the colonial era, but during the 1930s and 1940s (Chase-Dunn, 1985b). Thus, the type of urbanization experienced by peripheral countries has been very different from that in the core. Kentor (1981) has shown that one cause of urbanization in the periphery is dependence on foreign investments by transnational corporations. And this dependence has also been shown to cause rises in the levels of tertiary employment (services) which are much greater than the growth in secondary (industrial) employment (Evans and Timberlake, 1980; Kentor, 1981).

World Classes and World State-formation

Although it has been difficult to maintain in the recent period of international squabbles, warmongering, and neomercantilism, some have made the argument that the world bourgeoisie is becoming more integrated as a class (Sklar, 1980; Borrego, 1982). International organizations such as the Trilateral Commission are alleged to form the core of an emergent monolithic world bourgeoisie based on the global transnational corporations. This is a new formulation of the old debate which started at the end of the last century among members of the Second International about superimperialism versus continued interimperialist rivalry. Many of the issues discussed above in the section on the transnationalization of capital are relevant, but here we shall focus on changes in the interstate system.

There has been a world bourgeoisie since the beginning of the modern world-system, but it has been a very differentiated, competitive, and conflictive class. Peripheral capitalists employing coerced labor have produced for export to the core. Core capitalists, divided by nation state, sector, and access to state power, have made alliances and fought wars among themselves. Often these alliances have crossed the boundaries of core states. It is undeniable that the frequency and importance of intracore capitalist alliances has increased as the scale of transnational firms has grown.

The question is, does this lower the competitiveness of the system (addressed above) and does it alter the operation of the interstate system? Recent attempts to forge a core-wide common policy against OPEC (spearheaded by the internationally oriented portion of the United States bourgeoisie) were not notably successful. The Trilateral Commission has attempted to co-ordinate the economic policies of European, North American, and Japanese states in an era of economic contraction, again without much success. That these kinds of international organizations exist is not unique to the contemporary period, and neither is their ineffectiveness novel.

Some may discern a trend toward international political integration in the emergence of the United Nations. Indeed, international organizations have proliferated as the world-economy has become more integrated. The Concert of Europe fell apart to be reorganized as the League of Nations, which was rent by world war, to be followed by the United Nations. Although there undoubtedly has been some progress toward institutionalization of international conflict resolution and collective security in this sequence, the United Nations remains quite limited in its ability to prevent wars among states. The question we must ask is whether or not the importance of military competition among core states has been reduced.

The effect of the spread of nuclear weapons must be discussed here. Do these weapons make continued competition among subgroups of world capital by means of war obsolete? Clearly a world war involving nuclear weapons would disrupt the operations of the capitalist system, hardly the most tragic of its consequences. Such a war would lead to social devolution, if not the end of our species. This outcome is a real possibility because the separate contenders who are risking nuclear holocaust are not in control of the outcomes of their combined interaction. Is the world-system a headless horseman, or rather a horse with many heads, galloping toward the edge of an abyss?

State managers, world bankers, and transnational firms create war machines as a mechanism to provide investment opportunities, to be sure, but the weapons also have a potential "use value" as threats to maintain or extend political hegemony. These threats involve the risk of a holocaust even though none of the major actors desires this outcome.

The presence of nuclear weapons does not, in itself, change the basic logic of system interaction. Commodity production and geopolitical competition remain the main forms of competition. But the existence of these weapons does imply that the normal operation of the system, with the usual sequence of hegemonic decline followed by world war, followed by the emergence of a new hegemonic core power, cannot continue. A real world war among core powers would undoubtedly bring the final holocaust. Thus the mechanism which has formerly resolved the contradictions of uneven development can no longer operate. Or rather, if it does operate, the game is over.

The combined effects of increases in the ability of international organizations to mediate conflicts and the increasing destructiveness of weaponry have decreased the probability of the outbreak of war among core states to some extent. But it should be remembered that neither international organization nor increasing destructiveness is unique to the post-World War II era. Many turn-of-the century observers believed that the "Great War" was unthinkable because of the brutal destructiveness of industrial warfare technology. My point is that, while the probability of war among core states may have decreased somewhat, the basic logic of competition and conflict in the world-system has not changed and there are no existing institutions which are strong enough to guarantee the peace.

In a purely mechanistic system doom would be the most certain prediction. But we are dealing with a human system, a somewhat intelligent set of actors who can surely see the way out of such a dilemma. Perhaps a sufficiently large, but not entirely devastating, nuclear conflagration will jar the peoples and leaders of the world into consciousness and create the political will necessary to outlaw warfare. The existence of such a threat to the survival of the human species could provide the motivation for the mobilization of a movement to create a real basis for collective security, a world federation capable of preventing warfare among nation states. The current manifestations of this potential are, however, a long way from that goal.

A Socialist World-system

Another version of the claim that the current world-system has undergone or is now experiencing transformation focuses on the emergence of the socialist states. I have elsewhere presented an interpretation of these states as territories in which intentionally socialist movements have come to state power, but have not yet successfully introduced a self-reproducing socialist mode of production (Chase-Dunn, ed., 1982b).

Polanyi (1944) discussed the dialectical interaction between the market principle and the needs of society for protection against certain of the consequences of market rationality, but his analysis focused primarily on national societies. At the level of the world-system and its anti-systemic movements we see that the attempts to create non-commodified relations of cooperation become encapsulated politically within organizations: co-ops, unions, socialist parties, and socialist states. The market principle has, so far, been able to expand its scale to reincorporate these collectivities into the logic of competition within the larger world-system.

Thus the contemporary socialist states are important experiments in the construction of socialist institutions which have been perverted to some extent by the necessities of survival and development in the context of the capitalist world market and the interstate system.

The large proportion of the world population now living in avowedly socialist states, and victories within recent decades of socialist national liberation movements in Africa, Asia, Latin America, and the Caribbean, have been interpreted by Szymanski (1981) as a kind of domino theory of the transition to world socialism. Szymanski contends that the Soviet Union and Eastern Europe constitute a separate socialist world-system and that the logic of world capitalism has been seriously weakened by the growing number of socialist states.

My own interpretation disputes this contention. I see the socialist states (including China) as having been significantly reincorporated into the capitalist world-economy. Whether or not this is true, one of the most disconcerting features of current socialist states is their most unsocialist behavior toward one another. I interpret this as a continuation of the nationalism and interstate competition which is normal behavior in the capitalist world-system.

Frank (1980: chapter 4) draws the same conclusion from recent trends in which the socialist states have increased their exports for sale on the world market, imports from the avowedly capitalist countries, and made deals with transnational firms for investments within their borders.

National economic planning, which is most highly developed in the socialist states, may be simply the most complete expression of the trend toward state capitalism which is occurring in most core and peripheral countries. And while distribution is more equal within socialist states, this does not change the competitive logic with which they interact with other states. Thus one possible world is composed of states which are internally socialist but which compete with one another in international markets and geopolitics.

The increasing number of socialist states does not seem to have weakened the logic of world capitalism. Rather the political constraints on the free mobility of capital which these states have created push the logic of capitalist organization to expand its scale. States become firms, and transnational corporations deal with all players in a competitive world which remains subject to the anarchy of investment decisions.

DISCUSSION AND CONCLUSIONS

To argue that the world-system's logic has not fundamentally altered does not imply that this is impossible or even unlikely. Nor is it to argue that the massive expansions, emergent institutions, and shifts of capital from place to place have not had drastic effects on the lives of people. I would like to revisit some of the questions raised in the earlier sections to speculate about the possible consequences of changes which have not yet occurred, but which might occur in the future.

What if it were true that recent trends were the beginning of the end of the core/periphery hierarchy? World-system theory has claimed that *peripheral* capitalism is a normal and necessary part of the capitalist mode of production, and that the reproduction of expanded accumulation in the core requires the existence of primary accumulation in the periphery.

This idea is not based on the claim that peripheral production creates the bulk of surplus value in the system, but rather on the insight that the relative harmony of classes in the core, the somewhat peaceful accommodation between capital and labor which exists as social democracy, corporatism, or "business unionism," is based on the ability of core capital to emphasize nationalist bases of solidarity. Nationalism in the core is sustained by competition among core states and by the ability of core capital to pay off an important segment of core workers with higher wages, better working conditions, more welfare provisions, and greater access to political power through democratic processes. This is possible, at least in part, because core exploitation of the periphery provides a measure of additional surplus value through unequal exchange (e.g. cheap bananas for core workers), profits derived from investments in the periphery, and the status-based effects of comparison with "less developed" countries.

In a pregnant sentence Wallerstein predicts that "When labor is everywhere free we shall have socialism" (Wallerstein, 1974:127). This implies that, if the core/periphery division of labor disappears, capitalism will no longer be able to overcome its own contradictions, and the political structures maintained by the core/periphery hierarchy will crumble. Socialist transformation, which Marx predicted would occur first in the core nations, will finally visit them.

If the above analysis is correct the imminent approach of metanational capitalism would be good news for the world socialist movement, as Borrego (1982) contends. But the formal proletarianization of the world work force (the end of coerced labor and the decreasing availability of alternatives to dependence on the world market) does not necessarily mean the end of "segmented labor markets." Political and ethnic stratification have proven effective in maintaining wage differentials among formally "free" proletarians. The core/periphery hierarchy could become increasingly based on inequality between politically protected labor and "free" labor.

If a contraction in the magnitude of the core/periphery hierarchy were to occur, this would exacerbate the contradictions of capitalism, which have been softened in the past by what David Harvey (1982) has called the "spatial fix," the ability of capital to find fresh room for accumulation by moving to where opposition and constraints are fewer. The expansion of the capitalist world-system has been driven by the search for new markets, cheap inputs, and profitable investment opportunities. Lenin (1965) pointed out that by the end of the nineteenth century the core states could no longer find new worlds to conquer and were forced to divide and redivide the already conquered world. This extensive expansion has been supplemented by intensive expansion, the conversion of more and more aspects of life to the commodity form, and thus the expansion of profit-making opportunities in the provision of fast food breakfasts, etc. The potential for further commodification is great, especially in the periphery, where a substantial terrain of production and consumption for use remains.

Increases in the extent and depth of commodification must eventually reach limits. Only so much of human activity can be commodified and the ability of markets and capital to expand beyond political regulation must decline as the density and scale of political regulation begins to catch up. Anti-systemic movements create obstacles to the manueverability of capital and place claims on profits. The seesawing back and forth motion of capital must eventually generate consciousness and co-ordination among groups who have an interest in collective rationality at the world-system level. Capital flight has pitted workers against one another for 500 years, but the growing scale and density of political claims must eventually decrease the incentive to move and the level of profit. The systemic crisis of capitalism will involve the creation of democratic and collectively rational control over investment decisions in a context in which "private" wealth no longer has the power or the motivation to continue directing the production process.

The growth of welfare states, decolonization of the periphery, and the emergence of states in which socialist parties control state power should be understood in this light. Despite the failure of these to change the logic of the world-system so far, developments of this kind which manage to co-ordinate their efforts on a global scale can indeed transform that logic. These questions are addressed in more detail in chapter 16.

5

World Culture, Normative Integration, and Community

A structural approach to the modern world-system necessarily raises questions about the role of culture and of normative integration. This chapter discusses the extent to which world culture exists, and the role that ideologies, consciousness, and collective solidarities play in the reproduction and transformation of the contemporary world-system.

Critics of the world-system perspective have complained that cultural factors are treated as epiphenomenal, and a number of recent efforts have been made to remedy that situation (e.g. Wallerstein, 1984b: chapters 15 and 16; Robertson and Lechner, 1985). My own theorizing rests on historical materialism, but I do not accept a general model in which the "base" mechanically determines the "superstructure." This chapter argues that world culture and normative integration play secondary rather than primary roles in the reproduction of contemporary world order because of the nature of the capitalist mode of production as it operates on a global scale. But I am not arguing that culture and normative integration are secondary in all systems, nor that they will always be so in the future.

In this discussion of the structure, functions, and content of contemporary world culture I will argue that consciousness, ideology, and consensual definitions of reality and the good are not the primary institutions which integrate the modern world-system. Rather, in comparison with earlier whole socio-economic systems and with contemporary subunits such as families and national societies, the capitalist world-economy is integrated more by political–military power and market interdependence than by normative consensus. This is not to contend that there is no such thing as world culture, but rather to argue that its nature and structure depend on more potent economic and political institutions. After consideration of the role played by normative integration in the contemporary world-system I will discuss the structure of the emerging consensual world culture and the resistance to core cultural domination by peripheral groups.

A culture is defined broadly by many anthropologists as a constellation of socially constructed practices (e.g. Fox, 1985). I will use the term more narrowly to refer to consciousness and symbolic systems of belief and knowledge. In this sense culture is composed of collectively held definitions of reality and understandings of what constitutes good and evil. Thus we are talking about ideology, although this is understood broadly to include all belief systems – religion, but also science and secular economic and political ideas.

The construction and sharing of complex symbolic systems is the most important feature which distinguishes human beings from other forms of life. Symbolic systems allow us to collectively accumulate knowledge. The relatively great capacity for learned behavior (as opposed to instinctual behavior), which is based on the unpreprogrammed cortex of the human brain, allows individuals to internalize some of the accumulated cultural heritage of past social development. As Marx says in *The Eighteenth Brumaire* (Marx, 1978:9), this happy possibility has a dark side as well: "the tradition of all the generations of the dead weighs like a nightmare on the brain of the living." The institutions and ideologies we inherit not only empower us, they also constrain us and reinforce structures of domination. Structures of power mold the cultural heritages which individuals receive.

This is not the whole story, of course. If individuals only received heritages nothing would ever change. The very process by which individuals are confronted with competing and contradictory cultural elements, and the decisions between alternative possibilities, builds an element of freedom into the daily reconstitution of consciousness. Large-scale processes may carry on according to a systemic logic which seems to steamroll across individuals, but individuals and groups of people nevertheless choose their actions. Structural change, especially the transformation of systemic logic, occurs at least in part because people become aware of alternatives and struggle in their behalf.

Solidarity, the conscious identification of individuals with one another and with larger collectivities, is an important aspect of all social systems. Solidarity is based on identification and the sharing of cultural agreements, of definitions, of values and norms. It is this aspect of culture, its integrational function, which is the main focus of the following discussion. How does normative solidarity, which unites people into families, communities, and nations, function in the modern world-system?

A recurring issue which differentiates theories of social systems is the causal weight they attach to ideological versus infrastructural institutions. The shift in focus from national societies to the whole world-system has been accompanied by a new set of debates about this issue. Wallerstein (1979a) and Braudel (1984) have emphasized the importance of political and economic institutions at the world-system level which produce and reproduce material life, while others have stressed the cultural and normative bases of world-system integration (e.g. Parsons, 1971; Heintz, 1973; Inkeles, 1975; Meyer,

1987). This chapter will place the characterization of the importance of cultural institutions in a comparative context which employs a broad typology of whole socio-economic systems developed by Polanyi (1977).

Talcott Parsons was perhaps the most well known exponent of the idea that there exists a global social system which is normatively integrated. In his 1961 article, "Order and community in the international system," he argued that international law, shared assumptions about the desirability of economic development, rational bureaucratic organization, and political democracy form the basis of a world normative order. Parsons did not directly address the question of the role of the normative order in the larger system, because for Parsons all social systems are, by definition, normatively based. Social structures are defined in terms of shared assumptions about proper rules of behavior, and the value system is the most fundamental feature of a social system. In his short book, *The System of Modern Societies* (1971), Parsons applies his AGIL schema to the "international system," arguing that core states are differentiated in terms of their functions within the larger international system. The French specialize in fine arts and diplomacy, the British in democracy, and the United States in economic development and education.

TYPES OF INTEGRATION

Other students of comparative society, however, differ with Parsons's emphasis on the role of normative integration in all social systems. As discussed in the introduction to part I, Karl Polanyi (1977) and Eric Wolf (1982) distinguish between social systems in terms of the main type of glue which integrates them:

1 *Normative social systems* Polanyi discussed reciprocal systems in which production and exchange are based on consensually held norms of reciprocal obligation (Wolf's (1982) kin-based mode of production; Wallerstein's (1979a:155) mini-systems).[1] While most contemporary families are reciprocal subunits within a larger socio-economic entity, that larger entity, the modern world-system, is, I will argue below, held together by a different kind of glue.
2 *Politically coercive social systems* Polanyi also discussed "redistributive" systems which are integrated by political institutions which gather goods by means of taxation or tribute-payment.[2] States which organize threats and coercion are the main institutions in such systems.
3 *Market-based social systems* A socio-economic system is integrated by markets when a considerable share of its interactions, and the

> direction and nature of its development, are conditioned by the buying and selling of commodities in price-setting markets. A price-setting market is one in which the exchange rates – prices – are determined by competitive buying and selling by a large number of independent agents seeking to maximize their individual resources.

In reciprocal systems a consensual moral order defines reciprocal role obligations and mobilizes social labor. Distribution is controlled by a set of rights and obligations and social integration is guaranteed by socializing individuals into the belief systems which define their roles and regulate interaction. Internalized definitions of self and the peer pressures of a face-to-face community are the main glue which guarantees social order. Redistributional activity in such systems may confer prestige on benefactors, but authority structures are not very hierarchical. These societies are classless in the sense that kinship groups are not ranked and superior position is usually not inherited. And they are stateless in the sense that they do not contain a differentiated organization which exercises a monopoly of legitimate violence. Cultural integration based on consensus about what is real and what is good is the main basis of social order.[3]

In politically coercive systems there are classes and states. Surplus product is gathered and redistributed by a political–military ruling class which utilizes institutionalized authority backed up by force to accomplish appropriation. There are many institutional means used to reinforce the appropriation of surplus product in these "tributary modes of production" (Amin, 1980a:46–70) and they vary in the degree to which they are centralized (Wolf, 1982). European or Japanese feudalism represents a rather decentralized, so-called "stateless," type in which each manor is, in fact, a mini-state. More typically we think of the great agrarian empires in which a centralized state extracts resources from a wide territorial division of labor. In such socio-economic systems the political organization of force is the main determinant of societal dynamics, but normative integration continues to play a role. Religion is used to legitimate the rule of the temple and the palace. Codified law is created to centrally define correct behavior and deviance across local communities which have formerly relied on unwritten moral tradition. Such "world-empires" (Wallerstein, 1979a:156) are primarily integrated by the political competition which is articulated in a single state apparatus.

The three types of integration – normative, political, and market – exist in most world-systems, but world-systems differ in the extent to which these are dominant and in the particular ways in which they are combined. Normative integration has changed its locus and function over the long history of human social development. In the classless, prestate societies, clans and tribal groupings based on notions of kinship used normative integration (Durkheim's mechanical solidarity) to produce social order. Conformity was ensured by informal social censure; the deviant was often shamed into self-punishment (Malinowski, 1961).

When states emerged, societies became integrated predominantly by the coercive power of political institutions of various kinds. Military ruling classes monopolized the means of violence and "protected" peasants from other competing military centers in exchange for obedience and peasant-produced surplus product. The first urbanized civilizations may have been theocracies, integrated largely on the basis of normative legitimacy, but soon states, competing with one another in warfare, became integrated by political–military institutions. Normative integration through religious and ideological institutions continued as an important, but not central, adjunct to military organization. Subunits such as families, lineages, and peripheral communities remained integrated by normative means, but these were articulated within a dominant tributary mode of production.

It was the imposition of rule across normatively-defined communities which created the need for the law – codified rules. Normative integration in a consensual culture does not require codification because everyone knows what is right and what is wrong, just as the incest taboo in modern society does not primarily rely on legal enforcement. But when an imperial state seeks to impose a uniform set of rules across a set of normative communities which it has conquered, the written law becomes necessary.

In market systems integration stems primarily from the specialization of independent producers and their resulting objective reliance on one another (interdependence). Polanyi (1944) argued that pure market systems are unstable and tend to generate new political institutions to protect societal desiderata from the negative consequences of unbridled competition and narrow market rationality. In the Wallersteinian version "world-economies" are systems in which there are multiple cultures, multiple polities, and a single integrated division of labor. The *capitalist* world-economy combines commodity production for markets with political–military competition among unequally powerful nation states. Integration is due to interdependence and the dynamic interaction between uneven capitalist accumulation and the balance of power mechanism of the interstate system. The institutions of international capital investments and the interstate system are reciprocally interdependent and provide the structural center of what is an extremely expansionist and intensifying socio-economic system (see chapter 7).

Thus the glue which holds together the modern world-system is a combination of market-generated interdependence in the world division of labor and the political–military power of core states. Our global political economy is called a capitalist one because the market-based logic of accumulation constitutes a greater part of the dynamics of the whole system than in earlier (precapitalist) world-empires and world-economies. We know that markets and wage labor existed in the Roman Empire, but these institutions did not determine, or even much influence, the dynamic of imperial expansion and contraction. Rather it was political competition within the arena of a single state apparatus and the extraction of resources (tribute, slaves) by conquest which was the structural kernel of the Roman system (K. Hopkins, 1978).

The above characterization of the modern world-system does not imply that normative solidarities play no role in integrating our global system. Normatively integrated subunits such as families are important components of capitalist production because they operate as income-pooling units which allow people to combine different sorts of resources, and thus they play a crucial role in the reproduction of the labor force (Smith et al., 1984). Families, neighborhoods, village communities, and other face-to-face primary groups continue to play an important part in the generation and maintenance of individual personalities. Social psychological research shows that the cognitive relationships of individuals to larger solidarities such as ethnic groups or nations are crucially mediated by such primary groups (Shils and Janowitz, 1948).

Thus it is incorrect to see contemporary solidarities like the family as merely vestigial remnants of earlier modes of integration. Their functional importance in the modern world-system does not, however, mean that we ought to understand the larger system to be normatively integrated in the same sense that earlier socio-economic systems were. The system as a whole is not held together by consensual understandings. Most exchange in the capitalist world-economy is not specified by agreed-upon reciprocal obligations. Rather, exchange is primarily organized as market trade of commodities and as interorganizational and interstate political bargaining.

NORMATIVE SOLIDARITIES IN THE WORLD-SYSTEM

Normative integration plays an important but subservient role in the modern world-system. Normatively integrated subunits such as the family, the local community, ethnicities, and nations (national communities) serve important functions for the operation of the capitalist mode of production.[4] I already mentioned the importance of the household as an income-pooling group which bears the cost of child-bearing, child-rearing, care of the elderly, and psychological sustenance of the self.

Probably the most important resource-pooling solidarity in the modern world-system is the nation, not because of the direct effects of such pooling, but because of its linkage with the state. Most modern states are nation states in which the functions of formal political organization, authority, interest aggregation, etc. are blended with the ideology of national interests. Successful competition within the world market requires a strong and integrated state standing behind a strategy of competitive commodity production. Such a state must be able and willing to use force to guarantee the market share interests of its national investors (which may be state bureaucrats or "private" capitalists). The use of international force requires a certain degree of legitimacy, as does the maintenance of peace and order at home. Class conflicts and domestic resistance to the use of military power are often softened by the ideology of nationalism.

The viability of nationalism as a solidarity is, of course, reinforced by its frequent correspondence with the nation state. But nationalism is also reinforced by the core/periphery hierarchy, the structured inequality between "developed" and "underdeveloped" nations. Unlike class solidarity, which is usually crosscut by the core/periphery hierarchy, nationalism in both the core and the periphery is reinforced by the inequalities among "advanced" and "developing" countries.[5] National solidarity within core countries is reinforced by the perception by core workers that they share national interests with their "own" capitalists in exploiting peripheral countries and competing with other core countries. An example of this is presented in Sidney Mintz's (1985) recent study of the place of sugar consumption in the emergence of industrial capitalism in Britain, in which Mintz examines the linkages between slave-grown Caribbean sugar and the growth of sugar consumption by the British proletariat. Mintz's anthropology of food consumption emphasizes the social symbolism of what and how we eat, and its connections with power. He notes that cheap sugar provided fast calories for core workers at the same time as it enabled them to consume an item which, along with tea, had in the past been an imperial luxury available only to the rich.

CULTURAL PRESUPPOSITIONS OF THE WORLD MARKET

As the above indicates, there are various forms of community (solidarity) which are institutionally embedded in the operation of the modern world-system. Normative integration is important for families, neighborhoods, villages, cities, subnational regions, ethnicities, tribal groupings, clans, class and occupational groupings, political parties, and most importantly, nations. These various forms of community are not, however, the main type of glue which holds the contemporary world-system together. Neither is political organization, although this plays an important role in mediating competition. The main glue of our global system is the interdependence produced by a market-mediated network of economic differentiation, a division of labor which Durkheim called "organic solidarity." This form of integration is not a solidarity in the normative sense, because it does not require identification with a larger collective interest or the sharing of consensual definitions of proper behavior or the good.

Markets are constituted by the buying and selling activities of large numbers of individuals (or firms) operating on their own account to maximize returns. Normative evaluations of different persons are ideal-typically irrelevant. But, as Durkheim (1964) pointed out, contractual market exchange does require a certain level of normative consensus, as well as a certain kind of law. Actors must come to agreement on prices and on a generalized medium of exchange (money) and they should agree that one exchange partner is as good as another, or rather is as good as his/her ability to pay. The institutionalization of a price-setting market is problematic within a normatively integrated group, and it is even more problematic between different culturally-bounded groups.

Phillip Curtin (1984) has studied the world historical development of market exchange across cultural boundaries. Curtin observes that trade between culturally distinct groups is most often carried out by a separate normatively integrated group which specializes in crosscultural trade. Curtin terms these specialized trading ethnicities "trade diasporas" because they usually set up enclaves within the boundaries of the cultural groups that they link through trade. Curtin's work on sub-Saharan Africa led him to the idea of a trade diaspora, which he then used in a broader investigation of crosscultural trade ranging from ancient Mesopotamia to the trading outposts of the European colonial powers.

Without trust and credit long-term, long-distance trade is difficult to sustain, and trade between different cultural groups requires consensus about notions of fairness and equivalent values. A specialized trading group which is integrated on a kinship or ethnic basis provides the social organization which can sustain crosscultural market exchange. Curtin observes that trade diasporas decline as the separate cultures whose exchanges they mediate develop sufficient common understandings to allow direct trade, a situation he terms the emergence of a "trade ecumene." A certain level of cultural understanding facilitates the linkage of different cultural regions by market interdependence.

Of course, the emergence of a trade ecumene does not imply that a "perfect" market mechanism operates in international exchange. For one thing, much international exchange (even within a capitalist world-economy) is conditioned by political agreements similar in form to the "state-administered trade" which was typical in world-systems dominated by the tributary mode of production. And the "market universalism" assumption of the equivalence of all buyers and sellers is also violated by the fact that the capitalist world-system remains divided into separate normatively integrated groups – primarily nations. Also the universal equivalent, money, is imperfectly formed in international trade, as the history of international monetary institutions attests (Vilar, 1976). Nevertheless, the depth of the trade ecumene and the relatively strong operation of price-setting international markets is undoubtedly greater in the modern world-system than in earlier world-systems in which capitalism and commodified relations were less prevalent.

The normative relations which emerge among nation states and transnational actors in a market-integrated world-economy are primarily composed of expectations about fair trade and the protocols of diplomatic interaction. The analysis of these normative structures has been carried out under the rubric of "international regimes" (Keohane and Nye, 1977). Charles Lipson's study of the protection of private property in the periphery by core states describes well the limits of such international normative structures:

> . . . stable property rights and contractual relations are exceedingly difficult to establish across national boundaries. Although collective evaluations and expectations are an important feature of international relations, these normative properties are weaker because political, social, and cultural communities are constituted primarily at the domestic level, where they typically overlap and reinforce one another (as the term *nation-state* suggests). Thus, while it is difficult to establish the meaning and value of property rights domestically, it is far harder internationally. (Lipson, 1985:4, emphasis in the original)

Despite the limitations of international normative structures, the study of international regimes has revealed important things about the contemporary world order and the ideological premises and disputes which accompany world politics. The studies by Stephen Krasner (1985) and Craig Murphy (1984) demonstrate how arguments over world distributive justice in many respects parallel ideologies of inequality and inequity at the level of national societies.

Ideological support for socially structured inequalities also plays a role in justifying and rationalizing core/periphery differences. Some of the non-market barriers to wage equalization between core and peripheral workers are ideological, as is also the case with wage differences between men and women, or blacks and whites. Michael Hechter (1975) has shown that culturally based definitions of in-group and out-group (e.g. English versus Irish) played an important role in maintaining the structure of "internal colonialism" within the British Isles. But we must note that while attitudinal racism and nationalism certainly have a life of their own and undoubtedly play a supportive role in structures of domination, these are largely reinforced by economic and political institutions. And this is even more the case when the object of analysis is international inequalities. The political structure of migration control is a complex function of popular attitudes, the economic demand for labor, and the political power of competing organizations and states (Portes and Bach, 1985). And migration control is certainly one of the most potent institutions which reproduce core/periphery wage differentials.

THE STRUCTURE OF CONTEMPORARY WORLD CULTURE

Both the content and the level of consensus among participants vary across cultures. Consensus is never complete and it tends to decrease with complexity. As discussed above, Durkheim (1964) argued that there is a normative basis to contractual exchange in market society, although it differs greatly from the customary obligations prevalent in societies with a less complex division of labor. In societies with a complex division of labor in which individual producers exchange their products for the products of impersonal others through the medium of money, consensus still exists on some matters. But an elaborate division of labor tends to create an objective dependence of individuals and groups of producers on market exchange such that *broad consensual agreement is no longer required for social order*. People may believe anything they want to about religion or aesthetics. Market exchange only requires certain social agreements about the formally equal status of buyers and sellers, the legal obligations of contract, and the terms and content of exchange value.

This necessary consensus is somewhat minimal in comparison with the degree of consensus about ontology and sacredness which exists in simple societies, and this minimal consensus is backed up by law and formal sanctions. Complex societies are characterized by relatively individuated and voluntary forms of consciousness in the sense that individuals exercise many options in choosing among culturally available identities and ideologies.

Marx's (1967a:71–83) discussion of the "fetishism of commodities" implies that the institutionalized opaqueness by which market relations obscure the concrete relationships among producers is functional for the operation of capitalism because producers and consumers are alienated from the knowledge of their real interdependencies. More recent critics (Zaretsky, 1976; Bellah et al., 1986) argue that the consumerism and privatism which are associated with individuated identity in capitalist society alienate the individual from meaningful social action.

It is clear however that modern national societies continue to be integrated, at least in part, through collective consciousness. Durkheimian processes of moral boundary maintenance, as well as strong sentiments of solidarity are evident with regard to the "national community." The nation is probably the most important collective solidarity in the modern world-system. Ideological hegemony, as analyzed by Antonio Gramsci (1971), certainly plays an important part in legitimating political and economic hierarchies within national societies. To make this point, however, is also to recognize that consensus and cultural agreement are primarily organized along national lines in the contemporary world-system, and *not* at the level of the whole system.[6]

The organization of consciousness and identity along national lines is, in fact, an important characteristic of the capitalist world-economy. It is not only the multicentric character of the interstate system which allows capital to maintain its mobility and the capability of outmaneuvering oppositional movements. In addition, the tendency of world culture to be fragmented into national cultures, and for collective solidarities to be organized nationally, reinforces the structural mobility of capitalist accumulation. The poor record of proletarian internationalism and the bloody conflict among contemporary socialist states have resulted primarily from the institutional structuring of political power in the interstate system, but they have also resulted from virulent nationalism.

The point here is that nation-building, the formation of national solidarities out of formerly separate collective identities, is itself a product of the long-run operation of the interstate system and the commodity economy. That nations are better integrated in terms of collective identity in the core than in the periphery is largely a consequence of colonialism and economic exploitation which developed the core and underdeveloped the periphery. Colonialism often employed a divide and conquer policy which pitted peripheral ethnic groups against one another, while effective nation-building in core countries was facilitated by exploitation of the periphery.

The most salient feature of world culture is its multinational character. Natural language is the most important bearer of cultural meaning, and *there is no global language*. Language remains differentiated at the level of the world-system. And thus collective identity as expressed through intimately understood symbolic systems remains multinational. This is not to claim that consensual symbolic systems are not emerging at the global level. Cultural imperialism and the ideological hegemony of European religion, politics, economics, and science have produced obvious isomorphisms among the national cultures of the world-system. Robert Wuthnow (1980) has convincingly argued that the institutionalization of science and the emergence of different types of religious movements have been strongly conditioned by world-system processes. Economic development, political equality, and nationally delimited collective rationality compose an underlying set of consensual themes for world culture (Heintz, 1973). Each nation expresses its own identity in terms of some "uniqueness" which is nevertheless consistent with one or another version of these basic themes.

On the other hand the civilizational values which constitute European culture, and thus the culture of domination in the Eurocentered world-system, are by no means universally accepted despite the trend toward morphological similarities among national cultures. Important aspects of non-Western civilizational traditions with very different presuppositions about the universe are still strongly held by large numbers of the world's peoples (Galtung, 1981; Wallerstein, 1984b: chapter 16).

The study of international regimes (i.e. the evolution of agreements about specific issues such as aid, debt, foreign investment, the law of the sea, etc. (Krasner, 1985; Lipson, 1985; Wood, 1986)), as well as discussions of international distributive justice confronted in the debate over a "new international economic order" (Murphy, 1984), have certainly illuminated the process of consensus formation and disputation in the emergence of a world normative order. Stephen Krasner's (1985) study of debates between core and peripheral states reveals the feature, well known from studies of other cases of distributive justice, that peripheral states are much more likely to favor an international regime which controls resources on the basis of globally defined interests, whereas core states are more likely to favor the distribution of resources according to ability of individual states to pay.

Systems of linguistic equivalence have become institutionalized in the practices of international translators, and artificial world languages such as mathematics are accepted everywhere. A single method of time-reckoning is nearly universal, and pressure is exerted to standardize other measurements. Communications protocols, traffic signs, medical terminology, national economic accounting, social indicators, and even aesthetic and literary judgements are increasingly consensualized. World literature, world history, and even theory and research on something called the world-system, are perhaps expressions of the emergence of a unitary world culture (see also King, 1984).

Identification with the human species as a whole is not a very important solidarity in the integration of the contemporary world-system. The boundaries of human solidarities have been expanding their scope for a long time. The development of "world" religions such as Christianity and Islam separated kinship and blood ties from the definition of membership in the moral order. The actual content of the idea of universalism has expanded to include the whole human species – the "brotherhood of man," the "species-being" of nineteenth-century socialists. Contemporary discussions of the "global village," or "spaceship earth," stress the extent to which we share a common fate as a species. And most of contemporary social science assumes the oneness of the human species.

Of course ideas may be expressed or held by a minority without being institutionalized into social structures. When we discuss the nature of contemporary solidarity, the global community is revealed to be only weakly institutionalized. There are many competing world religions, including the variants of socialism. And international law, although stressed by Parsons (1961) in his discussion of normative order at the international level, is yet poorly institutionalized. Even the most central actors simply disregard the World Court when it suits them.

Durkheim used changes in legal systems as a measure of the type of solidarity found in a society. In a similar fashion, many people have examined the world legal system to see if global normative regulation is emerging. The functioning of the World Court has been the focus of much discussion and criticism (e.g. Falk, 1982). The importance of normative regulation at the global level undoubtedly oscillates with the level of conflict in the world-system. In addition it seems likely that international law has indeed increased its importance compared with earlier centuries. But this trend has not significantly shifted the overall logic of the world-system toward that of a normatively regulated system. That is to say, though normative regulation may have increased to some extent at the global level, it remains a very weak force.

Complex cultures are never very homogeneous. Parsons (1971) speaks of differentiated cultures in which subunits specialize in separate but interdependent forms of consciousness and meaning. Thus lawyers think differently from doctors (have a subculture) which is nevertheless part of a larger integrated culture. Perhaps the emerging world culture is such a differentiated civilizational whole. Many have argued that certain underlying cultural themes have penetrated everywhere in the modern world-system, or at least are shared by national elites everywhere. Variously called "modernism" or "Westernism," this world culture has been spread by colonialism and market relations to every corner of our earth. Its content has been described as focusing on economic development, rational bureaucracy, secular humanism and science, and political democracy, although the global status of the latter is questionable because of oscillation between democratic and authoritarian regimes in the periphery and semiperiphery. Nevertheless, it must be significant that there are few true monarchies left in the world. Legitimation of the state from "below," that is, as an organization operating in the interest of the "people," has become nearly universal. This is very different from the ideologies of tributary states and empires, which are agents of the gods (see chapter 6).

If there is something like a world culture then English is obviously one of its major languages. This has resulted from the far-flung expanse of the British Empire, but also from the fortunate (or unfortunate for Anglophobes) circumstance that the British hegemony was followed by that of a hegemon carrying a similar linguistic gene, the United States. A hegemonic core power promotes its own language and many speakers find it a necessary *lingua franca*.

Certainly the number of spoken languages has decreased over the last 500 years as a result of the European conquest of earth. And bilingualism has expanded to increase the size proportions of the world's population speaking one or another of the dominant languages. But synthetic languages (such as mathematics) and methods of time-reckoning, methods of measuring space, etc. have spread somewhat independently of natural languages.

Linguists such as Sapir (1949) and Whorf (1956) have argued that meanings are non-translatable across language groups employing incompatible assumptions about the nature of reality. We have all heard of the difficulties of translating certain German or French words into English. How much more difficult to express the Eskimo notions of snow or the Navaho attribution of modified action to what we think of as inanimate objects (e.g. "the log bumps," instead of "a bump on the log"). Problems of this kind are resolved (or obliterated) when translation equivalences become institutionalized, as when professional translators at the United Nations develop standard solutions to the problem of equivalences. The original nuances are lost, but this is nevertheless a form of global consensus creation.

CULTURAL IMPERIALISM

Culture usually reflects socially structured inequalities. That is, culture is itself hierarchical and comes to reflect, and to reinforce, hierarchy. Marx said that the dominant ideas of an age are the ideas of its rulers, and Gramsci analyzed ideological hegemony in terms of the ability of a ruling class to legitimate itself by propagating a dominant (but not totally exclusive) world-view. Much of what has been called world culture by Parsons (1961, 1971) and the modernization school, has been called Western cultural imperialism by others (e.g. Galtung, 1971).

William Meyer (1987) has performed an operationalization of "the structural thesis of cultural imperialism" which examines certain key propositions with data on 24 developing countries. He uses cross-sectional multiple regression analysis to examine the relationships between two indicators of the penetration of a country by Western news and information flows and three indicators of Westernization of the economy, education system, and consumption. Meyer does not find support for the hypotheses of cultural imperialism, but his study can hardly be cited as firm evidence. The small number of cases (small for regression analysis) and problematic operationalizations make the results untrustworthy. The same can be said of other comparative studies which have sought to examine the effects of media imperialism (see Stevenson and Shaw, 1984). These questions are important and relatively unplowed ground for careful comparative research.

While no one can deny the existence of hierarchical aspects of world culture, I will argue that this form of imperialism is not very central to the functioning and reproduction of inequality in the modern world-system. Cultural imperialism certainly propagates core popular culture and the "preference structures" which create demand for the consumption of core commodities in every part of the globe. This is accomplished in part through the centralization of communications and information-providing systems in core countries (Schiller, 1969). Coke, Pepsi, rock-and-roll, and American television programs are everywhere.

But just as oppressed groups within nations have often found it possible to redefine themselves, to throw off the styles and identities provided by dominant groups and to assert their own "traditional" or "unique" definitions of self or group, this kind of resistance also operates in the core/periphery hierarchy. The psychology of national liberation is essentially the creation of new national identities in reaction to the colonial ideologies of the past. This form of resistance has been fairly successful, although not unproblematically so.

The secular trend toward unifying cultural understandings remains subject to important resistance. Groups and nations which feel short-changed by the accretion of allegedly "universal" culture may often redefine themselves (Wuthnow, 1980). The traditionalism of the Khomeini regime in Iran, and the claims to non-Western civilizational values put forth by many peoples, show that oppression which is symbolically organized is much easier to combat than oppression which becomes institutionalized in a material division of labor or a costly military apparatus. Blacks may redefine themselves as beautiful; Jehovah's Witnesses may proclaim themselves the closest to God; and these "ethnic" forms of resistance may help people feel better about their situations, but the material bases of oppression and exploitation are more difficult to overcome. The nationalism of peripheral countries is thus an attempt by elites and peoples to redefine themselves on a more equal footing in a system which consistently operates to marginalize them, and as such these forces may often be understood as opposition to exploitation (Fox, 1987). The nationalism of core countries, on the other hand, appears as an atavistic denial of the best universalist tendencies of modern society. Yet both kinds are the product of a world political economy which divides peoples from one another and promotes conflict over resources.

Albert Szymanski's (1981:257–88) chapter on "ideological hegemony as a mechanism of imperial domination" shows the important extent to which core culture has been promoted in an effort to legitimate core/periphery exploitation. Szymanski also reveals the ease with which nationalist regimes in the periphery may produce their own television programs, etc. The falling cost of communications technology has provided the means to counter the centralization of the provision of information and entertainment. In the modern world-system it is much easier for oppressed people to redefine themselves, to adopt a more positive self-definition even in the face of "hegemonic" cultures, than it is to change the position of a nation in the economic and political–military hierarchy.

Thus we have the phenomenon of "overmodernization." Many developing countries adopt the trappings of development: state planning, mass education, national monuments, etc. without being able to create the material bases of economic development. Meyer and Hannan (1979) show that all countries, regardless of the rate of economic growth, expanded their education systems in the period between 1950 and 1970. The worldwide education explosion, however, is unmatched by worldwide economic development because it is much easier to create students, schools, and teachers than it is to institute productive and/or profitable economic enterprises in the context of a competitive world market.

Of course some countries have rejected modernization as Western imperialism and sought to recreate "indigenous" institutions and ideologies. The Iranian revolution is an obvious example, but many other peripheral and semiperipheral countries have similar elements in their national ideologies. It is fairly easy to accomplish such a redefinition and rejection of the dominant world culture because *the world culture itself is pluralistic.* Participation in the world market, or even in the international system of diplomacy, does not demand much in the way of cultural uniformity.

The above points support the contention that world culture is not the main way in which order is sustained in the contemporary world-system. But a counter-argument could contend that the world-system is not well integrated, and that this is due to a lack of normative consensus. Many have perceived international relations not as a system, but rather as an "anarchy of nations" each out to get as much as it can. It is clearly the case that warfare is an institutionalized part of the competition among states. Warfare is nearly continuous on the earth, and war among core states is periodically produced by the process of uneven capitalist economic development (see chapters 7 and 8).

While warfare indicates that competition regularly breaks into conflict, it is misleading to characterize the world-system as an "anarchy of nations." The system reveals many regular patterns of interaction despite the fact that it is not strongly integrated by consensual culture. The market interdependence and the related political–military balance of power mechanisms operate to produce certain features which contradict the hypothesis of a disordered Hobbesian war of all against all. First, the core/periphery hierarchy is fairly stable. Despite a certain amount of upward and downward mobility, any area is most likely to remain in the position in which it has long been. And the number of sovereign states has increased rather than decreased. In a system based purely on conquest we would expect the number of sovereign states to decrease as empire-formation takes place.

One of the most persuasive arguments in favor of a strong world culture is that by John W. Meyer. Meyer claims that certain values, primarily those of economic progress and rationality, are institutionalized as normative rules in the world polity. As he puts it:

> Explanations of the world-wide state system that stress cultural factors are on the right track. Yet their commitment to a narrow conceptualization of culture caused them to miss the awareness that modern world culture is more than a simple set of ideals or values diffusing and operating separately in individual sentiments in each society. The power

> of modern culture – like that of medieval Christendom – lies in the fact that it is a shared and binding set of rules exogenous to any given society, and located not only in individual or elite sentiments, but also in many world institutions (interstate relations, lending agencies, world cultural elite definitions and organization, transnational bodies, and so on). The United Nations, although a weak body organizationally, symbolically represents many of the rules of the modern world polity. . . . It symbolizes the rules of a political system in which national states are constitutive citizens. (Meyer, 1987:50)

Meyer contends that a strong set of institutionalized norms accounts for the stability of the interstate system, supports the sovereignty of existing states, and legitimates the expansion of state regulation within national societies in both the core and the periphery. He notes that peripheral states expand their internal jurisdiction and adopt the trappings of "modernity" (welfare systems, educational systems, etc.) even in the absence of much domestic economic development, and there is considerable empirical support for this contention (see Meyer and Hannan, eds, 1979).

I agree with Meyer that the normative rules institutionalized in the United Nations and the protocols of diplomacy support the interstate system and the sovereignty of states. But I do not agree that these norms are the main source of support for these important central structures of the modern world-system. Meyer's assumption that the norms are "shared and binding" is simply incorrect. When norms are binding the cost of deviance is opprobrium from a valued other (shame) or self-punishment motivated by guilt. Deviance from the norms of diplomacy or the UN Charter is not sanctioned in these ways in the contemporary world-system. My own explanation of the expansion, stability, and reproduction of the interstate system also refers to institutions, but not to rules and values embodied in the world culture. In chapters 6, 7, and 8 I argue that the features of states and the interstate system to which Meyer refers (and others) are produced by an institutionalized capitalist mode of production and by the efforts of groups to protect themselves from market forces and exploitation by core powers.

I agree that normative and value-based consensus has increased at the global level, and that world culture is evolving as a differentiated complex system of institutionalized values. But I also contend that these emergent features do not yet play a strong integrative role in the dynamics of the contemporary world-system. System integration is primarily mediated by markets, and this is backed up by the functioning of the interstate system, a political–military balance of coercive power which regularly (but not randomly) employs warfare as a means of competition. World culture operates to legitimate commodity production and the interstate system, but is not an important determinant of the dynamics of our world-system. Consciousness may, however, play an important role in the transformation of the current system to one based more on consensus and normative integration.

THE FUTURE OF WORLD CULTURE AND COMMUNITY

The trend toward world cultural integration which can be discerned in an increasing convergence around basic themes and the isomorphism of national cultures has not yet reached the point at which normative processes have a central role in world-system processes. The capitalist world-economy is an historical system with contradictory tendencies which will eventually lead to its transformation into a qualitatively different kind of system. My argument above should not be interpreted to mean that ideas will have no importance in the transformation of this system. On the contrary, it is my hope that a scientific analysis of the deep structural tendencies of the system will be useful in transforming it. As Polanyi (1944) suggested for national societies, the enormously productive forces of capitalist development are also enormously destructive of certain human values which do not easily enter into the calculus of "private" (or partial) profit-making. The normative assertion of these collective values is an important part of constructing a world polity which can democratically and rationally plan world production, distribution, and development. Thus the "universalism" generated by capitalist culture needs to be carried forth to a new level of socialist meaning, albeit with a sensitivity to the virtues of ethnic and national pluralism (see Chase-Dunn, ed., 1982b: chapter 14). The claims made by Parsons (1971) and the other culturalist theorists that normative universalism is a central feature of the existing capitalist world-system must be debunked, but the possibility of such a world society in the future should be recognized.

Now we turn to a consideration of the role of states and the interstate system in the capitalist world-economy. A summary of the conclusions reached in part I is contained on pages 5 to 7 in the Introduction.

PART II

States and the Interstate System

Economics and politics are not really separate phenomena despite the needs of academic disciplines to maintain their boundaries. Political economy is the study of the interaction and interdependence between economic and political activities. We cannot understand any social system without knowing how both power and production are organized. A debate has emerged about the nature of the modern world-system and the relationship between its economic and political aspects. Some authors stress the autonomous nature of geopolitics (Skocpol, 1977; Zolberg, 1981) and others, like Modelski and Thompson (1988) analyze long cycles of power concentration in which the long-range military capabilities of the "great powers" are the main focus. The world-system theory developed here looks at the specific ways in which economic and political action are intertwined within the capitalist world-economy. It is argued that the interstate system of unequally powerful and competing states is the political body of capitalism, and that capitalist institutions are central to the maintenance and reproduction of the interstate system, as well as vice versa.

According to Levy's (1983: table 3.1) compilation there have been 64 wars involving two or more states classified as "great powers" since 1495. Several different definitions and lists of wars are reviewed and critiqued by Levy (1985). Here I am defining world wars as major conflicts among core powers for control of core areas of the world-system. Rather than simply counting wars, students of international conflict have devised measures of the intensity of warfare. Goldstein (1985, 1988) uses a measure based on the number of battle deaths per year to study cycles of core war severity.

Though individual conflicts may have many causes, the cycles of world war among core states are understood here as a normal part of the restructuring of political relations which follows the uneven development of capitalist accumulation. The rise and fall of hegemonic core powers is also seen as a consequence of uneven development and associated processes of class conflict and core/periphery interaction.

Contrary to the arguments of some analysts (e.g. Schumpeter, 1955), capitalism is not a pacific mode of production. Rather, warfare appears as a normal and periodic form of competition within the capitalist world-economy. In the modern world-system warfare is in large part an adjunct to strategies of trade and investment, whereas in the precapitalist world-empires it was itself the primary form of competition. For capitalism the interstate system of sovereign nation states, which presumes the legitimacy of warfare, is a crucial institution. It is contended here that the emergence of a system-wide world state, even a confederation limited solely to the prevention of warfare among nation states, would be the beginning of the end of capitalism as a dominant mode of production.

Chapter 6 reviews recent neo-Marxist and neo-Weberian studies of states as organizations. The process of state-formation, the size of states, and differences between core and peripheral states are considered. Chapter 7 examines the arguments that claim that geopolitics is a separate game from economic competition. I contend that these two forms of competition constitute a single integrated logic in the modern world-system. The ways in which the interstate system and the world economy are intertwined with one another in the modern world-system are examined. Chapter 8 continues this discussion by focusing more explicitly on the institutions of capitalism and their role in reproducing the interstate system; it compares the modern interstate system with earlier world-empires, and considers the patterns and linkages between different kinds of wars. Chapter 9 outlines an explanation of the rise and decline of hegemonic core states, the most successful states within the capitalist world-system.

6

States and Capitalism

It has been implied that the world-system perspective is a vulgar "economistic" approach which contends that political action is determined by economic structures. It is undeniable that the relationship between political action and socio-economic structures is somewhat loose. This is quite evident when we consider the extremely complicated connections between class interests and political action. They are by no means as simple and direct as Marx and many Marxists have assumed (and wished). Analogously, if we examine the link between the world-system position of states and the policies, organizational forms, and regime structures of those states there is not a simple and complete fit. To be sure, we cannot explain everything about political action and state structures by knowing how and where a country is inserted into the world hierarchical division of labor. As John Willoughby's (1986:43) excellent discussion of core and peripheral state formation in the context of the internationalization of capital concludes:

> Neither imperial nor subordinate state behavior can be explained without reference to more specific national and international historical processes. No narrow focus on the tendencies of capital can by itself explain state behavior. The method does account for certain general structural trends in the evolution of the global polity, but these findings only provide a basis for understanding the subject of imperialism proper. It is still necessary to develop a framework that can model the interactions among core and peripheral nation-states and international organizations. Otherwise, it will not be possible to anticipate the shifting contours of political-economic subordination and conflict so basic to the capitalist world.

This said we can, however, observe certain general regularities which may be helpful in understanding the world-system as a whole, and also the constraints and possibilities of particular states.[1]

Those who wish to take a less deterministic, more voluntarist, approach to the state and politics often take the Weberian methodological route which emphasizes variability, and seeks to explain why it is different in such and such a place. Charles Ragin and David Zaret (1983) have recently clarified the distinction between Durkheimian variable-based and Weberian case-based explanation. The latter emphasizes explaining the genesis of diversity, while the former focuses on explicating the general model rather than the deviant case. Both strategies are useful and ought to be combined, as Ragin and Zaret contend. What they do not point out, and what is often missing in those analyses of particular states which emphasize historical contingency, is that explanation of variability or diversity assumes the adequacy of the general model with which the particular case is being contrasted. What I wish to do here is to focus on the formulation of a general model.

This chapter considers recent studies which compare core, peripheral, and semiperipheral states, and which discuss generalizations about the connection between the core/periphery hierarchy and features of states. It also discusses the question of the nature of the state within a capitalist mode of production, this in the context of the world-system perspective. The interconnections among the interstate system, geopolitics, and capitalist institutions are examined in two following chapters. Here we will focus on individual states.

Is it true that the typical capitalist state is one which only provides social order and does not intervene in markets or production decisions? Or, to ask the question another way, is capitalism a system which is best conceptualized as operating within the context of such a minimalist state? What is the real relationship between states and markets within the capitalist mode of production? Are core states typically stronger than peripheral states, and does this hold for both internal power and power *vis-à-vis* other states? Are core states typically more democratic, less centralized, and less authoritarian than peripheral and semiperipheral states? If there is such a correspondence between regime form and world-system position, what explains this correspondence? These and related questions are discussed in this chapter.

STATE STRENGTH: INTERNAL AND EXTERNAL

Immanuel Wallerstein (1974) contends that core states tend to be strong, both internally and *vis-à-vis* other states, while peripheral states tend to be weak. And he argues that these tendencies are reinforced by certain structural features of the world-system, by ongoing processes of exploitation and oppression which reproduce the core/periphery hierarchy (see also Rubinson, 1976; Kick, 1980). The strong state/weak state formulation has been criticized by neo-Weberians, as has the alleged “economism” of Wallerstein’s approach (e.g. Skocpol, 1977). It is contended by critics that some non-core states are very strong *vis-à-vis* internal oppositional forces, and that some core states look rather weak internally. It is generally agreed that in external state-to-state relations Wallerstein's generalization holds. Core states are always more powerful than peripheral states *vis-à-vis* other states in terms of military power and economic power deriving from position in the hierarchical international division of labor. These different types of power may not be perfectly correlated, as some states emphasize one or the other, and attention must be paid to the fact that some states change their relative position, moving up or down in the core/periphery hierarchy. The thing which distinguishes a capitalist world-economy from earlier world-systems is the extent to which states in the core rely on comparative advantage in production for the world market instead of political–military power. This does not imply, however, that the normal or typical capitalist state is one which does not interfere with market exchange. The *laissez-faire* state is, in fact, rather atypical, corresponding to those hegemonic core states who are big winners in the world market without needing to resort to strong mercantile interference, or small states greatly dependent on international exchange who do not have the option of exercising effective political–military influence.

The rough correspondence between external state strength and relative status in the core/periphery hierarchy is a matter of definition for those who understand geopolitics to be the main arena of competition in the modern world-system. It must be admitted that political–military competition is important, but if we seek to understand how the modern world-system differs from earlier world-systems we must examine the interaction between states and capitalist commodity production.

The question of internal power is admittedly more complex than the question of external power. I will argue that the form of the government, (whether it is constitutionally democratic, monarchical, or one or another form of centralized authoritarianism) is not simply related to the question of internal state power. A democratically constituted state may be weak or strong *vis-à-vis* internal opposition groups, as may an authoritarian state. And state strength *vis-à-vis* potential and/or actual internal opposition varies over time (relative to itself) in both core and peripheral states, as do the formal constitutional forms taken by states and the composition of class alliances backing particular regimes.

The question of the internal power of states is, like all discussions of power, both theoretically and empirically problematic. Much of the recent literature focusing on states analyzes the "capacities" of the state to implement policy decisions in specific realms of social, political, and economic activity (Skocpol, 1985). This is a useful conceptualization of internal state power, but it needs to be clarified in several ways. The quantity of various kinds of resources directly controlled by governmental agencies (assuming these can be quantitatively measured) needs to be compared with the resources available to internal groups that are prone to resist state policy. And both the state itself and its contending oppositional groups need to be analyzed, not as monolithic, but in terms of the degree of united action versus competing or even conflicting subsections. One important determinant of the power of a state *vis-à-vis* internal opposition is the degree to which state managers and state agencies support each others' actions. Indeed, Arthur Stinchcombe has made this his definition of legitimacy (Stinchcombe, 1968: chapter 4).

It should be noted that it is a characteristic of the most successful hegemonic core states to be relatively decentralized in form. Thus the Dutch Republic has been a confederation of provinces in which the central government has formally limited powers. The United Kingdom of Great Britain and Northern Ireland is also a confederation which, in addition to its stable institutions of representative democracy and constitutional limitations on central state authority, confers a relatively large share of governmental authority to local jurisdictions. The United States, similarly a relatively decentralized federation (though the power of the federal state has increased greatly over time), still does not have a nationally directed education system or a serious public central institution for national economic planning. The US shares with the other previous hegemons stable institutions of representative democracy at local, single state, and federal levels of government.

Peter Evans's discussion of transnational linkages and the economic roles of core and semiperipheral states suggests that core states often display internal weakness at the same time that they have external strength. He argues this as follows:

> Presiding over an economy in which transnational capital is the dominant fraction of the "local" bourgeoisie inhibits the expansion of the state's domestic economic role in capital-exporting countries. The interests of transnational capital coalesce with the geopolitical concerns of state elites around an "externally strong, internally weak" state apparatus. The United States is the prime example, Britain and Switzerland provide supporting evidence. (Evans, 1985:217)

Evans's usage applies best when we are considering processes such as those that occur in declining hegemonic core powers (see chapter 9). It is then that capital exports become relatively great as domestic opportunities for profit contract. In these states formerly convergent interests among different types of capital, and between capital and significantly large groups of core workers, show signs of increasing divergence. No doubt the state becomes weaker (relative to itself at an earlier time) in such a situation as the coalition of interests behind the state becomes increasingly problematic. But it would be inaccurate to characterize core states as typically internally weak relative to semiperipheral or peripheral states. The power of a state as an organization really comes down to the amount of resources it can mobilize relative to the amount of resources which can be mobilized against it. In core countries there are more total resources to be mobilized, and thus a state may need to mobilize great resources against an actual or potential internal challenge. But decentralization and democratic political forms are not direct indications of state weakness. In fact, these forms may help create legitimacy and consensus among significant supporters of a state, and thus undermine challenges and resistance to state authority.

As implied by the above discussion, legitimacy is an important component of internal state strength. Robert Philip Weber (1981) has demonstrated that there is an association over time in changes in the content of political rhetoric and the Kondratieff cycle. Weber performed a content analysis of British Speeches from the Throne from 1795 to 1972 which reveals a 52-year thematic cycle, and this closely corresponds to the K-wave. Weber argues that this shows that problems of political legitimacy are linked to the contradictions produced by capitalist development. Regardless of how this empirical relationship is explained, the finding confirms the existence of a connection between "internal" legitimacy processes and the long economic cycle of the world-system.

We normally think of autonomy and "sovereignty" as definitionally involved with state strength. Sovereignty is a very problematic thing when we turn to a consideration of peripheral states. The most extreme and obvious example of lack of sovereignty in the periphery is the formal colony, an extension of the state apparatus of a core power. Although such an apparatus may be very powerful *vis-à-vis* oppositional groups in the periphery, we would not consider it to be, in itself, an internally strong state. It is likely to lack legitimacy, and it always lacks autonomy. External and internal state strength are thus not completely independent of one another even at the level of definition. Sovereignty *vis-à-vis* other states is a requirement for internal strength as well as external strength because it would be nonsensical to characterize a comprador state or formal colony (whose very existence is guaranteed primarily by the forces of a core state) as being an internally strong state. Internal state strength must be defined in terms of those resources which are autonomously controlled by the particular state under consideration. In practice this is a difficult distinction to make, but we must make it in order to distinguish colonies and comprador regimes from strong states.

A related point, first outlined by Richard Tardanico (1978), is suggested by the conventional use in comparative research of government revenues or expenditures as measures of state strength. While these are obviously direct measures of some of the resources commanded by a state, a better measure would be the amount of resources commanded by the state *during a period in which state power is challenged.* Though the seventeenth-century Dutch Republic had a fairly small regular budget, the Stadtholder of Amsterdam could sell enough state bonds in a single visit to the Amsterdam securities market to fund the mobilization of the nation for effective war against its core state rivals (Barbour, 1963). Similarly, British government revenues per capita (or per national income) were lower than the French revenues throughout the nineteenth century, *except during years of war mobilization*, when the British state resources suddenly jumped to a level much higher than that of the French state. The relatively low level of per capita revenues, I would contend, does not signify that the British state was weaker than the French state during most years of the nineteenth century. On the contrary, the ability of the British state to mobilize greater resources *when they were needed* means that the state as an organization was probably internally stronger in Britain than was the French state in France.

A strong state, then, is strongly supported by an alliance of capitalists which is itself unified and has relatively convergent interests, and is the source of important resources. There are analytically two elements here: the magnitude of resources, and the relative unity within and among classes. Richard Rubinson (1978) has analyzed the political processes by which powerful coalitions among capitalists and landed property owners were forged to form a strong bloc behind upwardly mobile semiperipheral states in Germany and in the United States in the nineteenth century. Although core states themselves vary in terms of the unity and magnitude of resources to which they have access, in both these regards they are usually in better shape than are peripheral states, which generally suffer from higher levels of political disarticulation as well as a scarcity of resources.

An important difference between a capitalist state (which mainly provides order and other conditions for profitable commodity production and commerce) and precapitalist states (which directly engaged in the tributary mode of production in which political–military power was itself the main source of surplus appropriation) suggests reasons why a low-budget state may be, at the same time, very powerful *vis-à-vis* both internal and external opposition. Capitalists want effective and efficient states – that is, states which supply sufficient protection for successful capitalist accumulation *at cost*. A state which does this will be strongly supported by groups with large resources, and yet these states may have relatively small bureaucracies and sparse budgets.

The above arguments notwithstanding, most crossnational studies of internal state strength use some measure of the resources available to the government and compare this magnitude to some measure of the overall resources available in the country. The most common measure is the ratio of government revenues to the GNP. Most of this research has examined the causes of the relative growth of states and the effect of state strength on other variables (e.g. Rubinson, 1977b). A recent cross-national study by Su-Hoon Lee (1988) demonstrates that growth in the *extractive capacity* of peripheral and semiperipheral states (revenues), their *coercive capacity* (the military), and their *integrative capacity* (mass education) are primarily the consequence of international interactions (such as involvement in interstate wars and the international market) rather than internal factors. Cameron (1978) finds that the extractive capacity of core states is highly related to their degree of involvement with the international market.

Here is some additional evidence which bears on the question of the internal strength of core and peripheral states. Table 6.1 is taken from information contained in the World Bank's World Tables (1983). This table shows the average levels of government consumption as a percentage of GDP for groups of countries from 1960 to 1981. The country groups are composed by the World Bank. In our terms, the 21 so-called "industrial market economies" correspond almost exactly with the core. "Low income developing economies" (those 43 countries with less than $405 GDP per capita in 1981) are all peripheral, while "middle income developing economies" includes 106 countries, both peripheral and semiperipheral. So-called "East European non-market economies" and "high income oil exporters" are excluded from the above groups.[2]

TABLE 6.1 *General government consumption as a percentage of GDP at current market prices: means*

Groups of countries	*1960*	*1965*	*1970*	*1981*
Low income developing economies	8.3[a]	10.3[a]	11.1[a]	10.7
Middle income developing economies	11.2	9.7	12.3	13.5
Industrial market economies	15.1	15.4	16.4	17.3

[a] Excludes People's Republic of China
Source: World Bank, *World Tables*, 1983 volume 1, p. 502

The item, general government consumption, is defined as follows:

General government consumption comprises all current expenditure for purchases of goods and services by government bodies: that is, central, regional, and local governments; separately operated social security funds; and international authorities that exercise tax or governmental expenditure functions within the national territory. It excludes outlays of public non-financial enterprises and public financial institutions. The current expenditure of general government covers outlays for compensation of employees, purchases of goods (excluding the acquisition of land and depreciable assets) and services from other sectors of the economy, military equipment, and other purchases from abroad. Capital expenditure on national defense (except for civil defense) is treated as consumption, whereas all expenditure on capital formation (including civil defense) is included in gross domestic investment. (World Bank, 1983 I:xi)

Government consumption as a percentage of GDP is by no means the ideal measure of internal state strength. It does not take account of the resources which would become available to a state in the face of an emergency, an important component of state strength suggested in the argument above. Neither does it at all capture the dimension of unity (or disunity) among state agencies or potential opposition groups, nor does it include certain capital expenditures (e.g. land purchases) or the expenditures of state-owned firms, which probably are indications of internal state strength. Undoubtedly this measure is affected by differences in accounting procedures and other things which are unrelated to state strength. It does, however, take roughly into account the magnitude of the economic resources normally available to states and weights this by the total value of final economic transactions in the society (GDP). As such this ought to be a rough proxy (in crossnational comparison) for the normal extractive power of a state *vis-à-vis* its national society.

Table 6.1 shows that the percentage of GDP attributable to government consumption has risen since 1960 in all groups. This supports other research (Boli, 1980; Lee, 1988) which has demonstrated increases in state-formation in both the core and the periphery. Of more relevance to the question of differential state strength, however, is the indication in table 6.1 of considerable differences between zones of the world-system with regard to the extractive capacity of states. The level of average extractive capacity among core states is significantly higher than that found in either middle or low income developing countries, and this difference continues over time despite the rise of each group.

The differences between the low and middle income groups indicate, with one exception, that semiperipheral states may be internally stronger than peripheral states. This conclusion is uncertain however, because the group of middle income countries includes both semiperipheral and peripheral countries.

A STATE-CENTRIC VIEW OF EXPLOITATION

The recent literature which emphasizes the relative autonomy of state managers, and their inclination to expand the state bureaucracy and to organize stable and protected access to resources – to expand state power and control as far as they can – needs to be considered within a context of different modes of production. Charles Tilly (1985) has characterized modern nation states as predatory accumulators on their own account, as legalized protection rackets operating to obtain the largest possible share of resources. It is important to remember that, although there has been a trend toward the growth of states in both core and periphery, there still remain important differences between the operation of states within a capitalist world-system and the operation of states within systems in which tribute-gathering is the main form of accumulation. States within the contemporary world-system certainly have a tendency to expand their resources. State managers often and regularly attempt to extend their power by finding or creating constituencies which allegedly need their services, and by expanding state access to resources. But the objects of state policy and the continuing limitations on the use of state power need to be considered in the context of a world capitalist system.

The expansion of core states has been analyzed by certain Marxists in terms of necessary correctives to contradictions produced by "monopoly capitalism." Baran and Sweezy (1966) noted that the post-Korean-War expansion of the US military budget to wartime levels, which created a permanent state-sponsored demand for important sectors of US private industry, was proportionally the same share of the US economy which was idle due to overcapacity before the outbreak of World War II. James O'Conner's (1973) analysis of the fiscal crisis of the state extends this kind of thinking to the expansion of welfare services by the US state, arguing that the social contradictions of monopoly capitalism require ever larger state expenditures to subsidize the continuation of private accumulation.

But O'Conner's work also contends that there are important limitations on the further expansion of state expenditures, and this idea of constraints is often neglected by statecentric analysts. Contrary to the tone one often finds in the literature on the predatory expansiveness of state managers, there remain powerful forces which limit the tendency to state expansion. Taxation has been resisted in all historical systems, but in a capitalist system the ruling class itself lives primarily on profits from commodity production rather than tax revenues. Tax payments constrain profit-making in many ways. Taxes on capitalist firms raise the cost of products and reduce competitiveness, and thus profits. Taxes paid by consumers lower the effective demand for commodities. Thus, as Fred Block (1978) and many other analysts have pointed out, the very structure of capitalist accumulation limits states to activities which promote an atmosphere of "business confidence."

States themselves are often major purchasers of products from the private sector, of course. And, increasingly, modern states are themselves directly entering into the production of commodities. Bennett and Sharpe (1985:71) usefully summarize the differences between privately and publicly owned firms. Public firms may operate at a loss if there is sufficient political support to subsidize them. But even state capitalism is eventually subjected to cost considerations emanating from competitive markets. If states produce for export they must compete with foreign producers, and so cost considerations are important. And even when they produce only for their own monopolized domestic market, there are important constraints. If they produce for a protected internal market the political costs of maintaining an internal monopoly vary with the disparity between the internal price and the world price. Above a certain differential the costs of preventing smuggling, and/or illegal internal production, become exorbitant. As long as the interstate system remains a competitive arena there is a tendency toward the "equalization of surplus profits" in which the political conditions for the maintenance of monopolies are subjected to a logic of cost efficiency.

The historian of Venice, Frederic Lane (1979) has analyzed the interaction between state power and the economic growth of firms in terms of the notion of "protection rent." States, which he calls "violence-controlling enterprises," are differentially successful in providing effective and efficient protection to merchants and commodity producers. In the context of a competitive interstate system and an international price-setting market, protection rent is an important component of the profits which are gained by firms. Lane explains:

> An essential charge on any economic enterprise is the cost of its protection from disruption by violence. Different enterprises competing in the same market often pay different costs of protection, perhaps as tariffs, or bribes, perhaps in some other form. The difference between the protection costs forms one element in the income of the enterprise enjoying the lower protection cost. This element in income I will call *protection rent.* (Lane, 1979:12–13, emphasis in the original)

Though Lane's notion has been applied primarily to "mercantilist" states, protection rent, and competition among states to provide relatively efficient protection for their international merchants and producers, continues to be an important constraint on state expenditures in the contemporary world-system because capital can migrate to where effective protection costs are lower.

Of course, as William H. McNeill (1982) has argued, there is a contextual effect by which the level of expenditure of any single state will be justified in rising along with the general level. McNeill contends that market-based industrialism and rapid innovations in military technology have, in the context of the continuation of an extremely competitive interstate system, created a virtual explosion (excuse the grim pun) of military expenditures.

The expansion of states everywhere, and their increasing tendency to become directly involved in the process of economic development, may have somewhat weakened the constraints on state expenditures which emanate from the world market and the competition for investment capital, but these forces still remain important limitations on the expansion of state appropriation of resources.

Raymond Duvall and John R. Freeman (1981) present an excellent theoretical analysis of state entrepreneurship in dependent capitalist states, mainly semiperipheral ones. They make the important point that there is no such thing as "the capitalist state" in general. The particular articulation of each state within the larger world-system must be taken into account in any theory of state economic policy. Peter Evans's (1979) analysis of the Brazilian *tripé*, the alliances, bargaining, and competition among state managers, local capitalists, and transnational firms operating in Brazil, strongly supports the Duvall and Freeman contention that the role of the state in accumulation cannot be understood without attention to the particular insertion of each country in the larger system.

It is extremely difficult for states to cut themselves off from the larger world-system and to create a closed internal economy, although many have tried. The most successful in some respects are the large semiperipheral states, especially China and the Soviet Union, which have adopted state socialism. Because of the actual or potential great size of internal demand and access to internal natural resources, these states have been able to directly use political power to mobilize internal industrialization. They have been able to buffer themselves from world market forces and political–military threats that tend to undercut autarchic industrialization. Mercantilist state power (*àla* Friedrich List) was also used to protect infant industries from foreign competition in earlier successful industrializers – England, the United States, Germany and Japan (Senghaas, 1985) – and state power has been very important in the recent industrialization of Brazil, Mexico, India, and of course South Korea and Singapore.

Contrary to the implications of Gershenkron's (1962) analysis, it is not only late industrializers that employ mercantilist protection and state intervention in order to foster capitalist accumulation. Both England and the US, allegedly the models of *laissez-faire* industrialization, employed state power during crucial periods. In England state intervention was used in the seventeenth and eighteenth centuries to reinforce enclosures of agricultural properties and to protect the woolen textile industry against Dutch competition. In Elizabethan England the government acted to constrain the businesses of foreign merchants in London in order to open up additional opportunities for domestic commercial and industrial interests. The emergence of free trade ideology and policy occurred only *after* the initial successes, and were largely motivated by the desire of the new industrial capitalists to reduce the state-guaranteed prerogatives of the land-owning capitalists.

Similarly the United States employed state power to protect capitalist development, contrary to the image of the *laissez-faire* state. The anti-imperial revolution against Britain set the stage for a series of political struggles over the use of state power. State intervention occurred, for a long time, primarily at the level of the separate states rather than at the federal level (Lunday,

1980). This involved state-sponsored infra-structural development, the granting of commercial monopolies, and the regulation of land and water use. Intervention at the federal level turned toward an increasingly mercantilist "American System" policy in a series of struggles and not a few setbacks, which were finally settled by the Civil War. My own study of tariff politics in the US between 1812 and the Civil War shows, in this single policy terrain, how shifting coalitions of core capitalists, peripheral capitalists, farmers, and urban workers eventually led to the firm establishment of core capitalism in the United States (Chase-Dunn, 1980).

It is obvious that some states are able to move upward in the core/periphery hierarchy. These include Gershenkron's so-called late industrializers. The world-system analysis of "national development" views these cases of upward mobility as exceptions against the background of the more frequent "development of underdevelopment." This is not just a matter of vocabulary. Discussions of the state and national development which focus only on the industrialization of national economies have difficulty accounting for the phenomenon of a reproduced core/periphery hierarchy based on uneven development, with dependent industrialization occurring, but little or no reduction in the overall magnitude of world-system inequality.

As Peter Evans and John Stephens (1988) have persuasively argued, state control and market freedom are not mutually incompatible alternatives. States increasingly act to both control markets and create them. Indeed, the policies of states that successfully promote capitalist development are oriented, not only to the efficient supply of social order, but also to the creation of structures which promote profitable enterprises. State capitalism does not simply wait for entrepreneurs to succeed so that it can tax them. It acts to create opportunities for entrepreneurs, and sometimes it takes on the entrepreneurial role itself. Evans (1986) has analyzed the Brazilian creation of a domestic microcomputer industry by some state "technicos" who managed to create a constituency for themselves by spawning domestic computer-producing firms. "Japan, Incorporated," the state-level organization of an entire nation's education system toward research and development of new products for the world market, is another example of the aggressive capitalist state.

It is not simply a question of intervention versus the free operation of markets, but rather of the goals and content of state policies. It is undoubtedly true that economic intervention has increased and become much more sophisticated than when states imposed import and export tariffs primarily as a mechanism for raising revenues. But the larger point is that this kind of intervention is neither precapitalist nor anti-capitalist, but is rather the normal operation of states within a capitalist mode of production. The definition of capitalism as private business conducted in the context of a minimalist state was a mistaken representation produced by focusing on a core state (Britain) at the height of its hegemony, a rather atypical situation.

PERIPHERAL AND SEMIPERIPHERAL STATES

Rather than focusing on the exceptional success stories, the upwardly mobile states, attention should be given to the more usual patterns revealed by the relative stability of the core/periphery hierarchy and its constraints on state action. As many have argued, even core states are limited in terms of their possible actions by the fact of their interdependence in the larger world-system. Political–military conflicts and economic competition restrict the range of policies which a core state can adopt. And of course, the long-run operation of the whole system conditions the kind of class structure, political institutions, etc. which we find "internal" to core states as well as peripheral states (e.g. Walton, 1981). Nevertheless, the room for manuever is considerably greater for core states than it is for peripheral states because their access to resources is relatively greater and less dependent on external forces or constrained by internal opposition. The observation that peripheral capitalism relies more heavily on political coercion to maintain class relations and to accomplish production and distribution can be linked to an analysis of the organizational forms of states and regimes in the periphery.

Marx's examination of "primitive accumulation" (Marx, 1967a: part 8) discusses the plunder and dispossession which occurred in the expansion of European hegemony. In a sense capitalist accumulation was always, and still is, more "primitive" in the periphery. Its reliance on political coercion is more than a passing phase which occurs during the creation of capitalist institutions. The precapitalist world-empires utilized political coercion directly in the maintenance of master/slave or lord/serf relations. The gathering of tribute, taxes, and rents was a relatively visible form of surplus appropriation compared to the more opaque form of exploitation in the capitalist/proletarian relationship. So peripheral capitalism does bear a greater similarity to precapitalist societies based on the tributary mode of production than does core capitalism.

And yet it is misleading to conceptualize the developmental process we observe in peripheral areas as a separate precapitalist mode of production, or a period of transition to full capitalism. These usages are more than merely semantic differences because a mode of production ought to be largely self-reproducing, and a period of transition should not last for centuries. But peripheral capitalism, though it changes its form and, in some ways, does take on aspects of core capitalism (more proletarianization, more commodification, more state-formation, more nation-building, etc.) never arrives at the destination of "advanced capitalism." That is, the relative gap between the core and the periphery is reproduced, not eliminated (see chapter 12).

Thus peripheral states do develop, just as the economy of the periphery does. But they very rarely become core states. Peripheral areas experience state-formation. Decolonization creates formal sovereignty. The state arrogates greater powers over other social and political organizations such as tribes, village communities, ethnic and religious organizations, etc. The expansion of mass education performs the magical rituals of nation-building by producing and distributing national ideology and the political status of the citizen (Ramirez and Rubinson, 1979).

And yet other features of peripheral states seem more reticent to "develop." The literature on modernization and democracy argues that economic development is necessary in order to institutionalize a democratic polity. Yet, though there has been a good deal of industrialization in many peripheral and semiperipheral countries, this has not resulted in stable democratic government in most cases.

If we want to analyze the possibilities and constraints of peripheral and semiperipheral states the first thing we must notice is that many of these states depend on core states, transnational banks, or core-based transnational firms for a significant share of their resources, and these forms of support come with certain explicit or implicit limitations on state action. Bruce Moon's (1983) comparative study of the foreign policies of peripheral states demonstrates that patterns of voting in the UN can best be interpreted in terms of rather stable structures of core power domination based on the dependency of peripheral states rather than in terms of a more flexible set of bargaining relationships. And Nora Hamilton's (1982) study of Mexican social movements and the state in the 1930s shows the effects of changing core state policy on the limits of peripheral state action. One of the biggest factors allowing a significantly populist and nationalist state action (the expropriation of US-owned oil companies) by the Cardenas regime was the advent of Roosevelt's much more liberal policy toward Latin America. Cardenas could never have gone so far if the US had maintained a hard line.

Maurice Zeitlin's (1984) careful study of the class backgrounds of nineteenth-century Chilean statesmen and the class forces behind two civil wars in Chile is intended as an antidote to a vulgar world-system theory in which the policies of peripheral states are determined by direct manipulation by core states or core-based capitalist firms. Zeitlin effectively disproves earlier interpretations, which claimed that manipulations by British imperial agents defeated Jose Manuel Balmaceda's attempt to use Chilean state power to support a more autonomous type of economic development. But his findings, supposedly demonstrating that local class struggles (rather than "external factors") explain the failed "bourgeois revolution" of Balmaceda, actually reveal a clash of interests between two sets of peripheral capitalists: those vested in copper mines (who were suffering from declining prices and stiff foreign competition for export markets); and those rising producers of nitrate exports (who were enjoying grand profits).

Balmaceda's intended policy of state mobilization was supported primarily by the copper interests who wanted to tax the nitrate exporters in order to invest in infrastructure which would improve their position in the world market. Yes, this is a class struggle explanation, but one in which the interests and actions of the important class fractions are heavily influenced by their points of insertion and varying fortunes in the world market. The "rounds of accumulation" notion, which is useful in understanding regional uneven development in core areas (e.g. Smith, 1984), can be seen operating in the rise and fall of extractive and agriculture export products in peripheral areas. These boom and bust sequences account for a great part of the political changes which occur in the periphery (Bunker, 1985).

The world-system perspective also has implications for the nature of politics in semiperipheral states. In addition to these states being relatively intermediate in terms of their levels of internal and external power, it is thought that the relative balance of peripheral and core types of production within some semiperipheral states tends to create combinations of class interests and regime form which, it is argued, differentiate semiperipheral from both core and peripheral states. A recent volume edited by Giovanni Arrighi (1985) presents a collection of studies which examine the applicability of the semiperiphery concept for understanding twentieth-century political changes and patterns of economic development in most of the countries of Southern Europe.

These studies exhibit the many problems of trying to understand the particular histories of countries with a concept which has emerged from the attempt to describe and explain features and processes which appear when we focus on the world-system as a whole. When we use a telescope we see different patterns from when we use a magnifying glass. Nevertheless the studies are illuminating, not only because we learn a lot about the countries which are examined, but because the exercise clarifies some of the confusing aspects of the semiperiphery idea and some of the limits of its usefulness (see chapter 10).

REGIME FORM: DEMOCRACY AND AUTHORITARIANISM

It is a common observation that, though both core and peripheral states exhibit authoritarian regime forms, this feature is much more frequently found in peripheral or semiperipheral states. Kenneth Bollen (1983) presents a crossnational study of the relationship between world-system position and political democracy which demonstrates that both semiperipheral and peripheral states are less likely to have democratic regime forms than core states. Bollen's findings also show that peripheral states are even more likely to be undemocratic than semiperipheral states (Bollen, 1983: table 2). This striking larger pattern requires theoretical attention.

There has been much recent study of peripheral and semiperipheral states, their organizational characteristics, and the ways in which the state is linked to the local class structure. Michael Timberlake and Kirk Williams (1984) use crossnational data to examine the relationship between the level of penetration by transnational firms, exclusion of non-elite groups from politics, and levels of repressiveness of peripheral and semiperipheral governments. Their results show that dependence on foreign capital does not have a direct effect on government repressiveness, but is associated with political exclusion, and affects repression indirectly through its effects on exclusion. Thus, among peripheral and semiperipheral countries, it is those most dependent on foreign capital that are most likely to have authoritarian states.

Guillermo O'Donnell's (1978, 1979) analysis of bureaucratic authoritarianism in the Southern Cone countries of South America examines the links between industrial phases of semiperipheral economic development, the emergence of strong demands from a large and active middle stratum composed of formal sector workers and urban small businessmen, and the reactive emergence of an authoritarian regime. The democratic institutions of Brazil and Argentina were utilized by politically aggressive "middle class" interests to press their demands upon the state apparatus. It is the relatively developed countries in Latin America which have exhausted the import-substitution process and have relatively large and active middle strata which are most likely to develop bureaucratic authoritarianism. The cyclical ups and downs of the world economy, interacting with different phases of national development, produce a political crisis. According to O'Donnell, bureaucratic authoritarianism takes over when the military steps in to impose a technocratically legitimated order, allegedly representing the nation as a whole. This occurs in reaction to the political crisis, and may be exacerbated by a downturn in the world economy requiring fiscal austerity measures.

Clive Thomas (1984) has examined the authoritarianism of more recently decolonized peripheral states in Africa and the Caribbean. Thomas focuses on states in which the middle class of business entrepreneurs and the class of urban formal sector workers are miniscule or absent. In these peripheral states, Thomas argues, authoritarianism is a consequence of the absence of opportunities in the local economy. Political forms of exploitation articulated through the state apparatus are virtually the only game around, and so fierce competition over control of the state undercuts the emergence and maintenance of democratic institutions. Regimes tend to form around an authoritarian one-party state.

When we compare the analysis by O'Donnell with that of Thomas the first things that strike the eye are the important differences between the semiperipheral Southern Cone countries with their relatively developed national economies and significant middle classes, and the more peripheral Caribbean and African states with their small urban sectors. O'Donnell's arguments for the emergence and reproduction of authoritarian regimes are based on completely different (and opposite) causes from those of Thomas. For O'Donnell it is the large middle-class groups and urban workers clamoring for shares of the pie which reactively stimulates bureaucratic authoritarian regimes, while for Thomas it is the absence of these groups which results in authoritarian regimes.

While these explanations may seem to be at odds, they are easily reconciled if we employ two explanations suggested by the literature which compares regime types. A recent review of this literature by Peter Evans and John Stephens (1988) suggests a useful synthesis of the approach suggested by Barrington Moore's (1966) study of democracy and dictatorship and recent Marxist analyses which focus on the organizational power of the urban working class.[3] Moore's analysis focuses on the agrarian class structure to explain differences in regimes. He argues that those countries in which large agricultural landowners formed a significant political block tended to prevent the emergence of democratic state structures or to break down democratic regimes which had emerged. On the other hand, in countries where the landowners were either too few to be politically important or the agrarian class structure was composed mostly of peasant freeholders, the emergence of an industrial urban working class was able to create and sustain a democratic regime. It is necessary to examine the stability of democracy as well as its existence at any point in time. The historical studies of European states which examine their political histories over long periods of time are most useful for comparisons with contemporary peripheral and semiperipheral states. John Stephens's (1987) most recent study, which finds considerable support for Moore's thesis by comparing European states, is exemplary in this regard.

The class power approach is complementary with Moore's approach in that it focuses on the organizational power of the urban working class. Crudely stated, industrialization expands the urban working class, which engages in class struggle, building strong autonomous political organizations (unions and parties) which exert power on the state to extend citizenship rights and welfare rights. This is, of course, a restatement in Marxist terms of T. H. Marshall's (1965) thesis.

The relative size of the urban working class and middle stratum is known to vary with the level of national industrialization and the position of each country in the core/periphery hierarchy. When we add this to Moore's focus on agrarian class structure we provide a fairly powerful account of why core states have more stable democracies than peripheral and semiperipheral states. Of course, this does not explain every case, and it does not explain why these differences persist despite the increasing industrialization of the periphery and semiperiphery.

Evans and Stephens (1988) add two other factors. They argue that late industrialization is more capital intensive and thus creates a relatively smaller industrial working class, and this weakens the association between industrialization and democracy. Also they argue that state strength and democracy are inversely related, contrary to the argument I have made above. In support of this last contention they interpret Mouzelis's (1986) study of semiperipheral oscillation between populism and authoritarianism (see below) as the consequence of a precociously overdeveloped state apparatus. Similarly they attribute the authoritarian nature of the East Asian NICs to their relatively strong and interventionist state apparati. And conversely, they characterize the formerly British Caribbean states (the same ones analyzed by Thomas as authoritarian) as being democratic because of the weakness of the military and state apparatus inherited from British colonialism.

The contention that state strength is inversely related to the stability of democratic regimes is another instance of the confusion (discussed above) of state strength with authoritarianism. I argued above that democratic states are more likely to be internally strong than authoritarian ones. I know of no crossnational comparative research which has directly addressed this question. The easiest empirical test is the relationship between government revenues per capita (or per GNP) and regime form. This would not completely answer the question because of the problem mentioned above – there is a potential discrepancy between the actual amount of resources a state obtains through taxation and the amount it might obtain from supporters if its power were challenged. Even so I would guess that the correlation between this somewhat faulty proxy for internal state strength and authoritarianism would be negative in crossnational comparison.

Some support for this surmise is had from the study by Thomas, et al. (1973: table 11.3). They demonstrate that the level of economic development has a negative effect over time on the centralization of the party system and the likelihood of having a military regime. If internal state strength is associated with the level of economic development (as indicated by table 6.1 above), then it is likely that authoritarian regimes are associated with (and perhaps caused by) weaker states, not stronger ones.

To the agrarian class relations and working-class power explanations we can also add some other features which come from our analysis of the capitalist world-system. We have already mentioned the worldwide long business cycle (K-wave) which affects political developments in all states. There are several major forces operating which, in combination, account for the overall core/periphery differences in regime form. All states are more likely to take an authoritarian form when they are significantly threatened by internal or external opposition. Thus authoritarianism is a sign of weakness, not of strength. This applies to both core and peripheral states. Most analyses of fascism understand it as a reactive response to strong opposition from the Left. Socialist states are thought to move toward authoritarianism as a result of both internal opposition and threats from foreign capitalist states. Political and economic crises in the core and in the periphery tend to evoke a rise in centralization and authoritarian actions by states. Even the strongly institutionalized core democracies do this during time of war, and recent political commentary from the Trilateral Commission has suggested that democracy in the core may have to be tightened up as the increasing "cacophony of equity demands" produce an "ungovernable" situation (Wolfe, 1980).

Against this tendency for states to become more authoritarian in the face of increasing opposition is an opposing tendency which affects all states in the capitalist world-economy (but not equally). This is the tendency for capitalism to structurally sustain a political ideology of egalitarianism. Commodity production and markets assume that buyers and sellers have equal political standing, and the process of the commodification of labor power supports an ideology in which both capitalists and workers are defined as equal citizens freely exchanging labor for wages. These institutional supports for democratic ideology exert pressure on states to adopt a form of government based on legitimation from below, from the "people" or citizens. Most modern states are constitutionally defined as agents of the people rather than agents of God. This institutional push on modern states stems from the process of commodification. It has resulted in the nearly worldwide shift from legitimation based on the divine right of kings to legitimation based on the consent of the governed. Authoritarianism is, of course, contrary to democratic ideology, but most contemporary forms of authoritarianism are defined as temporary and necessary exercises, rather than the restoration of legitimation from above.[4]

The ideological pressure toward democratization affects the core and the periphery to different extents precisely because commodification is more complete in the core than in the periphery. This partly explains core/periphery differences in both the degree and the form of authoritarianism. Not only are authoritarian regimes more common in the periphery, but some of these are legitimated by traditional hierarchical ideologies. The world's few really powerful remaining monarchs are in Saudi Arabia, Thailand, and Nepal. But equally important as a cause of the core/periphery correlation with democracy and authoritarianism are the differences in both internal and external state strength. The relative weakness of peripheral states means that they are more likely to confront strong opposition and to face crisis situations.

Recent studies demonstrate that peripheral states in which the majority of citizens are freeholding peasants have difficulty enforcing policies and appropriating resources when peasants are opposed (Hyden, 1980). Stephen Bunker (1983) has shown that it is not really land tenure as such, but rather the combination of local effective control of land use with the production of export crops on which state development plans depend. This is a crucial combination that allows local oppositional groups to effectively resist the peripheral state. These and many other possible combinations which create openings for either state autonomy or effective local resistance may account for a good deal of the variation in state strength, and thus affect the tendency to form an authoritarian regime.

In addition to the ideological effect which commodification has on politics, there is another connection between core capitalism and democracy. It is an interesting fact that all the hegemonic core powers, both city states and nation states, which have been analyzed as hegemonic centers of the European capitalist world-economy by Braudel (1984) have been republics or federations, or both. This could be explained by the ideological connection with commodity production, but it may also be due to the need for a hegemonic core state to have a responsive state apparatus which can adjust quickly to changing needs for appropriate state policy in a rapidly changing world market and geopolitical environment. If this sounds too functionalist, run it the other way. Those core states that happen to have such a democratic, pluralist regime are better able, in combination with other necessary ingredients, to take on the role of a hegemon in a world-system in which commodity production is an important form of competition. Thus Venice, Antwerp, Genoa, Amsterdam, London, and New York were (are) world cities in states which are relatively democratic, or at least pluralistic, compared to the states with which they were (are) in competition.

This factor does not contradict Moore's analysis because none of these states, save England, had a significantly powerful landed aristocracy to sustain a centralized monarchy. The city states, as Braudel says, had the advantage of leaving primary production to others. Amsterdam struggled with the land-based House of Orange, but this did not much interfere with the mercantile use of the Dutch state. Indeed, this was part of what made it a strong nation state with an important internal market. The English landed aristocracy was itself heavily involved in both agricultural and urban capitalism, and played an important and complementary role in geopolitics.

The matter of working class power must be reinterpreted, but not discarded. It is not so much a matter of the industrial revolution *àla* the factory system creating an industrial proletariat as usually conceived. Many of these core powers did contain a significant industrial and productive sector which facilitated their centrality in the expanding world market, but in addition to this, the fact of being at the center of a world-system, with higher rates of profit and more opportunities for "clean" work, made class struggle a less contentious matter than it was in other areas (see chapters 10 and 11). This extension of Lenin's aristocracy of labor thesis back in time adds a consideration to the explanation of regime form which is not suggested by analyses which focus only on national development and ignore the core/periphery hierarchy.

Wallerstein suggests that the internal strength and spatial scope of state power is an important difference between semiperipheral and peripheral areas. Evans (1979) analyzes the strengthening of the semiperipheral Brazilian state after the military coup of 1964, and the way in which the state effectively mediated bargaining between transnational firms and national capitalists. Evans notes that the effectiveness and autonomy of the authoritarian Brazilian state varied across different sectors of the economy depending upon the production and market characteristics of different industries. Bunker (1985: chapter 4) shows that the Brazilian state's autonomy was quite limited when it attempted to regulate an internal extractive periphery, the Amazon region.

O'Donnell's (1978, 1979) work on bureaucratic authoritarianism contends that the semiperipheral states in South America have been quite effective in regulating their national economies, and have demonstrated a high degree of autonomy *vis-à-vis* both internal private power groups and transnational firms. The recent reversion of these same states back toward populist and democratic constitutional forms supports the idea that they are relatively strong states, at least if my argument about the relationship between regime form and state strength is correct. Portes and Kincaid (1985) have argued that the recent shift back toward democratic forms in Argentina and Uruguay resulted from a "crisis of authoritarianism" in which the economic policies of the authoritarian regimes were exhausted and largely ineffective, and the level of opposition had risen high enough to promote a return to democratic government, albeit under difficult economic and political conditions.[5]

Nicos Mouzelis (1986) has explicated a theory of semiperipheral politics which accounts for an apparent long-run cyclical swing between authoritarian and populist regimes based on the contradictory tendencies of dependent capitalist development. Mouzelis applies his theory to interpret the political history of Greece since World War II, but it is intended for wider application as well. His explanation is based on the idea that semiperipheral states differ most significantly from both core and periphery because they have a relatively large "modern" capitalist sector which is nevertheless strongly linked with the reproduction of a more traditional sector of petty commodity producers. Mouzelis argues that the late development of industrial capitalism in the semiperiphery, which followed rather than preceded the political shift from oligarchic patrimonial to bourgeois state forms, created a contradictory situation in which "civil society" (especially autonomous trade unions) is weak, and thus the state shifts back and forth between populist and authoritarian regimes depending on the short-run successes or failures of particular development schemes, and ups and downs in the world market.

This explanation differs from that of O'Donnell in two ways. First it tries to explain semiperipheral politics in long-run structural terms rather than focusing on the details of particular conjunctures. Secondly, Mouzelis and O'Donnell differ in their portrayals of the strength or weakness of "civil society." O'Donnell claims that it is the middle-class groups demanding more from the state which precipitate authoritarianism, while for Mouzelis it is the lack of strong and supportive middle-class organizations which underlies the instability of democracy. Of course both could be correct if there is a nonlinear relationship between middle-class strength and authoritarian regimes. A middle class may be strong enough to press political demands, but not sufficiently strong to resist the opposition which such demands engender.

The growing scale of economic production has stimulated greater involvement of states in the economy and the increasingly frequent use of the ideology of corporatism. As local economic circuits become more completely integrated into national and international networks, states come to be the only organizations which are large enough to exert leverage in the economy. Corporatist ideology, the notion of an interclass organic unity of interest which is mediated by the state, takes many forms. In semiperipheral countries both the bureaucratic authoritarian and populist democratic regimes have utilized corporatist ideology.

Some of the apparently contradictory implications of case studies of particular states with the analysis of states located in the core/periphery hierarchy may result from confusion between different types of comparison. Many case studies compare a state to itself at an earlier point in time, whereas world-system studies most often compare states to one another. Thus a state may indeed gain in internal strength relative to itself, as Evans and O'Donnell have claimed for Brazil, but not much change its level of internal strength compared to other states. Another possible example of this is Evans's "externally strong, internally weak" characterization of core states which export a lot of capital (see page 112 above). There is considerable evidence that all states are increasing their powers *vis-à-vis* internal opposition, but that core/periphery differences in internal state strength are not changing. This contention is supported by table 6.1 and other findings. John Boli has shown that state authority *vis-à-vis* other groups in society, as formalized in national constitutions, has increased since 1870 in core, semiperipheral, and peripheral states (Boli, 1979: table 13.5). Thomas et al. show that the centralization of regimes has increased in peripheral and semiperipheral regions since 1950, but this has not occurred in core countries, which remain much less centralized and exhibit no trend (Thomas et al. 1979: figure 11.2).

To summarize, I have argued that core states are stronger internally and externally than peripheral states, and that they are more democratic. These features of states are thought to result from a combination of several world-system processes interacting with nation-building, state-formation, and class struggles. Only further comparative research can place weights on these various factors and settle matters of controversy. The matter of internal state strength needs further conceptual clarification and empirical operationalization, as does the relationship between state strength and regime form. For now we have established for certain that important characteristics of states are associated with their position in the larger world-system. Let us now turn to the analysis of a larger structure, the interstate system which is composed of these contending and unequally powerful states.

7

Geopolitics and Capitalism: One Logic or Two?

As we have seen in previous chapters, the focus on the world-system has raised anew the issue of the relationship between economic and political processes in the capitalist mode of production. This has coincided with a new emphasis on the autonomy of political processes by neo-Marxists seeking to correct the overemphasis on economic determinism in earlier Marxist analyses.[1] While focusing most directly on the capitalist state and class relations within the core of the world-system, Nicos Poulantzas (1973) and Perry Anderson (1974) have stressed the autonomy of political processes and the "relative autonomy" of state managers from determination by capitalist class interests.[2] This emphasis on the autonomy of politics, long central among political scientists, has been extended to a critique of the alleged "economism" of the world-system perspective. At the international level this critique argues that geopolitics is an autonomous game in its own right which can be understood separately from an analysis of world economic structures. Theda Skocpol (1977, 1979) is the neo-Weberian sociologist who has most explicitly made this argument, but it has also been made by several political scientists who share a statecentric approach to social science, e.g. George Modelski (1978), Aristide Zolberg (1981), and Kenneth Waltz (1979).

All these authors claim that Immanuel Wallerstein has reduced the operation of the "international" system to a consequence of the process of capitalist accumulation. Indeed some have contended that geopolitics and state-building are themselves the main motors of the modern world-system (e.g. Winckler, 1979; Gilpin, 1981). Here I will argue that the capitalist mode of production exhibits a single logic in which both political–military power and the appropriation of surplus value through production of commodities for sale on the world market play an integrated role. This chapter discusses a metatheoretical issue, and presents an argument about the interdependence of the interstate system and the capital accumulation process.

First I will present a case for a change in terminology. The world-system scholars of the Braudel Center have employed the term "interstate system" in their discussions of geopolitics. The term most frequently used by other students of geopolitics is "international system." The units which compose the system I wish to focus upon are states, not nations. In addition to nation states, in which the state encompasses and represents a single "nation" (in the sense of a national community of culture-sharing people) there are modern states which represent only part of a nation (e.g. South Korea) and other states which rule over several nations. The phenomenon of nations and the processes of nation-building are certainly related to states and the interstate system, but this important distinction ought not to be confused by our terminology. *Interstate system* refers exclusively to the relations (economic, political, social, and military) among the formal organizations which monopolize legitimate violence within a specified territory. Interstate systems as entities themselves vary historically as to the kinds of states which compose them, the relative distribution of power among states within them, and the nature of the institutions which regulate relations among the states. In this chapter we are focusing on a particular interstate system, the one which emerged in Europe in the long sixteenth century, and which has subsequently spread to encompass the earth.[3]

A METATHEORETICAL ISSUE

In this chapter, rather than arguing at a metatheoretical level about economics, politics, and political economy in general, I shall ground the discussion in the particular processes which have been operating in the capitalist world-economy since the sixteenth century. But before I advance arguments for my contention that the interstate system and the capitalist accumulation process are part of the same interactive socio-economic logic I would like to briefly discuss a metatheoretical problem raised by this issue.

In order to know whether it is most elegant to conceive of capitalism as a singular process which incorporates both economic and political dynamics, or, on the other hand, if it is more powerful to emphasize the autonomy of these processes, we should be able to specify formally and compare a unified theory with a theory which posits separate economic and political subsystems.

Ideally these two theories should have different implications for concrete social change, and for our understanding of the dialectical transformation of capitalism into a qualitatively different system. Unfortunately my argument here does not proceed at this level of theoretical clarity. Rather I only adduce a case for the superiority of a unified theory. But it is important to cast this argument in the context of the attempt to develop the world-system perspective into a formalized theory of capitalist development.

Why have most of the theorists who focus on politics tended to adopt a narrowly historicist approach to capitalist development? Marx made a broad distinction between the growth of the forces of production (technology) which occurs in the capital accumulation process, and the reorganization of social relations of production (class relations, forms of property, and other institutions which structure exploitation and the accumulation process). Samir Amin (1980a) has applied this broad distinction to the world-system. The widening of the world market and the deepening of commodity production to more and more spheres of life has occurred in conjunction with a series of 40- to 60- year business cycles, the K-wave. The K-wave is associated with "non-economic" political events such as wars, revolutions, etc. This has caused some economists (e.g. Adelman, 1965) to argue that long waves are not really *economic* cycles at all, but are set off by "exogenous" political events.

The causal links between wars, revolutions, and long business cycles are not precisely understood despite a vast literature on K-waves (see Barr, 1979), but Amin (1980a) and Mandel (1980) have made the insightful argument that the accumulation process expands within a certain political framework to the point where that framework is no longer adequate to the scale of world commodity production and distribution. Thus world wars and the rise and fall of hegemonic core powers can be understood as the violent reorganization of production relations on a world scale which allows the accumulation process to adjust to its own contradictions and to begin again on a reorganized political foundation. Political relations among core powers and the colonial empires which are the formal political structure of core/periphery relations are reorganized in a way which allows the increasing internationalization of capitalist production and the spatial shifts which accompany uneven development. The observation that capitalism has always been "international" (and transnational) does not contradict the existence of a long-run increase in the proportion of all production decisions and commodity chains which cross state boundaries – the upward secular trend of the transnationalization of capital.

The above discussion does not establish causal priority between accumulation and political reorganization. But it implies that these are truly interdependent processes. The tendency to a narrowly historicist approach on the part of those who focus on political events may be due to the low predictability of politics and the apparently more direct involvement of human collective rationality in political action. On the other hand, the over-emphasis on determinism and mechanical models on the part of those who focus exclusively on economic processes may be due to the greater regularity of these phenomena and their law-like aggregation of many individual wills seemingly independent of collective intentions.

These perceptions are correct to a considerable extent precisely because capitalism as a system mystifies the social nature of investment decisions by separating the calculation of profit to the enterprise from the calculation of more general social needs. Anti-capitalist movements have tried to reintegrate economics and politics in practice, but up to now, the expanding scale of the commodity economy has evaded them. The interaction of the world economy and the interstate system is fundamental to an understanding of capitalist development and also to its potential transformation into a more collectively rational system. Neither mechanical determinism nor narrow historicism is useful in this project.

STATES AS PRODUCTION RELATIONS

The critiques of Wallerstein's work mentioned above contain implicit assumptions about the nature of capitalism which tend to conceptualize it as an exclusively "economic" process. Skocpol (1979:22) formulates the issue by arguing that Wallerstein "assumes that individual nation-states are instruments used by economically dominant groups to pursue world-market oriented development at home and international economic advantages abroad." She continues, explaining her own position:

> but a different perspective is adopted here, one which holds that nation-states are, more fundamentally, organizations geared to maintain control of home territories and populations and to undertake actual or potential military competition with other states in the international system. The international states system as a transnational structure of military competition was not originally created by capitalism. Throughout modern world history, it represents an analytically autonomous level of transnational reality – *interdependent* in its structure and dynamics with world capitalism, but not reducible to it. (Emphasis in the original)

Modelski (1978) and Zolberg (1981) argue even more strongly for the autonomy of the interstate system in opposition to what they see as Wallerstein's economic reductionism. These authors raise the important question about the extent to which it is theoretically valuable to conceptualize economic and political processes as independent subsystems, but in so doing they over-simplify Wallerstein's perspective.

Wallerstein's work suggests a reconceptualization of the capitalist mode of production itself such that references to capitalism do not point simply to market-oriented strategies for accumulating surplus value. According to Wallerstein the capitalist mode of production is a system in which groups pursue both political–military goals and profit-making strategies, and the winners are those who effectively combine the two. Thus the interstate system, state-building, and geopolitics are the political side of the capitalist mode of production.

As discussed in chapter 1, Wallerstein argues that a mode of production is a feature of a whole world-system, not of parts or subunits. His distinction between world-economies and world-empires as different types of world-systems emphasizes important structural differences in formal political organization across economic networks. In Wallerstein's view it is very important that modern capitalism became dominant in the context of an interstate system of competing states. This view is shared by many other analysts of the rise of the West, who focus on the decentralized features of European feudalism which were conducive to the emergence of a strong commodity-producing economy. In the more centralized world-empires the logic of the tributary mode of production was able to fend off the emergence of capitalism.

Max Weber was most explicit about the connection betwen capitalism and the competitive interstate system. Inspired by Leopold von Ranke's study of early European states[4] (von Ranke, 1887; see Weber, 1978:354) Weber added the interstate system to his list of necessary structural conditions for the emergence and reproduction of modern capitalism (see R. Collins, 1986: chapter 2). After mentioning in his *General Economic History* (Weber, 1981:337) that the European states were "competing national states in a condition of perpetual struggle for power in peace or war," Weber continues:

> This competitive struggle created the largest opportunities for modern western capitalism. The separate states had to compete for mobile capital, which dictated to them the conditions under which it would assist them to power. Out of this alliance of the state with capital, dictated by necessity, arose the national citizen class, the bourgeoisie in the modern sense of the word. Hence it is the closed national state which afforded to capitalism its chance for development – and as long as the national state does not give place to a world empire capitalism also will endure.

In *Economy and Society* Weber elaborates:

> Finally, at the beginning of modern history, the various countries engaged in the struggle for power needed ever more capital for political reasons and because of the expanding money economy. This resulted in that memorable alliance between the rising states and the sought-after and privileged capitalist powers that was a major factor in creating modern capitalism and fully justifies the designation "mercantilist" for the policies of that epoch. . . . At any rate, from that time dates that European competitive struggle between large, approximately equal and purely political structures which has had such a global impact. It is well known that this political competition has remained one of the most important motives of the capitalist protectionism that emerged then and today continues in different forms. Neither the trade nor the monetary policies of the modern states – those policies most closely linked to the

> central interests of the present economic system – can be understood without this peculiar political competition and "equilibrium" among the European states during the last five hundred years – a phenomenon which Ranke recognized in his first work as the world-historical distinctiveness of this era. (1978:353–4)

To this I can only add that the neo-Weberians ought to pay more attention to Weber.

Some Marxists, such as Colin Barker (1978) also recognize that the political basis of capitalism is not the state but the interstate system. Particular states vary in their emphasis on political–military aggrandizement or free market accumulating depending, in part, on their position in the larger system. And the system as a whole alternates between periods in which there is greater emphasis on competition based on state power versus periods in which a relatively freer world market of price competition comes to the fore (see chapter 13).

Core states with a clear competitive advantage in production are usually the most enthusiastic advocates of free trade. And, similarly, peripheral states under the control of peripheral capitalist producers of low wage goods for export to the core usually support the "open economy" of free international exchange. As Stephen Krasner (1976) points out, smaller core states heavily dependent on international trade also tend to support a liberal economic order. Semiperipheral states and larger second tier core states contending for hegemony utilize tariff protectionism and mercantilist monopoly to protect and expand their access to world surplus value. Periods of rapid worldwide economic growth are generally characterized by a relatively unobstructed world market of commodity exchange as the interests of consumers in low prices come to outweigh the interests of producers in protection (Chase-Dunn, 1980). In periods of stagnation protectionism is more frequently utilized to protect shares of the diminishing pie.

According to the model proposed in chapter 1, the capitalist mode of production includes commodity producers employing both wage labor in the core areas and coerced labor in the peripheral areas. Peripheral areas are not seen as "precapitalist" but rather as integrated, exploited, and essential parts of the larger system. Capitalist production relations, in this view, are not limited to wage labor (which is nevertheless understood to be very important to the expanded reproduction of the core areas) but rather production relations are composed of the articulation of wage labor with coerced labor in the periphery. This articulation is accomplished not only by the world market exchange of commodities, but also by the forms of political coercion which the core powers often exercise over peripheral areas. The direct and indirect use of political–military power by core states is emphasized by James Petras et al. (1981) as the most central way in which imperialism operates to constrain political action in peripheral areas. Petras's research clearly reveals the operation of this kind of coercive power, and its importance is without doubt. Albert Bergesen (1983) in combating charges that the world-system perspective is "circulationist" (i.e. a theory based on relations of exchange rather than class relations of production) has emphasized the importance of colonialism, core ownership, and other direct forms of control.

The states, and the system of competing states, which compose the world polity, constitute the basic structural support for capitalist production relations. Marx saw that the state stood behind the opaque exploitation of wage labor by capital in nineteenth-century England. The much more direct and obvious involvement of the state in the extraction of peripheral surplus value from slave labor or serf labor was another important way in which the state was essential to production relations. And this kind of direct political coercion over labor continues to operate under different forms within the contemporary periphery, and in core/periphery relations. The power of core states reinforces the commodified capital/wage labor relationship in the core, the coerced labor extraction in the periphery, and the extra-economic forms of exploitation between the core and the periphery. This constitutes the basis of production relations for the capitalist system.

States are the organizations which are often utilized by the classes that control them to help appropriate shares of the world surplus value. Market forces are either reinforced or regulated depending on the world market position of the classes controlling a particular state. When I say "classes that control the state" I am including state managers. I am not a vulgar instrumentalist arguing that the state is simply the executive committee of the bourgeoisie. The extent to which business interests directly control a state apparatus versus a situation in which state managers successfully achieve a certain autonomy by balancing different economic interests is an important variable characteristic of states.

Richard Rubinson (1978) has made the important point that state managers are most capable of effectively pursuing a policy of national development and upward mobility in the world-system when there is a considerable convergence of political interests within the dominant class in a nation. This clarifies an issue which is posed by the "relative autonomy" theorists, who ask whether or not the state represents the "general interests" of capital. As Barker (1978) reminds us, the world capitalist class exhibits a high degree of intraclass competition and conflict. There is no single world capitalist state to represent the interests of capital as a whole, so the various national states represent the interests of subgroups of capital. The extent to which they do this effectively depends on the degree to which the interests of the subgroups within a state converge or diverge as a consequence of their market position and options within the larger world economy. Fred Block (1978) reminds us that state managers are often able to expand the capabilities of the state in response to the demands of workers and peasants, and thus states not only come to institutionalize the interests of capitalists, but also, especially in the core, they take on redistributive functions which benefit workers.

Both political organizations and economic producers are subjected to a long-run "competing down" process in the capitalist world-economy, whereas in the ancient empires the monopoly of violence held by a single center minimized both market and political competition between different organizational forms. This accounts for the much more rapid transformation of both production technology and political organization by capitalism. State structures themselves are submitted to a political version of the "competing down" process which subjects firms to price competition in the realm of the market. Inefficient state structures, ones that tax their citizens too heavily or do not spend their revenues in ways which facilitate political–economic competition in the world-economy, lose the struggle for domination. In Marxist theoretical terms, the interstate system produces an equalization of surplus profits, the profits which return due to the use of political power to enforce local monopolies. There are no core-wide monopolies. Even the largest organizations (both states and firms) are subjected to the pressures of political–economic competition.

THE EMERGENCE OF CAPITALISM AND THE INTERSTATE SYSTEM

It has been pointed out by Zolberg (1981) and many others (e.g. Ekholm and Friedman, 1982) that not all precapitalist world-systems were world-empires. Wallerstein's discussion implies that earlier world-economies were short-lived, tending to either dissolve into economically delinked local systems or to experience empire formation. But Ekholm and Friedman (1982) have noted that many ancient world-systems had interstate systems which were quite stable in the sense that a balance of power mechanism operated to prevent empire formation for rather long periods. Their most important example is the Sumerian world-economy of city states, but others have described rather stable interstate systems in ancient China (Walker, 1953) and ancient India (Modelski, 1964).

The fact that there have been long-lived interstate systems prior to the emergence of the European world-economy raises the question of whether or not these were structurally or behaviorally different. Clearly the normative rules of diplomacy were different (see Modelski, 1964), but it is unclear if these are important determinants of the dynamics of an interstate system. A comparative study of interstate systems which employs a world-system perspective could perhaps answer this question, but such a study has not yet been done (see Chase-Dunn, 1986). My guess is that the most important difference between ancient and modern interstate systems is the nature of the competition among states, and therefore the substantive content of state policies. The modern interstate system is composed mostly of states which are significantly controlled by capitalists, which means that the goals of market protection and expansion constitute a larger proportion of state action than in precapitalist interstate systems. This characteristic probably also leads to other differences. It is likely that threatened hegemons in ancient interstate systems engaged in a policy of empire-formation, while in the capitalist world-economy this does not happen.

Feudalism is another type of precapitalist system which is not a world-empire. Zolberg (1981) is correct to point out that classical European feudalism (i.e. around the ninth century) was not a world-empire, but additionally it was a very strange kind of world-system. As a devolved residue of the Roman world-empire classical European feudalism was characterized by a regional political and cultural matrix organized across an economy which was almost completely delinked into self-subsistent manors. The medieval states were so weak that in most places most of the time the lord of each manor constituted a mini-state. Anderson (1974a) and many others have pointed out that it was the "parcellization of sovereignty" within this very decentralized system which allowed the capitalist mode of production to expand in institutional interstices, and to begin to dominate exchange, production, and politics.

The growth of commodity production for both local, urban/rural, and long-distance exchange was stimulated by the limitations of the manorial economy and the opportunities for profit-making presented by a system which had little regional political ability to regulate production and exchange. The constitution of cities as relatively autonomous elements within the segmented matrix of manors enabled merchants and artisans to obtain "state power" within a jurisdiction (the medieval city) which could then be used to legitimate and militarily back capitalist exchange and production. The fact that successful cities soon tried to protect their market advantages with politically guaranteed monopolies simply drove the market economy to expand elsewhere and to increase its spatial dimensions. This process of capitalist urban growth also spurred the strengthening of the nation state, as kings were able to gain resources from capitalists to use against recalcitrant local lords. Thus the nation states and the European interstate system came into existence. It was the dynamic of mercantile and commodity production competition between both state and private enterprises in the long sixteenth century, together with the emergence of a core/periphery hierarchy, which led Wallerstein to argue that the capitalist world-system was then born.

Anderson (1974b) insists that absolutism, the formation of strong centralized monarchies, was primarily an expression of feudal reorganization in the face of the crisis of feudalism in Western Europe. In Eastern Europe, according to Anderson, state-formation was a response to the formation of a militarily threatening international state system emanating from Western Europe. His emphasis downplays the role which the growth of commodity production and the emergent core/periphery division of labor between East and West played in the formation and extension of the European interstate system. He subsumes mercantilist international policy and state-sponsored development of crucial sectors of production into his complex definition of "absolutism." I would argue that these developments can be better understood as variants of state capitalism which were appropriate to the first epoch of the capitalist world-economy.

In the competitive interstate system it has been impossible for any single state to monopolize the entire world market, and to maintain hegemony indefinitely. Hegemonic core powers, such as Britain and the United States, have in the long run lost their relative dominance to more efficient producers. This means that, unlike the agrarian empires, success in the capitalist world-system is based on a combination of effective state power and competitive advantage in production. The extraction of surplus value stands on two legs: the ability to use political power to protect (and expand) profitable commodity production; and the ability to produce efficiently for the competitive world economy. This is not the statecentric system which some analysts describe, because states cannot escape, for long, the competitive forces of the world economy. States that attempt to cut themselves off or who overtax their domestic producers condemn themselves to marginality. On the other hand, the system is not simply a free world market of competing producers. The successful combination of political power and competitive advantage in production is a delicate balance.

There have been important differences among European states in terms of the strategies of development that they have followed. Some have relied more on continental military advantage and centralized fiscal structures while others, the more successful ones, have employed a low overhead policy of strategic protection of the vital business interests of their national capitalists. Again, I don't claim that all states equally employ a policy of support for their capitalists. Frederic Lane's (1979) concept of protection rent is again relevant here. Some states provide effective protection at or near "cost" and allow the profitable expansion of the businesses under their protection. Others are less efficient and promote less economic growth even though they may be quite able to extract taxes from their own citizens. All states pursue both military and market objectives, but the mix differs. What makes the game differ from precapitalist systems is the relatively larger proportion of the sum of all efforts which is devoted to strategies of profit-taking rather than tribute-taking.

The most successful core states have achieved their hegemony by having strong and convergent business class interests which unified state policy behind a sustained drive for successful commodity production and trade in the world economy. Second-runners have often achieved some centrality in the world economy by relying on a more directly state-organized effort to catch up with the hegemonic state.

It could be argued that the existence of states which successfully follow a more political–military development path is evidence in favor of the thesis that geopolitical and economic processes operate independently. The existence of such a development path is unquestionable (e.g. Prussia, Sweden, Japan, USSR) but the upward mobility of these states was certainly conditioned by its context, a world-economy in which commodity production and capitalist accumulation were becoming general. If *all* states had followed such a path the modern world-system would be a very different kind of entity. It is argued below that the reproduction and expansion of the kind of interstate system which emerged in Europe *requires* the institutional forms and dynamic processes which are associated with commodity production and capitalist accumulation. First, though, let us discuss the ways in which the interstate system helps to preserve the dynamics of the capitalist process of accumulation.

THE REPRODUCTION OF CAPITALIST ACCUMULATION

There are several ways in which the competitive interstate system allows the capitalist accumulation process to temporarily overcome the contradictions it creates, and to expand. The balance of power in the interstate system prevents any single state from controlling the world-economy, and from imposing a political monopoly over accumulation. This means that "factors of production" cannot be politically controlled to the degree that they could be if there were an overarching world state. Capital is subjected to some controls by states, but it can still flow from areas where profits are low to areas where profits are higher. This allows capital to escape most of the political claims which exploited classes attempt to impose on it. If workers are successful in creating unions which enable them to demand higher wages, or if communities demand that corporations spend more money on pollution controls, capital can usually escape these demands by moving to areas where opposition is weaker. This process of "capital flight" can also be seen to operate inside of countries with federal states.

Class struggles are most often oriented toward and constrained within particular territorial state structures. Thus the interstate system provides the political underpinning of the mobility of capital, and also the institutional basis for the continuing expansion of capitalist development. States which successfully prevent domestic capital from emigrating do not necessarily solve this problem, because foreign competitors are likely to take advantage of the less costly production opportunities outside the national boundaries, and thus push the domestic products out of the international market.[5]

The implication of the above is that capitalism is not possible in the context of a single world state, as Weber claimed. The transformation of the interstate system into a world state would eventually develop the political regulation of resource allocation. If this world state were socialist it would more regularly and fully include social desiderata in the calculation of investment decisions. The dynamic of the present system, in which profit criteria and national power are the main controllers of the use of resources, would eventually be transformed into a system in which development combines efficiency with a calculation of the individual and collective use values of human society. Such a collectively rational system would not constitute a utopia in which the problems of production and distribution would be completely solved, but the political struggles for resources which would be oriented toward a single overarching world government would exhibit a very different long-run dynamic of political change and economic development than that which has characterized the capitalist world-economy.

Of course this is an optimistic assessment. It is also possible that world state formation would bring about a transformation to a new version of the tributary mode of production. Both socialism and the tributary modes utilize primarily political means of accumulation, but the tributary modes employ large amounts of coercion, while socialism produces, distributes, and invests democratically. Either way though, capitalism would no longer be the dominant mode of production.

CAPITALIST REPRODUCTION OF THE INTERSTATE SYSTEM

Thus the interstate system is important for the continued viability of the capitalist accumulation process. But is the accumulation process equally as important for the generation and reproduction of the interstate system? First, what do I mean by reproduction of the interstate system? I am not making fine distinctions between types of interstate systems such as those introduced by Partha Chatterjee (1975). By an interstate system I mean a system of unequally powerful and competing states in which no single state is capable of imposing control on all others. These states are in interaction with one another through a set of shifting alliances and wars. Changes in the relative power of states upset any temporary set of alliances leading to a restructuring of the balance of power. When is such a system not reproduced? If an interstate system either:

1 disintegrates due to the dissolution of the individual states;
2 dramatically reduces to nearly zero the amount of material exchange and political–military interaction among the states; or
3 becomes dominated by a single overarching state,

the system can be said to have fundamentally changed (i.e. it has been transformed, not reproduced). In this definition the stages of classical, imperial, bipolar, and "contemporary" interstate systems identified by Chatterjee are subsumed into a single broad type which is nevertheless quite different from the precapitalist agrarian empires or the economically self-subsistent and "stateless" system which existed in feudal Europe.

WHICH CAME FIRST?

Skocpol (1979) contends that the European interstate system predates the emergence of capitalism[6] and she implies that this is evidence of its relative autonomy.[7] No one denies that states predate capitalism. At issue is the genesis of a dynamic interstate system which is self-reproducing rather than a transitional stage on the way toward empire-formation. It is clearly the case that multistate systems exhibiting some of the characteristics of the European interstate system existed prior to the emergence of the dominant capitalist mode of production. The multicentric "international system" which developed among the Italian city states and their trade partners in the East and West invented many of the institutions of diplomacy and shifting alliance which were later adopted by the European states. As Lane says of the sixteenth century: "The Italian state system was being expanded into a European state system" (1973:241). While this constitutes prior development, it may not be evidence in favor of the autonomy of the interstate system, as we shall see.

Many of the capitalistic financial and legal institutions later elaborated in the European capitalist world-economy were invented in the Italian city states. The Christian Mediterranean was part of an interstitial protocapitalist regional economy. Analogous to Marx's analysis of merchant capitalism, the Mediterranean regional economy, though developing the seeds of capitalist production with labor as a commodity, was primarily based on the exchange of "unequals" between social systems which were not integrated into a single commodity economy.[8] Nevertheless this protocapitalist regional economy succeeded in developing several institutional features which were only later fully elaborated in the capitalist world-economy which emerged in Europe and Latin America in the long sixteenth century. One of these was the interstate system which, as Zolberg (1981) agrees, only became stably formed after its emergence in Europe.

But doesn't the continuity of the Italian interstate system, and its failure to develop into a world-empire, constitute a case for the independence of the interstate system? Two factors militate against this conclusion. The states of the Italian system were already rather capitalistic, thus explaining the weakness of attempts at empire-formation, and the Italian system became incorporated into the larger European world-economy, which was already becoming dominated by production capitalism in the sixteenth century.

I am not arguing that capitalist institutions are the only factors which enable an interstate system to resist empire-formation. It is likely that a common cultural matrix also works against empire-formation by facilitating the diffusion of military and other technologies, and thus maintaining a relatively equal distribution of power among contending core states. The European system shared this feature (an interstate common cultural matrix) with earlier long-lived interstate systems such as those in ancient Mesopotamia, China, and India (Mann, 1986). Nevertheless the widespread existence of capitalist institutions such as international markets, money, banking, and opportunities for investment further stabilize an interstate system by inhibiting efforts at empire formation.

Skocpol's contention about the prior emergence of the interstate system also receives support from Anderson's (1974b) interpretation of the rise of absolutist states in Western and Eastern Europe. But this contention rides on one's definition of capitalism. Anderson holds with the school which sees the "fully formed capitalist mode of production" as becoming dominant only in the eighteenth century. Wallerstein's interpretation contends that "agrarian" capitalism became dominant in the long sixteenth century. Anderson's interpretation of the absolutist states in formation downplays the importance of capitalist production in the growing cities of feudal Europe and ignores the "protoindustrial" emergence of agricultural and artisan production for the market in rural areas (see Kriedte, et al., 1981).

Wallerstein's interpretation implies that the capitalist mode of production became the most important stimulus for change well before the "bourgeois revolutions" in which explicitly capitalist interests came to power in nation states. Anderson's account does not deny the importance, especially in the West, of the emergence of bourgeois sources of power and financial support, but he chooses to call the cup half empty instead of half full. His discussion of state formation in Eastern Europe correctly identifies the extent to which it was reactive to the competitive and aggressive interstate system which emerged first in the West. He ignores, however, the importance of the developing core/periphery division of labor for the shifts in class structure which influenced state formation in the East.

AN OUTSIDE ALLIANCE

One clue to the dependence or independence of the interstate system is its ability to reproduce itself, or to weather crises without becoming transformed into either a world-empire or experiencing disintegration of its network of international economic exchange. Wallerstein's analysis of the effort by the Habsburgs to transform the still shaky sixteenth-century capitalist world-economy into a world-empire (1974:164–221) demonstrates the importance of capitalism in reproducing the interstate system. I will discuss the later points at which similar challenges to the interstate system were mounted (Louis XIV's wars, the Napoleonic wars, and the twentieth-century world wars) and the causes of continuity of the interstate system, but first I want to consider another point made by Zolberg (1981).

Zolberg argues that the European interstate system occasionally incorporated powers that were outside the capitalist world-economy into alliances which affected the outcome of politico-military struggle. His main example is the alliance between France and the Ottoman Empire against the house of Habsburg. Wallerstein argues that the Ottoman Empire was itself a separate world-system, an "external arena" outside of the economic network that was the European world-economy until the nineteenth century. Zolberg contends that the French–Ottoman alliance, which was important in France's ability to resist the Habsburgs' move to enclose the emerging European world-economy within a single overarching empire, proves the autonomy of the interstate system. It is true that this alliance, and other less important ones between European states and states located in areas outside the European-centered division of labor, affected the course of development of the modern world-system. It may even be true that without this crucial outside alliance the emergence of core capitalism in Europe would have been long postponed.

Once again this shows that the interstate system was important for the survival and growth of international capitalism. On this there is little disagreement. But what would have happened to the European interstate system if international capitalism had been encompassed by the Habsburg empire? Obviously both international capitalism and the interstate system would have been transformed into a world-empire, and probably one in which capitalism as a mode of production was subordinated to the logic of imperial tribute and taxation. Though I agree that capitalism had become dominant over the logic of the tributary mode of production in the long sixteenth century it is obvious that its domination in that first epoch was somewhat shaky. The attempt to convert the nascent capitalist world-system into a tributary world-empire was stemmed, not by the institutional strength of capitalism alone, but in conjunction with the somewhat fortuitous alliance between the French and an "outside" power, the Ottoman Turks.

As we shall see below, later challenges to the interstate system were undercut by the logic of international capitalism alone. Zolberg is right in pointing to the French–Ottoman alliance as evidence of the importance of the interstate system, but in later challenges it was the strengthened institutions of international capitalism by themselves that prevented the interstate system from becoming a world-empire.

Another reason why Zolberg argues for the existence of an autonomous logic of the interstate system is his confusion over the difference between colonial empires and world-empires. It is perfectly correct that core states engage in imperialism in the sense of using military power to dominate parts of the periphery. These colonial empires expand cyclically with the growth of the modern world-system (Bergesen and Schoenberg, 1980). But this phenomenon is very different from the imposition of a single state over the whole system, including other core states.

MORE RECENT CHALLENGES

The European world-system became a global world-system in a series of waves of expansion which eventually incorporated all the territories and peoples of the earth. Although political–military alliances with states external to the system occurred after the sixteenth century, they were never again so crucial to the survival and development of capitalism as was the French–Ottoman alliance. But the capitalist world-economy continued to face challenges of survival based on its own internal contradictions. Uneven economic development and the vast expansion of productive forces outstripped the structure of political power, causing violent reorganizations of the interstate system (world wars) to accommodate new levels of economic development. This process can be seen in the sequence of core competition, the rise and fall of hegemonic core states, which has accompanied the expansion and deepening of the capitalist mode of production (see chapter 9).

After the failure of the Habsburgs there have been three other efforts to impose a world-empire on the capitalist world-economy: those of France under Louis XIV and Napoleon, and that of Germany and its allies in the twentieth century world wars (Dehio, 1962; Toynbee, 1967). Each of these came in a period when the hegemonic core power was weak. Louis XIV tried to extend his monarchy over the whole of the core powers during the decline of Dutch hegemony. Napoleon's effort came while Britain was still emerging to hegemonic status. The German attempts came after Britain's decline and before the full emergence of the United States. These three instances constituted threats to the existence of the interstate system and to the capitalist world-economy.

WHY HEGEMONS DON'T TRY IMPERIUM

It may be argued that one or another of these did not really constitute a serious effort at imperium. There has been much dispute about German intentions in World War I (see Fischer, 1967, and his critics) but the real issue is not intentions, but the structural consequences which a German victory would have had for the interstate system. If the balance of power system, and thus the multicentric nature of the core, could have survived such a victory, then these events did not represent real threats to the interstate system as such, but merely a challenge to the extant balance of power. If none of these efforts presented a real possibility of world imperium (i.e. the formation of a core state large enough to end the operation of the balance of power system) we must ask why there have been no strong challenges to the interstate system since the Habsburgs.

Some authors imply that the size of the European states has been limited by the range of effective territorial control, but this cannot explain the absence of empire formation in Europe. After all, the Roman Empire, using obviously more limited military technology, ruled most of the territory later occupied by the core states of the European world-economy. The mode of production greatly effects optimalities of state size and the tendencies toward empire formation.

It is the dynamic of uneven development of capitalism which systematically undercuts the possibilities for empire-formation, thus reproducing the interstate system. One of the striking things about these ineffective challenges to the interstate system is that they were not perpetrated by the hegemonic core powers themselves, but rather by emerging second runners among the competing core states. This raises the question of why hegemonic core powers do not try to impose imperium when it becomes obvious that their competitive advantage in commodity production is waning. Similarly we may ask, as Zolberg did of the sixteenth century, why opposing forces were able to prevent the conversion of the system into a single empire. To both of these questions I would answer that it is the transnational structures associated with the capitalist commodity economy which operated to tip the balance in favor of preserving the interstate system.

Hegemonic core states often use state power to enforce the interests of their "own" producers, although typically they do not rely on it as heavily as other competing core states. But, when a hegemonic core power begins to lose its competitive edge in production because of the spread of production techniques and differential labor costs, capital is exported from the declining hegemonic core state to areas where profit rates are higher. This reduces the level at which the capitalists within the hegemonic core state will support the "economic nationalism" of their home state. Their interests come to be spread across the core. Another way to say this is that hegemonic core states develop subgroups of their capitalist classes having divergent interests; there comes to be a group of "international capitalists" who support free trade, and a group of "national capitalists" who seek tariff protection. This explains the ambivalent, contradictory, and zigzagging policies of hegemonic core powers during the periods of their decline (Goldfrank, 1977; see also chapter 9 below).

Schumpeter (1955) pointed to the lack of patriotism shown by many capitalists[9] as proof that capitalism itself is a peace-loving system. He claimed that modern warfare is caused by atavistic survivals of the precapitalist era which periodically grip the world and lead to violent destruction on a massive scale. It is important to distinguish between capitalism as a system and the sentiments of those who make investment decisions. While some capitalists may be peace-loving, it is the export of investment capital to other core states during hegemonic decline which is the major factor which explains why hegemonic core states do not try to impose imperium. And it is the reproduction of the interstate system, which presumes the legitimacy of warfare, that guarantees recurrent bouts of violent destruction.

WHY DO CHALLENGES FAIL?

Why have the second-running core powers who have sought to impose imperium on the world-economy failed? Most theorists of the interstate system have not addressed this question as such. The balance of power idea explains why, in a multicentric system, alliances between the most powerful actors weaken. Coalitions in a triad, for example, balance the power by allying the two weakest actors against the strongest. But this alliance falls apart when the stronger of the partners gains enough to become the strongest single actor (hegemon) because the weaker power can gain more by allying with the declining former hegemon than by sticking to the original alliance. This simple game theory is extended to the interstate system by the theorists of power equilibrium, but it does not answer our question substantively. Again, in the modern world-system it is not the most powerful actor that tries to impose imperium, but rather upwardly mobile second runners with less than their "fair" share of political influence over weaker areas of the globe. Organski's (1968) theory explains why these second runners try, but not why they fail.[10]

Of course one might employ strictly historical explanations which make use of unique conjunctural factors, a theoretical maneuver (or rather an atheoretical maneuver) which is easy to accomplish when one is explaining only four "events." Here we seek an explanation of what seems to be a regularity of the world-system based on our hypotheses about its deep structural logic.

Morganthau (1952) invokes the notion of a normatively organized liberal world culture which successfully mobilizes counterforce against the threat to the balance of power system. This conceptualization of a normatively integrated world-system has already been described and critiqued in chapter 5. While I do not deny that some normative patterns are generalized across the system, I emphasize the fact that culture tends to follow state boundaries and that the larger system remains significantly multicultural. From this perspective it is far fetched to explain the failure of empire-formation in terms of commitment to internationally shared norms.

Craig Murphy (personal communication) contends that another reason why hegemonic core powers do not try to impose imperium on the whole system is the enlightened view of certain core statesmen that the multistate system is necessary for the survival of capitalism. Disraeli is suggested as an example. This type of consciousness can be understood as a response to the dispersion of investment capital and consumer interests which accompanies the declining hegemony of the leading core state. I doubt that liberal internationalist ideology plays much of an independent role in the reproduction of the interstate system.

On the other hand, I have suggested above that interstate systems in which the states share a consensual regional culture are more likely to resist empire-formation because new organizational and military technologies will rapidly diffuse and maintain rough power equality among the contending core states. This explanation does not invoke normative integration (the regulation of behavior by consensual belief in rules), nor is it dependent on the specific content of cultural forms. It simply argues that information is more likely to flow across state boundaries when the states have somewhat similar ideological and cultural systems. Such a condition existed among the core states of the European world-system and this could have partly explained the failure of empire-formation in Europe.

It is my argument, however, that both the attempts at and the failures of world imperium can be primarily explained as reactive responses to the pressures of uneven development in the world-economy. We have already noted that the attempts were fomented, not by the most powerful states in the system, but rather by emerging second-tier core powers contending for hegemony. One striking thing about all four cases is that they appear, in retrospect, to have been wildly irrational. The countries who adopted the strategy of aggrandizement reached far beyond their own capacities, and failed to generate sufficient support from allied countries.

I agree with Modelski (1978) that the predominantly land-oriented continental expansionism of the French monarchy was not a strategy which could lead to hegemony in the capitalist world-economy. It is notable that the overhead costs of purely geopolitical expansionism (Oliver Cox's (1959) "Florentine model" of domination) could not successfully compete with the low overhead strategy of allowing a more decentralized political system to bear the costs of administration while surplus value appropriation is accomplished by trade. It was this "Venetian model" (Cox again) which was followed by the states which became hegemonic core powers (Netherlands, Britain, and the United States) while the land-oriented political centralizers have been relegated to the role of second-runners among the core states.

Why didn't the French or German attempts at imperium receive more support? Probably in part because potential allies doubted the extent to which their interests would be protected under the new imperium, and because the path of capitalist growth in the context of the multicentric system appeared preferable to the emerging bourgeoisies of potential allied states.

If I am correct, the interstate system is dependent on the institutions and opportunities presented by the world market for its survival. There are two main characteristics of the interstate system which need to be sustained: the division of sovereignty in the core (interimperial rivalry) and the maintenance of a network of exchange among the states. The commodified nature of the capitalist world-economy assures that states will continue to exchange due to natural and socially created comparative advantages in production. Withdrawal from the world market can be accomplished for short periods of time but it is costly and unstable. Even the "socialist" states which have tried to establish a separate mode of production have eventually returned to production for and exchange with the larger commodity market.

The maintenance of interimperial rivalry is facilitated by a number of institutional processes. At any point in time national sentiments, language and cultural differences make supranational integration difficult, as is well illustrated by the EEC. These "historical" factors may be traced back to the long-run processes of state-formation and nation-building, and these processes have themselves been conditioned by the emergence of the commodity economy over the past 500 years.

But the main institutional feature of the world-economy which maintains interimperial rivalry is the uneven nature of capitalist economic development. As discussed above, hegemonic core powers lose their competitive advantage in production to other areas and this causes the export of capital, which restrains the hegemon from attempting to impose political imperium. Second-running challengers, who may try to impose imperium, cannot gain sufficient support from other core allies to win, or at least they have not historically been able to do so. This is in part because the potential for further expansion and deepening of the commodity economy, and development in the context of a decentralized interstate system, appears greater to potential allies than the potential for political and economic power within the proposed imperium. Success stories in the development history of the interstate system are frequent enough to undermine empire-formation.

Now let us further consider the ways in which the transnational institutions of capitalism interact with geopolitics to reproduce the interstate system.

8

Warfare and World-systems

Part of this chapter is a response to William R. Thompson's (1983c) valuable criticism of an earlier version of chapter 7. The issues raised by Thompson's article are addressed and a problem on which his analysis is conspicuously silent is considered. Thompson's discussion fails to address the argument that the reproduction of the interstate system is due to the operation of specific institutions characteristic of a capitalist mode of production. His comparison of generally "political," as opposed to "economic," variables ignores the role of historically specific economic institutions such as commodity production, wage labor, commodified wealth, and capital in the dynamics of the modern interstate system. I shall make further comparisons of the modern capitalist world-economy to precapitalist world-empires and world-economies in order to demonstrate the importance of capitalist institutions for the reproduction of the modern interstate system. In addition I will examine the arguments and research on the relationship between the long economic wave (K-wave) and world wars.

Thompson and George Modelski (1978; see also Modelski and Thompson, 1988) have contributed theorization and important research to the study of the modern world-system. While their conceptualization of that system is somewhat different from mine, they nonetheless recognize it as a hierarchical structure in which unequally powerful nation states contend with one another for position. In this they have moved well beyond the still widely held view that nation states can be understood as either "advanced" or "developing" without regard to the larger context in which they are interacting.

On the other hand both Modelski and Thompson proceed without any discussion of capitalism. They instead focus on the issue of the primacy of either "economic" or "political" variables (Modelski, 1982; Thompson, 1983c). While this may be a convenient shorthand, an understanding of the

An earlier version of this chapter was co-authored with Joan Sokolovsky.

underlying dynamics of the modern world-system requires comparison of its *specific institutional structures* with those of other historical, large-scale social systems. I do not claim that "economic" variables are more important to the dynamics of the modern system, but rather that several specifically capitalist features of the political economy act to reproduce the interstate system. The notion of "historical systems," which differ from one another in fundamental ways, is absent from Thompson's analysis, but central to mine.

COMMODITIES AND MARKETS

Thompson reduces the discussion of capitalist institutions to "economic growth" and "uneven development." This may be, in part, due to a lack of clarity in the work he was criticizing (Chase-Dunn, 1981), which uses such concepts as *commodity production* without benefit of explanation. In Marxist theory commodity production refers to the production for sale in a price-setting market of somewhat standardized commodities (including services). Everything is not a commodity. Some items are produced, not for exchange in a market, but for direct consumption by the producer. Other items are produced for exchange in a normative reciprocal system or in a politically administered redistributive system, but not for sale in a market. Other things are produced for sale, but are sufficiently unique that their conditions of production are not regularly and systematically subjected to price competition, e.g. art objects. Other things are sold but are not produced for sale, such as untransformed land or other resources appropriated directly from nature. Commodification is a process by which social relations become mediated by markets. A price-setting market is one in which the competitive interaction of a large number of independent buyers and sellers determines the ratios (prices) at which particular commodities exchange.

Capitalist commodity production exists when wealth, land, and labor have become largely (but not completely) commodified. Capitalist production implies a hierarchical division of labor between controllers of commodified means of production (capital) and the workers whose labor produces commodities for profitable sale.

Empirically there are no perfect price-setting markets. Prices are always influenced to some extent by normative and political factors. And there are no completely capitalist social systems, even our own. Capitalist commodity production and markets have been present to some extent in most of the historical systems since at least the emergence of cities some 5000 years ago in Sumer (Ekholm and Friedman, 1982). In some *parts* of the precapitalist world-systems capitalists became politically dominant and capitalist relations predominated (e.g. in city states such as Dilmun, Sidon, Tyre, Carthage, Malacca, and Venice), but not until the long sixteenth century of our own era did capitalist institutions come to dominate the developmental logic of the core zone of a world-system.

We should note that commodities and markets are, in the final analysis, human institutional artifacts. As such, they are historically variable. Most human societies in the history of social development have been predominantly based on either normative reciprocity or politically determined production and exchange in which markets have played only a very limited part.

CAPITALISTS IN POWER

Weber's analysis of capitalism (1978) stresses the importance of political control by capitalist merchants and producers. The medieval European cities which, by revolution or accretion, came under the autonomous control of merchants, were important early examples of institutionalized capitalist control of legal systems and coercive power. The capitalist cities of Northwestern Europe provided political and economic resources which enabled kings to gain power over feudal lords and to construct the absolutist monarchies which first formed the European interstate system (Anderson, 1974b). The first modern nation state (as opposed to earlier city states) to become largely controlled by capitalists was the Dutch Republic, which was dominated by the merchants of Amsterdam. Later, the English Civil War created the second bourgeois nation state.

Capitalist merchants and producers have gained power within most of the nation states of the modern world-system, but capitalist control of states has never been complete. Some states have been directly dominated by capitalists, while others are in the hands of state managers who aggregate contradictory class interests, but all states include other classes in their ruling coalitions to some extent. Both the class content of the ruling coalition and the constraints of the world-system are important determinants of state policy.

PRECAPITALIST WORLD-SYSTEMS

When I say that commodity production dominates world-system dynamics I do not mean that it is all-inclusive. We must look at the way in which commodity production is systematically interrelated with normative and political institutions. All social systems are built on a specific articulation of normative, coercive, and economic institutions. In the modern world-system capitalist commodity production is integrated with a set of political processes: state-formation, nation-building, and the geopolitical game which we know as the interstate system. Like markets and money, these political institutions are not natural or ahistorical. They are products of human invention, and their stability, change, and/or transformation must therefore be understood historically.

We know that the process of state-formation has occurred in various forms since the emergence of agrarian civilizations 5000 years ago, and that for most of the history of civilization this has been the most important process by which societies have increased in complexity, hierarchy, and size. Kinship systems were elaborated vertically into class systems in which various forms of taxes or tribute were appropriated to support a non-producing ruling class. Temples and palaces thus became controllers of property and surplus product. Interregional economic exchange networks were most often controlled by states in the precapitalist world-economies. These often became incorporated by conquest into world-empires based on the extraction of tribute. In these world-empires competition over political power and status was predominant, although the particular institutional forms varied greatly across the precapitalist world-systems. Most systems based on the tributary mode of production tended toward empire-formation in which a single state apparatus came to exercise domination over the core area. This facilitated politically organized extraction of surplus product. The wage labor that existed in some of the tributary empires was limited to certain sectors and was a very small proportion of the work force. Slave labor, a partially commodified form of labor control which is directly dependent on political coercion, was important not only in the peripheral regions but also in the core of many tributary empires.

The relatively large role played by private property, markets, wage labor, and commodity production in the Graeco-Roman world led to the invention of legal institutions particularly appropriate for a capitalist society. This law later became the basis for municipal legal systems in many of the capitalist cities of the European Renaissance. But in classical Rome, the main dynamics of expansion and decline remained based on military conquest, tribute, taxation, and the use of captive slave labor (K. Hopkins, 1978b). Ruling-class activities were based much more on private accumulation of profit than in earlier precapitalist world-empires,[1] but political maneuver and competition for status remained the main game (Finley, 1973).

THE MODERN WORLD-SYSTEM

In the capitalist world-economy system dynamics are produced by a single logic in which capitalist commodity production interacts with the processes of geopolitics, state-formation, class-formation, and nation-building. Relative to the precapitalist world-systems, the weight of commodity production is much greater. The business cycles, rapid technological change, and the relatively rapid changes of fortune of different regions are due to the operation of a world market which is much less constrained by political–military structures than were the trade networks of earlier systems.

This is not to say that political structures are unimportant, but rather that a particular kind of political structure is most suitable for the continued operation of this competitive economic system. A centralized system tends to articulate political and normative constraints on resource allocation and to enhance the possibility for long-run monopolies of advantage in which production cost considerations are not important determinants of income. Decentralized and competitive political systems allow market efficiency to be a much greater determinant of prices and the distribution of returns.[2] The multicentric structure of the interstate system allows competitive advantage in production to be an important continuing determinant of success.

Some states succeed in becoming more central in the capitalist world-economy through a mode of operation which bears some resemblance to that of the Roman Republic, i.e. conquest. But even these operate in the context of a system in which they must ultimately consolidate their gains by developing productive capacity for success in the world market. The paths to upward mobility are several: military expansion, mercantile armed trade, and commodity production have all been utilized in various mixes. But the most successful states, the hegemonic core states, have increasingly relied on their ability to gain large shares of the markets for the most profitable commodities, and loss of market advantage has ultimately led to their geopolitical decline. Thus the multicentric interstate system is important to the maintenance of a capitalist systemic logic, and to the specific institutions which most directly embody this logic: markets for labor, capital, and commodities. On this Thompson agrees.

CAPITALIST INSTITUTIONS SUPPORT THE INTERSTATE SYSTEM

More problematic is my contention that capitalist institutions *reproduce* the contemporary interstate system. I need to define clearly what the interstate system is so that we may tell when it has been reproduced or fundamentally changed, and I need to specify clearly my claims about attempts to transform that system. Thompson (1983c) correctly points out that my definition of the interstate system overlaps somewhat with my definition of a world-economy.

A world-economy is any territorial division of labor (network of exchange of fundamental goods) in which there are multiple political entities and multiple cultural systems. Thus world-economies always have interstate systems. An interstate system, by contrast, is defined as a system of three or more states in direct or indirect competition with one another in which none of the states is powerful enough to dominate the whole system. An interstate system could exist in which political interaction occurred without exchange of material goods. In a sense the European system of classical feudalism in the eighth and ninth centuries was such a system. The "states" were the manors, economically self-subsistent units interacting with one another in a shifting set of military alliances. While such a system is not a world-economy, it is an interstate system.

The modern interstate system is composed of nation states, culturally integrated countries which contain more than one city, whereas world-economies of the past most usually contained interstate systems composed of city states and empires.[3] Precapitalist world-economies have had interstate systems in which the political and military competition among several states determined the nature and extent of most material exchanges among states. This is Polanyi's (1977) "state-administered" trade. Precapitalist world-economies composed of city states were most often based on class relations in which each urban ruling class utilized political institutions to extract surplus product from its own rural hinterland. Empires were formed when one of these city states succeeded by warfare in conquering others and extracting tribute, and on forming a core/periphery system based on military domination. Today warfare is less central (though still important) to the workings of the modern world-system.[4]

Modelski's (1978) and Thompson's (1983c) explanation of the rise and fall of hegemonic core powers invokes a systemic need for order. International order is conceptualized as a "public good" which is most effectively provided by a single hegemonic core state. This functionalist explanation has difficulty accounting for the decline of core states or decreases in the amount of systemic political order. In my model relative peace among states is conditioned by a long period of economic growth in which a single hegemonic core state supports both economic and geopolitical order. This stability has costs, however, and periods of increased conflict emerge with the spread to other states of those economic and technological advantages which enabled the 'great power' to become hegemonic. World wars represent a reversion to military competition and a restructuring of the world political order which, up to now, has subsequently allowed for the further expansion of capitalist production.

My contention that capitalist institutions acted to prevent the interstate system from evolving into a world-empire led in the previous chapter to three questions:

1 Why have attempts to create a world-empire been so few, and seemed, in Thompson's and Modelski's eyes (and the eyes of the most central actors), so unfeasible?
2 Why have hegemonic core states never attempted imperium?
3 Why have second-running challengers to hegemonic states been unwilling or incapable of creating a world-empire?

Here I will elaborate some further considerations which these questions raise.

An interstate system is basically a game in which multiple players engage in shifting alliances in order to gain advantages. In a simple three-state version of such a game the two weakest states ally against the stronger, but if their combined resources are fewer than those of the strongest state it (the strongest) will eventually take over. Thus an interstate system will become a world-empire any time a willing single state or coalition of states can coordinate resources greater than the possible coalitions against it (them). Why has this not happened during the 500-year history of the capitalist world-economy?

Some would argue that state-formation on a sufficient scale is unfeasible due to technological or cultural constraints. I have already mentioned in the previous chapter that the Roman Empire, utilizing relatively primitive technology and a very different *raison d'état,* succeeded in unifying an area which included most of the territory later occupied by the core states of the European world-economy. The optimality of state size varies greatly with the logic of each socio-economic system. When tribute is the main form of surplus extraction the expansion of a single state to encompass an entire world-system is a strategy which pays. In a system in which surplus value is extracted mainly through capitalist commodity production, overhead costs are more crucial for success in the short run.

Of course, in the long run they are crucial in all systems, as the demise of the Roman Empire and many other empires illustrates. But in a market system capitalists themselves often enforce limitations on the tax-collecting abilities of states. Overhead costs are more crucial to profitable commodity production than they are to successful tribute-gathering and taxation, and the pressure to keep the cost of political order down operates effectively in the short run. Most states in such a system are seeking to protect internal markets and to extend trade advantages in the international market to their own capitalist producers and merchants. Successful state-building itself is somewhat conditional on the ability of each state to provide effective and cost-efficient protection to its commodity producers. Lane's (1979) analysis of states as "violence-controlling enterprises" which compete with one another to provide protection is as applicable to the contemporary interstate system as it was to the merchant capitalist city states of Venice and Genoa which Lane studied.

The more direct and powerful constraints on state budgets in a capitalist world-economy are part of the reason why there are so few attempts to take over the system and to create a world state. The overhead costs of such a state would be greater than the costs of supporting competing nation states, especially to capitalist producers. And such a centralized world state, while it holds the attractive possibility of world wide monopoly, also holds the potential for anti-capitalist social movements to coordinate their activities and to concentrate political action toward a single center. Transnational corporations might enjoy some advantages of centralized control, but they would have much less flexibility to pit political organizations and states against one another.

Why don't declining hegemonic core states change the rules of the game and attempt to retain their hegemony by organizing a world imperium? It is curious that no one, not even among marginal political ideologues, ever suggests such a project. The greatest support for international organizations (of a limited kind) comes from a hegemon during its golden age of hegemony. Its dominant ideology of free trade, firmly supported at first by its relative advantage in commodity production for the world market, appears later to have a life beyond its basis in competitive advantage. There is an element of institutional and ideological momentum which carries free trade ideology and liberal internationalism along as a guiding policy in declining hegemons long after most other core states have shifted back toward economic nationalism.

But the structural basis behind this apparent ideological inertia is the power of "international" capitalists within hegemonic core states. As a hegemon loses its comparative advantage in production (because competitors abroad adopt and improve upon production techniques, and because labor costs and taxes go up in a successful hegemon as workers and other interest groups use political power to obtain a share of the profits) a significant amount of capital from the hegemonic country gets exported to where greater profits are to be had. This gives the "international capitalists," those who have invested abroad, a continuing interest in free trade and a liberal international order. They oppose political thrusts toward protectionism, and they also would be unsupportive of a policy of aggressive political–military expansion over other core powers if, indeed, anyone suggested it. They do, however, support maintenance of the interstate regime as currently structured against possible challengers who want to create imperium or carve out a protected region. Some of the interests of workers, national capitalists, and international capitalists diverge during the period of hegemonic decline, but because these groups are somewhat evenly balanced, the result is a zigzagging domestic and international economic policy in the declining hegemonic core states. This topic is explored further in chapter 9.

But why do the rising powers which militarily challenge the dominance of declining hegemonic powers not go on to establish imperium? They may be ambivalent about the returns of imperium. Germany developed a competitive advantage in production but was denied direct access to cheap raw materials from peripheral areas and to markets by the international trade regime dominated by Britain. The Germans needed to loosen up the existing core/periphery structures but they did not need to take on the overhead costs of world imperium. As mentioned in the previous chapter, if a challenger did propose the creation of a world-empire it would be difficult to mobilize sufficient support because most potential powerful allies would likely calculate their opportunities for profitable commodity production in a world market to be greater than their potential returns from participation in an imperium.

WORLD WARS AND THE RESTRUCTURING OF THE WORLD-ECONOMY

Jack Levy's (1985) discussion and critique of different conceptualizations of world wars is a valuable review of recent scholarly works, including the world-system perspective, the long cycle theory of Modelski and Thompson, and Robert Gilpin's (1981) theory of hegemonic war. Levy compares different criteria for defining world wars, and criticizes those approaches which define these conflicts in terms of their consequences – the restructuring of the international system. Levy claims that this builds a logical circularity into the definition of world wars which makes it impossible to test important propositions about the relationship between wars and system structure. His proposed criteria are independent of outcomes and result in a list of ten "general" wars since the sixteenth century. The disputes over definitions and lists of wars have generated a profuse literature. The following argument lays out a typology of wars and their hypothesized roles in the world-system.

Without denying the importance of the periodic emergence of hegemonic states in the development of the modern world-system, I am not prepared to accept an explanation for the dynamics of the system that is grounded solely in terms of the ascension to military dominance of these leading states. This necessitates a reinterpretation of the concept of world wars as presented by Thompson and Modelski. While I agree with Thompson that world wars represent attempts to restructure political relations among states to correspond with changing economic realities, I also think they may be seen as a way in which states try to convert political–military strength into a greater share of world surplus value. In part, this is a function of the interdependence of political and economic factors in the capitalist mode of production. In either case, world wars, defined as those conflicts in which one state attempts to take over and thus destroy the interstate system or struggles in which leading power status is determined, are not the only important wars in the struggle among states in the capitalist world-economy.

Extending our consideration beyond the great powers to include the entire hierarchical division of the world-economy since 1500, we can identify three structural roles which wars have played. Most fundamentally, they may represent struggles for control or dominance over the entire interstate system. Although disagreements clearly exist over the analysis of particular cases, the world wars identified by Thompson all reflect struggles for pre-eminence to a greater or lesser degree. The Napoleonic Wars and World Wars I and II may be considered extreme examples of this type. There is no definitive answer to the counter factual question of what would have happened if the unsuccessful coalition in one of these wars had managed to achieve its goals; yet it is difficult to argue that the interstate system as we know it could have continued to exist if either the Napoleonic or German attempts to conquer most of the core zone had succeeded.

Secondly, wars may be used to facilitate the upward or downward mobility of individual states and the creation of a new structure of power that more accurately reflects the strengths and weaknesses of key actors. Examples of wars of this nature are legion.

During the eighteenth century, when economic and political power was quite evenly distributed throughout the core of the system, wars of this second type were more prevalent. The War of the Spanish Succession resulted in the exhaustion of Dutch resources and the fall of the Netherlands from leading status but did not lead to the immediate creation of a successor state. France was weakened but still strong, maintaining possession of some of its European conquests including the rich province of Alsace and city of Strasbourg. Its colonial empire was still extensive and Louis XIV's grandson retained the throne of Spain. England was strengthened but not yet preponderant. Spain held on to its American empire and Austria gained extensive territories on the European continent. Hinsley, for example, emphasizes the relative degree of equality that characterized the leading states in the eighteenth century (1967: 176). Similarly, Davis contends that the British economic hegemony achieved in the nineteenth century could not have been predicted a century earlier (1973: 288). Under these conditions, the hierarchical structure of the core was fluid and wars like the Seven Years War facilitated the rise to prominence of expanding states like Prussia and Russia.

Finally, wars may be used to restructure relations between core states and the periphery in keeping with relative changes in power among actors. The trade wars between Britain and France during the eighteenth century represent the most obvious examples of this kind. Yet all important wars have resulted in changes in the status of core powers *vis-à-vis* peripheral areas. World wars followed by the emergence of a new hegemonic core power have facilitated decolonization. The Napoleonic Wars and World War II stand out in this respect. Free trade works to the advantage of the leading state when its competitive advantage assures market dominance. The hegemonic power is able to minimize the cost of political control represented by formal empire. Conversely, when wars have resulted only in changes in relative position within a more equal framework, victories have been accompanied by changes in formal control of particular peripheral areas to reflect the new balance of power. Bergesen and Schoenberg (1980) have documented the close relationship between periods of multicentricity within the core and the development of formal colonial empires as contrasted with periods of hegemony and the movement toward free trade and decolonization.

Clearly, none of these categories of wars are mutually exclusive, and historically world conflicts have usually involved a combination of them. Indeed the growth of exchange networks and interlocking alliances within the world-system have insured the spread of conflicts to encompass states with widely divergent motives. Thus the Seven Years War linked the conflict between Prussia, Austria, and Russia for core status with the struggles between Britain and France for control of the resources of the periphery.

In analyzing the trajectory of military conflicts it is often nearly impossible to distinguish between the real aims of participants, their stated aims, and the effect that the victory of one or more actors is perceived as portending for the whole system by other states. To make matters more complicated, war aims regularly change with initial successes or defeats. However it should be possible to determine the impact of global conflict on the restructuring of the interstate system.

When examined in these terms wars have operated to reduce discrepancies between economic and military power structures in the world-system. Some states, like Prussia or Russia, have used military power to increase their share of world surplus. When this path results in an expanded economic base for capital accumulation, as the addition of resource-rich Silesia did to the Prussian polity, then the improved position of the state may be maintained and extended. However, the costs of military expansion reduce the percentage of national resources available for productive investments. When military power is not converted to economic productivity or when the fiscal costs of maintaining the state's international position become too high, core status may be ephemeral. Thus the outmoded organization of the Russian economy and social structure was eventually reflected in the loss of military superiority in the decades beginning with the Crimean War.

Conversely, states like Great Britain and the United States, which did not have to contend with the expense of maintaining a threatened land frontier and were able to keep the costs of government down, had more capital to devote to the tasks of economic development during their periods of expansion within the system. This may help to explain the success, noted by Thompson and Modelski, of the naval route to global power. States without exposed borders were able to devote resources to the maintenance and development of sea power. When a continental power like France under the direction of Colbert attempted to develop a comparable fleet, the added drain on national resources needed to maintain both a large land army and an expanded navy provoked considerable resistance within the nation.

Overall, then, I share basic agreement with Modelski and Thompson on the existence since the sixteenth century of a multicentric world-system tied together by political relations among states and economic exchange networks. I concur as to the importance of the periodic emergence of a preponderant economic and political power.

I differ from the "power cycles" approach in my effort to go beyond a systemic need for order to the construction of a causal model that will explain both the reasons for the recurrent rise of these global powers and their failure to hold their position within the structure of world power. I believe that these causes lie in the institutions of capitalist development. Upward mobility within the system has been conceptualized as a two-sided process. While productive advantage has frequently been converted to political strength by leading states in the system, other states have been able to use the increased share of world surplus value gained through military force to stimulate their own economic expansion.

The waning of dominant status has also been linked to the operation of the capitalist world-economy. Changes in competitive advantage, costs of control and diverging interests among capitalists, workers, and state bureaucrats within declining hegemons have been advanced as some of the mechanisms through which this relationship is articulated.

THE K-WAVE AND WARS

One aspect of the link between the interstate system and the world economy is revealed in the connection between the Kondratieff cycle (K-wave) and warfare, first posited by Kondratieff himself. An impressive research literature has blossomed in recent years investigating this linkage, and, although considerable disagreement still exists about the causal connections involved, quite a bit is now known.

An entire industrial sector of international relations scholars have been working for scores of years to code the timing, participants, territory, costs, and destructiveness of warfare in the interstate system. Levy's (1983) book, *War in the Modern Great Power System, 1495–1975*, presents a recent complete compilation of the data on warfare. Although visual inspection of the frequency of wars and other measures reveals an obvious sequence of periods of more and less war, Levy reports that warfare does not exhibit any strictly cyclical features. Joshua Goldstein (1988:244) however, demonstrates that a statistical test (the Auto-Correlation Function) applied to Levy's data on war severity (the number of battle deaths per year) produces clear evidence of a 50- to 60-year cycle over the period from 1495 to 1975.

Thompson and Zuk (1982) and Goldstein (1988) use time series analysis techniques to examine the relationship between wars and the K-wave. Goldstein uses several price and production series and the dates given by four earlier scholars (Braudel, Frank, Kondratieff, and Mandel) to produce a set of trough and peak dates for K-waves between 1494 and 1975. He argues that strict periodicity is an inappropriate standard for social cycles. Thus he analyzes sequences of phases with unequal periods in his measure of the K-wave. Goldstein's results reveal a clear association between the K-wave and the severity cycle (battle deaths per year) of war among core powers. He argues that severe wars are more likely to occur *during the upswing phase* of the K-wave and his empirical work finds support for this. This conclusion is dependent on the dates Goldstein uses to distinguish between upswing and downswing phases of the K-wave (1988: figure 11.3). Thompson (1986) doubts the soundness of Goldstein's periodization of the K-wave before 1790. Nevertheless Thompson finds support for the relationship between war and K-wave price upswings in his own analysis of the period between 1816 and 1914. What is not in doubt is the finding that the K-wave and the war cycle are linked in some systematic way.

The business cycle is most often measured by price series. Goldstein argues that there is a production–stagnation cycle which precedes the price cycle by 10 to 15 years. The war cycle peaks in between the peaks of the production cycle and the price cycle in Goldstein's model. The data on long-run series which indicate real production and related indicators are rather scanty, so most empirical work has focused on the relationship between price series and war. Some of that relationship is undoubtedly a rather simple matter of the effects of warfare on inflation, a matter studied by Thompson and Zuk (1982). They conclude that most K-wave price downturns can be attributed to the ending of major wars, but that K-wave price upswings regularly occur before the outbreak of wars.

Goldstein's causal model of the connection between war and the K-wave production cycle posits a negative feedback loop. According to Goldstein wars occur during K-wave production upswings because, though states always desire to go to war, warfare is expensive and so states do it when economic growth is providing them with more resources. Goldstein argues that warfare, on the other hand, has a negative effect on economic growth through non-productive expenditure and destruction of people and property. Thus the two cycles spur one another on.

Like Thompson, Goldstein does not consider the capitalist nature of the institutions and processes which link warfare and economic growth in the modern world-system. For him states are simply war machines that go after one another when they have the resources to do it, and since capitalist economic growth provides great resources, warfare is endemic.

Goldstein's study reveals empirical details of the relationship among business cycles, wars, and the rise and fall of hegemons which must be taken into account in any theory of the world-system. He shows that Kondratieff waves and peaks in the severity of wars among core powers are closely associated in time, with nine out of ten peaks in world war since 1500 occurring *near the end of an upward phase* of the price cycle. The somewhat surprising finding here is that, according to Goldstein, world wars regularly occur during a period of economic expansion. This is surprising for two reasons. Most people think first about World War II, which is the single exception among the ten core war peaks since 1500. And many theories of core war are based on the idea that war is caused by increasing competition among core states, (so-called "lateral pressure" (Choucri and North, 1975)) which has been assumed to be most severe during periods of economic stagnation.

Examining data series on prices and several indicators of production, innovation, and investment, Goldstein concludes that the production cycle and the price cycle are somewhat out of phase with one another, with the production cycle lagged about 10 to 15 years behind the price cycle. In Goldstein's model (1988:259) the war cycle peaks just between the production cycle and the price cycle. This model is, of course, an idealized depiction of the exact features which are only generally supported by Goldstein's analysis of actual data. Nevertheless, if Goldstein's representation is correct we may be able to explain why there has been considerable disagreement about the timing of the relationship between warfare and the K-wave. Goldstein follows Kondratieff and many other theorists in arguing that warfare is most likely to be severe during the upswing phase, but his own model implies that warfare actually peaks in between the peak of the price cycle and the production cycle. If we believe that the psychology and logic of production decisions as well as statecraft are involved in the relationship between warfare and the K-wave, as the Wallersteinian world-system perspective would emphasize, then it is most interesting that the warfare peak is alleged to occur *after* the peak of the investment cycle, in other words *during the beginning of the investment and production downswing*. This is simultaneously a period in which states have a lot of resources available for war and capitalist investors have begun to slacken investments, presumably because they perceive limitations on profit-taking. Increasing competition for markets and investment opportunities is due to overproduction by producers of core goods for the world market relative to effective demand, and this kind of competition leads to pressure for the use of extra-economic power, that is state power, to protect and/or expand market shares and investment opportunities.

Goldstein does not distinguish the prices of different kinds of commodities, but other researchers have shown that price cycles vary across different kinds of commodities. Michael Barrat-Brown's (1974) study of the terms of trade between core and peripheral areas demonstrated that there are differences in the degree of price changes such that terms of trade of peripheral goods *vis-à-vis* core goods rise and fall over time, and this finding is confirmed by Paul Bairoch (1986:205–8). This supports Wallerstein's (1984b) argument that core commodities are overproduced in some periods relative to effective demand, that is relative to the politically structured distribution of resources in the world-system. This causes military conflict among core states, and sometimes results in the restructuring of the international order under a new hegemon.

Goldstein's demonstration of the link between war cycles and the K-wave is extremely important evidence in support of the contention that geopolitics and the world economy are interdependent processes. The connections between the war cycle, the K-wave, and the hegemonic cycle are examined in the next chapter. Here I would like to quote Goldstein's observations of four trends based on his analysis of warfare over the last 500 years:

> First, the incidence of great power war is declining – more and more "peace" years separate the great power wars. Second, and related, the great power wars are becoming shorter. Third, however, those wars are becoming more severe – annual fatalities during war increasing more than a hundred-fold over the five centuries. Fourth (and more tentatively), the war cycle may be gradually lengthening in each successive era, from about 40 years in the first era to about 60 years in the third. The presence of nuclear weapons has continued these trends in great power war from the past five centuries – any great power wars in this era will likely be fewer, shorter and much more deadly. (1985:432)

Now let us turn our attention to the hegemonic sequence.

9

The Rise and Decline of Hegemonic Core Powers

Here it is argued that three states have been hegemonic in the capitalist world economy since its consolidation in the long sixteenth century – the United Provinces of the Netherlands, the United Kingdom of Great Britain, and the United States of America. The periods in between these hegemonies were characterized, I contend, by a *relatively* equal (multicentric) distribution of military power and economic competitive advantage among core states, and by relatively higher levels of conflict and competition within the core. I also think that these periods were characterized by more bilateral and politically controlled relationships between the core and the periphery in which each core state attempted to monopolize exchange with its "own" colonial empire. Stephen Krasner (1976) has contended that periods in which a single great power has been hegemonic have been characterized by relatively more free trade among different areas of the world economy. The interaction between the hegemonic cycle, with its rise and fall of hegemonic core powers, and changes in the structure of the core/periphery hierarchy is analyzed in chapter 13. This chapter focuses on the core zone itself, and processes which cause the rise and fall of hegemons, and it considers the current situation of the United States as a declining contemporary hegemon.

RISE AND FALL IN DIFFERENT SYSTEMS

In order to understand the dynamics of the current US decline I will primarily compare hegemonies *within* the modern world-system. But it may also be fruitful to compare the current situation to long-run cycles of centralization and decentralization which occurred in precapitalist modes of production such as the rise and fall of the Roman Empire. This has been done in a recent article by Galtung et al. (1980). They compare the decline of Rome in antiquity with what they call the "decline of Western imperialism." They find some similarities at the level of cultural processes, but in my view they fail to grasp the important structural and systemic differences between the modern world-system and the Roman world-system.

One important difference between the Roman world-empire and the capitalist world-economy is the organization of the state. In Rome a single overarching state apparatus came to encompass nearly the entire economic network, whereas in the capitalist world-economy there is no single state, but rather there is the interstate system described in previous chapters. The Roman world-empire had a single center while the capitalist world-economy is politically multicentric. It is true that at various times within the modern world-system there has been a single most powerful (hegemonic) state, but the hegemon has never been powerful enough to impose imperium over the whole core.

The main consequence of this structural difference is its effect on the dynamics of competition, reproduction, and growth in these two types of systems. In the Roman world-empire, competition was primarily mediated through a single state apparatus and, although monetarization of the economy was extensive (K. Hopkins, 1978a), the competitive price-setting market was not strong enough to regularly encourage increases in economic efficiency on the part of producers. The main way to gain and hold income was through obtaining access to political power. Roman property and contract law was quite "modern," but markets remained dominated by political power, and this power was centralized in a single state apparatus. The main type of growth was *extensive*, through the addition of control over lands and slaves. As Keith Hopkins (1978b:62) shows, the dynamic of the Roman economy was fueled by conquest. Roman military organization and transport technology, by far the most advanced in antiquity, eventually reached their cost-effective spatial limits, and territorial expansion halted.

The slave mode of production required new inputs as slaves were worked to death on the latifundia of Italy. Tribute as a form of surplus extraction was most remunerative in newly conquered lands. The ending of territorial expansion of the empire created a scarcity of slaves and tribute, and led eventually to a reversion to serfdom in the countryside. The Roman political constitution was unique in the extent of its ability to incorporate oppositional groups into the state by the extension of citizenship. While the political system was always more oligarchical than the earlier Athenian democracy (Anderson, 1974a) the definition of membership was much more flexible, and allowed power and status to be shared with those in a position to mobilize effective opposition. The dynamic of co-optation of opposition led to changes in political forms – from republic to empire (Brunt, 1971) – but the necessity of integrating organizational forms within a single state apparatus slowed the rate of organizational innovation and discouraged experimentation. Over time the weight of the political superstructure became greater than the underlying economy could bear. Because the Roman system was so centralized, the demise of Rome also meant the demise of the system. It was not possible, in the short run, for a new center to emerge to revitalize the mode of production and to restart its expansion on a new basis.[1]

By contrast, the capitalist world-economy, with its more decentralized polity, allows for much greater economic *and political* competition. The existence of the price-setting world market (which includes both national and international markets), while it is not a "perfect" market, does regularly encourage investors to increase the efficiency of production (to produce at lower cost) in order to gain a greater share of income. Thus technical development of productivity is facilitated by the fact that there is no central state that can impose monopoly control on the whole arena of economic competition. Similarly, the multicentric interstate system encourages the "export of capital" because political opposition to profitable investment and labor exploitation is mediated by the individual nation states and often can be escaped by crossing state boundaries.

Political competition in the capitalist world-economy is also much more dynamic than in world-empires. The interstate system allows different paths to "success" in the competition among states. Some emphasize political–military expansion, while others emphasize a strategy of competitive commodity production for the world market. In such a decentralized political system new forms of political organization can emerge unconstrained by any central state and are thereby free to compete with one another for dominance. What makes the modern world economy a *capitalist* world-economy, however, is its unique combination of an interstate system with the institutions of commodity production for profit on a market, and a high level of the commodification of labor power. These institutions are interwoven, along with the "private" nature of investment decisions, into a competitive interstate system; and it is the institutional combination of all these elements that creates the qualitative uniqueness which differentiates the capitalist world-system from earlier world-systems.

The modern system has shown its flexibility over the 500-year period of its expansion and deepening. Unlike the Roman world-empire, it has changed its center without going into devolution as a system. Thus the present period is most probably not a demise of "Western imperialism" (*à la* Galtung et al. 1980) but rather the demise of the hegemony of the United States. The main challenges to US supremacy are posed by other core powers, not by the periphery. The possible outcomes, a new hegemony and continuation of the system, or real transformation of the capitalist world-economy into a qualitatively different system, are options that bear only broad and somewhat superficial similarities to the decline and fall of the Roman Empire.

The main difference between the modern world-system and earlier world-systems is that commodity production has become the dominant logic of competition *at the center of the system*. In the Roman world-empire and many other precapitalist world-systems there was much commodity production, but it flourished mainly in the interstices. It was the business of clients, freedmen, or the specialty of semiperipheral trading states, while the "perspective of the world" was a game played exclusively by men more interested in expanding state power as the primary means to wealth, power, and status. It was the emergence of a different kind of state in the core region of the European world-economy, the hegemonic Dutch state employing its military capabilities primarily to provide protection rents to its capitalists, which signaled the consolidation of a world-system in which capitalism had become the dominant mode of production.

DEFINITIONS OF HEGEMONY

Wallerstein (1984a) defines hegemony in terms of economic comparative advantage – the concentration of a certain type of commodity production within the borders of a single core state. Remember that "core production" is commodity production which utilizes relatively capital intensive technology and skilled, highly paid labor. Hegemony in this sense is comparative advantage due to a combination of product development – producing the most sophisticated and desirable products – and competitive prices – the ability to price the exported core products at levels which make it hard for competing national economies to avoid purchasing them, and yet, at the same time, to make a profit while selling at such prices. Wallerstein observes that economic comparative advantage enables one core country to penetrate the home markets of other core countries with capital intensive commodities. The production of these types of commodities has, of course, relatively denser forward and backward linkages, and spinoffs which multiply the growth effects of investments within the national economy.

Very different conceptualizations of global power are utilized by political scientists studying the "international system." George Modelski and William R. Thompson (1988) propose a theory of a long cycle of political–military power in which great powers rise and fall. Their theory is similar in some respects to the Wallersteinian perspective. They claim to be studying the world system (without the hyphen – see Thompson, ed., 1983) and they agree that periods of concentrated power correspond with relatively lower levels of conflict among core powers, while periods in which there is a more equal distribution of power among core states tend to be more conflictive. But they have a very different notion of what constitutes concentrated power (they do not use the term "hegemony"). For them the central matter is naval power, which is an indicator of the ability of a great power to exercise "global reach." Predominant naval power enables a great power to maintain order at the level of long-distance international interactions. Modelski and Thompson contend that land armies and general military expenditures are not useful indicators of "global reach" because these resources are usable primarily in regional or continental warfare, not for domination of the global power system. This argument illustrates Modelski and Thompson's "layered" conceptualization of the world system, in which the global level of interaction is analyzed as importantly distinct from local and regional interactions.

Modelski has defined "world powers" as "those units monopolizing (that is controlling more than one half of) the market for (or the supply of) order-keeping in the global layer of interdependence" (1978:216). The global system since the sixteenth century is said to have experienced the rise and fall of four of these "world powers:" Portugal, the Netherlands, Britain, and the United States (Modelski and Thompson, 1988). According to Modelski (1978) the power of the "world power" is not really based on controlling the actions of other leading states. Rather a world power produces order by manipulating alliances to produce relative stability in the core while dominating European interactions with the rest of the globe.

Other political scientists speak of hegemony in terms of "power capability," which is defined broadly as the ability of one state to control or influence the behavior of other states using rewards and punishments. Robert Gilpin (1981) explicitly conceptualizes hegemony in terms of relative overall military power, although he analyzes the concentration of economic innovations which provide the economic wherewithal behind superior military advantage.

For Wallerstein hegemony comes to include productive, commercial, and financial dominance within the world economy. But productive efficiency must be accompanied by state power. The creation and maintenance of economic preeminence requires the political and military capacity to preserve a domestic class structure favorable to capitalist accumulation, innovative production, and the prevention of external restrictions on flows of capital or goods. In this sense political–military power is a necessary but not a sufficient basis for the attainment of hegemony in a capitalist world-economy.

The free market, which initially favors the competitive advantages of a leading power, eventually results in the flow of capital and technological innovations to competing states. This results in the loss of productive advantage by the hegemonic power. Further, the costs of maintaining the global order are borne disproportionately by the leader, resulting in rising production costs and an excessive expenditure of national resources in the non-productive military sector. Recent efforts by the United States to encourage Japan and Western Europe to increase their military budgets reflect a recognition of the disproportionate costs of maintaining world order borne by the hegemon. Additionally, formerly convergent interests of different groups of capitalists in a hegemonic core power become more divergent as important sectors of the national economy lose competitive advantage.

When they seek to operationalize power capability many researchers have used what Thompson (1983b) somewhat disparagingly calls an "omnibus" measure which combines a number of different indicators of economic and military resources. Organski and Kugler (1980:30–8) have argued strongly for "total output," that is total GNP, as the best measure of power capability of the great powers. They also argue (1980: 68–84) that total output should be combined with a measure of political development, which they define as the ability of the state to mobilize the resources of its own society. Another study which has explicitly tried to measure variation over time in the degree of concentration of power among the "great powers" is that by Singer et al. (1979). They combined a number of economic and military indicators of the capacity of states. A similar composite measure was constructed by Ferris (1973). Curiously, none of the indicators used are measures of economic development as usually understood, but are rather indicators which combine size and development, as does total GNP. Of the studies I have reviewed, only that by Doran and Parsons (1980) utilizes measures of economic development, and they combine these into a single composite index along with size indicators.

Some surprises emerge from my review of the studies which have tried to empirically measure changes in the relative power capabilities of states. Although these have been done by political scientists, only Modelski and Thompson focus exclusively on military power, and they examine only a particular kind of military power – naval power. Organski and Kugler argue that total GNP is the best overall measure of power capability, although later they combine it with a measure of *internal* state strength. None of the studies measures hegemony in terms of total military power. None of the studies examines measures of development separately from measures of size. And none of the studies tries to examine the relationship between economic and political types of power.

CAUSES AND CONDITIONS OF THE RISE AND DECLINE OF HEGEMONIC CORE STATES

In this section a set of causes and conditions of the rise and decline of hegemonic core states is hypothesized. Then I present a brief overview of the three hegemonies. Later I describe the few quantitative studies of the hegemonic sequence which have been conducted.

The rise and fall of hegemonic core states can be understood in terms of the formation of leading sectors of core production and the concentration of these sectors, temporarily, in the territory of a single state, which hence becomes the most economically and politically powerful of the core states. Decline sets in when the hegemon loses its ability to develop lead industries ahead of its competitors. This process can be understood as a feature of the world-economy as a whole in so far as it involves the interaction of systemic variables such as the Kondratieff wave, the application of new technologies to production (Mandel, 1978; Rostow, 1978; and Bousquet, 1980); and the violent reorganization of the interstate system through warfare. As noted in the previous chapter the strong association in time between long business cycles and wars among core powers has been empirically demonstrated.

The uniqueness of the world-system perspective is that it examines the system-wide dynamics of these cycles as well as the exclusively national processes involved. The cycles that occur are the consequences of the relative over-production in different periods of different types of commodities (core commodities and peripheral commodities) and the limits on effective demand that particular political structures impose on consumption. During periods of the expansion of core production labor unions, guilds, and other politically organized interest groups increase their demands for shares of income. The expansion of core production increases the need for raw material inputs, many of which are produced in the periphery. The terms of trade between core and periphery shift in favor of the periphery, enabling peripheral producers and the states they control to attain a relatively more favorable market position and to make more effective demands for a larger share of surplus value. This redounds on the struggle for shares among core states, where wage increases (and the "cacophony of equity demands") are less easily met by increased exploitation of the periphery. This dynamic leads to heightened class struggle within core countries and to increased competition among core countries for shares of a no longer growing pool of world surplus value. It is striking that hegemony in the core is consolidated after wars in which potential contenders have destroyed one another, leaving an opening for the emerging dominance of the new hegemon. The pattern which is documented by Thompson (1986) and Goldstein (1988) is as follows: a rising challenger (B) initiates war against the declining hegemon (A). (A) makes an alliance with another rising core state (C) to combat the military challenge by (B). (A) and (C) win the war and (C) emerges as the new hegemon.

Goldstein's study examines the relationship between the war/growth cycles and the rise and fall of hegemonic core powers. Utilizing the Wallersteinian conceptualization of three hegemonies – the Dutch, the British, and the American – he demonstrates that they are related, but not in a very regular way. As Goldstein (1988:287) puts it:

> I find the connection between the causal dynamics of these two cycles – long waves and hegemony cycles – to be weak. They are not synchronized, and there is no exact number of long waves that makes up a hegemony cycle. Rather, I see the two cycles as playing out over time, each according to its own inner dynamic but each conditioned by, and interacting with, the other.

And further along he concludes:

> Each hegemony cycle contains several long waves, but not a fixed number. Each of the long waves *within* the hegemony cycle ends in a war peak that re-adjusts the international power structure without bringing in a new hegemony. (Goldstein, 1988:288, emphasis in the original)

In a footnote Goldstein continues: "All great power wars affect relative positions in the international 'pecking order.' Hegemonic wars determine the top position in that order" (1988:288).

Although Goldstein does explicate a causal model which explains the relationship between economic growth and periodic wars (see chapter 8), his explanation of the linkage between these cycles and the three hegemonies is more historical. He argues that many contingencies link the particular outcomes which are revealed by the hegemonic sequence and the particular countries which become hegemons, challengers, and "also-rans." Goldstein does not, however, address the more system-wide questions which were the focus of chapters 7 and 8 above: why is the interstate system reproduced, rather than evolving into world-empire; why do the successful hegemons rely more on accumulation through trade than military expansion; and why don't hegemons facing decline opt for worldwide imperium? Also, why are the direct military challengers of hegemons never successful? As argued in previous chapters these questions require attention to the peculiar nature of competition and accumulation in a capitalist world-economy.

Though Goldstein treats the hegemonic sequence historically, it is possible to try to delineate the systematic conditions and processes which contribute to the rise and demise of hegemonic core states. Let us discuss some similarities of the three hegemons which suggest the kinds of processes which can account for their rise and decline.

THE THREE STAGES OF A HEGEMONY

Hegemonies have three stages. The first is based on competitive advantage in mass consumption goods that can penetrate the markets of core producers in competing countries and also can expand the size of the market by lowering the price of the product. The second stage is based on the expansion of capital goods production, and the third stage is based on the export of financial services and the performance of central place functions for the world-economy (See Wallerstein, 1984a).

In terms of the cities that became hegemonic world cities over the history of the modern world-systems we may compare Amsterdam, London, and New York to peripheral cities and to other non-hegemonic core cities (e.g. Seville, Paris, etc.). We should examine the conditions that promote the development of production in key core industries and those that facilitate the development of the necessary state strength to back up the expansion of world market shares.

A number of conditions may contribute to the determination of which country becomes a hegemon. Geographical location would appear to play some role in facilitating hegemony. Hegemonic powers have been centrally located within the economic networks they come to dominate. This is obviously an advantage in terms of transport costs, but may become less important as transport costs decrease. Technology adequate to a breakthrough in competitive core production must be available, either from local inventors or through borrowing. All three hegemonies have involved "industrial revolutions" in the sense that new, more economically efficient technologies were applied that allowed the production of mass consumption goods more cheaply than by competitors. Another necessary condition is the existence of investment capital sufficient to develop the new types of production in the hands of those willing to risk it in entrepreneurial ventures. Each rising hegemonic power has early on developed diversified, capital intensive agriculture for home consumption and for export. They have eventually developed access to cheap imports of some staple foods and raw materials, most often produced in the periphery, which have been important inputs to industry. Human capital, that is, labor with skills relevant to the new type of production, must be available. All these conditions contribute to the ability of an emerging core state to form a leading sector of core production that can serve as the basis for hegemony.

The political conditions of rise to hegemony are rather more complicated. A hegemonic state must be powerful *vis-à-vis* other states and must also have the strong support of the class coalition that composes its regime. The quality and unity of this class coalition are also important. It must strongly include classes with an interest in pursuing a strategy of profitable production for the world market. Although the ability of the state apparatus to appropriate resources is undoubtedly important (Tilly, 1985), the conception of state power I am using is not reducable to the extractive power of government. As discussed in chapter 6, a state is powerful if the classes that support it will grant it great support during emergencies (Tardanico, 1978). Its ability to extract surplus through taxation does not automatically show that it is strong in the sense that I mean here. The Dutch state could raise a navy overnight by convincing the Amsterdam merchants that their interests were at stake, whereas the French state, whose peacetime government revenues per capita were much greater than those of the British throughout the nineteenth century, could not raise so great a subscription during time of war.

The size of the state is also important, and as Wallerstein is fond of pointing out, it is possible to be too large as well as to be too small,[2] especially if economic regions with contradictory interests are part of the same state, as was the case with France. It should also be added that most hegemonic core states have a relatively egalitarian and pluralistic political system compared to those of their competitors. This pluralism allows rapid adaptation to changes in the interests of classes in the center coalition, as well as some flexibility in response to the demands of workers and farmers. These characteristics can be advantageous in the world economy, at least during the period of upward mobility. The relative egalitarianism of the polity incorporates a larger percentage of the population into the development process and provides some (again temporary) solutions to the Keynesian problem of effective demand. Another way of saying this is to point out that upwardly mobile core states have larger home markets than their competitors because of relatively more equal distributions of income.[3] Nation-building, the formation of a strong social solidarity at the national level, is a process which characterizes the emergence of all three hegemons. This contributes to political stability and to the expansion of the home market. It should be pointed out that these political qualities do not preclude the existence of a domestic underclass (e.g. Hechter, 1975; Zinn, 1980). Typically this serves both as an outcaste status group that reinforces the solidarity of the larger nation, and as a domestic source of economic exploitation.

What, then, are the conditions that lead to the decline of a hegemonic core state? First it should be pointed out that core states do not decline absolutely. The entire world-economy continues to grow, albeit at different rates. What happens is that core states *relatively* lose their hegemony, but they do not plunge into the periphery. The most important cause of relative decline is the spread of leading core industries to other competing core countries, and to parts of the semiperiphery. Hegemonic states attempt to monopolize the new types of production, but unsuccessfully because of their inability to politically control the diffusion of techniques, skilled labor, and investment capital. Competing producers in other states attempt first to win back their home markets, often employing political regulation of trade (protectionism) as well as the adoption of the new production techniques (Senghaas, 1985). Later some of them will successfully compete with the hegemonic power in international markets.

Another factor that contributes to the loss of hegemony we may term the turnover time of fixed capital, especially investment (both private and public) in infrastructural inputs to the production system. This obviously operates at the level of heavy investment in technologies such as plant construction and expensive large-scale machinery. Latecomers have an advantage in that they can adopt newer technical innovations, while earlier investors must wait to recoup initial investment. Steel plants in the United States and Japan are well known examples of this. But the same problem may be seen in other investments in the built environment which are less obviously subject to the logic of profits, but that nevertheless have an effect on competitive production.

Transportation systems, urban structures, communications systems, and energy systems involve investments of resources that, once made, tend to be relatively permanent or not easily reorganized. The canal system of Amsterdam, more systematic and spacious than that of Venice, is a permanent feature of the city. The advent of other forms of transportation, more economically competitive ones, does not produce the rebuilding of Amsterdam, but rather the removal of some of its economic activities to other locations. Similarly, the location of cities on rivers is heavily influenced by the transport costs relative to a particular stage of transport technology. The advent of larger ships does not produce the removal of cities downstream, except in the sense that ports with deeper water become the new centers of trade. At the level of nations, national transport systems, energy systems, communications systems, and the locations and division of functions between cities, as well as the types of technology utilized in factories, are all forms of investment subject to the turnover time of fixed capital. A second-running core state that is developing a new type of core production can more easily incorporate the latest, most competitive techniques and features of overall social production than the already-invested hegemonic core state. This is one of the components of Gershenkron's (1962) "advantages of backwardness."

It can be asked why entrepreneurs within a declining hegemonic core state do not invest *within* their national economies to revitalize material production and increase productivity. It may be that a particular steel company must wait for its sunk capital to be depreciated before building a new plant that uses more productive technology, but why don't other corporations make such investments? Here we may point out that the structure of national tariffs plays a role in the determination of investment locations. Tariff protection of national industries increases in a period of slower growth as states seek to protect their national markets against international competition. It may be in the strategic and national interest to make new investments in steel, and indeed states often adopt policies that subsidize such undertakings. But the purely profit-oriented logic of investment is unlikely to help a country which is losing its competitive position in the world market. Building a new steel plant next to the old plant means that the national market will have to be shared, while buying steel from more competitive producers abroad and investing in more immediately profitable enterprises (often located in other countries) is the most attractive strategy for private investors.

Thus economic nationalism by itself might prevent the relocation of certain industries, but declining hegemonic core states are usually ambivalent about the choice between nationalism and internationalism. This reflects the contradictory interests of their "national" and "international" capitalists as well as the contradictory interests of workers as consumers and job-holders (Hart, 1980). The road of state-sponsored "revitalization" advocated by those in hegemonic core states most concerned with the interests of national producers (both labor and capital) may be taken, but other competing states will also employ this strategy, and they are more likely to do it effectively because the coalitions of classes that control these other states are less dominated by those who have international investments (Evans, 1985). The international capitalists within a declining hegemonic core state can often convince consumers that it is better to try to hang on to centrality in world exchange and to benefit from low-cost imports than to adopt an expensive (and risky) program of economic revitalization.

In addition, organizational features tend to have a certain inertia (or momentum, if organization is a process). Once a national economy becomes organized in a certain way there is a tendency to crystallization around patterns which are then not easy to change. While organizational forms may be more malleable than the infrastructural features discussed above (because material sunk capital is less malleable), social rigidities do crystalize around organizational forms.

A frequently cited explanation for the British decline at the end of the nineteenth century was the reticence of family-held firms to adopt the newly emerging corporate form (Crouzet, 1982). In many sectors family firms apparently preferred continued control to additional profits, and thus British industry was late to adopt the expanded scale and new organizational forms becoming widespread in Germany and the United States. Albert Bergesen (1981) has argued that US corporations in the twentieth century have displayed a functionally equivalent reticence to adopt a new organizational innovation which is becoming widespread, the state–firm merger. Also, the US federal government lags behind almost all contemporary states with regard to national economic planning in an era when state capitalism is being successfully employed by most competitors.

Another factor is the opposition that successful capitalist accumulation creates. The very political pluralism and relative egalitarianism that was earlier a competitive advantage allows the formation of constraints on the maneuverability of capital and increases the costs of production. The most obvious example of this is the formation of political organizations that protect and expand the interests of workers. Wages, both direct and social, tend to go up in a successfully hegemonic core state. Capitalists who are making big profits are more likely to accept a higher wage bill accompanied by a stable labor supply. This changes when competition increases and profits decline.

Similarly, other constraints on the continued revolution of production become politically articulated. The state begins to respond to the needs of core workers and other groups (e.g. consumers, environmentalists, etc.), and these "non-economic" demands on capital may reduce the relative profitability of production within the country, at least compared to offshore locations where workers and other groups are less well organized.

Mancur Olson's (1982) *The Rise and Decline of Nations* stresses rising wages as the most important among the "social rigidities" which cause the decline of formerly successful national economies. Olson's analysis points to some interesting organizational features which reduce relative efficiency of production and increase the obstacles to economic growth and revitalization. Nations in which interest groups are fragmented and specialized, such as the US, have more obstacles and inefficiencies than nations in which general organizations such as labor or socialist parties represent broad constituencies (i.e. Sweden) because these latter broad-based groups are better able to incorporate matters of national interest into their political agenda. But Olson's analysis proceeds from the assumption that purely economic efficiency and the ability to compete effectively in world markets are the best measures of progress. Thus the policy implication of his analysis is that states and firms should remain as independent as possible of the demands of workers, or other interest groups. A more balanced definition of progress would suggest that the logic of growth ought to include the needs of workers, consumers and the environment. "Efficiency" across the world-system should take these needs into account without pitting workers in different countries against one another. This can be accomplished only by democratically regulating major investment decisions at the world level.

Another condition, one that is often related to increasing politically articulated constraints on capital, is the export of investment capital. Capitalists respond to differentials in profit rates, and so increasing costs of operating in the home economy produce the incentive to invest elsewhere, and thus the phenomenon of the export of capital or "capital flight." This means that fewer new investments in material production are made in the home economy, although new lead sectors do continue to emerge, especially in the provision of financial services to the larger world economy. Thus the world cities located in hegemonic core states typically become more important to the economy of the country in the latter days of the hegemony. This is because the centrality in exchange that developed from the earlier centrality in production is an important resource for the national economy and for the functioning of the larger world economy.

It may be the case that, although benefiting from centrality to a certain extent, the hegemonic core state comes to bear too great a proportion of the costs of maintaining order in the larger world-economy. The smooth operation of the world-system requires the repression of deviance and the maintenance of order, as does any social system. In the contemporary system an important degree of order is maintained through political–military expenditures. Military expenditures may serve some economic functions (e.g. Baran and Sweezy, 1966), but several studies demonstrate that they do not contribute to national economic growth (e.g. Szymanski, 1973; Väyrynen, 1988). The small or non-existent military expenditures of Japan and Germany since World War II have allowed resources to be concentrated on research and development of profitable commodities. The costs of maintaining world order tend to be borne disproportionately by the hegemonic core state, and this burden cannot easily be spread across the core as a whole, although a declining hegemon will try to lessen its share of the costs. At some point the costs of centrality come to outweigh its benefits, usually after competing core states, which have been operating under the umbrella of the hegemonic state, begin to effectively challenge the hegemon's dominance in world markets.

COMPARISON OF HEGEMONIES

Let us now assess and qualify the generalizations of the previous section by reviewing the characteristics of the three powers that have been hegemonic in the modern world-economy (the United Provinces of the Netherlands, the United Kingdom of Great Britain, and the United States of America) and by comparing them with the prior hegemony of Venice and with the powers that contended for hegemony but did not attain it.

The Habsburg Empire (which included the core "dorsal spine" of the European world-economy in the first half of the long sixteenth century) (Bousquet, 1980) was based primarily on political–military, rather than economic, centrality. The mercantile aggressiveness of the Portuguese (Modelski, 1978) served as the first wave of European expansion, but like the later centrality of Seville, Portugal did not develop centrality in production.[4] The Portuguese expansion, and the "primitive accumulation" of money-capital by the Spanish, had important, although complicated, effects on the emerging European world-economy (Wallerstein, 1974:67–84), but they did not lead to the development of core production in Lisbon or Seville. Somewhat like the case of France later on, Spain included areas with interests unconducive to the development of core activities, and the state was weighed down by the necessity of holding together centrifugal regions (Wallerstein, 1974). The attempt by the Habsburgs to impose imperium on the not yet fully integrated capitalist world-economy represented a precapitalist logic of domination partially reflected in the *wholly* mercantile model of exploitation that was the main feature of Portuguese and Spanish expansion to external arenas. These powers, while very important to the formation of the newly emerging system, were not themselves fully formed hegemonic core states of that system. Capitalists had state power in smaller city states in this period (Venice, Antwerp, Genoa, Florence) but the larger states were still dominated by tribute-oriented classes.

The United Provinces of the Netherlands much better fits the Wallersteinian conception of hegemony in a capitalist world-economy. The Dutch Revolution created a republican federation in which the seafaring capitalists of Amsterdam held considerable power. The religious wars brought refugees to

Amsterdam with their skills and what other capital they could manage to convey. Citizenship in Amsterdam was to be had for the price of eight florins (Barbour, 1963). Competitive advantage in production was first evinced in the herring fisheries, which captured a large share of this staple market in the Baltic and the expanding Atlantic economy. Shipbuilding was another leg of Dutch core production that enabled merchants to out-compete Hanse and English pliers of the carrying trade. The cost-efficient Fluyt was easily adapted to many specialized uses and effectively manned by small crews (Wallerstein, 1980a). Angus Maddison (1982:35, table 2.2) shows that the Dutch economy was much more industralized in 1700 than was the British economy. Both Maddison and Wallerstein demonstrate that the Dutch hegemony was based on production capital in lead industries, contrary to those who have seen the Dutch as primarily merchant capitalists.

The Dutch state is often seen as small, but in terms of the notion of state strength employed in chapter 6, it was estimable (Braudel, 1984:193–5). Johan DeWitt, the Stadtholder of Amsterdam, could raise sufficient funds in a day on the Amsterdam bourse (stock and commodity exchange) to defeat any sea power in the world. It has been said that the state was split between the capitalist cities and the land-oriented House of Orange, but in comparison to the other core states, the capitalists had great sway indeed. During national calamities the princes of Orange rallied the populace to defend the nation, while during the peace the less patriotic urban capitalists had their way. The federation and the republican form of government enabled the state to adapt easily to changing economic and military contingencies and the changing interests of its center coalition.

The ideology of free trade and the rights of all nations to use of the seas were propagated by the Dutch intelligentsia during the period in which economic competitive advantage enabled the Amsterdam capitalists to undersell all competitors (Wilson, 1957). This did not prove incompatible with a policy of "armed trade" employed in the periphery to deprive the Portuguese of their monopoly of spices from the East Indies (Parry, 1966).

Barbour (1963) contends that in many respects Amsterdam is the last city state, more similar to Venice and Genoa than to England or the United States, and Braudel (1984) concurs. The Dutch orientation toward the seafaring international market was undiluted by commitments to continental territorial aggrandizement. In this respect it was much like Venice, and Peter Burke's (1974) comparison of Dutch and Venetian entrepreneurs and rentiers is revealing. The Venetian city state was the hegemonic core state of a protocapitalist Mediterranean regional economy (Braudel, 1984). Barbour's comment on city states and nation states in the core suggests the observation that hegemonic core states are larger the larger is the system as a whole.

Lane (1973) observes that the Venetian ruling classes became land oriented during the period of their decline, and he interprets this as an attempt to form a nation state that could compete with the larger states of the European world-economy in formation. The United Provinces seems rather small in terms of land area and population size compared to the other states of Europe, but it nevertheless played the role of hegemonic core state rather effectively during the seventeenth century.[5] The United Provinces may be seen as a kind of midpoint between Venice and England. The hegemonic state became increasingly a nation state, and the size of the national market became larger and larger, with the US national market being an immense share of the world economy it dominates.

The Dutch decline exhibited the tendencies mentioned in my description of hegemonic stages: the shift toward financial services, the export of capital, and the transformation of the capitalists from entrepreneurs to rentiers (Burke, 1974; Riley, 1980). Amsterdam remained an important center of international commerce and finance 300 years after it lost first position. World cities decline relatively, not absolutely.

The United Kingdom fits the stages of hegemony best.[6] Eric Hobsbawm's (1968) study, *Industry and Empire*, depicts the three stages of hegemony in the rise of English cotton textile production, its replacement in the middle of the nineteenth century by the production and export of machinery, railroads, and steamships, and the increasing importance of London in the later nineteenth century as a center of world financial services. The Dutch hegemony, however, matches the three stages formulation rather well, although the middle period of export of ships, arms, and land reclamation projects fits the notion of "capital goods" somewhat loosely.

The English Revolution, like the Dutch, exhibits relative egalitarianism, pluralism, and the firm incorporation of diverse capitalist interests into a flexible state capable of mobilizing immense resources for international war while maintaining a somewhat sparse and inexpensive peacetime bureaucracy. It should be repeated here that we are describing features of the core of a larger capitalist system, not features of capitalism as a whole. We do not want to repeat the mistake of identifying capitalism as a system with the *laissez-faire* state.

The unity of the center coalition in the United Kingdom was not without contention, as can be seen by the history of the rise and fall of the Corn Law. But the agrarian capitalist landowners were much more integrated into successful production for the world market than were the aristocrats of France. France was a case of too large a nation state in which the formation of the absolute monarchy was necessitated by the divergent interests of economic regions (Braudel, 1984: 315–51). The cities of the West were anxious to participate in the expanding Atlantic economy, while the older Mediterranean-oriented Occitania (Wallerstein, 1974:262–9; 1980a) displayed the tendencies of downward mobility characteristic of other areas that had become semiperipheral to the system. The mercantilist and industrializing policies of

Colbert were undercut by the renewed focus on continental diplomacy and political–military aggrandizement (Lane, 1966). The "bourgeois revolution" was delayed until 1789, by which time England had stolen the march on the newly emerging core industries. Paris remained the cultural and diplomatic center of Europe, while London became the hegemonic city of the global economy.

The export of capital from England in the latter half of the nineteenth century is legendary (Crouzet, 1982). English capital went both to the periphery and to other core states. That this phenomenon was by no means new is shown by the earlier Dutch case. It must be seen less as a cause of the spread of the new types of core production to other areas than as a response to that spread. The discussion of the "climacteric" of British maturity (Phelps-Brown and Handfield-Jones, 1952) often alleges a loss of entrepreneurial spirit among business leaders, which reminds us of Pareto's foxes, but this, like the Dutch shift toward low-risk, steady rentier incomes, can be understood mainly as a response to changing opportunities for investment. Venture capital did not disappear; it was sent abroad.

Sometime after 1850 the average incomes of workers in Britain began to rise (Emmanuel, 1972; Braudel, 1984). This was largely the result of the successful formation of trade unions and political organizations of the working class, which succeeded in obtaining some influence in the British state. The increasing power of organized labor raised the cost of exploitation in Britain and created political resistance to the maneuverability of capital. These factors further encouraged the export of investment capital.

The United States exhibited many of the general characteristics I have attributed to hegemonic core states. The infant core industries of New England in the eighteenth century (shipbuilding, salt cod, distilling of rum made from Caribbean sugar, and light manufacturing) emerged in tandem with profitable opportunities provided by the semiperipheral location of New England merchants as carriers between core and periphery in the expanding Atlantic economy – the so-called "triangle trades." An alliance between the merchants of New England, farmers of the middle colonies, and planters of the South, with the help of the French army and navy, managed to create a sovereign state out of a collection of British colonies. The policy of the federal state toward the protection and development of core industry varied with the price of wheat in the world market.[7] Alexander Hamilton's "Report on Manufactures" recommended a protectionist and import substitution policy which would develop the home market and enable the United States to become a core power, but Hamilton's policy was not immediately adopted. The merchant capitalists of New England were ambivalent at first, gaining much of their profit from carrying Southern cotton to the English Midlands. They allied with the South to oppose protection until, "In 1825, the great firm of W. and S. Lawrence of Boston turned its interest and capital from importing to domestic manufacturing, and the rest of State Street fell in behind it. So did Daniel Webster, who was now to become Congress' most eloquent supporter of protection" (Forsythe, 1977).

In general the Southern peripheral capitalists, exporting raw materials to core industry in England, opposed protectionism because it raised the cost of imported manufactured goods and risked British tariff retaliation. Northern manufacturers generally supported tariffs. Henry Clay's "American system" was a policy of protection for domestic manufacturers combined with state-sponsored expenditures on transport infrastructure to integrate agriculture and manufacturing in the home market. Farmers supported this policy when the world price of wheat was low. During price booms the farmers sided with the South, as they too became primarily interested in exports.

The slave South was the most successful peripheral economy the world has ever known, and it sought to extend its political control over the West and over the federal state. After a series of confrontations and compromises the "irrepressible conflict" was settled by the Civil War, which resulted in the consolidation of control by core capital in alliance with core labor and Western farmers. In the 1880s the United States attained core status in the world-system.

The further rise to hegemony by the US was due to a combination of production for the home market and the international market. It is somewhat harder than for the earlier Dutch and British hegemonies to identify a single mass consumption commodity that led to the development of a new sector around which economic hegemony was consolidated. Agricultural commodities were important exports throughout the rise of the United States, as they still are. Agricultural commodities may be either core or peripheral products depending on the way they are produced. Slave-grown cotton was clearly a labor intensive peripheral commodity. Western wheat and other agricultural exports became more and more capital intensive, such that now they are definitely core products relative to the kind of agricultural production occurring in the rest of the world-economy.

The success of core production in the industrial North during the nineteenth century led to the early export of cotton textiles, and not long after, to the export of machinery. Electrical appliances and automobiles became important mass consumption exports, along with other industrial products. As discussed above, the home market seems to have played a relatively larger role in the early development of the United States than did the home market of earlier hegemonies. This was possible because of the successful and relatively egalitarian territorial expansion of the United States (egalitarian in the sense that land acquisition by small and middle-size owners was substantial).

Let us compare the US hegemony with the Dutch and British hegemonies. The size of the home market of the hegemonic core power increased with the size of the world market. All three hegemonies rose after competing core powers weakened themselves in intracore war. Their success relied more on economic competitive advantages in the production of material commodities than on military superiority, although both were important. The maturation of hegemony brought increasing political and military centrality, as well as economic advantage. Decline in each case has had more to do with the catching up of competing core powers than absolute decreases in levels of production or consumption.

The US hegemony differs from the Dutch and British hegemonies in some important ways, however (Goldfrank, 1983). The length of US hegemony will probably be relatively short, and this may correspond with the increasing frequency of other world-system cycles which has been noted by Albert Bergesen and Ronald Schoenberg (1980:271). Thus it does not make sense to mechanically extrapolate from the earlier sequences of core rise and decline. Such an extrapolation based on the late nineteenth century would go as follows: The downswing of the Kondratieff, which began in 1873, could be compared with the period of the early 1970s. The United States would still have relative centrality but would begin worrying about its economic competitiveness and its ability to have its way in the world polity. A period of increased core competition would bring rising tariffs, increased colonial expansion, division (and redivision) of the periphery. This period would be followed by the Edwardian Indian summer, the economic upturn which began in 1895. The world economy would appear to regain stability and growth, but shifting alliances and uneven development would result in a bid for political–military hegemony by an upwardly mobile power that had not succeeded in attaining much integration into the structure of world power (Germany in 1914, perhaps a United Europe in the second decade of the twenty-first century). This extrapolation would predict the outbreak of a new world war sometime early in the twenty-first century, and a resulting reorganization of the world political structure that would allow a new hegemonic core power – not the Soviet Union but perhaps Japan – to emerge and a new period of capitalist accumulation to begin.

The apparently shortening period of world-system cycles may reveal imminent changes in the dynamics of the system which could alter the above scenario. Since the late nineteenth century the system as a whole has begun to experience certain natural and social "ceiling effects." Previously the contradictory aspects of the logic of capitalist development have led to conjunctural reorganizations of the political structure of the system through intracore war. This is what has pushed the decline of old hegemonic powers and the rise of new ones able to operate on scales more appropriate to the expanded size and intensified nature of the system. These reorganizations have allowed the capitalist accumulation process to begin again on a new basis, that is, to adapt to the problems created by its contradictory nature, and to continue expansion and intensification. In the twentieth century the ceiling effects have resulted in much deeper structural problems for the system than previously (Chase-Dunn and Rubinson, 1979). The inclusion of virtually all global territory and population into the capitalist world-economy in the late nineteenth century eliminated the possibility of expansion to previously unintegrated areas. And the formal decolonization of the periphery, even though it has not eliminated (or even reduced) the hierarchical core/periphery division of labor, has increased the costs of exploiting the periphery. This reduces the amount of surplus value from the periphery available for resolving class conflicts within core countries.

How do these ceiling effects create a situation which is different from the one faced by the Dutch or the British in similarly late phases of their hegemonies? One difference is a consequence of the increased density of political regulation of the capital accumulation process across the system. While most of this regulation is nationally controlled, and thus is more an increase in state capitalism than a change in the logic of the competitive accumulation process (Chase-Dunn, ed., 1982b), there are incipient forms of supranational economic regulation, and this provides a greater chance than ever before for the hegemonic core state to engineer a political solution to the trend toward increasingly bloody confrontation. Ulrich Pfister and Christian Suter (1987), in their excellent study of recurrent international financial crises, argue that the ability of the contemporary world debt structure to prevent (or postpone) collapse is due to the increased level of international co-ordination among banks provided by such institutions as the International Monetary Fund and the World Bank. The process of world state formation may be unlikely to realize an effective monopoly of legitimate violence in the next 40 years, but this outcome has a greater probability of occurrence than ever before. The hegemonic core state, and especially that sector of its ruling class with the greatest dispersion of investments across the globe, has the greatest interest in maintaining both the present order and the global peace (Goldfrank, 1977).

From the point of view of this cycle of core competition, where is the United States presently? The US hegemony in core production probably began in the 1920s. But it was not until after World War II that the United States actively adopted the role of hegemonic political leader. This leadership matured in the 1945–70 period of the Pax Americana. Economic hegemony began to decline from about 1950 on. In 1950 the United States produced 42 percent of world goods and services: by 1960 this had dropped to 35.8 percent and by 1970 it was 30 percent (Meyer et al., 1975: table 2).[8] The decline of the US position *vis-à-vis* other core states is convincingly demonstrated by Rupert and Rapkin (1985).

Albert Bergesen and Chintamani Sahoo (1985) show that the dominant position of US-based firms has declined relative to the position of European and Japanese firms in various world industries since the 1950s. Financial centrality did not begin to slip until 1971, although signs of unrest due to balance of payments deficits were visible earlier, as were pressures to engage in trade protection (Block, 1977).

Examining trends in their network measure of the structure of world trade of commodities at different levels of processing, Smith and White (1986) show that the core became increasingly multicentric (less hierarchical) between 1965 and 1980. This finding supports the notion that the decline of US hegemony corresponds to a more equal distribution of competitive advantage in core production.

The defeat in Vietnam is often seen as an indicator of declining US political and military centrality. Perhaps more important have been the rifts in NATO. Various attempts to regain US-led unity, such as the Trilateral Commission, have been less than successful. Reagan's effort to warm up the Cold War with the "evil empire" and to act tough with Libya, Grenada, and the Sandinistas in Nicaragua can be largely understood as an attempt to re-establish US political hegemony in a world which is becoming less economically centralized.

Thus the golden age of US hegemony has clearly passed, but the United States will remain the largest national market and the most powerful military power for some time to come. The internal operation of the process of uneven economic development (to be seen in the emergence of sunbelt cities) will prolong the US hegemony, as will the fact that US-based corporations have advantages of scale that cannot be easily matched by the firms (private or public) of other core states. And, although the United States is dependent on raw material imports due to its high level of consumption, it is less dependent than many of its competitors because of remaining internal resources. Thus we can expect the United States to maintain its economic and political centrality, but it can never recover the heights of hegemony reached during the score of years following World War II.

It would seem probable that the United States would attempt to organize a core-wide approach to the problems of a stagnating world economy because it still has the most to lose from increasing levels of core conflict. But this attempt is likely to be undermined by increasing intranational and international competition in a period of world economic stagnation (Kaldor, 1978). The relative harmony of labor and capital that has characterized US class relations since the 1950s is likely to move in a direction more similar to other core states – increased class consciousness and struggle between labor and capital.

Two trends may portend a reorganization of US politics. The US political party system has undermined class politics in a number of ways. The "winner take all" electoral system undercuts the discussion of issues, as all "serious" electoral contenders play for the middle. The major parties have been supported by crossclass alliances formed on a sectional basis stemming from the regional political history of the US dating back to the Civil War. And class-based politics have been undermined by the "diamond-shaped" distribution of income in the US, which locates the majority of families in middle-income ranges, and also, of course, by the identification of people from all classes with the "American" nation.

Crosscutting sectional differences are being evened out by the development of the sunbelt, a trend which undercuts the domination of the South by "Dixiecrats." This makes the South more similar to the North, and may reduce the regional crosscutting which has been an important reason that the major parties have resisted organization along class lines. Another factor may also increase the salience of class interests in US politics – the trend toward a "shrinking middle class" discovered in the income distribution statistics since 1978 (Rose, 1986: table 5).

These trends may well change the vocabulary of US politics toward serious consideration of working-class interests and issues of democratic control of the economy, and in this regard the US may catch up with other core states. On the other hand, recent research has shown that the US class structure has not experienced increasing proletarianization in recent years. Wright and Martin (1987) show that between 1960 and 1980 the proportion of the currently employed work force composed of non-supervisory wage-earning workers declined from 54.3 percent to 50.5 percent. Managers, supervisors, and "experts" all increased their weight in the work force. While Wright and Martin interpret most of this trend as due to the rise in the US of a "post-industrial" economy, they also contemplate a world-system explanation:

> The Marxist theory of proletarianization is a theory about the trajectory of changes in class structures in capitalism as such, not in national units of capitalism. In a period of rapid internationalization of capital, therefore, national statistics are likely to give a distorted image of transformations of capitalist class structures. If these arguments are correct, then one would expect that changes in the class structure of world capitalism would be unevenly distributed globally. In particular, there should be at least some tendency for managerial class locations to expand more rapidly in the core capitalist countries and proletarian positions to expand more rapidly in the Third World. (1987:22–3)

This continued shift toward a more core-like class structure may work against the other trends noted above with regard to possible changes in US politics. While the decline of hegemony and the increasingly unequal distribution of income may stimulate some polarization along class lines and alter the focus of politics, it is unlikely that the US will experience any sharp turn toward socialism in the near future.

Conflicting class interests over international economic policy will continue to make it difficult for the US to engineer a core-wide alliance. In the face of increasing competition for raw materials, the most likely strategy will involve the solidification of economic and political ties with some areas of the periphery. This would be the functional equivalent of an old-time colonial empire, although the terms of the alliance are likely to be less exploitative for the peripheral areas than earlier colonial empires were. For one thing, formal recolonization is impossible (although it is interesting to think about why), so trade agreements and military pacts must exhibit, at least on the surface, the formalities of a relationship between equals. Of course, the ideology of international liberalism has never prevented overt interventions in peripheral "back-yards." But we can surmise that the level of peripheral resistance is now greater, and so is the level of resistance to imperial adventures within core countries compared to earlier eras of the world-system.

The tendency for core states to solidify relations with particular peripheral areas may undercut the tendency, observed since World War II, for violent conflicts among core powers to be fought out in the periphery. The export of violent confrontation to the less powerful areas of the globe has been the rule during the period of the Pax Americana. But in a period of multicentricity, wars that break out in the periphery may more easily become world wars.

MEASURING THE HEGEMONIC SEQUENCE

Most of the studies of the hegemonic sequence have been of the type carried out above, a narrative which tends to confirm the theoretical views of the narrator. The classic example is *The Precarious Balance* by Ludwig Dehio (1962), a diplomatic history of the clashes among the great powers of Europe. Charles Doran's *The Politics of Assimilation: Hegemony and its Aftermath* (1971) is a fascinating analysis of the way in which changes in the relative power of core states affect the decisions of statesmen. Even Goldstein (1988), who does a sophisticated quantitative analysis of Kondratieff waves and cycles of war severity, simply adopts the Wallersteinian designation of the Dutch, British, and United States hegemonies, and launches a narrative when he comes to the hegemonic sequence.

There have, however, been a few studies which have attempted to measure the sequence of concentration and dispersion of power among core states. These have been carried out primarily by political scientists studying the international system, and they have employed very different ideas about what constitutes hegemonic power, as reviewed above.

It would be important, given that there are very different theoretical claims made by students of the hegemonic sequence, to compare different measures, to study the timing and the magnitude of hegemonic rise and decline, and to discover the causal interactions between economic and political–military types of power. It should be noted here that only one of the existing studies

(Thompson, 1986) has employed a measure which could be understood as even a rough proxy for the Wallersteinian notion of hegemony (see below). It is, of course, difficult to measure comparative advantages in core production and the ability to penetrate foreign markets, especially if we want to quantitatively compare our measures over long periods of time. I will contend, however, that certain measures of national economic development are good proxies for the idea of comparative advantage in core production. After all, GNP per capita is highly correlated with national labor productivity (GNP per worker), especially when we compare a large number of countries. Other measures known to crossnational researchers to be highly correlated with GNP per capita may also serve fairly well as estimates of comparative advantage in capital intensive production. It is well known that the distribution of the national product across economic sectors – especially the percentage of the total product in agriculture – is highly negatively correlated with other measures of economic development in crossnational comparisons with large numbers of countries, as is the percentage of the work force in agriculture.

I will contend that these measures of economic development can serve as rough proxies for relative core status in the Wallersteinian sense, at least until we can find the resources to unearth data more directly related to the notion of comparative advantage in core production. Some results of the analysis of the distribution of economic development measures among core countries for the nineteenth and twentieth centuries are presented below.

But first let me report what other researchers have found. George Modelski and William R. Thompson (Modelski and Thompson, 1988) have completed a monumental coding project which estimates the amount of naval power controlled by each of the great powers of Europe from 1494 to the present. In order to be categorized as a "global power" a nation must control either 10 percent of the total "capital ships" or 5 percent of the total naval expenditures of the great powers. The "world power" (hegemon in my terminology) initially possesses at least 50 percent of the naval resources available to all the global powers. In the Modelski/Thompson theory the long cycle of global power moves from one core war to the next. After a core war a "world power" theoretically controls a preponderate amount of naval power, enough to enable it to serve as the policeman of the interational system and to keep the peace. This preponderance of power, however, deteriorates over time until it is challenged by a country whose power is growing.

Because Modelski and Thompson are focusing on naval power and not land-based armies, their list of hegemons and the timing of hegemonic cycles comes out being fairly similar to the sequence posed by Wallerstein. They are focusing on the highest level of global control, which is the arena of ships of the line, capital ships, and later, aircraft carriers. The reason that the Modelski/Thompson list of hegemons is similar to that of Wallerstein is that naval power and global reach are especially important forms of control in a capitalist world-economy in which international markets and core/periphery trade are important in the determination of who wins and who loses.

There are, however, some important differences between the "long cycle" and the Wallersteinian narrative of hegemons. Modelski (1978) claims that Portugal was the first "world power." And, like many other political scientists studying the "great powers," he sees Russia as an important player beginning in the eighteenth century. The British are depicted as having enjoyed global power status in two "long cycles," one in the eighteenth century and a second in the nineteenth century, following the Napoleonic Wars. Several smaller European states, which became "developed" core countries in the nineteenth century, never make it to the list of great powers.

The Modelski/Thompson approach is similar in some respects to the "transition" theory of Organski and Kugler (1980). They argue that important core wars occur when a rising dissatisfied great power challenges the international regime (from which it has been largely excluded) by making war against a declining or stagnating formerly most-powerful state. Organski and Kugler do not formulate a world-system level hegemonic sequence, but they do see uneven rates of economic growth as the main cause of changes in the relative power among core states. As mentioned above, they operationalize this by measuring total GNP.

I have always thought of hegemony (in the sense of comparative advantage in core production) as exhibiting a wave-like pattern in which troughs are periods of relatively equal distribution of comparative advantage among core powers and peaks are the golden age of a hegemon's economic and military power. This picture is typified, following Eric Hobsbawm's (1968) *Industry and Empire*, by the rise of British productive advantage during the late eighteenth-century industrial revolution, consolidated after the victory over France in 1815, with a peak around 1860 and the beginning of a slow downturn in the 1870s.

The picture painted by Modelski and Thompson is very different. For them the peak of the cycle is right after a core war in which the new victorious global power is at the zenith of its naval advantage over contenders. Slow deterioration begins right away (in 1815 in the above example) and core war breaks out again when a new power is able to imagine defeating the old hegemon. Modelski and Thompson note that the military challenger never wins, but that the conflict results in a reorganized international power structure, usually centered on a country which was allied with the former hegemon.

Thompson's (1983a) analysis of his own data leads, however, to a modification of the above hypothesized transition model. He notes that the pattern of an increasingly powerful naval challenger is not regularly revealed in his analysis of the relative power of core states, although there is a tendency for the advantage of the hegemon to deteriorate. He posits, instead, a "two-step transition model" in which a secondary core power tries to expand regionally through land-based military adventures, and this regional war becomes a global war when the old hegemon and another allied core power perceive the regional challenge as a global challenge.[9] As Thompson puts it:

> It is most unclear, moreover, whether the primary challengers realize, at the outset, the full extent to which their regional activities will be viewed as threatening by either the 'reigning' world power or its eventual successor. How else are we to account for the repeated surprise with which the primary challengers confront the intervention of English, British and American military forces? How else are we to explain, especially in the twentieth century, war breaking out before the primary challengers have achieved the capability base that they themselves have projected as necessary for global competition? (Thompson, 1983a:112)

Before commenting more on the Thompson/Modelski project I will describe another study of the concentration of power among core states, that by Singer et al. (1979). This is one of the studies which devises what Thompson (1983b) calls an "omnibus" measure of power concentration which combines six separate indicators. The indicators used are:

> "demographic" – the number of people living in cities having population sizes larger than 20,000; and the nation's total population;
> "industrial" – total energy consumption; and total iron or steel production; and
> "military" – military expenditures and the number of persons in the armed forces (Singer, 1979:273).

It should be noted here that none of the variables used in the composite measure is an indicator of the level of development. They all combine aspects of a nation's size with its level of development. Thus simply being a large country can give a high score on any of the indicators.

The resulting scores were used to calculate a measure of the relative concentration or dispersion of power among the "great powers." This was done by summing the values of each indicator for all the nations thought to compose the circle of great powers, and then calculating the percentage of that sum held by each country, and then averaging the percentages across the six indicators to determine an individual country's final score. These country scores were then used to calculate a statistic invented by Ray and Singer (1973) to estimate the concentration of power in an international system. The resulting concentration scores are presented for five-year time points from 1820 to 1976 (Singer et al., 1979:277).

Thompson (1983b) uses the same concentration formula (the Ray–Singer index) to compare his data on naval power with the Singer (et al., 1979) measure. He calls the Singer measure the C.O.W. measure after the

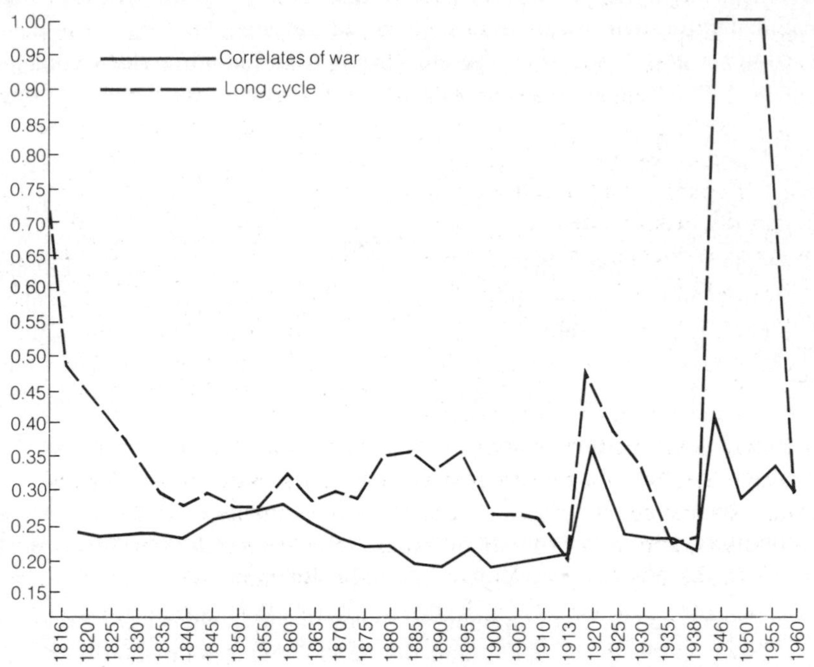

FIGURE 9.1 *Two capability concentration indexes: 1816–1960*
Source: W. P. Thompson (1983b:152)

Correlates of War Project, a usage I shall adopt. Figure 9.1 is taken from Thompson (1983b:152) and shows the relationship between the concentration index as calculated using Thompson's naval data and the C.O.W. indicator from 1816 to 1960. Inspection of this graph reveals that the concentration indices go way up during periods of core war. Thompson's index drops dramatically following the Napoleonic War, contrary to the notion of a slow deterioration, and both measures seem to rise slowly, "mounding" rather than peaking during the nineteenth century before they zoom up during World Wars I and II.

Although the above raises questions about the pattern of concentration hypothesized by Modelski and Thompson it does not really tell us much about the Wallersteinian version of hegemony. This is because none of the indicators used in the above studies examines the distribution of development among the core powers. A paper by Kugler and Organski (1986) presents data showing the relative distribution of total GNP across the circle of "great powers" from 1870 to 1980. Kugler and Organski utilize part of the C.O.W. methodology, summing the total GNP for all the countries and then calculating each country's percentage of the total. They use the results of this table to dispute the contentions of many authors who have written about hegemony. They show, for example, that Russia had a greater percentage of the total GNP among major powers in 1870 than did the United Kingdom.

The problem with this "economic" measure is that it confounds size with development. By this same measure India is a "major power" while Belgium is not. Of course, it all depends on what you mean by hegemony. Below I have begun the task of assembling some indicators which examine the distribution of core production among core states. I have recalculated the percentages in Kugler and Organski's (1986:table 1) presentation of GNPs, weighting by the population sizes of the countries. This produces a set of numbers which shows the relative GNP per capita instead of total GNP (see table 9.1). While this is by no means an ideal indicator of the concentration of core production, it ought to be a much better estimator of Wallerstein's type of hegemony than the total GNP measure employed by Kugler and Organski.[10]

Table 9.1, being a transformed version of the Kugler and Organski table, contains some countries which were not core countries in 1870, such as Japan and Russia, and does not contain other countries which were core countries by 1870, the Netherlands, Switzerland, and Belgium. While this table shows that, by the measure of GNP per capita, Britain was indeed the most developed country in 1870, it also indicates that the United States had caught up by 1880. We know that GNP per capita can be high because of the production of valuable raw materials as well as core production. Although the US had achieved a good deal of industrialization by 1880 its GNP was also raised by an agricultural sector which was bringing extremely fertile virgin soils into production. This, and the well known higher wages paid in the US, may account for part of the early high US GNP per capita.[11]

Table 9.1 also indicates that, in terms of GNP per capita, British

TABLE 9.1 *Relative distribution of Gross National Product per capita among the major powers (proportions of the sum of GNPs for all countries have been weighted by each country's population)*

	UK	*France*	*Germany*	*USA*	*Japan*	*Russia/USSR*
1870	25.2	19.1	16.8	20.2	9.1	9.6
1880	23.5	19.3	16.8	24.2	7.1	9.1
1890	26.7	19.1	16.5	23.2	6.7	7.8
1900	25.3	19.3	17.1	23.6	6.9	7.6
1913	22.5	18.5	18.0	26.4	7.4	7.1
1925	21.2	18.1	14.7	27.9	10.3	7.8
1938	21.1	14.6	18.7	23.9	11.1	10.5

Source: Adapted from Kugler and Organski (1986:10). Populations are from Banks (1971)

predominance peaked in the 1890s. This is well after the slowdown of British growth studied by Crouzet (1982: chapter 12) which ostensibly began in the 1870s. Crouzet (1982:377) shows that British growth rates between 1870 and 1913 in total output, output per head and output per man-hour were lower than in Germany, Sweden, and the US, and even France increased its output per head and output per man-hour slightly faster than Britain in this period. But the British growth rates are not significantly different from the average figures for ten European countries during this period. The depression of the 1870s was hard on all the countries, and it may be that the British relative decline did not gain real momentum until the 1890s.

Another rough proxy for the development of core production is provided by the figures on the distribution of product across economic sectors (Mitchell, 1975). Table 9.2 contains information on Britain and France as far back as 1790 showing the transformation of the structure of European and US national economies in terms of the proportions of national product in agriculture. This measure is known in recent crossnational comparisons utilizing large numbers of countries to be highly negatively correlated with GNP per capita. The industrial revolution of the eighteenth and nineteenth centuries occurred primarily in manufacturing, although we know that important productivity increases also occurred in agriculture. Nevertheless, all core countries, as table 9.2 shows, have experienced a structural change such that agriculture has become a decreasing proportion of total product. Table 9.2 shows the timing of that transformation across countries.

As we can see, the United Kingdom already had a lower proportion of product in agriculture in 1790 than did France.[12] This is probably due to the changes in structure which had already occurred as a result of the prior growth of industry in Britain. The proportion of product in agriculture decreased rapidly in Britain between 1790 and 1830, while in France it varied around 50 percent. By 1850 the French proportion began to come down, and it continued to do so slowly until 1969. The British proportion continued a rapid decline until it reached 4 percent in 1930. In 1850 Germany's proportion was 47 percent, comparable to that of France, while Britain's had already dropped to 21 percent.

In 1860 we have data for Italy, Sweden, and Norway, as well as Germany. The German transformation had slowly begun. Italy was still predominantly agricultural and did not begin to change until 1890. Norway and Sweden were already less agricultural in 1860 than the other countries, except Britain. Sweden did not change much until the 1890s, while Norway was steadily being transformed from 1860 on. In 1870 we have data for Denmark and the United States. Denmark was still very agricultural, although it begins its transformation immediately. The US had only 21 percent of its product in agriculture in 1870. Only Britain was more industrialized, with 15 percent. The early catching up to Britain by the US is further supported by Gilpin's

TABLE 9.2 *Percentage of national product in agriculture*

	Britain	*France*	*Germany*	*Italy*	*Sweden*	*Norway*	*Denmark*	*USA*	*USSR*	*Netherlands*	*Belgium*
c.1790	40	49									
c.1810	36	51									
c.1820	26	48									
c.1830	24	51									
c.1850	21	45	47								
c.1860	18	45	45	57	38	34					
c.1870	15	43	39	57	39	33	48	21			
c.1880	11	41	36	57	37	–	44	16			
c.1890	9	37	32	51	32	27	35	17			
c.1900	7	7	30	51	28	22	29	17			
c.1910	–	35	25	42	25	23	30	17			
c.1920	6	–	–	48	22	–	23	15			
c.1930	4	–	18	31	13	17	19	9	39		
c.1940	4	22	15	30	12	12	17	9	29	11	
c.1950	6	15	10[a]	32	11	14	20	6	25	13	9
c.1960	4	9	6[a]	15	8	10	14	5	20	11	7
c.1969	3	6	4[a]	11	4	6	9	4	19	7	5

[a]West Germany only

Sources: Mitchell, 1975:799, table K2. For US, *Historical Statistics of the United States*, volume 1, p. 238

(1975:89, table 7) calculation of the percentage distribution of the world's manufacturing production, and also by Thompson's (1986) study of the concentration of lead industries (see below). On the other hand Maddison (1982: table C5) indicates that 50 percent of the US work force was still in agriculture in 1870.

I have examined the relative concentration of several specific types of economic production and other indicators (Chase-Dunn, 1976). Several of these indicators were presented by Eric Hobsbawm in *Industry and Empire* (1968: diagrams 23–25c). Hobsbawm calculated his figures in terms of ratios, the percentage of various things such as world trade, industrial output, coal production, pig iron production, steel production and cotton consumption which occurred in, or were attributable to, Britain. When these concentrations are calculated in this ratio form two things are striking. Except for pig iron production and the percentage of world trade which is British trade, all the indicators of British economic hegemony decline from the time of earliest measurement, usually around 1800. I submit that this does not mean that the peak of British economic hegemony was before 1800, but rather that the way in which the indicator has been calculated makes it very difficult for British advantage to increase. This is because, for most of the indicators, the British were the first producers. For example, we may wish to examine the changing distribution of railway lines. Since the British developed the first steam-driven railway, the ratio of British advantage to the other core powers starts at infinity. The British have one and the other powers have zero. It is difficult to go up from there. For this reason I have constructed an alternate measure which examines *difference scores* rather than ratio scores. Thus, with a difference score the first instance is a value of one instead of infinity.

When we examine the same distributions utilizing difference scores we indeed find peaks during the nineteenth century, or more usually "mounds." The British advantage over the sum of French, German, and US quantities generally rises to some point between 1870 and 1890 and then declines. For example, installed railway line per kilometer of land area peaks around 1870. Crude steel output peaks in 1890. Raw cotton consumption peaks twice, once in 1880 and again in 1890. Pig iron production peaks in about 1880. Coal output peaks in about 1885. National income per capita peaks between 1890 and 1900, but then rises again between 1910 and 1913. Foreign trade does not really peak in the nineteenth century but rather rises and continues to rise, as Hobsbawm (1968:diagram 26) shows, until about 1930. Similarly, steam engine power peaks in 1880 and then rises even higher after 1890.

Two things can be inferred from the above. The generalization about an overall peaking of British hegemony in the 1870s must be considered a sort of average. When we look at particular sectors or particular types of production the peaks come at different times. And in some respects the British hegemony continued on into the twentieth century. This was especially true in terms of

British centrality in international trade. The US did not begin to be the hegemon with respect to international trade until the 1930s.

A study which focuses on leading industries as the measure of economic advantage in the hegemonic sequence has been presented by Thompson (1986). He uses Rostow's (1978) description of leading sectors in national development to construct a list and periodization of leading sectors in the development of the world economy (Thompson, 1986: table 3). He then computes national proportions for several great powers beginning in 1790 for each of the lead industries, and then averages the proportions across industries for each core country to produce a measure of the concentration/dispersion of core production in lead industries (Thompson, 1986: table 5). Thompson's results produce a rise and decline for both the United Kingdom and the United States, and he compares this measure with the Thompson/Modelski measure of the concentration of global naval and air force reach. This important empirical work is accompanied by an insightful discussion of the interaction between economic and military power in the hegemonic sequence.

Thompson's measure of leading sector concentration is undoubtedly the best effort so far to operationalize the rise and fall of economic competitive advantage in the hegemonic sequence. And, like most good empirical studies, it produces some surprises. Contrary to the description found in Hobsbawm (1968) and suggested by my analysis above, Thompson's measure shows the British hegemony peaking earlier, between 1810 and 1830, and his measure also indicates that the US hegemony peaks earlier than most analysts have supposed. According to Thompson's measure the US surpasses Britain around 1890 and the US hegemony peaks in 1920, and then again to a lesser extent in 1950 (Thompson, 1986: figure 6).

Even though his study is much better than any earlier study because of more complete data for earlier time points and a better operationalization of core productive advantage, Thompson's study still cannot be considered the final word. His choice of leading sectors and his periodization of them is controversial. One of his sectors, pig iron production, was an old industry in 1790. A better choice would have been steam engine power (Landes, 1968: 221). Also, the countries which Thompson includes in his comparison to compute a concentration index are controversial. He includes Russia, for example, from 1790. Russia may have been a "great power" in the interstate system but it was hardly a core country by any measure of economic development. Thompson leaves out other countries which were undoubtedly core areas, such as the Netherlands – long a core power; Belgium, industrializing rapidly by 1840; and Switzerland, which was quite industrialized by 1870 (see Senghaas, 1985).

Since our definitions of coreness are partly what is in dispute we need to have data on as many countries as possible as far back in time as we can get them. This will enable us to compare different methods of measuring the concentration of leading core production and produce a more certain understanding of the concentration/dispersion sequence. It will also enable us to study the causal relations between economic competitive advantage and political–military power, a matter which is central for all the theories of hegemony but which has yet only been scratched empirically. Thompson's study is an important step forward, but much more needs to be done.

The above comparison of hegemonies reveals that most features of the three cases examined fit our general description of the causes and conditions of rise and demise. But here more research which compares the successful hegemons with less successful core contenders also needs to be done. If the hegemonic sequence is indeed a structurally-based phenomenon produced by the dynamics of the larger world-system, we may wonder how the future operation of system processes will affect the rise and demise of hegemons.

The United States should be expected to maintain economic internationalism longer than other core states, just as the British refused to adopt protection long after all other core states had. It should also be the biggest proponent of core-wide cooperation because it has the most to lose from conflict. The recent international policy of the United States has been decidedly ambivalent. At the same time that the Trilateral Commission has continued to proclaim intracore cooperation and free trade, the Reagan administration has increased military expenditures and there are growing pressures for protectionism. Most of the moves toward industrial revitalization have taken the weak form of "lemon socialism," bailing out a few large firms that could not continue without government subsidies. The structural contradictions within hegemonic core powers outlined above make moves in either policy direction ineffective. This is not to declare that US decline is *inevitable*, but it does imply that, given the tendencies of the larger world-system, a real reversal is extremely unlikely.

The main conclusions of part II on states, the interstate system, and the hegemonic sequence are summarized on pages 7 to 9 of the introduction. Part III focuses more closely on the core/periphery hierarchy, and chapter 13 discusses possible causal connections between world-system cycles, including the hegemonic sequence, and periodic changes in the structure of core/periphery relationships.

PART III

Zones of the World-system

The following four chapters examine the notion that one of the most important structures of the modern world-system is the core/periphery hierarchy, a socially structured spatial system of power/dependence relations.

In chapter 10 we discuss how related terminologies have been employed by other scholars and consider various possible analytic definitions of the core/periphery hierarchy. I propose a definition of the semiperiphery and a usage of the imagery of zones which avoid the search for empirical boundaries among categories. The nested nature of the core/periphery hierarchy is considered, as are the reorganizations which have been characterized as several "new international divisions of labor." The problem of the homogeneity of the periphery is discussed, and research is reviewed which reveals consequential differences among peripheral areas depending on the type of indigenous society which was present before incorporation into the Europe-centered world-system. The idea that the form of incorporation varied with changes in the organizational nature of the core at the time of incorporation is also discussed. Then we review efforts which have been made to measure the position of countries in the core/periphery hierarchy, the problems involved, and some proposed solutions.

In chapter 11 the question of the function of the core/periphery hierarchy for the reproduction of capitalism is confronted. Have colonialism and imperialism been necessary aspects of capitalism in the core, or have these been only unfortunate by-products resulting from misunderstandings or vestigial atavism? Was primitive accumulation simply a stage by which capitalism was brought to the periphery, or has it been a form of primary accumulation which was and is necessary to the reproduction of capitalism in the core? Rather than solving this problem by definition, an explanation based on the importance of peripheral exploitation in reproducing capitalist class relations in the core and the multicentric interstate system is proposed. Various mechanisms which are alleged to reproduce the core/periphery hierarchy are reviewed, as is the crossnational research which examines the effects of those mechanisms on national development.

In chapter 12 we examine recent changes in social structural characteristics which have occurred in core and peripheral countries. Such phenomena as dependent industrialization, overurbanization, and the burgeoning urban informal sector are considered. Then we review the evidence regarding trends in the magnitude of core/periphery inequalities. Has there been an absolute immiseration of the periphery, as some authors claim, or have both core and periphery developed, but at different rates, resulting in a growing relative gap?

Chapter 13 examines hypotheses which link cycles in the whole world-system with cyclical changes in the core/periphery relationship. The Kondratieff wave, waves of core war severity, and the hegemonic sequence are discussed in connection with alleged oscillations in the core/periphery structure such as alternate tightening and loosening of regional trade networks, periods of trade protection versus periods of relatively more free world market exchange, waves of colonial expansion, waves of capital exports from the core to the periphery, and cyclical international financial crises which are triggered by defaults on peripheral debts.

10

Core and Periphery

This chapter discusses the analytic meaning of core and periphery. These conceptual categories are unpacked into their underlying dimensions, and the controversy over different usages is discussed. The notion of the semiperiphery is also defined, and the nested quality of the core/periphery hierarchy is considered. The problem of boundaries between the core, peripheral, and semiperipheral zones is described, and various approaches to operationalizing the core/periphery relationship are reviewed. Then we shall consider the problem of peripheralization as a process, and discuss literature which considers the incorporation of different local modes of production into the capitalist world-economy. Recent research by economic historians disputing the importance of exploitation of the periphery for core industrialization is critiqued. And we review the literature about reorganization of the form of the core/periphery relationship which has been characterized as the "new international division of labor."

TERMINOLOGIES

Regional differences have long been of interest to sociologists, anthropologists, geographers, political scientists, and economists. The relationship between "civilization" and "barbarism" is perhaps the oldest form of the comparison of developed and less developed regions. The modernization theorists utilized the distinction between modernity and tradition to compare societies thought to be at different levels of development.

It has been discovered that the so-called developed and undeveloped regions are often in interaction with one another, and that this interaction often importantly alters the structures of both partners (e.g. Lattimore, 1940). The idea of regional hierarchy has been applied to the contemporary international system by dependency theorists who discuss dominance and dependency, by political scientists who study the interactions between the countries of the "North" and those of the "South" (e.g. Doran et al., eds, 1983), and by Marxists who study imperialist countries and exploited ones. Authors such as Raul Prebisch (1949), Johan Galtung (1971), and Samir Amin (1974) have employed the terms "center" and "periphery," while Andre Gunder Frank (1969) originally spoke of the "metropole" and "satellites." Various other terms, such as great powers, rich and poor countries, First World, Second World, Third World, and Fourth World, have been used.

The terms I shall employ have been proposed by Immanuel Wallerstein. These will be defined below, but here I will simply list the words. We speak of a hegemonic core power, other core powers, and second-tier core powers. We speak of semiperipheral countries, including those which have moved down from the core and those which are moving up from the periphery. We speak of peripheral areas, of extreme peripheries and of external arenas – those areas outside the boundaries of the world-system. Core is preferred to center because it suggests an area rather than a point. Periphery means a large category, not just an outside edge. The scheme refers to a socially structured stratification system which is spatially differentiated because of the territorial forms taken by important organizations, especially states. As implied by the above, vertical mobility is possible within this structure of inequality, although the overall hierarchy is understood to be reproduced by several processes which operate in the world-system. These processes are examined in chapter 11. Here we will focus on the nature of the spatial inequality which is produced by a capitalist world-economy.

CORE AND PERIPHERY IN GENERAL

The contemporary world-economy is not the only world-system which has had a core/periphery hierarchy. Indeed, Kasja Ekholm and Jonathan Friedman (1982) have argued that all world-systems, past and present, have core/periphery hierarchies and are based on a similar general "capital imperialist" mode of production. They point out that all world-systems seem to go through periods of concentration and dispersion of power and wealth, to experience uneven development, and to exhibit the domination and exploitation of peripheral areas by core areas. Much of the literature about the evolution of states and empires supports the notion that core/periphery systems have been important dimensions of organization in the ancient world-systems (e.g. Rowlands et al., eds, 1987). It is typical for a core area to extract surplus product from peripheral areas. It seems likely however, that there have been important qualitative differences in the ways in which these core/periphery hierarchies have been organized. One interesting difference between the modern world-system and most precapitalist world-systems is the relative degree of inequality within core and peripheral societies. Core countries in the modern system have relatively less inequality, while in precapitalist systems the core societies tended to be more stratified. I have recently outlined the beginning of a comparison of core/periphery hierarchies in different types of world-systems which seeks to determine their similarities and systematic differences, but this work is only at the stage of a prospectus (Chase-Dunn, 1986). Here we will define core and periphery in a way which is specific to our contemporary world-system, although a more general definition will be needed for the comparative study of different types of world-systems.

CORE AND PERIPHERY IN A CAPITALIST WORLD-SYSTEM

The analytic question which must be discussed is the essential nature of the core/periphery hierarchy in a world-system in which capitalism is the dominant mode of production. It is relatively easy to compile a list of social structural features which distinguish core areas from peripheral ones. Thus, core states are internally and externally strong, contain relatively integrated nations, and have articulated national economies in which production is relatively capital intensive and wages are relatively high. Core states have relatively less internal economic and political inequality than do peripheral states.

These generalizations are true but they do not tell us what the essential quality of the core/periphery hierarchy is. Of course it may be that there is no single, most important, underlying dimension. Nevertheless, some authors have specifically postulated a central analytic definition of coreness and peripherality, and it would be theoretically valuable to have a clearly specified definition. Here we shall discuss the various previous formulations and present a new synthesis.

In general the core/periphery hierarchy is a structure of domination and exploitation, of course. As in all class-based socio-economic systems, surplus product – the material product of direct producers beyond that which is required to reproduce those producers – is appropriated by a class of non-producers. But how is this appropriation organized and accomplished in the modern world-system?

It is easiest to begin with the ways in which it is not accomplished. First, as argued in chapter 5, it is not organized primarily through normative mechanisms. This is not to say that these have no importance but, in comparison with political coercion and market exchange, normative mechanisms of control and appropriation play only a supportive role. Secondly, political coercion, though still important, is much less central to the appropriation process than in earlier world-empires and world-economies in which various forms of the tributary modes of production were dominant. Taxation is certainly important as the source of resources for states, but taxation and tribute are not the most central forms of appropriation in the modern world-system.

I disagree with those who focus on political–military power as the main dimension of the "North/South" relationship. Political coercion is more directly operant in peripheral areas than it is in core areas, and political coercion (including the rule of law and police forces within nation states and the use and threat of military force in relations between states) certainly plays an important role in maintaining the power relations which are necessary conditions for the operation of capitalist commodity production. But, in comparison with historically previous world-systems, this world-system is much less reliant on direct political–military coercion, and more reliant on economic exploitation which is organized through the production and sale of commodities. The problem becomes: how can we analytically define the typical mix of political coercion and economic remuneration which allows core areas to dominate and exploit peripheral areas in the contemporary world-system? And once we have defined coreness and peripherality, how can we measure this dimension?

Several problems emerge from a review of the definitions and discussions we find in the literature on core/periphery relations. One concerns the units or actors which are the nodes of core/periphery relationships. Another is, of course, the nature of the relational qualities alleged to be central. And another is the hypothetical shape of the distribution of core and peripheral activities.

Many authors have claimed or implied that the main economic dimension of the core/periphery hierarchy is the division of labor between industrial production of processed goods versus the extractive production of raw materials or agricultural commodities. Several important pieces of research have been done which examine differences in the "level of processing" of commodities. These often imply that the level of processing distinction is the main dimension of the core/periphery hierarchy. This argument stems from a 1945 study by Albert Hirschman (1963) which examined the effects of the level of processing of exports and imports on national economic power. Hirschman, and later Galtung (1971), reasoned that a national economy which produces mainly highly processed goods will have a higher rate of growth because of more integrated forward and backward linkages within the constellation of economic activities in the national economy, and thus greater spinoffs and multiplier effects caused by new investment. Regional economies in which primarily extractive raw materials or agricultural products are produced are likely to be less internally differentiated, less internally linked, and thus new investments are unlikely to stimulate much local growth.

Another argument in support of the level of processing contends that it is easier to apply innovations and new technology to the industrial sector than to the raw materials and/or agricultural sector because the industrial sector is less dependent on "natural" factors, and is thus more amenable to reorganization. Stephen Bunker (1984) contends that extractive economies export large amounts of environmentally derived energy, and thus rapidly deplete the local ecosystem, which in turn tends to undermine the possibility for more diversified economic activities. These negative effects of extractive activities can (in theory and sometimes in practice) be overcome by large investments to guard or reconstruct the local ecosystem, but the owners of extractive enterprises are unlikely to make such preservationist investments. Thus extractive activities tend to prevent the development of core-type diversified industrial activities in the same region.

The Braudel Center scholars have a somewhat different approach. Wallerstein defines core activities and peripheral activities as distinct characteristics of nodes on commodity chains. As described in chapter 1, commodity chains are tree-shaped interconnections between processes of production, distribution, and consumption, which often cross state boundaries. Each final product may be analyzed in terms of materials, labor, sustenance of labor, transportation, intermediate processing, final processing, and final consumption. Wallerstein argues that nodes or loci of activity along these commodity chains can be distinguished in terms of the returns they receive. Core activities receive disproportionately high returns, while peripheral activities receive low returns. And this distinction is conceived as dichotomous, so that each activity is *either core or peripheral*. A core area is one in which a relatively high proportion of economic activities are core activities, and vice versa for a peripheral area. A semiperipheral area is defined as a region containing a relatively equal mix of core and peripheral activities.

Giovanni Arrighi and Jessica Drangel (1986) have made a valuable effort to clarify the analytic definition of core and peripheral activities. They agree with Wallerstein that the core activity/peripheral activity distinction should be conceived as dichotomous, but they disagree with Wallerstein's tendency to equate core activity with capital intensive (machine) production. Wallerstein and other theorists (e.g. Chase-Dunn and Rubinson, 1977) have criticized the notion (discussed above) that equates the core/periphery dimension with a division of labor between processed manufactures and the production of raw materials or agricultural commodities – the level of processing. Both raw material and agricultural production may be carried out as core production if capital intensive technology is combined with skilled, well paid labor, it is argued. Thus the distinction between core agriculture and peripheral agriculture, and also core industry and peripheral industry, is made possible, with the underlying differences having to do with the level of profits and wages, and these are assumed to be associated with the relative degree of capital intensity.

While Arrighi and Drangel (1986) agree that it is a mistake to simply identify core activity with the level of processing, they also question the identification of core activity with relatively capital intensive production. Rather they define core activity as that economic activity (not necessarily production) which receives relatively high returns regardless of what the substantive nature of the activity is. Arrighi and Drangel adopt a Schumpeterian definition of core activity based on entrepreneurial innovation. Schumpeter (1939) argued that the driving force behind capitalist accumulation is the ability of organizational entrepreneurs to develop new activities which enable them to capture a large share of the returns to economic activity. This may occur in the realm of product development and production, but it may also occur in financial or commercial activities. Arrighi and Drangel argue that core activity consists in the ability of some actors to capture relatively greater returns by protecting themselves to some extent from the forces of competition. Peripheral activity, on the other hand, is exposed to strong competition and thus the level of returns (profit, rent, and wages) is low.

The Arrighi and Drangel definition is provocative, and it bears similarities with other recent work on the nature of core capitalism. Braudel (1984) focuses on *haute finance*, a combination of finance and commercial capital aided by state-abetted monopolies, as the essence of core capitalism. This similarly differentiates coreness from any particular type of production. We are also reminded of Raymond Vernon's (1966) notion of the product cycle in which core innovators create new products which they are able to sell for high prices (technological rents) until the products are copied by other producers who cut the price and utilize cheaper inputs, thereby shifting production of the product toward the competitive (peripheral) sector. Also Arrighi and Drangel's discussion is reminiscent of the distinction made by James O'Conner (1973) between the monopoly sector and the competitive sector, and the related distinction between the primary labor market and the secondary labor market employed in labor market segmentation theories.

While these approaches may seem to be similar on the surface, they differ in terms of the underlying mechanisms by which differential returns are generated. The product cycle idea implies that research and development costs for developing new products are recouped through technological rents – the ability of an innovator to receive a high price for a new product. There is no exploitation here. Those capable of creating new products for which potential markets exist receive a fair profit on their research and development investments. On the other hand, monopolized or oligopolized industries may receive an exploitative return because of their ability to control prices, thus resulting in "surplus profits." It is implied that protection from competitive forces is not due so much to innovation as to the ability of firms to gain political protection from states, or because of the prohibitively high cost of entry into the production of goods which have attained high capital intensity and great returns to the scale of production.

CORE PRODUCTION

I will define core activity as a certain kind of production, the production of relatively capital intensive commodities (core commodities) which employ relatively skilled, relatively highly paid labor. This is a relational idea because the level of capital intensity which constitutes core production during a specific period is defined as relative to the average level of capital intensity in the world-system as a whole. Since average capital intensity is a rising trend, forms of production which once were core production may become peripheral production at a later time.

Capital intensity involves the utilization of techniques which facilitate high productivity per labor hour. Thus a large component of capital intensive production is the utilization of machinery, or capital goods, in the production process. Capital intensity is similar to Marx's idea of the organic composition of capital – the ratio of capital to labor which is employed in the production process. It is also closely related to the idea of labor productivity, although both capital-intensity and the speed and skill of human effort are involved in labor productivity. Capital intensity and the usage of skilled labor are usually combined, at least when we consider the overall production process. It may not take skilled labor to operate the machines, but it takes skilled labor to build them and to keep them running.

A core area is an area in which relatively capital intensive production is concentrated. Capital intensive production is often in the manufacturing or industrial sector of a national economy, but it may also be in the service sector, the agricultural sector or other sectors. The definition of core production is not restricted to "industry" even though this is often the most capital-intensive sector. Agriculture in core areas is usually also capital intensive relative to agriculture in other zones of the world-system, and the same is true of services.

It makes no sense to me to dichotomize the distinction between core and peripheral production. Dichotomization creates the false problem of where to place the cutting point. Rather the core/periphery dimension is a continuous variable between *constellations of economic activities* which vary in terms of their average relative levels of capital intensity versus labor intensity.

What is the unit which can be designated as engaging in core or peripheral activities? Wallerstein uses the term "node" to designate the locus of core or peripheral activity on a commodity chain. This term is intentionally vague because all of the more specific designations have problems. One possibility is the firm, the unit of capital, the organization which appropriates profit. But some firms are transnational and combine both core and peripheral types of production. And some important aspects of core production, such as relatively dense forward and backward linkages, may not be characteristics of single core firms. Cities are a possibility because they are also loci of accumulation, and they can have the crossfirm characteristics often associated with core production. But not all regions have cities, and some aspects of relations among cities are important to the core/periphery distinction.

A third possibility is the nation state. The trouble with focusing on a national economy, defined as a juridical unit, is that the real economic networks often do not follow state boundaries. Indeed, in the sense of completely self-contained economic systems, there are no national economies in the world-system. But regions and nation states do differ in terms of their relative levels of economic integration, as pointed out by dependency theorists and Marxist scholars such as Amin and de Janvry. Amin (1974) and de Janvry (1981) define core capitalism as self-reproducing, relatively integrated, capitalist accumulation, whereas peripheral capitalism is understood as a disarticulated regional economy which is highly dependent on imports from, and exports to, the core. It is worthwhile to remember that core states are also dependent on the existence of the larger world-economy, but it is important to recognize the very different extent and nature of this dependence.

The differential integration of regions and nation states has long been, and remains, an important feature of the core/periphery hierarchy, and this aspect of the hierarchy requires that we focus on regions rather than the activities of individual firms in defining core and peripheral formations.

The unit of coreness or peripherality will be the "region" then. This is still vague but it is clearly not the firm, nor the nation state. Cities, but also systems of cities and rural areas, can be regions of relatively capital intensive or labor intensive production.

Arrighi and Drangel dispute the identification of core activities with capital intensive production because industrial production is becoming an activity which is located in the semiperiphery and the periphery, and they also point out that "non-productive" activities are often more profitable and yield higher salaries than activities which are directly associated with industrial production.

Arrighi and Drangel (1986:54) show that the average proportion of the work force in the industrial sector has diminished in core countries while it has risen in semiperipheral and peripheral countries. Industrialization has certainly occurred in the semiperiphery and much of the periphery, but I contend that this has not diminished the level of inequality between core and periphery in terms of the capital intensity of production. The proportion of the work force employed in the industrial sector in core countries has gone down precisely because capital intensity has risen. Robot manufacturing does not require a large work force in the factory. Because capital intensity has continued to rise in the core during the industrialization of the semiperiphery the overall distribution has not much changed. If the distribution of capital intensity were to become more equal there would also be a decentralization of economic power which would threaten the operation of capitalism.

As for the Arrighi and Drangel observation that capital intensive production does not always yield the highest returns, this is true, but again it is necessary to examine economic constellations of activities. Speculators on the stock exchange may enjoy the highest rate of profit, and this activity may increase in a period of uneven development in the core and stagnating growth throughout the world-system, because money-capital cannot find profitable productive investments in a world in which productive capacity greatly exceeds effective demand. But this should not lead us to the conclusion that these "innovative entrepreneurs" have succeeded in moving on to a new form of accumulation which will be successful in the long (or even medium) run. Rather this form of speculative activity is more a sign of world-level crisis than a new form of core accumulation (see chapter 4).

On the other hand, it must be admitted that the association between capital intensity and the level of returns is not exact. Successful accumulation may or may not lead to a diversified, relatively capital intensive regional economy. The rise and fall of peripheral boomtowns and extractive enclaves are evidence of this. Successful development of a core economy involves all sorts of investments which are not immediately profitable, as well as the sort of political regulation and state policy which facilitates long-term development rather than simply short-term accumulation. The fact that Arrighi and Drangel (1986:44) claim that Libya has moved into the core (based on their use of GNP per capita as a measure of core status) reveals the weakness of their identification of core activity with short-run returns based on any kind of activity. Libya sits on a fortune in oil but, by any other measure besides GNP per capita, Libya is clearly not a core state. This brings us to the next problem, that of operationalizing the core/periphery distinction. But before we review the studies which have been done and the controversies over measurement let us consider the problem of the core/periphery hierarchy as a nested multilevel structure.

NESTING

The core/periphery hierarchy is a system-wide dimension of structured inequality, but at the same time it is also a regionally nested hierarchy. The states of the interstate system are obviously important units in this hierarchy, but states are not internally homogenous. As suggested by Galtung's terms, "the periphery of the center" and "the center of the periphery," there are important regional inequalities within countries. Many of the processes of uneven development which we study at the level of the world-system also occur within countries (Hechter, 1975; N. Smith, 1984) and these are not only analogous processes. They are often historically linked with one another.

In the US the Civil War transformed the South from a peripheral area of the Atlantic economy into an internal periphery of a rising core state. And recently the sunbelt has become a new center of core capitalist accumulation which is helping to sustain the declining hegemony of the US (Feagin, 1985). Appalachia has long been a subsistence refuge region, parts of which became specialized in extractive peripheral production. The urban hierarchies which characterize national city systems are another manifestation of regional stratification within countries, as is the urban/rural dimension.

In addition, the world-system is nested into international regions as well as regions within countries. An analysis of the world-system hierarchy must not ignore the nested forms of inequality which occur in continental subregions. The discussion of subimperialism (e.g. Marini, 1972) suggests that regional powers, such as Brazil in South America or Nigeria in Africa, sometimes play the role of the core *vis-à-vis* contiguous peripheral countries.

Another nested hierarchy is the world city system. This includes national urban networks, the great world cities of hegemonic core states (Amsterdam, London, New York), the important core cities within other core countries, and the metropolises of the peripheral countries, which are often primate within their national urban networks (Chase-Dunn, 1985a; D. Meyer, 1986). Thus nesting occurs at several levels and it is this set of shifting network boundaries, often at odds with one another, which constitutes the institutional terrain on which competition takes place in the world-system.[1] On the other hand, the nested quality of the core/periphery relationship is not transitive. John W. Meyer once quipped that "everybody is somebody's periphery." Even with substantial nesting the multilevel core/periphery structure forms a highly stratified hierarchy of dominance and dependence. Evidence regarding the magnitude of this inequality is discussed in chapter 12.

THE SEMIPERIPHERY

The idea of the semiperiphery is one of the most fruitful concepts introduced by Immanuel Wallerstein. It has been widely used but there are important disagreements about definitions and some scholars have criticized Wallerstein for vagueness and contradictory usage (see Lange, 1985). The suggestions I have made above regarding the core/periphery hierarchy imply a re-examination of the semiperiphery concept.

Wallerstein employs two elements in his definition of the semiperiphery – the dichotomy between core and peripheral activities, and the notion that a state boundary encompasses an approximately equal balance of both core and peripheral activities. Thus, by this definition, there are no semiperipheral activities as such. Rather there are semiperipheral states which contain a balance of both core and peripheral activities.

Wallerstein also argues that the existence of semiperipheral states acts to depolarize the core/periphery hierarchy by providing intermediate actors whose very presence reduces the salience of potential conflict along the core/periphery dimension of inequality. He has also discussed the opportunities for upward mobility of semiperipheral states during the stagnation phase of the Kondratieff cycle (Wallerstein, 1979a: chapter 5).

Since I have reconceptualized core and peripheral activities as a continuum of relatively capital intensive/labor intensive forms of production, it is hypothetically possible, according to my usage, for a semiperipheral area to contain a uniformly intermediate level of production with respect to the core/periphery continuum. The semiperiphery idea is an important one because it enables us to focus on how the existence of intermediate regions affects core/periphery dynamics in the world-system as a whole. It also encourages us to examine the ways in which intermediate actors have different strategies, and intermediate states have different developmental possibilities – different in the sense of systematically differentiated from either typical core or typical peripheral regions. Wallerstein does not claim that the semiperiphery is a homogenous zone or set of states. Rather he contends that being in a semiperipheral location *vis-à-vis* the core/periphery hierarchy is a condition which encourages certain kinds of behavior.

The idea of semiperipheral states containing a balance of both core and peripheral activities is useful because this condition is likely to produce contradictory economic and political interests within the boundaries of a single state. Wallerstein argues that this was an important reason why France was unable to make a more effective bid for hegemony in the seventeenth and eighteenth centuries. Though France was definitely a core power, the effort to hold together a vast territory with conflicting regional interests reduced the resources available for competition with England for hegemony, and produced an ambivalent and vacillating international economic policy.

The notion of a mix of core and peripheral activities is useful, but there is another type of semiperiphery, that which contains activities which are predominantly intermediate in terms of the relative level of capital intensity/labor intensity. This does not have exactly the same consequences as the mixed form. Wallerstein's usage sometimes suggests that some kinds of class relations are intermediate in form, and thus indicate semiperipherality. In his discussion of the semiperipheral Christian Mediterranean of the long sixteenth century Wallerstein (1979a: chapter 2) contends that share-cropping was a form of rural class relations which was intermediate between the yeoman agriculture of core areas and the serfdom and slavery of peripheral areas. This idea of an intermediate form of labor control is similar in some ways to my notion of intermediate levels on the capital intensity/labor intensity continuum. This suggests that there are indeed some activities which are usefully conceptualized as semiperipheral, and that the prevalence of these activities in a region or state can constitute a semiperipheral area.[2]

I am arguing that there are two analytic kinds of semiperipheries: Type one covers those states in which there is a balanced mix of core and peripheral activities, and type two covers those areas or states in which there is a predominance of activities which are at intermediate levels with regard to the current world-system distribution of capital intensive/labor intensive production.

Obviously much is left out in terms of the kind of specification we will need in order to operationalize these definitions of the semiperiphery. For now I wish to look at the implications of the above for our expectations about semiperipheral behavior.

I have argued in previous chapters (and will elaborate in chapters that follow) that the core/periphery hierarchy supports the reproduction of capitalist accumulation by depolarizing class conflict within core states, and also within those peripheral states in which the state has come under the control of politicians who are willing to use anti-imperial rhetoric to smooth over domestic conflicts. This general argument also applies to competition within ruling classes. We expect more national solidarity among different groups of capitalists in the core, and anti-imperial rhetoric may have an integrating effect on different types of peripheral capitalists within peripheral states.

These harmonizing effects of the core/periphery hierarchy on intraclass and interclass relations are less likely to operate in the semiperiphery. The harmonizing effects work differently on different groups. Among core capitalists national solidarity is easier to achieve because there are more opportunities to go around, and thus competition is less intense. For core workers wages are higher, working conditions are better, and core capitalists are more likely to make economic and political concessions to workers precisely because they are less pressed by competitive forces.

These generalizations apply only *grosso modo*. Within individual core countries, depending upon the heritage of institutional forms left over from past struggles, the current state of the world-economy, and the future prospects of the national economy, these effects may vary considerably. The same holds for the following generalizations about peripheral and semiperipheral states. It is also important to know the particular trajectory of an area in trying to understand its political and economic behavior. Downwardly mobile countries are likely to be quite different from upwardly mobile ones even though they might be at the same level in the core/periphery hierarchy.

Peripheries in which the state is substantially controlled by core powers or dependent on core-based transnational corporations experience heightened levels of competition among contending groups of peripheral capitalists, and exacerbated class conflicts, though these may be largely invisible most of the time because of externally supported repression. These conditions explain the high levels of political instability and likelihood of authoritarian regimes, as well as the internal weakness of the peripheral states. When peripheral politicians come to state power who are willing to employ anti-imperial rhetoric this reduces these domestic conflicts somewhat, depending on the degree of implementation of anti-imperial policies. Peripheral states that implement radical anti-imperial policies reduce the level of domestic class conflicts, but they face the grave peril of intervention by an offended core power.

In semiperipheral states the effects of the core/periphery hierarchy are different. Both types of semiperipheral states defined above may have opportunities for upward mobility in the core/periphery hierarchy, and this will affect national politics and state policy. Type one, a balance of core and peripheral activities, will experience political conflict over state policy because of the conflicting regional interests. Type two, a relatively uniform but intermediate level of semiperipheral activities, will be much less likely to experience conflict among different kinds of capitalists. Type two may, however, experience exacerbated class conflicts because workers in intermediate industries may be able to organize nationally because of the similarity of their working conditions, and they are unlikely to enjoy good wages or social benefits, at least compared to core workers.

Class conflict in type one semiperipheries may also break out, especially during periods of state crisis, but there are likely to be problems of solidarity between the workers in the core sector and the workers in the peripheral sector. We can note the similarity here between Wallerstein's definition of semiperipheral states (type one above) and Trotsky's notion of combined and uneven development, which he employed masterfully in his history of the Russian Revolution (Trotsky, 1932: chapter 1).[3]

The most important thing about semiperipheries is that interesting political movements are more likely to emerge in them. Movements of both the right and the left have often found fertile ground in semiperipheral and second-tier core states (Goldfrank, 1978). The basis of this political fertility stems from the contradictory location of semiperipheral areas in the larger world-system.

Semiperipherality both produces challenges to the dominant mode of production from anti-systemic movements and is fertile ground for upwardly mobile countries who achieve success within the system. All three hegemonic core powers were formerly semiperipheral areas (Chase-Dunn, 1988). One factor which may partly determine the path taken by semiperipheral areas is the relative degree and nature of internal stratification. More stratified semiperipheries are likely to produce social revolutions which challenge the logic of capitalism, while relatively less stratified and politically liberal semiperipheries can achieve the degree of class harmony necessary for upward mobility within the capitalist world-economy.

Anti-systemic movements are also likely to emerge in peripheral areas, but they are less likely to survive there because resources to resist core intervention are meager. The most important experiments with socialism have emerged in semiperipheral states, and there is reason to believe that semiperipheral areas will continue to produce powerful challenges to the capitalist mode of production in the future.

ZONAL BOUNDARIES

If the core/periphery hierarchy is really a set of discrete zones we should be able to determine the boundaries between the zones and to unambiguously know the zone in which each country or area is located. Arrighi and Drangel (1986) have discovered a fairly regular trimodal distribution of countries based on GNP per capita as a measure of position in the core/periphery hierarchy. Nemeth and Smith (1985) and Smith and White (1986) have used a network analysis of the level of processing of imports as a measure of the core/periphery structure, and this reveals a four-tier hierarchy with two distinct semiperipheries, one characterized as "strong" and one as "weak." For myself the vocabulary of zones is simply a shorthand. I don't see any advantage in spending a lot of time trying to define and empirically locate the boundaries between zones because I understand the core/periphery hierarchy as a complex continuum. Since there is upward and downward mobility in the system there must be cases of countries or areas which are in between zones, at least temporarily. For me it doesn't matter whether there are "really" three zones, four zones or twenty zones.

The vocabulary of zones is simply a useful metaphor, as is the notion of the semiperiphery. I don't think we need to reify our words to the extent that we waste time arguing over the exact boundaries of zones. There are many more important problems, such as the magnitude of inequalities, the operationalization of the core/periphery hierarchy, and the study of the relationships among different dimensions of world-system inequality, which should receive our efforts. For me the designations of second-tier core states or extreme peripheries are sometimes useful, but I would not want to try to locate subzones or claim that there are really four zones instead of three. Thomas Hall's (1986) work on the continuum of integration into the world-system similarly disputes the value of a simple dichotomy between those areas which are outside of, and those that are inside, a world-system.

A MULTIDIMENSIONAL HIERARCHY

The definition of core and periphery described above focuses on relative levels of the capital intensity of commodity production. This is an indicator of the economic basis of national power in a capitalist world-economy, but other theorists conceptualize the core/periphery hierarchy more directly in terms of power relationships among states. Thus James Petras et al. (1981) emphasize the military power of imperialist countries – their ability to use coercive force to control the behavior of other countries. We have discussed various attempts to measure the military power of core states in chapter 9. Such direct measures of military power could be utilized in the study of peripheral and semiperipheral countries. After all, most analysts agree that external state strength is an important component of the world-system hierarchy. The research which has been done on different types of economic dependency (reviewed below) demonstrates that these are often not highly correlated with one another in crossnational comparison. This implies that the core/periphery hierarchy may be *multidimensional*.

Another dimension has been studied by Singer and Small (1966; Small and Singer, 1973). They have coded a measure of international status ordering based on the exchange of diplomats among countries. What is needed is a long run empirical, crossnational study of the relationships among the different political, military, and economic types of power/dependence relations to determine how these dimensions interact with one another. Such a study might not solve the question of the best way to analytically define the core/periphery hierarchy, but it would be very helpful in further research on the causes and effects of a country's position in the hierarchy.

MEASURING WORLD-SYSTEM POSITION

Now let us turn to the problem of quantitatively measuring the position of areas in the core/periphery hierarchy. Students of the world-system are by no means agreed upon what units ought to be compared. Most empirical studies examine nation states or colonies, employing political boundaries to designate the units of analysis. This is problematic because these boundaries are themselves a creation of the system we are studying and they also have effects on the processes which we want to study. The reality we want to study is a multilevel, multidimensional, nested hierarchy composed of individuals, households, communities, cities, classes, unions, parties, firms, ethnic groups, states, international regions, zones, and the emergent characteristics of the whole world-system. However, the goal of science is to simplify a complex reality in a way which helps explain patterns and predict outcomes. Thus there is no point in making a map which is as complicated as the territory. We can simplify our analysis as long as we take into account the problems of inference which may result from our simplifications.

Arrighi and Drangel (1986) argue that their conceptualization of the core/periphery hierarchy can be adequately operationalized by using GNP per capita. This same indicator could be used for my conceptualization of core production as relatively capital intensive production. A better indicator of my concept would be the amount of product divided by the number of hours worked, because capital intensity is very nearly the same as labor productivity. But a fair proxy for the above is GNP per capita because, when we consider a large number of countries, there is a high correlation between the number of hours worked and the size of the population. A better proxy would be the ratio of GNP to the size of the active work force.

GNP per capita is also a relatively feasible measure for studies of world-system position because it is available for a large number of countries over fairly long time periods.[4] And, since we know that a number of other indicators are highly correlated with GNP per capita in cross-national comparison in recent decades, we might use those measures as proxies for GNP per capita (and thus world-system position) back into the nineteenth century or perhaps further. I have in mind the level of urbanization, the proportion of the work force in agriculture, and energy consumption per capita. The proportion of the national product in agriculture was used in this way in table 9.2.

It is somewhat ironic that the very measure which is most often used by modernizationists as an indicator of national "development" – GNP per capita – is also arguably an indicator of world-system position. And both schools of thought would have similar reservations. Kuwait's (or Libya's) GNP per capita is not due to its success in core production but rather to its small population combined with gigantic oil resources. Possession of a gold mine is not a good indicator of either economic development or world-system position. But again, though there are exceptions, in most cases high GNP per capita designates high productivity per labor hour due to the employment of capital intensive production techniques.

At the other end of the spectrum there are also problems. Non-marketed production is difficult to value. Dudley Seers (1983) tells enough horror stories from his days as a development economist in Africa to scare any user of GNP figures from peripheral countries. But when we compare large numbers of countries in order to group them into broad categories the problems associated with the valuation of garden produce are considerably reduced.

A better measure which successfully weeds out the extractive enclave booms is based on the idea of the level of processing. Some fairly sophisticated measures using information on world trade have been analyzed, as discussed below. While these are fairly highly correlated with GNP per capita when we compare all countries, they do not lead to the erroneous conclusion that Libya is a core state.

To my knowledge very little has been done to construct a quantitative measure of world-system position for countries and colonies in the nineteenth century. For more recent time periods we have much better data, of course, and recent research has attempted to operationalize world-system position as well as specific kinds of dominance/dependence relations. Because GNP per capita has long been thought of as a measure of economic development, most analyses of crossnational data have not employed it as a measure of overall world-system position. Rather several studies have examined specific types of international dependence. The first crossnational comparative analysis of penetration of peripheral countries by direct foreign investment was performed by Albert Szymanski (1971) in his doctoral dissertation at Columbia University. This type of dependence has now been extensively studied and its effects on national development are rather well understood (Bornschier and Chase-Dunn, 1985). These effects are reviewed in chapter 11.

International economic dependence stemming from asymmetrical trading patterns was first measured by Hirschman in his *National Power and the Structure of Foreign Trade* (1980) first published in 1945. Since then, the comparative study of trade dependence has developed into an extensive literature. Various sorts of debt dependence have also been studied, beginning with the work of Keith Griffin (1969).

The above studies, and many others, operationalized international dependence as variable attributes of each country, usually derived by determining the extent of some international connection and weighting it by some measure of national size. David Snyder and Edward Kick (1979) applied network analysis to international relations in order to develop a block model measure of world-system position. They used a dichotomous form of cluster analysis to determine the structural similarities among groups of countries based on four international interaction matrices. The four matrices they analyzed were the value of trade between countries; military interventions; the exchange of diplomats; and the existence of treaties.

The block-modeling technique used by Snyder and Kick wasted a lot of information for the metric measures such as trade because it reduced each cell to a zero or a one. And the interesting relationships between the economic and political dimensions were unanalyzed, as the four dimensions were combined to produce a single structure which grouped countries into categories which are positionally similar on the combined four dimensions. Nevertheless this network measure of world-system position has achieved wide usage in crossnational research, although later studies have modified it to correct apparently mistaken categorizations (e.g. Bollen, 1983).

Another network measure has been developed by Roger Nemeth and David A. Smith (1985). Using the idea that the level of processing is the key to the core/periphery hierarchy, Nemeth and Smith combine five trade matrices containing different commodity classifications of imports. The five trade categories were determined by factor analyzing the trade matrices of 53 two-digit commodity classifications. This produced clusters of commodities by empirically examining their associations in world trade patterns rather than by trying to decide ahead of time which commodities embody higher degrees of processing. This structural trade network measure produces a core, two semiperipheries, and a periphery.[5] Nemeth and Smith also show that being in the periphery, and what they call the "weak semiperiphery," is associated with relatively slower growth rates of GNP per capita, whereas being in the core or the "strong semiperiphery" is associated with higher levels of growth.

The question of the effects of different kinds of dependency relations and overall world-system position will be discussed in the following chapter. Here I want to point out that the measurement of world-system position has been carried out only for very recent times, and even for these there remains considerable controversy about how the core/periphery hierarchy ought to best be operationalized. We still know little about the interactions among different forms of economic and political dependency, but we do know that dominance/dependence relations in the world-system are empirically multidimensional. This is clear from the fact that many of the measures of different types of dependency are not highly correlated with one another in crossnational comparisons. Thus a peripheral country may be dependent in one respect but not in others. Also we do not have a good understanding of the interaction among different types of dependency and overall world-system position.

THE PROCESS OF PERIPHERALIZATION

Conceptualizing the spread of the European world-economy to the whole globe has raised a number of thorny theoretical issues as well as many difficult empirical ones. Amin (1980a) argues that we should not assume that the periphery which resulted from the incorporation of external arenas into the European-centered capitalist world-system is a uniform zone, and Eric Wolf (1982) has demonstrated this clearly. There were a number of important determinants of the particular local and regional social structures which were created in the process of peripheralization, most important of which was the nature of the existing social structure before the Europeans arrived.

The globe was already covered with world-systems of various kinds when the Europeans began their expansion. The nature of the indigenous social systems, their abilities to militarily resist, their susceptibilities to the trade goods (and diseases) offered by the Europeans, and their possession of things valued by the Europeans, all affected the nature and timing of incorporation. The most developed and powerful civilizations were able to hold the Europeans at bay longer, despite the strong attraction which their wealth exercised on the Europeans. And regions with very little wealth were not early incorporated because the Europeans were not interested, unless some strategic or transportation utility existed in a particular location. Because of the fact that European core powers were competing among themselves some areas were formally colonized simply to prevent competing powers from having them, a phenomenon which has been called "anticipatory colonialism."

The continuing importance of the pre-conquest social structures is indicated by the recent comparative research of Gerhard Lenski and Patrick Nolan (1984; also Nolan and Lenski, 1985). They show that countries which had a technological heritage of horticultural (digging-stick) methods of production in agriculture continue to show lower levels of development in the 1960s and 1970s than countries which had a heritage of more technologically advanced agriculture, employing the plow, animal energy, and irrigation. They also contrast, within the category of agrarian (more technologically advanced) societies those which have made the transition from horticulture to plow agriculture more recently and those which made that transition long ago. Interestingly, they show evidence in support of a version of the hypothesis of the "advantages of backwardness" by demonstrating that the growth rates and levels of development of the group of countries that have more recently developed plow agriculture are higher than those agrarian countries which developed it long ago (Nolan and Lenski, 1985). Although other factors probably account for some of the differences found by Lenski and Nolan, their findings support the contention that features of the pre-integration social structures continue to have relevance for contemporary development patterns.

Others have pointed out that the nature of peripheral social structures is also affected by the timing and particular circumstances of incorporation. It is held by some that the stage of capitalism which exists in the core at the time of incorporation has important effects on the kind of colonial structure which is created in the periphery. While my analysis of the stages of capitalism as cycles and trends of world-system development (chapter 3) would describe changes in the core somewhat differently, I would not dispute that the particular organizational forms which existed in a period, as well as the peculiarities of the conquering power and its situation *vis-à-vis* competing core powers, have had important consequences for the kind of peripheral social structures which emerged. These, as well as the original differences among indigenous social structures and the particular role performed by indigenous groups have recently been demonstrated by Hall's (1989) excellent study of the incorporation of the Southwestern United States into the capitalist world-economy.

Another matter which should be kept in mind when thinking about the periphery as a whole, and variations within it, is the question of ebb and flow of influence from the core. In chapter 13 we shall discuss waves of colonial expansion and the export of capital from the core to the periphery. It should also be noted that both the nature and intensity of core influence over peripheral areas vary over time. This is seen in the sequence of peripheral cash crop booms; the rise and fall of particular kinds of extractive economies; and the emergence, during periods of low interest by core powers, of more autonomous social and economic structures in the periphery. Andre Gunder Frank's (1979b) study of the transformation of agriculture in colonial Mexico (New Spain) from 1521 to 1630 shows how market forces generated by the expansion of silver mining linked many farmers and livestock raisers into the commodity chains connected to the European core. When the silver in an area ran out, these cash crop producers reverted to the hacienda economy, a largely self-sufficient rural system containing many of the social attributes of feudalism. The argument about whether or not the resulting peripheral social structure is "capitalist" needs to take account of the ebb and flow of core penetration of the periphery.

The assertion that the core/periphery hierarchy is an important structural feature of the world-system certainly does not imply that the core determines everything that happens in the periphery or that peripheralized peoples are inert objects of exploitation and domination. As with class structures, the core/periphery structure is a dynamic tension of domination and resistance. This has been demonstrated by a number of studies, especially by anthropologists, who have sought to understand the linkages between local and world-system processes and the methods by which peripheralized peoples resist core domination.[6]

The above points are important to keep in mind when we are doing a case study of a particular situation of peripheralization. I would, however, contend that despite the results of Lenski and Nolan cited above, it is likely that the secular strengthening of world-system level economic and political processes has resulted in an increasing homogenization of the periphery – a kind of convergence in which original differences have tended to be reduced. I realize that there seem to be contemporary forces, such as cultural nationalism and dependent industrialization, which might further differentiate the periphery. Nevertheless, the extent of commodification and the high level reached by the trend toward the globalization of production by transnational firms increasingly subject peripheral areas to forces which homogenize their social structures along the lines of peripheral capitalism. This also includes the consequences of the efforts of peripheral peoples to resist core exploitation and domination. While these resistance efforts may differ from one another in terms of the particular cultural forms they adopt, their organizational forms are becoming morphologically similar, and the overall relative homogeneity of social structures in peripheral areas is increasing.

THE NECESSITY OF IMPERIALISM

I have already claimed that the core/periphery hierarchy was and is a necessary feature of the world-system which allows the capitalist mode of production to adjust to its own contradictions. A number of contrary interpretations have been presented elsewhere. Some Marxists (e.g. Albert Szymanski (1981) and David Harvey (1982)), have argued that capitalist imperialism (the export of capital to peripheral areas, the extraction of raw materials, and the penetration of new markets) is simply an alternative which exists for core capital, but is not necessary to the reproduction and expansion of capitalist social relations. This supposes the possible existence of a world in which the core/periphery hierarchy has disappeared and yet capitalism remains the dominant mode of production.

Others (e.g. Chirot, 1977) have claimed that imperialism was simply a mistake. The European states allegedly conquered and subdued the periphery, not because it was profitable, but because they were suffering from a false ideology – the belief that colonialism would be profitable and the contagion produced by the knowledge that other powers were doing it. It was a kind of self-fulfilling prophecy. Some activists in the periphery apparently shared this delusion. We can recall the Irish revolutionary who, in 1916, declared that Ireland should be free of English rule so that she might become a sovereign nation "with colonies of her own."

My argument, discussed in greater depth in the following chapter, is that exploitation of the periphery by the core made an important and necessary contribution to capitalist accumulation in the core in earlier centuries and that peripheral exploitation continues to be important because of its effects on politics within and among core countries. Briefly, exploitation of the periphery, and the threat of capital flight to the periphery, has acted to prevent labor unions and socialist parties within core countries from successfully challenging core capital. Thus the core areas of the world-system remain dominated by capitalists. Socialist revolutions have happened, not in the core as Marx predicted, but rather in the semiperiphery and the periphery. The problems they have encountered with economic and political development in the context of a world-system still dominated by capitalism have further bolstered the political and ideological hegemony of capital. The implication here is that a future decrease in the magnitude of core/periphery inequalities will reduce the political dampening effects on class politics within the core, and make transformation of the world-system toward socialism more likely.

But let us return to the question of the importance of the core/periphery hierarchy for capitalist economic development. There are two recent studies published by economic historians, Patrick O'Brien (1982) and Paul Bairoch (1986), which dispute the importance of European colonialism for the industrialization of Europe in the nineteenth century. Essentially these authors claim that European colonialism before 1800 was not economically important for the development of industrial production in Europe. O'Brien contends that trade with Africa, Asia, and Latin America constituted only a small proportion of economic production in Europe, and a small proportion of international trade as well. He also claims that the items imported from the periphery were not important to European economic development, consisting mainly of luxury goods and bullion. And he argues that the profits made on investments in peripheral trade and production were not abnormally high once the risk factor is taken into account, and that these profits did not play a very large role in the capital formation which spurred the industrial revolution. O'Brien also disputes the claim that the core/periphery trade was important in the diversification of core production in Western Europe, although he does not deny the adverse impact that colonization had on peripheral areas. He claims that the imports of gold and silver bullion from Latin America did not have significant growth-producing effects in Europe.

Bairoch (1986) takes the similar position that colonialism was not an important stimulus to European economic development before 1800. He argues that Europe did not become dependent on colonial energy and raw materials until after the industrial revolution. In addition to agreeing with many of the above points made by O'Brien, Bairoch shows that the colonies held by the European powers did not contain a numerically large population compared to the population of Europe before 1880.[7] Bairoch contends that prior to industrialization, European colonization was "traditional colonization" in which there were only small differences between the level of living of the colonizers and the colonized. Bairoch correctly points out, as we have noted above, that core/periphery hierarchies were found in many pre-industrial empires, but he contends that these societies were limited in their ability to exploit peripheral areas by "the military and economic constraints . . . which put a certain limit to the extent of an imperial system" (Bairoch, 1986:195).

The arguments of Bairoch and O'Brien can be disputed on several grounds. O'Brien uses world-system concepts in order to frame his argument but both he and Bairoch make several errors in their use of statistical categories, at least if their evidence is supposed to be relevant to world-system hypotheses. O'Brien's discussion of the small percentage of international trade composed of exchanges between Europe and the continents of Asia, Africa and Latin America, and his characterization of the items exchanged as unimportant for core development, ignore the sizeable Baltic trade,[8] and the role of closer peripheries such as Wales and Ireland. For Wallerstein an important chunk of the periphery of the early European world-economy was Poland, a region which was importing manufactured goods from Western Europe and exporting grain. Polish grain exports definitely contributed to the diversification and growing capital intensity of Dutch and English agriculture in the seventeenth century, as lands and labor in the core were freed from the production of wheat. Dutch trade with Sweden and its Baltic dependencies played a similar role.

Bairoch claims that "traditional" colonialism, a type which allegedly included European colonialism before 1800, did not involve significant core exploitation of the periphery, and did not result in very large differences in the level of living between core and peripheral areas. And he intentionally ignores city states such as Venice in his comparison of levels of living despite Braudel's (1984) focus on these as the core areas of the European world-economy. Bairoch's argument that "traditional" colonialism was unimportant for core development contradicts the claims of Ekholm and Friedman (1982) who find core/periphery exploitation playing a central role in the uneven development which occurred in the first state-based world-system, that in Sumer in the third millenium BC. The process of empire-formation carried out by the Assyrians, the Persians, and the Romans is thought by almost all historians of antiquity to have involved significant degrees of core/periphery exploitation.

Bairoch's claim that the magnitude of inequalities resulting from "traditional" colonialism was small may be due to comparing the wrong units. Lenski and Lenski (1982) claim that the agrarian empires were the most unequal social systems that have ever existed. But even if it were true that core/periphery inequalities were quantitatively smaller in the ancient world-systems, it does not follow that they were therefore unimportant in the process of the rise and fall of empires. We know, for example, that urbanization was at a very low level in "traditional" societies compared to industrial ones, but it was certainly significant that cities were built at all. Lumping all the "traditional" societies together in a heap is not something we have come to expect from historians. The geometric rates of change and the gross inequalities we see in the modern world-system should not prevent us from seeing the importance of quantitatively smaller but nonetheless significant differences among the precapitalist world-systems.

Bairoch looks only at the colonies of European states, ignoring most of the non-colonial dependencies such as Poland. O'Brien does not limit himself to colonies, but still excludes the Baltic and closer peripheries from his consideration of core/periphery relations. Bairoch and O'Brien continue to paint with broad strokes when they approach the core. Bairoch includes Europe as a whole, including Russia! Thus his figures showing the relationship between the populations of Europe and European colonies (see note 7) are quite mistaken if we are interested in core/periphery relations. He might at least have limited himself to those European powers which held overseas colonies. Instead he includes peripheral Poland along with semiperipheral Italy and Russia, as well as Greece (part of the Ottoman Empire which according to Wallerstein was an external arena until the nineteenth century) in the category of "Europe."

O'Brien points out that his statistics indicating the small importance of core/periphery trade contain some deviant cases, small countries like Portugal, the Netherlands, and England! The Netherlands and England were not just small countries, at least in the world-system perspective. They were hegemonic core powers specializing in the production of core commodities for sale to the world market and exercising global naval power in support of this strategy of accumulation through trade. What differentiated the European world-economy from earlier world-systems was that this kind of accumulation was dominant *in the core area.* Earlier systems had seen interstitial semiperipheral powers, such as the Phoenicians and Venice, play such a role, but the Dutch Republic was the first capitalist state to be hegemonic in a core/periphery system.

Both Bairoch and O'Brien seem to believe that the industrial revolution which began in Britain in the latter half of the eighteenth century was the first industrial revolution and the most important watershed between modern and traditional society. They ignore earlier periods of institutional change and economic growth such as the spread and deepening of commodity production across Europe, and the concentration of competitive core production in Holland in the seventeenth century. They also ignore important differences among the European states, some of which continued to pursue largely continental military expansion, while others were following the path of commodity production for the world market.

Both O'Brien and Bairoch claim that the tropical foods imported from colonies by the core were not important for core development. This might be disputed on two grounds. First, the provision of low-cost food for mass consumption lowered the cost of labor within core countries. Lowering the cost of living to workers made it possible (in theory), for wages to be lowered without killing off the work force. On the other hand, evidence indicates that average wages went up in the core. Tropical food imports contributed early on to relatively harmonious class relations within core countries. As Sidney Mintz's (1985) study of sugar consumption in England shows, sugar went from being an expensive luxury consumed only by the ruling class to an inexpensive basic staple contributing a sizeable share of the calories consumed by the working class. A similar pattern occurred with tea consumption, and these widening forms of consumption of former luxuries operated symbolically to allow core workers to acquire the symbols of wealth and to thereby "benefit" from imperialism and industrialization. The effects of this, combined with the reorganization of the international division of labor which expanded middle-class occupations in core areas, acted to sustain national class coalitions and to dampen political challenges to capital and the capitalist core states.

Bairoch admits that the small percentages which peripheral markets added to the demand for core exports "may have sizeable influence on the profitability of a particular industrial sector" (Bairoch, 1986:211). O'Brien estimates that "commerce with the periphery generated a flow of funds sufficient, or potentially available, to finance about 15 percent of gross investment expenditures undertaken during the Industrial Revolution" in England (O'Brien, 1982:7). He claims that this is not a significant amount and that Britain, and perhaps Holland also, are atypically high in this respect compared to the other Western European countries. He also claims that, though the British textile industry was significantly dependent on raw cotton imports and on export markets in the periphery, this industry was not crucial to the overall growth of industrialization in Europe.

Many of these facts could be easily reinterpreted to support the importance of the periphery for core industrialization. Fifteen percent of capital formation is not a small share. And, as argued above, Holland and Britain are not simply deviant cases, nor are they unimportant ones. Also most economic historians give the cotton textile industry a much more central importance in the transformation to the factory system and urban industrial production which occurred in the nineteenth century (e.g. Braudel, 1984:571–4; Crouzet, 1982: chapter 7). Bairoch and O'Brien ignore a number of the finer distinctions made by the world-system perspective, and they allow the geometric rates of change which occurred in the later nineteenth century to overwhelm the importance of smaller, but still significant, developments which occurred earlier in the history of the European world-economy. These factors contribute to their mistaken conclusion that the periphery played no role in the development of the core.

REORGANIZATIONS OF THE CORE/PERIPHERY HIERARCHY

The overall core/periphery hierarchy is a socially structured system of economic and political–military inequality. The forms which this hierarchy has taken have changed while the hierarchy itself has been preserved. The first forays which began the peripheralization process in many areas involved pillage and plunder by the European powers.[9] Marx described this "primitive accumulation" thus:

> The discovery of gold and silver in America, the extirpation, enslavement and entombment in mines of the aboriginal population, the beginning of the conquest and looting of the East Indies, the turning of Africa into a warren for the commercial hunting of black-skins, signalized the rosy dawn of the era of capitalist production. (Marx, 1967a:751)

This direct use of coercive force has moved slowly in the direction of institutionalized economic power based on law and private property, although the element of coercion in core/periphery relations and within the periphery is still greater than within the core. Slavery and serfdom have been largely abolished in the periphery. And other forms of obviously coercive labor control, such as contract labor, indentured servitude, debt peonage, village tribute workers (*mita*), etc. have declined. Other groups have increased: "semi-proletarians" living in village enclaves and working for wages seasonally or "temporarily" during their most productive years, rural proletarians, share-croppers, and formally free peasants owning their own small plots but forced to sell their cash crops to monopolies or state marketing boards (Paige, 1975:13). So has the "formal sector" of proletarians working in large firms, often protected in some way by state regulations guaranteeing minimum wages, etc. But this has been accompanied by a burgeoning informal sector of unprotected wage earners, often working for small firms in the "competitive" sector (Portes, 1981).

The categories of free labor and coerced labor do not fully capture the kinds of labor control which occur in the core/periphery hierarchy. Rather, core labor is "protected" to a greater extent by state regulation and welfare institutions, although this seems less evident during the current period of attack on the wages of workers in both the core and the periphery. It is nonetheless still the case that core labor is more protected than peripheral labor. The uneven process of state-formation and economic development allows core workers access to the strongest states and the most profitable and capital intensive sectors in the world-system. The process of proletarianization has occurred in both the core and the periphery, with a lag in the periphery. And with the additional feature that proletarians in the core can gain not only "free" status but also a certain amount of political protection *vis-à-vis* capital and *vis-à-vis* competition from other workers.

It must also be noted that colonialism, the direct organization of formal political–military control over peripheral areas by core states, has largely passed away. This certainly does not mean that political–military forms of power have ceased to operate in the core/periphery hierarchy. We still see "gunboat diplomacy," the overt and covert use of force, and the use of military and economic aid to friendly peripheral regimes which support the core/periphery hierarchy. But perhaps the weight of political–military versus economic-based power has shifted a bit. The growth of the transnational corporations has shifted the use of core state power toward the support of property rights in the periphery, as demonstrated by Charles Lipson's (1985) study of the development of institutions protecting foreign capital.

Several authors have suggested the importance of major reorganizations in the core/periphery division of labor. John Walton (1985) speaks of the third "new international division of labor," and a similar discussion of stages of dependency is offered by Dale Johnson (1985:22–8). The first international division of labor corresponded to what others have called "classical dependency" – the export of raw materials from the periphery to the core and the export of manufactured goods from the core to the periphery. This involved the "deindustrialization" of those peripheral areas which were producing products which were in competition with core exports. This first international division of labor evolved over a long period of time in which various rounds of cash crop booms and mining booms, visited peripheral areas unevenly, in cyclical waves, and in ebb and flow.

The second "new" international division of labor, according to Walton, began in the 1930s when some peripheral countries began the process of dependent industrialization. Backed by state policies of import substitution, national capitalists tried to capture the domestic market for manufactured goods. Similar attempts had been made in the nineteenth century by groups in Chile (Zeitlin, 1984) and Mexico (Hale, 1968) without much success, but the political transformation of the United States, Germany, and several other hitherto peripheral areas in Europe, which occurred during the nineteenth century, made possible the formation of new centers of core capitalist industrialization (Chase-Dunn, 1980; Senghaas, 1985). These instances of upward mobility into the core were not the most typical pattern, however. Most areas continued to be peripheralized. It is doubtful if many of the newly industrializing countries (NICs) will be able to accomplish more than dependent industrialization. Peter Evans's (1979) analysis of the competition and bargaining among state bureaucrats, domestic capitalists, and transnational corporations (TNCs) over shares of the Brazilian national market shows that even in countries where import substitution has been most successful the TNCs have succeeded in controlling many sectors of the domestic market.

John Walton's third new international division of labor is the globalization of production by the transnational firms. This has been revealed in worldwide sourcing and the production of industrial components in the periphery for export to the core. Volker Bornschier (1976) shows evidence that the bulk of TNC manufacturing investment in the periphery remains focused on production for the domestic market, but there has also been an expansion of transnational production in "free enterprise zones" in the periphery. This is the "new international division of labor" studied by Fröbel et al. (1980).

While these reorganizations of the core/periphery hierarchy have altered some of the organizational forms and institutional mechanisms operating in the world-system (as discussed in chapters 3 and 4) the more basic dynamics of the system have not changed. Evidence in support of this view is presented in the review of formal comparative research contained in the next chapter.

11

Reproduction of the Core/Periphery Hierarchy

This chapter examines different arguments about how the core/periphery hierarchy is reproduced as a structural feature of the capitalist world-system. It has been argued above that underdevelopment is more than simply a transitional stage on the way to core capitalism. Many students of imperialism have examined the forces which drive capitalism to expand into the periphery. The forces of expansion – opportunities for cheap raw materials, lower-cost labor, and expanded market demand – tell us why the periphery becomes exploited, but they do not tell us why the processes of underdevelopment which recreate the core/periphery hierarchy are sustained. The real question is: why is the periphery necessary for the reproduction of core capitalism, or what would happen to core capitalism if the core/periphery hierarchy were to disappear? It is unsatisfactory to simply contend that capitalism and the core/periphery hierarchy are inseparable by definition. We need to examine the question of the "necessity of imperialism" directly, and the following discussion reviews several theoretical perspectives with the purpose of answering that question.

It should be stated at the outset that many, even most, of the theories reviewed do not hold to the proposition that the existence of the periphery is a requisite for the survival of core capitalism. Rather, most theorists hold that the periphery is simply a convenient way for the core to ameliorate certain contradictions caused by its own logic, but that these contradictions have other possible solutions, and so the periphery is fortuitous (for the core), but not necessary (e.g. Harvey, 1982). I shall review the extensive recent literature by loosely combining arguments according to their main emphasis, a method which causes some difficulties because most arguments are, in fact, multivariate. Nevertheless some order of presentation is necessary. Another difficulty is the different time-orientation of the various theories reviewed. Some are focusing on processes thought to be occurring only since World War II, while others are attempting to formulate a theory which applies to the core/periphery hierarchy over a much longer period. The consideration of various explanations cannot escape arguments found in chapter 3 about stages of capitalism, and in chapter 10 about reorganizations of the form of the core/periphery hierarchy. The intent, however, is to construct an explanation which accounts for the long-run reproduction of the core/periphery hierarchy.

The consideration of the driving forces behind expansion to peripheral areas does not, by itself, explain the consequences of that expansion. Expansion to some areas, such as the United States, resulted in the extension of core capitalism, a relatively self-generating process of capitalist accumulation, while expansion to other areas produced the more usual dependent peripheral capitalism and reproduced the world-level core/periphery hierarchy. What are the systematic mechanisms which give "backwash effects" – the cumulative underdeveloping properties of international inequalities (Myrdal, 1957) – greater weight than "spread effects," the more even development of core-type capitalist accumulation across space?

In addition to a discussion of the various theoretical mechanisms which have been proposed to reproduce the periphery, I will review the corpus of crossnational research which has been done on some of these mechanisms. For various reasons that research does not provide the final word, but it does shed some light on the larger question.

A number of mechanisms have been asserted to be the mainstays of the core/periphery hierarchy. Neil Smith (1984) claims that uneven development in the capitalist mode of production stems from the basic contradiction between use value and exchange value. Arghiri Emmanuel (1972) propounds a theory of unequal exchange which is said to account for the extraction of surplus value from the periphery by the core, and several authors have elaborated upon and criticized his theory. Others (e.g. Petras et al., 1981) have suggested that it is state power which is the main support of the core/periphery hierarchy. Thus the US imperial state acting as world policeman supports the operation of the IMF, the World Bank, and other institutions of the core bourgeoisie. Others (e.g. Chase-Dunn and Rubinson, 1977) see the process of state-building in the core as less monolithic, but they nevertheless argue that core/periphery differences in state strength account for the continuing underdevelopment of the periphery. And others (e.g. Biersteker, 1978) trace the international uneven development of commodity production to the monopolies and/or political machinations of the core-based transnational corporations. Immanuel Wallerstein (1983a) argues that differences in the process of class-formation between the core and periphery, and the political consequences of those differences, account for the reproduction of international inequalities. Alain de Janvry (1981) contends that the peripheral reliance on export markets reproduces a disarticulated economic structure in the periphery, which remains necessarily dependent on the core sector for markets.

It is of course possible that all the above mechanisms operate together, varying over time in their relative importance. We have already noted in chapter 10 that the form of organization taken by the core/periphery hierarchy varies over time, and to some extent from place to place. Here I want to review some of the arguments and discuss the problem of doing research to determine which are the most important mechanisms of core/periphery inequality.

The Marxist geographer Neil Smith (1984) has recently argued that uneven development at the urban, regional, national, and international levels results from the contradictory tendencies of differentiation and equalization inherent in the process of capitalist accumulation. Smith's valiant effort to ground a theory of uneven development in Marx's accumulation model does not contain a systematic explanation for the reproduction of the core/periphery hierarchy, however. He notes that capital's need for cheap labor and cheap raw materials are contradictory to the need to expand consumption in the periphery in order to widen markets, but he does not explain why capital continues to maintain international inequality rather than using the periphery as a new locus of core-type accumulation (Smith, 1984:141). It is implied in Smith's approach that there is nothing necessary about the core/periphery hierarchy for capitalism. As he says, "the emphasis on accumulation over consumption is just that, however – an emphasis" (Smith, 1984:141). Core capital continues to reproduce international inequality simply because it is stuck in its old ways. As Smith says, "Empirically, however, and despite the dramatic industrialization that has taken hold in the 1970s in select Third World economies, a general and sustained industrialization seems unlikely. This kind of restructuring is, so far, blocked by inherited patterns of capital accumulation" (Smith, 1984:158). While I agree with Smith's prediction, the purely contingent basis he asserts for it is somewhat disappointing, especially if we are searching for a systematic explanation for the reproduction of the core/periphery hierarchy.

Arghiri Emmanuel (1972) claims that unequal exchange is the mainstay of uneven development. Unequal exchange, as Emmanuel defines it, is asserted to be a main basis of the extraction of surplus value from the periphery by the core, and to result in the underdevelopment of the periphery. I shall summarize Emmanuel's theory and the other approaches which focus on core/periphery wage differentials or differences in the processes of class formation between the core and the periphery. I shall also review arguments which focus on:

- the nature of the core/periphery division of labor between raw material producers and manufacturers (trade composition);
- state-centric explanations;
- the disarticulation of peripheral economic structures; and
- the economic and political activities of transnational firms.

Then I shall present my own synthetic explanation of core/periphery reproduction. We shall then discuss recent cross national research which is relevant to the question of core/periphery reproduction.

WAGE DIFFERENTIALS

Emmanuel's theory of unequal exchange explains how surplus value is transferred from the periphery to the core by the operation of prices in the international market. Working from Marx's theory of the organic composition of capital, Emmanuel distinguishes between two kinds of unequal exchange: that which occurs due to differences among sectors in the organic composition of capital (the ratio of capital to labor in the production process); and that which occurs due to differences among sectors in the average wages paid for equivalent kinds of work. Emmanuel defines the first type as a normal transfer across sectors with differences in the level of organic composition. It does affect core/periphery exchange because average core production has a higher organic composition (more capital per wage hour) than does peripheral production. Amin (1977) and Mandel (1975) contend that this alone is a significant component of core/ periphery exploitation which is reproduced by the monopolization of more productive technologies in the core. But for Emmanuel the most important type of unequal exchange is that which is due to wage differences returning to workers who perform similar kinds of work. He notes that core workers receive much higher wages on the average than peripheral workers even when differences in productivity due to technology are accounted for. For example, a carpenter in the United States may earn ten times more than a carpenter in Mexico despite their use of similar work technology. Amin (1980b) has calculated that there is indeed a difference in wages between core and periphery which goes well beyond the differences in productivity.

Amin summarizes his estimates for 1976 as follows:

> For industry, while productivity is about half what it is in the center, wages are only one seventh; in agriculture, while productivity is 10 percent of what it is in the center, peasants' earnings are one twentieth of the center; and in other activities productivity of close to one third of the center compares with wages of one seventh. Since ratios of productivities are uniformly less unfavorable in the periphery than the ratios of remuneration, it follows that there is superexploitation of labor in the periphery which totals as much as $300 billion and which is largely hidden in the structure of prices. (Amin, 1980b:18–19)

De Janvry and Kramer (1979) have criticized certain logical difficulties in Emmanuel's formulation of the theory of unequal exchange. They contend that the theory only holds when there is complete specialization among countries in terms of the goods produced for export, and that initial wage disparities will tend to disappear if capital and labor are mobile. Bill Gibson (1980) shows that Emmanuel's theory can be generalized to account for trade in which specialization of exports is not complete. And he analyzes a 67-sector matrix of world trade which provides evidence that there is indeed a large transfer of value from the periphery to the core as a result of wage differences beyond productivity differences.

There is substantial agreement about the importance of wage differentials between core and periphery in the exploitation which occurs at the world level. But disagreement is wide on the question of the origins and processes which reproduce this wage differential. Emmanuel argues that wages are an exogenous variable. Original differences exist because nations have different "historical and moral" heritages, and these differences are reproduced because labor is relatively constrained from migrating across national boundaries. If really free mobility of labor were allowed, migration would eventually eliminate core/periphery wage differentials. Emmanuel suggests that, for various reasons, capital is more mobile than labor, but his theory does not include a systematic analysis of the processes which reproduce the core/periphery wage differential. Other theorists do address this question but their explanations differ. We shall review these below.

In addition to the causes, there is some dispute about the consequences of unequal exchange. While it is widely agreed that it accounts for a substantial transfer of value to the core from the periphery, the estimates of the actual amount vary considerably (see Gibson, 1980). And the consequences for the relative rates of growth in peripheral countries is also in dispute. Many neoclassical economists claim that exports to the core should have positive growth effects (export-led growth), while Emmanuel and others claim that specialization in low-wage exports has a retardant effect on growth. Evidence on this is discussed in the next section.

Another explanation of underdevelopment which focuses on wage differentials between the core and the periphery is that formulated by Raul Prebisch (1949). His argument focuses on returns to rises in productivity. He claims that core workers are institutionally able to tie their wages to increases in productivity because they have strong trade unions and important access to core-state power, while in the periphery increases in productivity lead to lower prices for peripheral products and increases in unemployment (and lower wages) as workers are made redundant by more productive technology. Peripheral capitalists do not have the market power to prevent price decreases, as core capitalists often do, and peripheral workers do not have the institutional power to tie increases in productivity to wage increases. Thus the core benefits from cheaper peripheral imports, while the periphery is hurt by more expensive core products, and peripheral workers experience continuing low wages and high unemployment. While Prebisch's theory focuses on wage differences, it can be seen that the key variable is differential access to state power and strong unions. Theories which explicitly focus on that dimension are discussed below.

CLASS-FORMATION

Other theorists focus on the differential processes of class-formation between core and periphery. Immanuel Wallerstein (1983a) sees the reproduction of non-wage forms of exploitation in the periphery as the key to the reproduction of the core/periphery hierarchy. Others focus on the interaction between core domination and the economic status of women in the periphery. Claudia von Wehrlof (1984) contends that the most fundamental dimension of oppression and exploitation in the capitalist world-economy (both core and periphery) is that which exploits the unpaid labor of women and peasant "semi-proletarians." The definitional blindness which fails to calculate the labor contribution expended within households and within the peripheral non-monetized sectors to the reproduction of the world work force is seen as fundamental to the nature of the modern system, rather than as a vestigial backwater of a former mode of production. Wallerstein (1983a) argues that the systematic reproduction of non-wage forms of labor is the main mechanism which prevents the equalization of core capitalist accumulation. Other authors (e.g. Ward, 1984), working from the "women and development" perspective, contend that it is the combination of Western health technology and the kind of dependent economic development occurring in the periphery which stunts the demographic transition and worsens the economic status of women. Research on these topics is discussed below.

TRADE COMPOSITION

Several authors have argued that it is the particular form of the international division of labor which accounts for the reproduction of the core/periphery hierarchy. Johan Galtung (1971) claims that it is the "level of processing" of exports relative to imports which differentially effects rates of national growth. The classical form of the core/periphery division of labor was the export of raw materials from the periphery to the core and the export of manufactured goods from the core to the periphery. Galtung and others (e.g. Hirschman, 1963) argued that the spinoffs and multipliers associated with diversified manufacturing are greater than those associated with raw material production, and thus the core will experience faster economic growth than the periphery, and the gap will be reproduced.

Stephen Bunker (1984) characterizes extractive economies as the main element reproducing the core/periphery hierarchy. Resource depletion and changing demand account for the costly boom and bust cycles of peripheral extractive economies. Because material resources are located randomly in relation to urban agglomerations, the restriction of spinoffs and multipliers in raw materials extraction is exacerbated by the high costs of relocation of social and economic infrastructure as resources are depleted or international demand changes. Use values are lost to the region both through exports of the resources and through the disruption of the ecosystems from which they are extracted. Unequal exchange of labor is accompanied by the unequal exchange of matter and energy. The dominant classes engendered by such economies tend to invest available capital in infrastructure and organization for transport and exchange rather than in industry. Political institutions are largely adapted to control access to natural resources. Neither is geared to the protection or rational exploitation of the resources on which the economy is based. The extractive region is ecologically impoverished by a process which does not generate alternative productive economies. The core's demand for raw materials, and the peripheral social organization which extracts them, combine to reproduce the core/periphery hierarchy.

Another type of trade-based mechanism which is argued to support the core/periphery hierarchy is the ability of core areas to maintain themselves as leaders in the development of new productive technology. This gives core producers the edge in international competition with non-core producers even when there is industrialization in the periphery. The product-cycle theory elaborated by Raymond Vernon (1966) describes the concentration of research and development in core areas, where new products are introduced. The technological monopolies which enable the developers to sell new products at a high price (technological rent) are eventually diminished as other producers introduce comparable competing products. Price competition eventually moves the production of the product toward the periphery, where labor costs are cheaper. Thus it is the greater returns to firms which can develop and introduce new products, and the process by which these products diffuse through the system, which reproduce international inequalities. The division of labor between "monopoly sector" research and development and "competitive sector" production of standard products becomes the key differential within the core/periphery division of labor.

DISARTICULATION OF PERIPHERAL ECONOMIC STRUCTURES

Osvaldo Sunkel (1973) was perhaps the first from the dependency school to focus on the disintegration and disarticulation of national economic structures which is characteristic of peripheral capitalism. Criticizing the modernization school, which focused on the "bottleneck" between modern and traditional sectors, Sunkel argued that the extreme inequalities and disarticulation of peripheral economies are functionally related to the reproduction of international inequalities. Sunkel and Andre Gunder Frank (1969) contended that the important social, economic, and political linkages between the "modern" and "traditional" sectors, rather than their separateness, were responsible for reproducing the traditional sector and slowing the development of peripheral countries.

Alain de Janvry (1981) has reformulated this early emphasis on disarticulation into a well specified theory of the features of peripheral and core capitalism. Core capitalism is a self-reproducing process of capitalist accumulation which is subject to certain contradictions, in particular, the tendency to produce more commodities than can be sold given a certain level of effective demand. The tendency toward market saturation can be temporarily resolved by the development of new products, the raising of wages and consumption levels, and/or the expansion to new markets in the periphery. Core capitalism therefore contains within it a tendency to resolve economic crises by expansion of consumer demand and/or state expenditures, although these forms of adjustment are limited by the competition among core states for shares of the world market. Peripheral capitalism, on the other hand, is primarily dependent on the production of products not sold in the domestic market. Thus there is no dynamic which encourages the expansion of domestic consumption. Rather the reproduction of low levels of remuneration for most workers is sustained by a political coalition between dependent peripheral capitalists and the transnational core firms and core states who benefit from the relatively cheap exports. This encourages the reproduction of forms of semiproletarianized labor receiving extremely low wages, often below the level needed to reproduce the worker over a lifetime. These low wages are often subsidized by non-market forms of subsistence production or an urban informal sector which operates at a low price level due to the incorporation of subsistence activities and unpaid family, or mutual aid, forms of labor.

De Janvry discusses the relationship between his model of core capitalism and peripheral capitalism in terms of features of necessity and possibility. For peripheral capitalism, core capitalism is both necessary as a source of market demand and needed imports, and it provides certain opportunities for profitable business activities. For the core, on the other hand, the existence of the periphery is not necessary. Rather, its existence only provides certain opportunities, but core capitalism could proceed to reproduce itself in the absence of a sector of the world economy in which peripheral capitalism is operating. This is because the opportunities for low wage production, cheap raw materials and food, and the expansion of markets are desirable but not essential. There are also possibilities to resolve these problems within the core economy itself. Thus, for de Janvry, "Peripheral capitalism and the associated pattern of primitive accumulation is not a *sui generis* reality with its own distinct laws of motion, *but is only a phase* – however historically exceptional and prolonged – in the development of capitalism in particular areas of the world system" (de Janvry, 1981:22 emphasis added).

De Janvry outlines versions of his model of disarticulated peripheral capitalism for both the export-enclave economy and import-substitution industrializing economies. In the second, certain circuits have been internalized and there is a growing domestic market, but the process of import substitution leads to new forms of dependence on capital goods imports from the core, and the disarticulated traditional sector remains. This extension was earlier outlined by Sunkel (1973) but de Janvry describes it dynamically as a struggle between comprador capitalists allied with the core and national capitalists who politically support the development of a home market. This struggle is alleged to account for the periodic oscillations between populist and authoritarian regimes in semiperipheral countries.

TRANSNATIONAL CORPORATE EXPLOITATION

Several explanations focus on the institutions of core-based transnational private banks and production firms (TNCs) as the key organizations reproducing the core/periphery hierarchy. Most of these focus on recent decades. It is argued that dependence on foreign (core-based) equity capital and loans retards economic development in the periphery. Core corporations decapitalize peripheral countries by repatriating much more than they invest, and they act politically to reinforce peripheral regimes which support the pattern of uneven economic development which produces great intranational inequalities in the periphery. The classical form of exploitation was the production of extracted raw materials and agricultural goods for export to the core. It is obvious that such producers have no interest in raising the income of the masses in the periphery because those masses are not a significant source of demand for their products. Though many transnational firms have begun producing manufactured goods *for the domestic market* in peripheral and semiperipheral countries, these firms still support regimes which perpetuate inequalities between the poor masses and the well-off ruling groups and their relatively small coterie of middle-class subalterns. Contrary to the theories of those who suppose that the growth of transnational manufacturing in the periphery gives the foreign firms an incentive to support policies which would increase the incomes of the masses (because they now are selling within the domestic market), Bornschier and Chase-Dunn (1985: chapter 2) have argued that the continuing near-subsistence level of incomes of the great majority of peripheral peoples does not present an opportunity for expanded markets for core-based transnationals. These firms continue to provide resources to support existing inequalities because most of their products are either capital goods consumed by the state sector or other large firms or else are relatively expensive goods (e.g. consumer durables) for which the masses do not, and cannot in the foreseeable future, constitute a source of effective demand. A quantity of TNC resources concentrated on maintaining the current pattern of uneven development receives a greater return than if those resources were used to alter the regime in favor of a more even distribution of income. Increasing the income of near-subsistence households does not create demand for expensive goods, but rather leads to greater consumption of food and other basics. Thus, even though transnational corporations are producing for the domestic market, they act politically to sustain a disarticulated peripheral economic structure which leaves a large proportion of the population out of the process of development.

STATE-CENTRIC EXPLANATIONS

Several theorists claim that it is the imperial structure of political–military power among states which reproduces the core/periphery hierarchy. This argument is made explicitly by James Petras et al. (1981). Underdevelopment in the periphery and the economic exploitation of the periphery by the core are supported by the political–military power of core states. During the period of formal colonialism core states exercised direct control of peripheral areas. In the contemporary world-system it is the United States, taking upon itself the role of world policeman, that overtly and covertly supports peripheral regimes which are open to exploitation by core capital. Other core states also perform a similar role in "their own peripheral backyards," and the maintenance of the hierarchy is also backed up by international organizations such as the World Bank and the IMF, which are under core state control.[1]

A more complicated version of the statecentric approach is outlined in Chase-Dunn and Rubinson (1977). Here the process of unequal exchange is theorized as linked to differential forms of state-building, power-block formation and class struggle which occur in core and periphery. This perspective combines the statecentric approach with elements of other explanations. It poses a question which is not asked by the imperial power theorists described above: what reproduces political–military inequalities among states? We know that some states change their positions in the world political–military hierarchy. Prussia, the United States, Japan, and the Soviet Union all joined the circle of "great powers," while Portugal, Spain, and Britain have experienced declines in relative military power. But why hasn't the distribution of military power itself become less unequal? What are the processes which concentrate great military power among a few core states, even while particular states rise and fall in terms of relative power?

Richard Rubinson (1978) also examines the processes which have made it possible for some states to move up in the core/periphery hierarchy in his analysis of the political transformations which occurred in Germany and the United States in the nineteenth century. These cases represented rare instances of successful upward mobility in the world-system. The more typical countries which remained in the semiperiphery and the periphery either did not have movements of political transformation or had movements which failed in their attempts to develop the institutional bases of core capitalism (e.g. Zeitlin, 1984).[2] The theoretical propositions developed in Chase-Dunn and Rubinson (1977) describe the interaction of four processes which reproduce the core/periphery hierarchy: power-block formation, state formation, unequal exchange, and class struggle. Unequal exchange has already been discussed above. Here follows a synopsis of power-block formation, state formation, and class struggle.

POWER-BLOCK FORMATION

A power block is a coalition of classes and subgroups of classes which supports a state. Power-block formation is the process by which the interests of a political–economic coalition are institutionalized within the state apparatus. Political means are necessary to secure stable economic advantages, and thus groups of capitalists constantly attempt to convert their economic power into political power. Consequently, a struggle over state power develops among subgroups of the capitalist class within particular states. Historically, in those areas where peripheral capitalists producing primary products for export controlled the state, this type of production became prevalent and the position of indigenous manufacturing and merchant classes tended to decline. In those areas where manufacturing and commercial capitalists dominated the state, those economic interests tended to be sustained. This is because the possession of political authority is an important mechanism which reproduces the international division of labor. Once a set of economic interests becomes dominant within a state apparatus those types of production become relatively secure and resistant to challenges from capitalists with contradictory needs *vis-à-vis* state economic policy. The political victory of core producers in core states is complementary with and acts to sustain the political victory of peripheral capitalists in peripheral areas. Consequently, the economic division of labor becomes structured into a geopolitical division of labor.

During the era of the "classical" division of labor between the core and the periphery, based on manufacturing industries and raw material production, the process of power-block formation reinforced this division of labor. In the core an alliance of commercial, financial, and industrial capital favored relatively flexible state policies which allowed for the continuous development of core capitalism. Powerful and flexible coalitions supported a strong state, and conflicts over state economic policy were settled relatively amicably. In the periphery the power block was usually composed of an alliance among raw material producers who were dependent on core markets. New producers who would challenge the market shares of existing core capitalists tended to be excluded from state power in the periphery, although challenges to this happy arrangement between core and peripheral capitalists occurred often. In most peripheral countries the challengers lost and the state continued to be in the hands of peripheral capitalists tied to the current core/periphery division of labor.

This model can be adapted to the more recent period of "dependent industrialization." In many countries the above characterization is still apt, but in others the level of import-substituting industrialization has risen such that we need to take it into account in the negotiations among local capitalists, transnational capitalists, and the peripheral and semiperipheral state managers. The work of Peter Evans (1986) makes it clear that the state managers are themselves often important actors, sometimes creating constituencies in the private sector to support programs which would develop core-type production. The case of semiperipheral states is considered more generally below.

STATE-FORMATION

State-formation is the process by which states increase or decrease their strength, both in relation to their own populations and in relation to foreign actors. The processes of power-block formation and state-formation are closely related. Core areas have strong states, states in which political authority is quite extensive and stable. Peripheral areas have relatively weak states, in which political authority is less extensive and stable (remember chapter 6). A strong state has the ability to mobilize great resources whenever it needs to. State strength, in this sense, is partly a function of the extent to which the support of a country's dominant classes is institutionalized within the machinery of the state. The relationship between power-block formation and state-formation arises from the political demands and requirements of the different kinds of economic interests institutionalized within states.

Before explaining why different types of power blocks produce different types of state-formation, it is necessary to recall the importance of state action in the competitive capitalist world-economy as discussed in part II. Strong states can be effective mechanisms for protecting economic actors from the risks and uncertainties which inhere in competitive commodity production in the world market. States as violence-controlling enterprises can provide important protection rents to their capitalists, and under some conditions states can effectively intervene to support new types of production which can maintain or increase the share of world surplus value which returns to domestic capitalists (Rueschemeyer and Evans, 1985).

Because of the importance of states in the process of capitalist accumulation, all capitalists desire to utilize state power for regulating the market to their own advantage. Thus, dominant groups of capitalists attempt to institutionalize their interests within the state. But the type of state-formation is dependent on the *nature* of the power block. *The industrial–commercial–financial block in core states produces strong states, while the export-oriented block in peripheral states produces weaker states.* This difference derives from the different political requirements and demands of these types of production.

The effects of the nature of the power block on the degree of state-formation can be separated into external and internal causes. There are two external mechanisms. First, where the interests in a state are composed primarily of industrial and commercial capital, great demands are put on the state to create an aggressive foreign policy. This is because such economic production requires access to foreign markets both for raw materials and for the selling of both capital and consumption goods. Capitalists engaged in this type of production will be competing for access to such markets. One of the most effective means to compete is to employ an aggressive foreign commercial and military policy. Thus, we can expect that the demands for such policy will lead to an increase in the authority and strength of the state, as commercial and industrial capitalists support increasing its strength in order to pursue such policies. Countries in which the dominant capitalist groups are producing primary products for export will experience many fewer demands on foreign policy. Peripheral capitalists producing raw material exports are unlikely to support an extensive foreign policy because their gains are not usually affected by an aggressive state economic policy. *It is almost impossible to affect the demand for such primary goods by state action.*[3] Thus, there will be fewer vectors of economic interest pushing the state toward an aggressive foreign policy, and consequently the authority and strength of the state will be less.

The second external consideration affecting the relative strength of states arises from strong states actively attempting to weaken peripheral states. Core states employ this process because weakening peripheral states is one way to further monopolize markets and to ensure a steady supply of raw materials.

Among the *internal* reasons, strong states arise in the core because extensive political regulation is needed to foster and protect core industrial and commercial activities. For example, a highly sophisticated trade and commercial policy is required both to protect home industries and to provide the infrastructure needed for industrial production. Since production in the core is much more extensive and diversified, there will be many more political demands placed on the state, and consequently a greater degree of state-formation.

Once strong states develop, they become a central mechanism for reproducing the core/periphery division of labor. As the world market changes, and new areas of profit are created, a strong state, which has incorporated a large variety of interests into itself, is in a position both to feel the pressures for shifting political advantage to some rising new area of profit and to have the ability – because of its greater authority – to effect such a shift of political advantage to new types of production.

Political coalitions between classes and state-formation may take on distinctive forms in the semiperiphery. Because of the mix of core and peripheral activities in some semiperipheral states, different kinds of capitalists tend to have very opposing interests. Some have alliances with core powers based on their control of peripheral activities, while others favor more independent policies which would expand core-type activities. Thus it is often the case that the state apparatus itself becomes the dominant element in forming the power block and is able to shape the political coalitions among economic groups. In semiperipheral countries with potential for upward mobility, state mobilization of development has often been an important feature. Those upwardly mobile countries that rely on alliances with core powers tend to develop rightist military regimes (e.g. Brazil from 1964 to recently) while those that attempt more self-reliant development move toward the left (e.g. China and the Soviet Union). Whether leftist or rightist, upwardly mobile semiperipheral countries tend to employ more state-directed and state-mobilized development policies than do core countries.

Peripheral countries tend to have high levels of political instability and either right-wing regimes backed by core powers or left-wing anti-core regimes. But in the periphery the opportunities for real upward mobility in the system (the expansion of core activities) are much more limited, and so the class forces backing core-type development tend to be weak. Anti-imperialist movements may take state power and try to mobilize for development (e.g. Angola, Cuba, Vietnam, Mozambique, Nicaragua, etc.), but the development of core-type activities requires resources that small peripheral countries usually do not have. Internal market size, state strength, natural resources, and sufficient political will to isolate the country from core powers are necessary if such anti-imperialist mobilization is not to become either an isolationist backwater or a CIA countercoup. Those areas that escape the system but do not economically develop are soon reconquered (e.g. Haiti, Burma). However, these constraints on successful development in opposition to the system are reduced the more it becomes possible to make alliances with other, more developed, socialist states.

CLASS STRUGGLE

The fourth mechanism by which the core/periphery division of labor is reproduced is the operation of class conflict on a world scale. Classes are conventionally understood in terms of their operation within national societies, and class struggle is therefore seen as taking place primarily within countries. Objective economic classes cut across national boundaries to form a structure that can only be understood in terms of the world-system. Amin (1980b) develops this type of analysis in his discussion of the world proletariat and the world bourgeoisie.

Since the major political organizations in the world economy are nation states, class struggles tend to be oriented toward these state structures. Hence there is contradiction between the economic basis of class-formation and the political basis of class struggle. Class struggle takes the form of competition for the control of particular state structures, and this fragments objective classes and stabilizes the larger system. Proletarian internationalism has not yet been an effective unifying force even between core workers of different states, let alone between core and peripheral workers. The interstate system tends to confine class struggle within nation states. This has the effect of reproducing the core/periphery division of labor by producing class alliances that politically stabilize the global mode of production.

Exploitation takes place along two main dimensions: between capital and labor and between core and periphery. The exploitation of the periphery by the core helps core capital to co-opt core labor into a national alliance. Similarly, opposition to core exploitation sometimes produces alliances between domestic capital and labor in the periphery. In many semiperipheral areas, on the other hand, interclass alliances are more difficult because the core/periphery hierarchy presents contradictory alternatives. There are real simultaneous possibilities in some semiperipheral countries for either an alliance with core powers or a mobilization for autocentric development. The state is the key organization and its control is hotly contested between groups with widely opposed interests. This results either in authoritarian regimes that strongly suppress class struggle or in class struggles that result in leftist movements taking state power. The contradictions between capital and labor are muted in the core and sometimes in the periphery by the operation of the core/periphery contradiction, but in the semiperiphery the class struggle may be exacerbated. This is part of the explanation for the emergence of social democratic class alliances and business unionism in the core. It also partly explains why socialist movements based on the power of workers and peasants have first come to state power in the semiperiphery (Russia and China).

The coming to power of socialist movements in the periphery does not contradict the above. These have most often been anti-imperialist struggles that have taken state power on the basis of anti-core class alliances. Of course, nationalist class alliances have been important in the semiperiphery also, but the intensity of domestic class struggle involved in the creation of socialist regimes has been greater in the semiperiphery than in the periphery. The point here is not to completely explain the class basis of all states but to point out that one consequence of core/periphery exploitation is to stabilize interclass alliances in the core and in the periphery. This reinforces the interstate system and helps reproduce the core/periphery division of labor. The political function of the semiperiphery, according to Wallerstein, is to stabilize the system by concentrating deviant political forms in an intermediate position. This also tends to depolarize and stabilize the core/periphery dimension of exploitation.

A POLITICAL THEORY OF THE NECESSITY OF IMPERIALISM

Beyond the simpler question of the mechanisms which reproduce the core/periphery hierarchy in the short run is the matter of the necessity of the existence of a peripheral sector for the reproduction of capitalist social relations in the core. We have already mentioned that many Marxist scholars (e.g. Szymanski, 1981; de Janvry, 1981; Harvey, 1982) contend that the periphery, and peripheral capitalism, is simply a phase on the road to the extension of core capitalism (fully developed capitalism) throughout the globe. Peripheral areas are alleged to present opportunities for profit-making, but are not seen as necessary for core capitalism. This is the case, it is said, because though peripheral areas allow the process of capitalist accumulation in the core to adjust to its own contradictions, these contradictions can also be periodically resolved within core capitalism itself. Thus, hypothetically, the whole world could become the realm of core capitalism without creating a systemic crisis for capitalism. The great inequalities among core and peripheral countries could become reduced, and the same form of accumulation could operate in all areas.

My own position is that the core/periphery hierarchy is necessary for capitalism because of the political effects which exploitation of the periphery has in the core. These have already been alleged in the above discussion of power-block formation, state-formation and class formation. It is my contention that capitalism as a mode of production must be understood in more than economic terms, and that political processes are more than simply conjunctural and historical. Capitalism as an historical system creates opposition to itself, and this opposition must be adjusted to and accommodated. This occurs in the form of slow adjustments, but also through economic and political "crises" which restructure certain relationships, but which allow the logic of capitalism to be reproduced. Thus the rise and fall of core powers, and uneven development (which occurs both within the core, between the core and periphery, and within the periphery) operate as an adjustment process which drives capitalism to expand to an even greater spatial scale. The anti-systemic movements which try to change the logic of the mode of production are outflanked and reincorporated, and often end up providing new ways for capitalism to adjust to its own contradictions.

The role of the periphery and semiperiphery in this process of expansion, intensification, crisis, and struggle is two-fold. The exploitation of the periphery by the core provides an extra measure of surplus value which can be used by core capitalists as a source of new capital-formation, or as a reward for core workers, or as a resource for sustaining powerful core states. It can also help resolve potential conflicts among different groups of core capitalists. The availability of cheap raw materials and, especially, cheap foodstuffs in the core is a benefit to core workers as well as core capitalists. The hierarchical division of labor which concentrates cleaner, more skilled jobs in core countries creates a class structure there which is more amenable to nation-building and a strong state apparatus. In a number of different ways the class struggle within core countries is made less antagonistic because of the existence of a world periphery. This operates directly by allowing for higher wages in the core, and indirectly by supporting nationalist ideology which compares (favorably) the core nation to peripheral areas, although these factors operate differently in different core countries (see Lipset, 1977, 1981).

Uneven development occurs within the core as well as between the core and the periphery, and the class structures within core countries are not homogeneous. My theory does not suppose that all core workers have benefited from imperialism, nor that class relations within the core have always been pacific. The structure of the working class within core countries is only partly composed of the labor aristocracy of primary sector workers. These have successfully organized business unions in which wages are tied to productivity in the context of an agreement for industrial peace. But this regime has been the outcome of a long struggle in which some militant workers sought to challenge the logic of capitalism and to build the logic of socialism. The radicals lost those battles to others who sought a less antagonistic relationship with core capital in large part because of the material incentives which core capitalism could provide to the labor aristocracy of primary sector workers.

On the other hand, there is still a large proportion of workers in some core countries (especially the United States) who receive low wages within the competitive sector and the underground economy, as well as a fairly large underclass of marginalized people. The "relative harmony" of class relations within the US results not from the uniform co-optation of all workers, but from the inequalities which pit different groups of workers against one another, converting each into a "special interest group" and undermining class-wide solidarity and socialist consciousness. In other core countries with more homogenous working classes labor parties have reached a *modus vivendi* with capital based on sharing the benefits of economic development.

Uneven development within the core is also evident with the long business cycle and the changing comparative advantage in commodity production which occurs among core states. It is not the case that the core is a uniform region, or that the political structures which shape the distribution of returns are unchanging. High wages, and the "social wage" which is built into the welfare state, are not invulnerable, as is obvious in the current period of economic relocation. When competition and high wages and taxes create a profit squeeze on core capital, the regime of business unions and welfare nets is attacked by austerity policies, capital disinvestment, and capital flight – this last often to the periphery or the semiperiphery (Walton, 1981; Ross and Trachte, forthcoming). Thus exploitation of the periphery undermines socialist challenges to capitalism in the core and allows core capital to limit the wage bill in the core by threatening job blackmail, or by actually moving production to the low wage periphery.

Several authors (Amin, 1980a; Braudel, 1984:614) have argued that the positive relationship between wages and increases in productivity in the core only began operating in the middle of the nineteenth century. If this is true it might be argued that the political explanation for the necessity of the periphery is not applicable before then. The evidence for this claim is based on a study of the wages of English building craftsmen and laborers from the thirteenth century to the twentieth (Phelps-Brown and Hopkins, 1955). Braudel shows that the wages of a stone mason were *inversely* related to rises and declines in the level of consumer prices until the mid-nineteenth century, at which time the relationship became positive (see Braudel, 1984:616, figure 58). Amin has contended that working-class wages in the core were at a subsistence level until well after the industrial revolution in the core, and he argues that the core/periphery relationship changed as a result of the introduction within the core of a regime which tied the wages of certain workers to increases in productivity. Amin contends that the political explanation of the function of the periphery for the reproduction of core capitalism outlined above applies only to the period after 1850.

I would like to suggest a different interpretation which extends the political mechanism further back in time. First, the political explanation does not focus only on the wages of workers in the core. The argument also extends to the shape of the overall class structure within core states, and to relationships among different subgroups of the capitalist class within core countries. Thus, even though stone masons, and perhaps broad sections of the working class, were receiving subsistence incomes up until the middle of the nineteenth century, the shape of the class structure in core areas was less hierarchical than in peripheral areas, and the quality of the relationship among different types of capitalists was different. The size of the middle class, the opportunity for larger amounts of skilled labor, and the ability of relatively successful capitalists to ally with one another in support of a (therefore) strong state, are conditions which predate the extension of greater than subsistence wages to a sizeable portion of the core working class.

The argument that colonialism and exploitation of the periphery helps resolve conflicts among different groups of capitalists within core states is supported by several different observations which have been made about the connection between imperialism and core politics. Volker Bornschier (1988) contends that colonialism "fostered non-revolutionary political change favorable to industrialization" by dampening the conflict between older sections of the core ruling class (whose incomes had been partly based on state-guaranteed privileges) and the newly arising industrial bourgeoisie. It has been observed by others (e.g. Schumpeter, 1955) that much of the British colonial bureaucracy was staffed by the second sons of landed aristocrats. But Cain and Hopkins (1986) show that the dominant party in the British imperial bureaucracy was composed of agricultural capitalists before 1850 (so-called "gentlemanly capitalism") and that, when the old colonial system was replaced by free trade, it was the commercial and financial barons of the City of London who took over imperial policy, not the manufacturers. In any case it seems plausible that the availability of resources derived from imperial exploitation can help smooth over conflicts between emerging sectors of capital and those groups which experience a decline in their fortunes as a result of the dynamics of uneven development within the core.

We do not have data on the relative distribution of incomes in early core and peripheral areas which might be used to detect the pattern now familiar – a diamond-shaped distribution of income in the core versus a pyramid-shaped distribution in the periphery. But Braudel does provide some documentary indications that wages were often higher in core states. Of fifteenth-century Venice he says,

> But the peacefulness of the Venetian social scene is nonetheless astonishing. It is true that even the humblest toilers fortunate enough to inhabit the heart of a world-economy might pick up scraps from the capitalists' table. Was this one of the reasons for the lack of trouble? Wages in Venice were comparatively high. And whatever their level, it was never easy to reduce them. (Braudel, 1984:136)

It may be that a version of Braudel's imagery of a layered world-system (capitalism at the top, eventually extending itself downward), is useful here. Perhaps the most important effects of core exploitation of the periphery were at first on relations among capitalists themselves, creating unity and support for a strong state, and encouraging state policies in the service of successful capitalist (as opposed to tributary) accumulation. Later, as the world-system became centered on core nation states rather than core city states, the incorporation extended to a middle class of subalterns, and even later it came to include core workers as well. Braudel's discussion of the Dutch hegemony implies that both rural and urban workers received relatively high incomes. He quotes Pieter de la Court (1662) as saying:

> Our peasants are obliged to pay such high wages to their workers and farmhands that (the latter) carry off a large share of the profits and live more comfortably than their masters; the same inconvenience is experienced in the towns between artisans and their servants, who are more insupportable and less obliging than anywhere else in the world. (Braudel, 1984:179–80)

Another problem with the extension of the political explanation for the necessity of the periphery back in time is the lack of any socialist challenge to capitalism before the existence of modern working-class trade unions and parties. Eric Hobsbawm (1959) has contrasted the modern organizations of the working class with the forms of action taken by what he calls "primitive rebels." It must be agreed that socialism was not a viable alternative to capitalism before the middle of the nineteenth century for many reasons. Even if the Chartists could have succeeded in establishing a democratic form of collective rationality in England, the low level of productive technology would have placed grave limits on the ability of such a regime to survive, especially in the context of a larger world-system still dominated by capitalism. But socialist challenges were not the only challenges (then or now) to the logic of capitalism. Wallerstein points out that the possibility of a reversion to the tributary mode of production, through the establishment (by the Habsburgs) of a core-wide world-empire, was only narrowly averted in the sixteenth century.

It has been argued in part II that the capitalist mode of production is dependent on the existence of a competitive interstate system in which the core remains politically multicentric. The formation of a core-wide world state would be likely to reduce the operation of those capitalist institutions which limit and disorganize the establishment of political control over investment decisions. Of course, political control over investment decisions can be of several kinds. Many have pointed out the structural similarity between a tributary world-empire and a hypothetical socialist world government. Both establish political regulations over major investment decisions in the world economy, although presumably one would operate at the behest of a democratic majority of the world's citizens, while the other would be the instrument of a new ruling class based on some modern form of the tributary mode of production. In practice these two situations are somewhat difficult to distinguish (because, as Marx and Engels said, every new class represents its own interests as universal interests), but that is not the problem I am addressing here.

Rather I am arguing that the existence of a peripheral sector of the world-economy is a necessary sustaining structure for the reproduction of the interstate system, and thus capitalism in the core. This is the case because of the effect of core/periphery exploitation on the nationalism of core workers and core capitalists, and because the competition over exploitation of the periphery intensifies interimperialist rivalries among core states. This last effect has certainly increased, as Lenin (1965) observed, since the whole globe has been brought within the capitalist world-economy because of the necessity of redividing territories which have already been claimed by one or another core state. But this interstate competition over peripheral areas and external arenas was already strong before the capitalist world-economy had become completely global.

The attempts to transform the interstate system into a core-wide world-empire were partly motivated by competition for raw material extraction from peripheral areas, and the failure of these attempts resulted in part from the superior access to peripheral raw materials held by the hegemonic core states and their allies, which enabled them to stave off the attempts at world imperium.

Thus the existence of a core/periphery hierarchy has allowed capitalism in the core to reproduce and expand by undermining political challenges to capitalism within core states and by reinforcing the multicentric structure of the interstate system, which is itself a necessary structural basis of capitalism.

CROSSNATIONAL STUDIES OF THE EFFECTS OF DEPENDENCE

While the above arguments are not all formulated at the same level of generality, they all do have implications for the way in which the core/periphery hierarchy is reproduced. Most authors do not ask the question in terms of the maintenance of a structural feature of the world-system, but rather they argue in terms of the consequences for national development. Here we must mention a point to be discussed in more detail in chapter 15 on methods – evidence which shows that something which affects national development is not directly evidence about the world-system level. This is the aggregation problem – the ecological fallacy in reverse. It is possible that a certain mechanism causes the underdevelopment of some national economies, but not the reproduction of international inequality. This could occur if the mechanism under consideration slowed the development of some countries relative to others, but nevertheless peripheral countries were, on the average, catching up with the core. Thus, though we will review below the crossnational research which examines the effects of various mechanisms on national development, no firm conclusions about the reproduction of the core/periphery hierarchy are possible from these results. We shall consider studies which examine recent trends in the magnitude of core/periphery inequalities in the following chapter. Formal studies which directly evaluate evidence about the causes of the reproduction of the core/periphery *at the world-system level* have not yet been done, but this should not prevent us from using the less formal evidence that we have to evaluate the hypothesized mechanisms.

Here we shall review crossnational comparative research which has been done on the effects of various kinds of dependence on economic growth in the periphery. Generally, dependency theory implies that having a high level of dependence causes a relatively slower rate of economic development. There are several types of dependence which have been studied by the method of crossnational comparison:

1 dependence on foreign aid and loans;
2 dependence on foreign equity capital;
3 the composition of trade in terms of the levels of processing of exports and imports (trade composition);
4 the concentration of exports in terms of specialization in particular commodities (commodity concentration); and the concentration of trade partners, usually the percentage of exports going to the largest export partner (partner concentration).

One study has examined the effects of the export of low wage goods hypothesized as central in the unequal exchange theory.

Foreign Investment Dependence

Dependence on foreign equity capital, as measured by the extent to which a national economy contains a high proportion of capital stocks owned by foreign corporations, has been found to have a retardant effect on economic growth, and also to be associated with a relatively greater degree of national income inequality (Bornschier and Chase-Dunn, 1985). Contrary to the arguments of some theorists of dependent industrialization, this also holds true for dependence on foreign capital invested in manufacturing (Bornschier and Chase-Dunn, 1985: chapter 7). Thus both classical dependence (investment in extractive and agriculture exports) and dependent industrialization probably reproduce the core/periphery hierarchy by slowing the rate of economic development in dependent countries. Studies of the several mechanisms which have been found to mediate the retardant effects of investment dependence on development are summarized in Bornschier and Chase-Dunn (1985). Evidence indicates that decapitalization resulting from repatriation of profits by TNCs is one important mechanism accounting for the negative growth effect.

Trade Dependence

Trade dependence has several dimensions, as outlined by Rubinson and Holtzman (1981). Galtung (1971) shows that export partner concentration and commodity concentration are negatively correlated with GNP per capita, while trade composition (the export of manufactured goods and the import of raw materials) is positively correlated with GNP per capita. Thus these measures of trade dependence are distributed as expected across the core/periphery hierarchy. This result is confirmed using a more sophisticated measure of trade composition developed by Firebaugh and Bullock (1986). But the question remains about the effects of these various forms of trade dependence on economic development. Rubinson and Holtzman (1981:93) review 13 crossnational quantitative studies of the effects of these various forms of trade dependence on the growth of GNP per capita. They conclude that commodity concentration does not have systematic effects. They also conclude that trade composition positively affects economic growth. Thus exporting manufactured goods and importing raw materials, as expected by Galtung and others, has been found to be associated with higher rates of economic development.

As described in the previous chapter, Nemeth and Smith (1985) have constructed a network-based measure of the position of countries in the world-system based on the composition of imports. Their network analysis produced four tiers of the world-system: a core, a strong and a weak semiperiphery, and a periphery. Using these categories in a crossnational panel analysis to determine the effects on economic growth, Nemeth and Smith generally confirm the results of other studies of trade composition. Both the weak semiperiphery and the periphery show negative effects on the percentage growth rate of GNP per capita, but the strong semiperiphery exhibits a positive effect which is similar in size to the positive effect associated with being in the core category (Nemeth and Smith, 1985:548–53).

Bornschier and Hartlieb (1981), however, find that, when attribute measures of trade dependence are entered into a multiple regression analysis together with a measure of foreign investment dependence and other appropriate control variables, none of the trade dependence variables have significant effects on the growth of GNP per capita between 1965 and 1977 (Bornschier and Hartlieb, 1981:38). This suggests that the apparent effects of trade composition indicated in other studies may have resulted from its association with penetration by transnational firms.

Low Wage Exports and International Split Labor Markets

Kristen Williams (1985) reports the results of a crossnational study which sets out to evaluate competing explanations of international uneven development:

neoclassical economics, Emmanuel's unequal exchange theory, and Prebisch's hypothesis of unequal returns to productivity increases. Williams examines data from both core and non-core countries for five-, ten-, and fifteen-year time lags between 1960 and 1975. She examines the causes of wage increases, productivity increases, changes in the organic composition of capital, and GNP per capita growth. Her results are surprising for all of the theoretical positions examined.

She tests the hypothesis that trade with high wage countries slows the rate of GNP per capita growth for non-core countries (derived from Emmanuel's unequal exchange theory) but finds no support for it (Williams, 1985:57). Neither is Prebisch's model of the periphery supported. Increases in productivity, and/or the organic composition of capital, increase both wages and growth in the periphery, a result which Williams interprets as support for the neoclassical model. She finds a negative effect of the growth of peripheral exports on productivity and wages, and thus economic growth. This is not the unequal exchange effect predicted by Emmanuel, but neither is it consistent with the neoclassical theory of "export-led" growth. Growth in the volume of peripheral exports lowers economic growth because it lowers both productivity and wages.

Williams finds that a quite different model explains the dynamics of the core. "The neo-classical model does not seem to fit. Increases in productivity do not seem to lead to either growth in wages or economic growth . . . Instead, one of the predictions of Emmanuel's model does seem to have some empirical support. Increases in wages appear to lead to growth. In fact, wage increases seem to have the largest impact on growth" (Williams, 1985:65). She later argues that this is probably due more to the Keynesian consequence of increasing demand than to anything connected with Emmanuel's theory of trade imperialism.

Williams suggests a version of split labor market theory to account for her findings. "For the periphery, low wages encourage labor-intensive development, which has low productivity, so wages stagnate" (Williams, 1985:68). This is indirectly related to international trade, rather than directly, as Emmanuel theorized. Wage differentials between core and periphery are maintained by immigration controls and by the ability of core producers to avoid having to compete directly with peripheral producers. Specialization in the development of new high-technology products, and the product cycle which shifts these to the periphery once price competition begins to operate, is consistent with the "monopoly sector/competitive sector" imagery which finds support in Williams' research.

Debt Dependence

A growing focus on aid dependence and dependence on foreign loans has accompanied the international financial crisis which has become evident in this decade. Excellent work has been done on long cycles of international financial crises by Ulrich Pfister and Christian Suter (Pfister and Suter, 1987; Suter, 1987; Suter and Pfister, 1986). This research is reviewed in chapter 13 on cyclical changes in core/periphery relations. Excellent research has also been done on the international aid regime and its relationship to the debt crisis by Robert Wood (1986). Here I shall review the crossnational evidence on the effects of aid and debt dependence on economic development.

Crude early attempts to estimate the effect of debt dependence (e.g. Chase-Dunn, 1975:734) provided some evidence that per capita external public debt – loans to the government and government-guaranteed loans in 1965 – had a negative effect on the growth of electrical energy consumption per capita between 1965 and 1970. The estimated effect on per capita GNP growth was also negative, but not statistically significant. Debt dependence was also found to be cross-sectionally associated with higher levels of income inequality among households. The reason these findings were weak was the limited availability of data.[4]

Ulrich Pfister (1984) more conclusively demonstrates that total accumulated foreign debt is negatively correlated with GNP per capita growth between 1975 and 1981, in a group of 77 developing countries. When accumulated *debts to private banks* are studied, the negative relationship is even stronger. This relationship holds when additional control variables are used in multivariate analyses. Interestingly, Pfister finds that inclusion of a measure of penetration by transnational non-financial firms (TNCs) does not lower the estimated effect of debt dependence, but the estimated effect of investment dependence (penetration by TNCs) is much smaller than when debt dependence is not included with it in the same regression equation. This implies that either the negative effect of equity investment dependence is spurious due to its association with debt dependence or, as Pfister (1984:11) suggests, it may be that bank credits are a "mediating variable in the process of decapitalization induced by the operation of multinational corporations."

Pfister also shows that current flows of foreign aid between 1975 and 1977 have a positive effect on GNP per capita growth and these effects are largest for a subsample of 31 low income developing countries. However, accumulated debt due to foreign aid does not positively affect growth, suggesting that "returns on this kind of financial flow are in fact rather low and that they do not set the economy of the recipient country on a more rapid growth path in the long run" (Pfister, 1984:16).

Pfister also examines the processes which mediate the negative growth effect of debt to private foreign banks. He presents evidence that this effect is not due to high levels of debt service because, though high debt service is associated with high accumulated debts, it is unrelated to economic growth.

Sell and Kunitz (1986–7) find that the level of indebtedness in the 1970s is associated with slower declines of the mortality rate among a group of peripheral countries in Asia and the Americas, but that growing indebtedness was associated with higher rates of mortality decline. They argue that the slowdown in the decline of peripheral mortality rates in the seventies and eighties was not due to asymptotic effects of having already reached high life expectancies, but rather to the increasing participation of countries in the world economy under conditions which introduce new kinds of health hazards at the same time that progress against older health hazards is slowing down.

One of the statecentric approaches (that by Petras et al., 1981) focuses on the power of the hegemonic core state as a main mechanism behind the reproduction of the core/periphery hierarchy. One way this is alleged to operate is through the effects on peripheral states of military aid programs supplied by the hegemon. Hartman and Walters (1985) have examined the effects of national dependence on US military aid (from 1946 to 1973) on GDP per capita growth in 32 non-core countries. Their crossnational analysis demonstrates that US military assistance has a strong and stable positive effect on economic growth between 1960 and 1973. While this might be thought to undermine the "imperial state" thesis because military aid causes development instead of underdevelopment, Hartman and Walters note that the "success" cases were a small number of countries (Taiwan, South Korea, Turkey, and Greece) that received an enormous amount of aid as a result of their connection to the US effort to "contain communism." They note that this path to development may be difficult for other countries to repeat because "the receipt of massive amounts of US military aid is not a reliable means of achieving sustained, long-term autonomous development since it is not under the direct control of the recipient nation" (Hartman and Walters, 1985:453).

The network measures of world-system position have been used in studies which examine the causes of economic growth and other aspects of development. Snyder and Kick (1979) used their block model measure which combined four different international interaction matrices (described in the previous chapter) in a crossnational analysis to determine its effects on economic growth. Peripheral and semiperipheral locations produced by their network measure are associated with relatively slower rates of economic growth, while core countries show higher rates of growth. Kukreja and Miley (1988) have used Snyder and Kick's measure (as corrected by Bollen, 1983) to demonstrate a cross-sectional relationship with a measure of industrial diversity of national economies. They show that peripheral and semiperipheral national economies are less likely to have a complex division of labor as measured by the distribution of the work force across nine economic sectors. Nemeth and Smith's (1985) network measure, which is based on international trade matrices (see previous chapter) has also been shown to be related to different rates of economic growth. Nemeth and Smith show that their core and "strong" semiperiphery categories are associated with relatively higher rates of economic growth, while their "weak" semiperiphery and periphery categories are associated with slower economic growth.

Other Effects of Dependence

A cross-sectional analysis by Volker Bornschier and Thanh-huyen Ballmer-Cao (1979) presented comparative evidence which supports the proposition that relative income inequality among households is associated with greater degrees of penetration by transnational corporations. This has been further confirmed in recent research by Charles Ragin and York Bradshaw which analyses data over the period from 1938 to 1980. Ragin and Bradshaw (1986) show that a multiple indicator measure of economic dependency stunts economic development, depresses the rate of improvement in the physical quality of life, and increases distributional inequalities within countries. Several other studies confirm similar findings (see Bornschier and Chase-Dunn, 1985: chapter 8).

Kathryn Ward's (1984) research on the effects of investment dependence on the status of women and fertility rates illuminates another way in which the core/periphery hierarchy may be reproduced. Ward's review of the literature on women and development provides several causal propositions about the effects of international economic dependence on the position of women in developing societies and the fertility rate. She postulates that the kind of economic development which occurs in a context of high dependence on foreign investment decreases the economic opportunities of women relative to men, and also maintains the economic value of children for subsistence production. This latter obstructs fertility reduction. Dependency, she predicts, will be associated with fewer economic opportunities for women in the wage labor sector. Further, some of the potentially liberating and anti-natalist cultural influences, which might otherwise diffuse from the core to the periphery, are blocked by the consequences of underdevelopment and the inferior economic status of women.

Analyzing data from 126 countries Ward finds that her hypotheses are generally supported. Both investment dependence and trade dependence are found to have negative direct and indirect effects on women's share of the labor force and the level of women's participation in the labor force. These findings also hold when agricultural and industrial sectors are examined separately. Fertility is shown to be largely determined by economic development and family planning programs (negative effects) and by infant mortality (positive effects). Lesser but significant causes of fertility are income inequality, investment, and trade dependence (positive), and the educational and economic status of women (negative). Thus Ward's research demonstrates that certain aspects of the core/periphery hierarchy are direct and indirect causes of the population explosion in the periphery as well as perpetuation of the patriarchal oppression of women. A more recent study by Patrick Nolan (1988) finds only a weak relationship between Nemeth and Smith's (1985) network measure of trade composition and fertility, however.

Peter Evans and Michael Timberlake (1980) showed that investment dependence in peripheral countries is associated with relatively large service sector employment, and Jeffrey Kentor (1981) demonstrated that investment dependence has a positive effect on measures of urbanization and over-urbanization, and that these effects are partly mediated by the expansion of the service sector. The effect on service sector growth was confirmed by Robert Fiala (1983) for the decade of the 1950s but weaker effects were found for the 1960s. Moshe Semyonov and Noah Lewin-Epstein (1986) have shown that investment dependence expands the part of the service sector which is associated with producer services, but not consumer services.

CONCLUSIONS

What can we conclude from the crossnational studies regarding the operation of mechanisms which reproduce the core/periphery division of labor? Unfortunately, due to the aggregation problem mentioned above, the studies of national development cannot be used as conclusive evidence about which are the most important processes producing international inequalities. Even though investment dependence has been shown to be an important cause of relatively slow economic growth in peripheral countries, it does not necessarily follow that it accounts for the reproduction of international inequalities. No one has studied the relationship between changes in the level of worldwide investment dependence and changes in international inequalities over time.

The crossnational findings reviewed above, however, do provide us with our best guesses at this point about which mechanisms reproduce the core/periphery hierarchy. Equity investment dependence and debt dependence are probably more important than the various forms of trade dependence. There is little support for the hypothesis (derived from Emmanuel's theory) that low wage exports directly retard national development. These findings are based on research on the last few decades, and thus ought not to be generalized to earlier periods. In order to be more certain we need studies over longer periods of time, and studies which examine the core/periphery dimension at the world-system level rather than at the level of national development. The few studies which have been done are descriptive in the sense that they examine changes in the magnitude of core/periphery inequalities but do not examine the causes of these changes. These are reviewed in the next two chapters.

12

Recent Trends

This chapter reviews studies which have examined recent changes in the distribution of social structural features among core, peripheral, and semiperipheral countries. Research has shown that great changes in certain social structural features have occurred in peripheral countries in recent decades. As mentioned in chapter 10, several authors have claimed that the international division of labor has moved into a new stage. Industrialization has begun in many peripheral and semiperipheral countries and some formerly peripheral countries such as Korea and Taiwan have shown strong signs of moving toward core status. Other organizational trends which have increased in peripheral and semiperipheral countries in recent decades are:

- urbanization;
- the increasing population primacy of the largest cities within developing countries;
- the growth of mass education;
- the expansion of state structures;
- the rapid growth of population; and
- the shift of the structure of the work force out of agriculture toward industry and services.

All these signs of "development" (in the modernization sense) are viewed with some skepticism however, by those who notice that some kinds of development are happening much faster than others, and the overall level of inequality between core and periphery has apparently not diminished. We shall examine studies which look at the magnitude of core/periphery inequalities. But first let us review the recent organizational changes within zones of the world-system.

In chapter 6 we discussed evidence about the internal power of states which revealed that the extractive power of states *vis-à-vis* their societies is increasing in both the core and the periphery, but that core states continue to have greater extractive capacity than peripheral states (see table 6.1).

Patrick Nolan (1984) presents the mean levels of several social structural characteristics in the core, periphery, and semiperiphery for 1960 and 1970, as well as average growth rates for the countries in these zones for various periods up to 1970. His tables (Nolan, 1984:112–16) generally reveal the expected differences among core, semiperipheral and peripheral countries on measures such as the percentage of the labor force in agriculture, industry, and tertiary employment, as well as the percentage of GDP in agriculture and manufacturing. Nolan shows that peripheral and semiperipheral countries are changing in the direction of the core on all of these measures between 1960 and 1970. Using a slightly different categorization of countries into world-system zones, Michael Timberlake and James Lunday (1985) show similar changes in the country averages of national labor force structures between 1950 and 1970 (Timberlake and Lunday, 1985:334). They also use national data to examine the structure of the world work force as a whole, rather than averaging country scores (Timberlake and Lunday, 1985:335). When they break the world work force into zones the results are very similar to the analysis produced by averaging country scores.

The Timberlake and Lunday study, though it examines the same kinds of data as did Nolan (1984), points to one feature not discussed by Nolan. Timberlake and Lunday compare the percentage of the work force in the secondary (primarily manufacturing) sector with the percentage of the work force in the tertiary (primarily services) sector. They make a ratio of these two proportions with tertiary in the numerator and secondary in the denominator, and refer to this as the T/S ratio. Their table 15.1 (1985:335) shows that the T/S ratio for the core and semiperiphery varies between 1.01 and 1.25 from 1950 to 1970. But the T/S ratio for the periphery is much higher, about 1.8. This fact is discussed in terms of the notion of "overdevelopment" and the "bloated tertiary," referring to the existence of a relatively larger tertiary sector in peripheral countries. Timberlake and Lunday theorize that it is the centralized pattern of capitalist accumulation in the world-system which creates this kind of economic structure in peripheral countries. A large portion of the peripheral tertiary sector mediates the relationship between extractive and cash crop exports in exchange for secondary sector imports from the core. Though the percentage of the peripheral labor force in industry grew from 10.6 percent in 1950 to 14.3 percent in 1970, this is still a very small proportion compared to core countries, where this percentage has apparently peaked out at about 40 percent. Interestingly, the 26 countries categorized by Timberlake and Lunday as being in the semiperiphery do not show higher levels of the T/S ratio than core countries.

Timberlake and Lunday (1985:337) also examine core T/S ratios from 1850 to 1970 and peripheral T/S ratios from 1900 to 1970. They show that the average T/S ratios of the core countries rose from 0.68 in 1850 to 1.24 in 1970, demonstrating the pattern described by the literature on "post-industrial" society. Both the service sector and the secondary (industrial) sector have grown, but the service sector has grown faster and continues to grow, while the industrial sector has grown relatively slower and seems to have reached a peak. For peripheral countries data are only available beginning in 1900, but these show that the average T/S ratio for peripheral countries was already much higher in 1900 – 1.25 for peripheral versus 0.81 for core countries. By 1970 the peripheral countries had increased their average T/S ratio to 1.76, although this had not increased since 1950, when it was slightly higher at 1.79.

A similar pattern is revealed when we examine levels of urbanization across zones of the world-system. Firebaugh (1985) shows that the level of urbanization (the percentage of the population living in cities larger than 20,000 in population size) has increased in both the core and the periphery since 1920, the first year in which Firebaugh is able to compute average urbanization levels for both groups of countries. Firebaugh's (1985:295) groups include 11 Western European core countries and an unspecified number of peripheral countries. In 1920 the average urbanization level for the core was 31 percent, while in the periphery it was 7 percent. In 1940 the core had increased its level of urbanization to 36 percent while the periphery had only changed to 10 percent. By 1960 the average level of urbanization in the core countries studied by Firebaugh had reached 44 percent while the level among peripheral countries was 17 percent. Firebaugh points out that the "urbanization gap" between core and periphery increased between 1920 and 1960, but that this trend is bound to be reversed as core countries reach ceiling levels of urbanization while peripheral countries continue to urbanize.

Another feature of national urban systems is the degree of urban primacy exhibited by the city-size distribution in a country. Some national urban systems are flat in the sense that the ranked population sizes of the cities do not form a size hierarchy because the cities are of similar size. Many countries have city-size hierarchies which conform approximately to the "rank–size rule." The rank–size rule specifies a city-size distribution in which the largest city is twice as large as the second largest, three times larger than the third largest, etc. A city system has a high level of "urban primacy" when the largest city is much larger than would be the case in a rank–size distribution. It has long been observed that many peripheral countries have greater urban primacy than many core countries, and that urban primacy seems to be a frequent, but not universal, feature of peripheral city systems.

Many authors have sought to explain this difference in terms of patterns of colonialism or the effects of dependency in the world-system. Recent research which examines the city-size distributions for countries in the world-system since 1800 reveals that, indeed, there are now significant differences between the core and the periphery in terms of average levels of urban primacy, but these differences are of relatively recent origin (Chase-Dunn, 1984, 1985b). For Latin American countries the difference emerged in the 1930s and 1940s. This suggests that structures of colonialism are not responsible for the high levels of urban primacy since Latin American colonialism ended in the 1820s. Whatever has caused this core/periphery difference is something which has had its effects in relatively recent decades.

Another urban-related feature of the core/periphery structure is the city-size distribution of the world-system as a whole. I have studied changes in the city-size distribution of the ten largest cities in the world-system beginning with the pre-modern Europe of AD 800 until 1975 (Chase-Dunn, 1985a). This shows that the level of urban primacy in the world city system varies cyclically and corresponds generally with changes in the distribution of military power and economic comparative advantage among core powers. However, there has been a trend in recent decades for some of the world's largest cities to be located in semiperipheral countries. By 1975 four of the ten largest cities in the world were located in semiperipheral countries. In addition the world city system has been flattening since 1875 and has reached a degree of city-size decentralization not seen since the twelfth century. In terms of population size, the world city hierarchy is becoming much less hierarchical, and much of this is due to the rapid growth of a few extremely large cities in semiperipheral countries.

CHANGES IN THE IMPORTANCE OF DIFFERENT TYPES OF DEPENDENCE

There is evidence of a shift in the relative balance of different forms of dependence over time. Bornschier and Chase-Dunn (1985:52) show that from the 1960s to the 1970s three measures of average trade dependence of peripheral countries declined (see also table 13.2 in the following chapter),[1] while dependence on private foreign investment by transnational firms and three measures of non-equity debt dependence increased greatly. The rising trends of investment dependence and debt dependence are found to hold for several subcategories of non-core countries. An examination of the World Bank categories of low income countries, middle income countries, newly industrializing countries and OPEC members shows that both an index of transnational corporate penetration (table 12.1) and the total debt outstanding as a proportion of GNP[2] (table 12.2) have increased substantially in each of these country groups.

TABLE 12.1 Transnational corporate penetration index[a]: group average

Year	LICs[b]	MICs	NICs	OPEC
1967	5.2	10.1	7.1	6.2
1971	5.7	11.1	8.2	9.1
1975	6.3	13.4	10.7	8.0
1979	13.0	28.3	21.4	19.4
Number of countries	33	31	10	7

[a]This index is a measure of the extent to which a country is dependent on transnational firms. It uses data on the book value of foreign direct investment weighted by an estimate of the stock of domestically owned capital. See Bornschier and Chase-Dunn (1985: chapter 4)

[b]LICs = low income countries, MICs = middle income countries, NICs = newly industrializing countries, OPEC = members of the Organization of Petroleum Exporting Countries

Source: Bornschier and Heintz (1979) and updates

TABLE 12.2 Total debt outstanding as proportion of GNP, market prices: group averages[a]

Year	LICs	MICs	NICs	OPEC
1970	0.18	0.16	0.10	0.09
1973	0.19	0.18	0.09	0.10
1975	0.26	0.22	0.15	0.12
1976	0.28	0.24	0.15	0.14
1977	0.31	0.27	0.17	0.17
1978	0.34	0.31	0.18	0.27
1979	0.36	0.32	0.18	0.26
1980	0.37	0.32	0.18	0.23
Number of countries	29–34	29–32	8–10	5–7

[a]Means are calculated for only those countries which had data available in 1975. Sample size varied from year to year within the ranges indicated.
Data for Iraq and Iran are generally not available for the OPEC group after 1977.

Sources: GNP from World Bank (various years) *World Debt Tables*. Debt, 1970–4, OECD (various years), Geographical Distribution of Financial Flows to Developing Countries: 1975–80 OECD (1982)

TRENDS IN THE MAGNITUDE OF WORLD-SYSTEM INEQUALITY

There has been much discussion of the extent of world-level inequality but very little empirical work. Authors argue over whether or not there is a growing gap, and some claim that the capitalist world-economy has brought absolute as well as relative immiseration to the periphery. Here I will review the few studies which allow us to estimate changes in the magnitude of world-system inequalities, and discuss the complicated question of the overall effects of capitalist development on the quality of life in peripheral areas.

The first thing to point out is that most of the quantitative studies focus on the post-World War II period, especially the 1950s and 1960s, in which the world economy was generally growing, albeit at different rates in different places. It is undeniable that many groups have experienced absolute immiseration, both material and cultural, as a result of their contact with the expanding European world-system. The demographic collapse of New World populations shortly after the conquest by Spain was a result of both epidemic diseases (Crosby, 1972) and socially structured exploitation (Frank, 1979b). And, since this first era of pillage and enslavement, there have been many other times and places when absolute disaster as well as relative deprivation has followed as a direct consequence of the incorporation of people into the expanding world-system. Cultural and material exploitation and immiseration are very difficult things to quantify. The destruction of indigenous cultures, like the extinction of genetic species, is unweighable.

We should evaluate the destructiveness and creativity of a mode of production by comparing it to other modes (Wallerstein, 1983a; Wallerstein, 1984b: chapter 14). When we compare the modern world-system with earlier world-systems I tend to agree with Marx. It is not the best of all possible worlds, but it does represent progress over earlier systems in many respects. Earlier systems were also exploitative, especially once states had been invented. They also destroyed indigenous cultures and spread diseases and killed people through over-exploitation and recurrent warfare. The quality of cultural and spiritual welfare is difficult to compare, but even here the critics of modern culture have not convinced me that the contemporary lowest common denominator is below that of earlier civilizations.

In material terms the problem is somewhat easier. We must consider population growth and the material level of living. Earlier modes of production allowed the human species to increase its numbers, but only slowly (Coale, 1974). As Marx pointed out, the ability of capitalism to revolutionize productive technology is its most progressive feature, although this is more of a mixed blessing than Marx realized. The rapid increase in the numbers of human beings in the twentieth century has been largely due to a combination of more productive technology and public health measures. While acknowledging that rapid population growth creates problems, I believe that population growth is a positive consequence. Certainly the carrying capacity of the earth is limited, but we have not yet come close to that limit. The main problems of pollution and resource depletion are caused by a lack of collective rationality with regard to long-term consequences. These are world-level political problems which capitalism as a socio-political system is probably unable to solve, but we should not allow these observations to blind us to the basically progressive developments in productive and medical technology. It is too easy for residents of the core countries to undervalue basic food supplies and non-animal energy sources. An appreciation of the overall collective rationality needed to wisely expand productivity and energy use is not enhanced by neo-Luddism.

When we examine the quality of individual lives across the whole periphery it is by no means clear that there has been absolute immiseration over the long run. Recent evidence (described below) suggests that the average material level of living has risen slightly even in the periphery of the world-system in recent decades. Earlier instances of absolute immiseration probably involved larger portions of the world population, whereas more recent episodes of absolute immiseration have become less frequent and less widespread. If this is true the problem has become more a matter of relative than of absolute immiseration. Evidence about recent changes in the distribution of certain resources is reviewed below.

There is, however, one sense in which the notion of absolute immiseration is undoubtedly applicable to the modern world-system, and that is the matter of the destructiveness and scale of warfare. The percentage of the total population involved in warfare, the severity of warfare in terms of the proportion of the total population which is injured and the proportion of social resources destroyed, have increased rapidly in the last centuries, and especially in this century (Galtung, 1980:7). The potential now, as everyone knows, is the destruction of not only the accomplishments of human endeavors but of three billion years of biological evolution as well. Any mode of production which brings about such a consequence is guilty of much more than absolute immiseration. It is in connection with the production of warfare that the historically progressive nature of capitalism is cast into doubt.

ABSOLUTE IMMISERATION OR RELATIVE DEPRIVATION?

What is the evidence about recent trends in world-level inequalities? Every region on earth experienced increases in production per capita during the post-World War II period. Of course, average levels of GNP per capita do not tell us about intranational distributions. It is well known that some groups in some regions have experienced declines in material welfare, and the extent of these absolute declines has certainly grown during the recent period of worldwide economic slowdown (Frank, 1981:125–31). But do these pockets of absolute decline outweigh the areas of growth such that the average level of living in the periphery has declined since World War II?

The question of absolute and relative levels of poverty is examined in a study conducted by Bourguignon et al. (1983). The conclusions with regard to changes in the relative distribution of income and consumption in this study are qualified by another paper by the same authors (Berry et al., 1983) which warns that measurement errors in the determination of relative levels of world inequality do not allow much certainty about trends. Nevertheless, the first paper is important because it combines both intranational and international data on inequality of household incomes to estimate changes in the level of world inequality from 1950 to 1977.

With regard to absolute immiseration, Bourguignon et al. (1983) report that the total number of poor people below the poverty line of $200 yearly income increased between 1950 and 1977. This might be understood as an indicator of absolute immiseration, but other facts lead to a different conclusion. While the absolute number of people below the poverty line increased, this was due largely to population growth in the poorest countries. When Bourguignon et al. examine the *proportion* of the world population below the poverty line, this *decreased* from 43 percent to 28 percent in the period studied. This means that although the number of poor people increased absolutely they decreased as a proportion of the whole world population.

Other studies indicate that immiseration has not increased. Studies of average life expectancies in peripheral countries show increases (Sell and Kunitz, 1986–7, table 1). Studies of calorific and protein content of food consumption in the periphery show stable levels, and an index of per capita consumption for the "low income economies" shows an increase from 1960 to 1981 (World Bank, 1983, volume 1:548). Ragin and Bradshaw (1986: table 1) show that an indicator of the physical quality of life in poor countries increased substantially between 1938 and 1980. Thus there is no evidence for absolute decline in the average material level of living when we examine the periphery as a whole. This may not hold for specific areas or groups, and it is possible that a more widespread decline has occurred since 1981 as the world economic crisis has caused severe dislocation in many countries. Sell and Kunitz (1986–7) argue that the recent debt crises and stagnation of the world economy have brought "the end of an era in mortality decline."

What can we conclude about trends in the distribution of relative shares of world resources? The Bourguignon et al. (1983) study found that the poorest 40 percent of the world's population received 4.9 percent of world income in 1950, but only 4.2 percent in 1977, and the gap between the poorest and the richest halves of the world population increased. Even though this is the only study to combine both intranational and international data on inequality, the revealed trends must be viewed with some uncertainty because of the measurement problems discussed by Berry et al. (1983). Nevertheless it is fairly certain that the magnitude of world income inequality did not decrease in this period. Ragin and Bradshaw (1986: table 1) examine two indicators of welfare, telephones per 1000 population and a composite measure of the physical quality of life. These both show an increase in the relative gap between core and peripheral countries between 1938 and 1980.

Let us now examine the distribution of some other resources. Most studies of global resource distribution compare the means of country groups. Studies which compute averages for country groups are informative, but they do not allow us much certainty about changes in the overall magnitude of inequality because the countries in each group are held constant over time. Since some individual countries are likely to be changing their ranks, estimates of this sort do not provide firm knowledge about changes in the magnitude of inequalities. Table 12.3 presents figures which show changes in the relative concentration/dispersion of several kinds of resources or social structural features across *percentile groups* of the world's population. The use of percentile groups in place of country groups allows for changes in the rank of countries to occur without disturbance to the estimates of percentile shares.

Table 12.3 uses data from countries to compute the proportion of world "resources" held by percentile groups of the world population. For each resource the countries included in the overall distributions are the same for all time points so that the addition or deletion of countries does not affect the proportions. The proportions are calculated by ordering the countries in terms of the per capita or "level" indicator, such as GNP per capita. All countries are listed from high to low in terms of GNP per capita and their total GNP and total population are also listed. Then the group of countries highest on GNP per capita that includes nearly 20 percent of the world's population is examined to determine what proportion of world GNP they produce.[3]

Table 12.3 shows the concentration of economic production as measured by GNP and energy consumption. It examines the world economic structure as indicated by the proportion of the agricultural labor force and the proportion of the industrial labor force, and it also examines the shape of world urbanization. It shows changes in the distributions of these features to the top and bottom quintiles of the world's population, as well as the middle 60 percent, and the shares accounted for by the United States.

The main conclusion indicated by the overall pattern in table 12.3 is that the distribution of these features has not changed very much in the 20-year period from 1960 to 1980. Certainly there has been no decrease in the relative distribution of productivity as indicated by GNP. Somewhat surprisingly the middle group has not gained in this period, and neither has the top group lost, despite the well known phenomenon of the "newly industrializing countries." The United States has fallen considerably from

32.1 percent of world GNP in 1960 to 26.9 percent in 1980. This is a continuation of the declining position of the US in world commodity production which was demonstrated to have been occurring since as early as 1950 by Meyer et al. (1975: table 2). The poorest quintile shows a decrease from 1.4 percent to 0.8 percent. Recall, however, that this is a relative share, not an absolute decrease.[4]

Energy consumption shows a similar distribution in 1960 to GNP, but in the following decades an important change occurs. The top quintile loses 13 percent of world energy consumption to the middle group. This might be due to the industrialization of semiperipheral countries. When we examine which countries grew the most or the least between 1970 and 1980 in per capita energy consumption we discover two factors which account for the change in the world distribution. First, three high consumption energy-producing countries in the top quintile experienced large declines in their energy consumption: Trinidad, Bahrain, and Kuwait. The United Kingdom and Luxembourg, both in the top quintile, also experienced large declines. On the other end of things, large increases were registered by a number of countries in the middle group: Libya, Austria, Yugoslavia, Japan,[5] Romania, South Korea, Hungary, Greece, Spain, Portugal, and Ireland. These, along with the milder growth of other semiperipheral countries in the middle group and the declining consumption in the countries within the top quintile (mentioned above) were great enough to overwhelm the increases experienced by other countries in the top quintile such as Norway, Australia, Canada, the United States, Saudi Arabia, Iceland, Finland, the Netherlands, Czechoslovakia, East Germany, and Belgium. A combination of declines on the part of some oil producers (plus the United Kingdom and Luxembourg), plus growth among Eastern European and semiperipheral industrializing countries (as well as Japan and Austria), accounts for the shift in the distribution of world energy consumption.

It is interesting that the shift in energy consumption, which is at least partly due to the spreading of industrialization to semiperipheral countries, is not reflected in the distribution of GNP. A sectoral analysis of GNP growth might help resolve this apparent inconsistency. It is possible that financial services and high technology/low energy industries located primarily in core countries have expanded enough in the period studied to offset the semiperipheral industrial growth component of the world distribution of GNP. Much of semiperipheral industrialization has been in heavy intermediate industries which consume great amounts of energy per unit of GNP. When we consider the distribution of economic structural characteristics there are some interesting trends. The world's agricultural work force is shifting toward those countries which are already highest in terms of the proportion of the work force in agriculture. From 1960 to 1980 the proportion of the world's farmers and farm workers located in the quintile of countries with the *lowest*

TABLE 12.3 *Concentration of resources among countries in the world-system: 1960–1980*[a]

Resources or social structural features	*1960* %	*1970* %	*1980* %
Economic production The proportion of world GNP going to:			
the countries highest on GNP per capita with 20% of world population	79.2	79.8	81.1
the middle countries on GNP per capita with 60% of world population	19.4	18.9	18.1
the countries lowest on GNP per capita with 20% of world population	1.4	1.3	.8
the United States	32.1	28.5	26.9
		N = 112	
The proportion of world energy consumed by:			
the countries highest on per capita energy consumption with 20% of world population	83.3	80.3	69.9
the middle countries on per capita energy consumption with 60% of world population	16.1	18.8	29.1
the countries lowest on per capita energy consumption with 20% of world population	.6	.9	1.0
the United States	36.0	32.4	27.8
		N = 126	
Economic structure The proportion of the world's agricultural work force living in:			
the countries lowest on % of work force in agriculture with 20% of world population	3.8	3.3	2.6
the middle countries on % of work force in agriculture with 60% of world population	63.0	58.0	57.0
the countries highest on % of work force in agriculture with 20% of world population	33.2	38.7	40.4
the United States	1.0	.6	.4
		N = 129	

The proportion of the world's industrial work force living in:			
the countries highest on % of work force in industry with 20% of world population	42.7	41.1	41.0
the middle countries on % of work force in industry with 60% of world population	51.1	53.3	51.8
the countries lowest on % of work force in industry with 20% of world population	6.2	5.6	7.2
the United States	12.9	11.6	9.5
		N = 129	
Urbanization The proportion of the world city-dwellers living in:			
the countries highest on % urbanization with 20% of world population	38.4	37.3	34.1
the middle countries on % urbanization with 60% of world population	56.2	56.6	58.9
the countries lowest on % urbanization with 20% of world population	5.4	6.1	7.0
the United States	14.3	12.9	11.0
		N = 133	

[a]Percentages are based in sets of countries for which data are available for all time points. Thus comparisons over time are not confounded by missing data.
N = Number of countries.

Source: All data are taken from World Tables, 1983, volume II, except for GNP which was supplied by the World Bank's Economic Analysis and Projections Department.

proportion of the labor force in agriculture declined from 3.8 percent to 2.6 percent, and declines were also experienced by the middle group. The countries in the quintile highest on the percentage of the labor force in agriculture – i.e. peripheral countries – increased their proportion of the world's farmers and farm workers from 33.2 percent to 40.4 percent. This finding suggests a different twist to the notion that national economies are developing by shifting workers out of the agricultural sector. It is true that this is happening in most countries, but it is happening much faster in the more developed countries, so that the structure of the world work force is shifting toward a greater concentration of farm workers in the least developed countries.

When we examine the relative global distribution of industrial workers the major feature is stability in each of the groups, although the lowest quintile has increased from 6.2 percent to 7.2 percent. This stability is interesting because the most developed countries are not increasing the percentage of their work force in industry, and many are experiencing declines in this proportion as the service sector continues to grow. The United States, as shown, experienced a reduction in its proportion of the world labor force in industry from 12.9 percent to 9.5 percent in the period studied. This "export of the proletariat" is rather small, however, when we examine the top quintile as a whole. Its proportion of the world industrial labor force declined from 42.7 percent to 41.0 percent.

Urbanization, on the other hand, reveals fairly substantial changes in its world distribution. The most urbanized countries declined in their proportion of world city-dwellers from 38.4 percent in 1960 to 34.1 percent in 1980. Both the middle group and the bottom quintile experienced increases. This means that the well known phenomenon of rapid urbanization in the periphery is redistributing the world's city-dwellers. Of course urbanization – the proportion of a population residing in cities – is subject to ceiling limits such that increases above 100 percent are impossible, and so concentration would be likely to decline in a world in which some countries have become completely urbanized while others are still on the road to urbanization. Similar ceiling effects, however, might be expected to reduce core/periphery differences in the distribution of the world's work force across economic sectors, but for these the inequalities are either stable or becoming greater. I would suggest that the reduction in core/periphery differences in urbanization levels is indicative, not of the periphery catching up with the core with regard to a structural feature of modernization, but rather of the increasingly direct integration of the populations of peripheral countries into the world labor market, including the rapidly expanding informal sectors in the large cities of the periphery (Portes and Walton, 1981). Thus this is not evidence of the reduction of core/periphery inequality, but rather a more direct inclusion of peripheral peoples into the structure of international dominance and dependence. As reported in the previous chapter Jeffrey Kentor (1981) has shown that dependence on foreign investment causes increased urbanization in the periphery and that this is mediated by the expansion of tertiary sector employment. Peripheral urbanization is thus a very different phenomenon from the urban–industrial pattern of development which occurred in core countries.

Another recent trend is the spread of the production of military weapons to the Third World. Some authors (cited in Neuman, 1984) claim that this is an indication of the dispersion of power in the "international system." Research by Stephanie Neuman (1984) confirms that the number of countries producing weapons and the number of weapons produced have increased since 1969, but the relative share of weapons production by non-core countries has not steadily increased. Neuman's (1984:170–1) table 1 shows that the dollar value of arms exports from Third World countries as a percentage of world arms exports over the period from 1969 to 1978 varied from 2.10 percent to 8.84 percent, but there was no regularly increasing trend over the period. Though the number of countries producing weapons increased dramatically from 1950 to 1980 (from 4 to 26) most of the major weapons systems are produced in a few industrializing semiperipheral countries. Argentina, Brazil, China, India, Israel, South Africa, Taiwan, and South Korea (30 percent of the 26 Third World producers) are responsible for 75 percent of the Third World production in the period from 1975 to 1980. With regard to the types of weapons produced Neuman (1984:174) concludes that they are ". . . fewer, older, and less complex defense items – the so-called 'vintage' and 'intermediate' military components and systems." Thus, like the spread of industrial production generally, the quantity and the type of development in the semiperiphery indicates perhaps some upward mobility on the part of a few countries but not a general decrease in the magnitude of core/periphery inequalities.

CONCLUSIONS

The most important conclusion from the evidence reviewed in this chapter is that, despite the undeniable industrialization of many peripheral and semiperipheral states, there is no evidence of a reduction in the magnitude of core/periphery inequalities. Thus, reports of the demise of the core/periphery hierarchy are certainly premature.

On the other hand, there is little evidence of general absolute immiseration of the periphery. Some studies show small increases while others show little change in various indicators of the average life chances and level of living in the periphery. Data are not yet available for the recent period since 1981, a period in which there have been famines and economic crises in several regions of the periphery. Periphery-wide data on this time period might yield a different result. My best guess is that it is relative rather than absolute immiseration which will have significant political effects in the long run.

13

World-system Fluctuations

This chapter examines empirical studies of world-system cycles and arguments about their causes and effects. Early theorizing about relationships among world-system processes posited both temporal models showing the relations among different cycles over time and models depicting causal relations among variables (e.g. Chase-Dunn, 1978:170–1). Subsequent empirical work has confirmed some of the original hypotheses and exposed others as overly simplified or completely wrong. This chapter reviews the state of a field which is rapidly changing because so much new empirical work is being done, and yet much more needs to be done before we will have a clear picture of the causal nature of world-system processes.

As was discussed in chapter 9, the distribution of competitive advantage in commodity production in the core of the world-system varies from a situation of hegemony, in which one core state has a clear advantage, to a situation in which profitable production of core products for the world market is more evenly distributed across the core states. For analytic purposes we can refer to the former situation as hegemonic and the latter as "multicentric." In chapter 9 we discussed the causes of the rise and fall of hegemonic core powers – the national-level and world-system dynamics which result in the cycle of core competition. We will now examine how this fluctuation between hegemony and multicentricity affects the structure of control and exchange between the core and the periphery.

One of the features of the core/periphery relationship which is hypothesized over time is the fluctuation between a more or less *multilateral* system of "free" trade between the various core states and the various peripheral areas on the one hand, and a more *bilateral* system of colonial empires on the other. These two hypothetical structures are graphically represented by figure 13.1.

This figure illustrates two different idealized structures of control and exchange between core states and peripheral areas. In a system of colonial empires each core state monopolizes exchange with its own colonies and

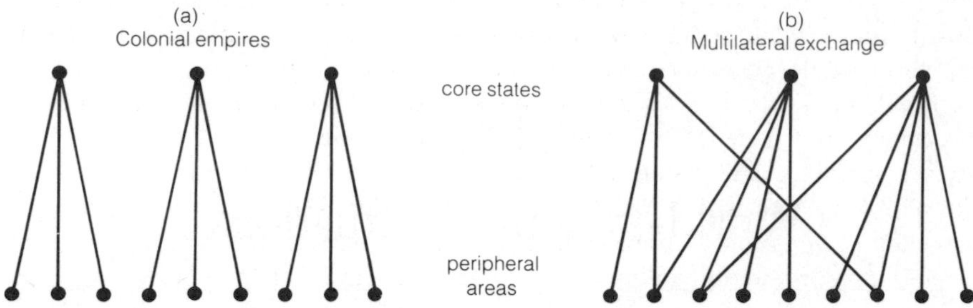

FIGURE 13.1 *Structures of core/periphery exchange*

excludes other core states from this trade. In the multilateral structure trade is less controlled by mercantilist state policies and the exchange comes closer to the ideal of a free world market. These schematic alternatives are, of course, only roughly approximated in complex reality. Some core countries never have formal colonial empires or have only small ones; truly price-setting international markets in which commodities exchange between core and periphery without regard to bilateral political considerations have never been completely realized; and, of course, the composition of the core and the periphery changes over time with the rise and fall of different regions and the incorporation of new regions into the modern world-system. Nevertheless, the above hypothesized structural types may have analytic utility.

Two additional features of the core/periphery relationship will be considered in this discussion. The first is expansion. The European world-system expanded to incorporate and peripheralize formerly external arenas in a series of waves since the sixteenth century. The nature of this incorporation varied depending upon the type of society being incorporated, as well as the particular features of capitalist accumulation and political organization which were current in the core at the time of incorporation (chapter 10). Nevertheless we may note that the rate of incorporation of new populations and territories varied over time such that incorporation occurred in waves. And another feature of the core/periphery relationship which has varied over time is the amount of resistance to core domination from peripheral areas. These variations, of course, can and should be studied in particular contexts to understand the conjunctural elements which nuance each situation; but here I want to examine them as features of the world-system as a whole.

The following discussion also incorporates two other cyclical variations which we have noted operating in the world-system: Kondratieff waves (K-waves); and the cycle of the severity of war among core powers. These cycles and variable features will each be discussed in turn below before we consider the temporal and causal relations among them.

As discussed in earlier chapters, in my view the core/periphery hierarchy plays an important role in the reproduction of capitalist accumulation. Let us now examine some of the ways in which the structure of domination between the core and the periphery changes and is changed by the process of capitalist accumulation in the core. Intensive and extensive development are alternatives for capital, and their relative profitability is determined in part by the level of resistance which is encountered. Thus, one reason that capital is exported to the periphery, and that colonial expansion is undertaken, is that resistance to capitalist exploitation is often weaker in the periphery than in the core. Also, expanded reproduction in the core creates demand for food products and industrial raw materials which can be cheaply produced in the periphery. And core producers seek market outlets in colonial areas in order to realize additional profits on product lines originally introduced in core markets.

According to Rosa Luxemburg (1968) the motive of market expansion is the key reason for imperialism, as capital seeks to escape the market saturation resulting from cyclical overproduction of commodities. All of the above processes – desire for expanded investment opportunities, desire for commodity markets, and the rising demand for cheap food and raw material inputs – stimulate capitalist core states to use political–military power to sustain the property relations and other institutional supports which facilitate core exploitation of the periphery. This general tendency is influenced by the cycles of economic growth, uneven development, periodic warfare, and hegemonic rise and fall which emanate from the arena of competition and conflict within and among core states. Economic and political competition among core states often produces defensive expansion in the periphery, a kind of "anticipatory colonialism" which appears to be unmotivated by existing economic opportunities, but which can be understood in terms of the "strategic" interests of competing core powers.

A HYPOTHETICAL MODEL OF TEMPORAL RELATIONS

This section focuses upon a specific world-system-level process: the way in which competition among core states and their national bourgeoisies affects the relationship between the core and the periphery. The descriptive form of the hypothesis is that a hegemonic distribution of productive advantage in the core, in which the bourgeoisie of a single core state is hegemonic in the world economy, leads to a relatively multilateral structure of exchange and control between the core and the periphery, and the relaxation of political controls over core/periphery exchange. Conversely, a more multicentric distribution of competitive advantage in the core leads to a bilateral structure of exchange and control between core states and their colonial empires, and also to the expansion of colonial empires into new territories.

The aggregate rate of growth in investment and production which varies over time to produce the Kondratieff wave is an average for the world-system as a whole, at least in principle. But development is, of course, uneven among core states, between the core and the periphery, and within the periphery as well. So-called "rounds of accumulation" based on the expansion of new types of production are obviously not uniformly distributed across space. And the overall rates of economic growth, as well as the levels of slowdown and stagnation, vary from country to country, and also regionally within countries. Thus capitalist development is spatially uneven, and it is this which produces the hegemonic cycles and the upward and downward mobility of countries in the core/periphery hierarchy. But let us ignore these spatial variations for a moment to focus on the average levels of growth and the overall system-wide variations in the severity of competition and conflict among core states.

In my 1978 article I argued that the K-wave and conflict among core states were inversely related (Chase-Dunn, 1978). This was before Goldstein's (1988) research, which shows that the severity of wars among core states varies not inversely but conjointly (with a small lag) with the K-wave. My earlier reasoning was influenced by my study of tariff politics. I argued that in periods of economic expansion capitalists are less likely to support state intervention, while during periods of stagnation they are more likely to support the use of state power to protect or extend their interests. A recent study of nineteenth century tariff politics (McKeown, 1983) agrees with my supposition that K-waves and tariff protectionism are inversely related. Goldstein's results show that warfare is most intense during K-wave upswings, while McKeown (1983) concludes that protectionism increases during downswsings. Apparently some kinds of competition are greater during upswings while other kinds increase during downswings. These lead to different sorts of state intervention.

The concentration of productive advantage in a single core state means that commodities are being produced at a low cost and in enough volume to invade the markets of competitors and to create new markets by affecting consumption patterns. When the price of these commodities is low enough, and demand in other core countries is high enough, the political barriers to trade across state boundaries are likely to be lowered, and a period of relatively free trade ensues. Stephen Krasner (1976) first described this consequence of "hegemonic stability" in his study of tariff barriers and trade patterns in the world economy during the nineteenth and twentieth centuries.

In the nineteenth century the period between 1820 and 1870 was one in which tariff barriers among core states were generally lowered. The Anti-Corn Law league carried on an extensive program of propaganda and political mobilization to abolish Britain's tariff protection and to convince other states in the international market to follow suit. French prohibition of imported British yarn had led to extensive smuggling as weavers demanded fine cotton and worsted yarns either not available or too expensive in the home market

(Clapham, 1966). Napoleon III was convinced by economic liberals and French consumers that open competition would stimulate industrialization in France. Even the United States, which was protectionist during most of the nineteenth century, dramatically lowered its tariff barriers between 1846 and the Civil War (Chase-Dunn, 1980). Tim McKeown's (1983) study of nineteenth-century British international economic policy and diplomacy shows that the British state was not a consistent or insistent propagator of free trade among the core states, contrary to Krasner's argument. My own explanation for the rise and fall of free trade among core states focuses on the vectors of political support for state policies which come from internal producers and consumers in the context of the world market. The British state was much pushier in "opening" the colonies of other core states and external arenas such as China and the Ottoman Empire. This "imperialism of free trade" was a major factor in the extension and multilateralization of the world market.

There is a constant tendency for all states to have protective tariffs because the returns to the protected producer are great, while the loss to individual consumers is small. Political policy is thus subjected to the influence of strongly motivated interests seeking protection, while the interests of consumers are dispersed and difficult to mobilize. But if the gap between home market prices and international market prices becomes too great either smuggling will occur, or political pressures will be brought to bear to lower tariffs. An additional element is the overall rate of economic growth. Producers are more adamant about protection during periods when profits are falling and alternative investments are difficult to find.

Just as tariff barriers among core states were lowered, barriers constraining core/periphery trade within colonial empires between an individual "mother" country and its colonies tended to relax as the advantages of buying cheap imports came to outweigh the forces supporting colonial trade monopolies. Consumers within core states wanted cheap sugar, for example, and the political support for monopoly faced strong opposition as the difference between the price of protected sugar and world market sugar grew. Similarly, consumers in peripheral areas had an interest in buying their imports from the core power that sold them most cheaply, and this tended to disrupt bilateral colonial exchange monopolies. Both colonial monopolies and home market monopolies were politically attacked during a period of overall economic growth of the world economy.

The diffusion of technological innovations from the hegemonic core state (Henderson, 1965) and the stimulus to more efficient production resulting from core competition leads, in combination with the right domestic political conditions, to the expansion of industrial production in other core states and in some semiperipheral states. In the nineteenth century these were the United States, Belgium, Germany, and France (Maddison, 1982; Senghaas,

1985). This resulted in a more even distribution of competitive advantage across the core.

The expansion of production of processed goods in the core caused the demand for raw materials to rise. Raw material production was more dependent on "natural" factors such as climate and the location of natural resources, so the geographical distribution of extractive production was necessarily more widespread than the production of manufactured goods. This dependence on natural conditions also slowed technological improvement in the production of raw materials relative to that which was possible in manufacturing production, which is more easily amenable to reorganization. In addition, the increased accumulation of capital in the core stimulated an organized labor force demanding higher wages and other amenities. This provided an incentive for capital to utilize cheaper peripheral labor when possible. All these factors expanded and intensified the economic exploitation of the periphery.

The evening out of competitive advantage across the core led to increased competition among producers for access to markets and raw materials. This was manifested within the core by the re-emergence of protective tariffs around home markets, and between the core and the periphery in the tightening of colonial monopolies and the expansion of colonial empires to new areas. The core/periphery trade network shifted back toward a more bilateral (colonial) structure. This "new" mercantilism and "new" imperialism occurred because the overall growth rate of the world-economy slowed down and so competition increased and groups intensified their utilization of state power to maintain shares of a shrinking "pie". Each core country increased its ties with its "own" colonial empire, and trade among core countries declined in importance (Woodruff, 1967).

Colonial expansion and economic penetration of the periphery mutually reinforced one another, although formal colonization was fiscally expensive and was often a defensive (or even preventive) result of core competition over access to peripheral resources and markets. The scramble for sub-Saharan Africa which culminated in its division among the imperial powers in 1885 was largely the result of *anticipatory* economic and political competition.

A period of conflict and disorganization of the world-economy brought about by increasing competition among core states created room for the emergence of peripheral resistance. Similarly, but during a different phase of the worldwide K-wave, the increased demand for raw materials improved the market position of producers in the periphery and thus may have encouraged peripheral resistance. Peripheral independence movements received support from those core powers in a position to benefit from breaking down the colonial monopolies of other core powers. British support for Spanish American independence movements is a case in point.

Decolonization and resistance from the periphery increased the costs of exploitation, and this forced core capital to reconsider the possibilities for more intensive exploitation at home. The creation of formally independent states in the periphery, although their sovereignty was compromised by neocolonial forms of core/periphery domination, nevertheless increased the cost of exploitation. It created barriers to further colonial expansion (or recolonization), and multilateralized the structure of trade as peripheral states obtained some latitude to play off core countries against one another. As in the core, however, opposition from one area drove capital to where opposition was less, and this provided the motive force for the continual expansion and deepening of capitalist exploitation.

Before reviewing the empirical studies which have been done, let us describe another model, this time in the form of a set of hypotheses about directional causal effects. The model below was presented in Chase-Dunn (1978) and a related version was formulated by Pat McGowan (1985) based on the arguments contained in Bergesen and Schoenberg's (1980) study of waves of colonialism.

A CAUSAL MODEL

Let us decompose the process of uneven development in the core into three parts: (1) the growth of production in the hegemonic core state resulting from the concentration of productive advantages; (2) the growth of production in competing core states resulting from the evening out of the distribution of productive advantage; and (3) the aggregate rate of economic development in the world economy.

Similarly, we can decompose the core/periphery structure into four components: (1) economic penetration of peripheral areas by core firms; (2) expansion of formal colonial control by core states; (3) the oscillation between a bilateral and a multilateral network of exchange and control between the core and periphery; and (4) the increase of peripheral resistance as manifested by decolonization movements and other forms of resistance to core domination.

The relationships among these variables are mediated in part by the level of conflict among core states. These variables and the hypothesized causal relations among them are illustrated in figure 13.2.

As specified, this model is not testable with quantitative data even if the proposed variables could be operationalized over a time period sufficient to include meaningful variation in world-system structures because it is underidentified – too many of the variables are endogenous in the sense that they are affected by other variables in the model. Nevertheless each proposed effect is adduceable. The model is presented to clarify my arguments. Further specification needs to be done to make it testable, and, of course there are

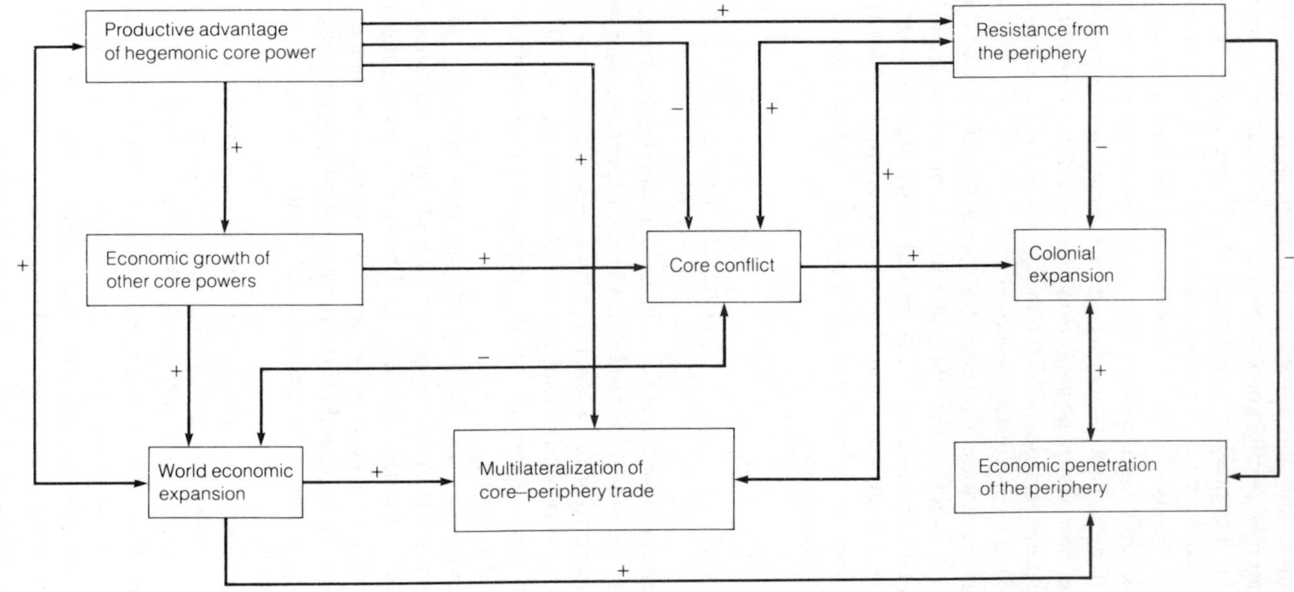

FIGURE 13.2 *A causal model of the effects of the hegemonic sequence on the core/periphery hierarchy*

difficult problems of data availability. For now let us simply use this model as an heuristic tool.

A REVIEW OF EXISTING EVIDENCE

There have been quite a number of interpretive studies which assert dating schemes for various of the world-system fluctuations but only very recently have researchers begun to actually measure world-system variables and study their interaction over time. The path-breaking study of waves of colonialism by Bergesen and Schoenberg (1980) has been followed by a number of other efforts. These are reviewed below and the implications for the above hypothetical arguments are discussed.

Cycles in the Core

The findings from Goldstein's (1988) study of cycles of core war, K-waves, and the hegemonic sequence indicate that some previous world-system hypotheses were incorrect. Hopkins and Wallerstein (1979) argued that each hegemonic sequence was composed of two K-waves, but Goldstein concludes that the K-wave is related only loosely to the hegemonic sequence. Each hegemony contains a different number of K-waves and associated war cycles, but the hegemonies all begin after an unusually large peak in core war severity. These matters are still in some doubt, however, because of remaining controversies over the conceptualization and measurement of the hegemonic sequence (see chapter 9).

Also, contrary to many earlier world-system arguments, Goldstein finds that war is more severe during K-wave upswings than during K-wave downswings, and so the K-wave and the war cycle vary conjointly rather than inversely. If it is true that tariff protectionism, on the other hand, does vary inversely with the K-wave then the variable "core conflict" in the middle of figure 13.2 needs to be decomposed into different types of conflict/competition among core states.

Colonial Expansion

I propose a slightly different approach to that employed by Bergesen and Schoenberg (1980) in their study of waves of colonialism from 1415 to 1969. Measuring the expansion of the modern world-system is not a simple matter. Expansion is carried out by states through formal colonization, but also by private entrepreneurs, and some areas become incorporated into the world-system through trade or treaty which does not involve formal colonial subjugation (e.g. Hall, 1986). As David Henige's (1970) compilation shows, many colonies were settled first by private parties and later received official colonial status. Bergesen and Schoenberg's operationalization treats each newly established colony equally, but surely some were more important than others in terms of the amount of territory or number of people subjugated. Unfortunately, only rough estimates of the territorial or population size of the colonial empires are available for the earlier centuries (Bairoch, 1986; Taagepera, 1978). The use of the number of new colonies established is, however rough, the best continuous measure we have available at this time.[1]

Bergesen and Schoenberg devote most of their analysis to the *net number of colonies*, an indicator which shows the cumulative number of colonies established minus the colonies which have been terminated. This indicator reveals the two waves of colonialism, an earlier one in the seventeenth and eighteenth centuries, and a later one in the nineteenth century known to many students of colonialism as the "new imperialism."[2] But Bergesen and Schoenberg should have paid more attention to the expansion of colonial empires separately from their termination. These are separate processes, one emanating mostly from the core and the other due largely to resistance from the periphery to core domination. Bergesen and Schoenberg present graphs of these phenonomena separately (1980:234–5), confirming what has also been noted by McGowan, that they have quite different patterns in time. Figure 13.4, from Bergesen and Schoenberg (1980:234), shows an 11-year non-cumulative moving average of the number of new colonies established.

This figure, I will argue, shows the periods in which the world-system is being territorially expanded due to colonizing by core powers. The figure reveals ten peaks of expansion since 1500, and visual inspection suggests that these may be related in a lagged fashion to the Kondratieff waves and war severity cycles demonstrated by Goldstein.

Pat McGowan (1985: table 4) analyzed the Bergesen and Schoenberg data using the method of time series regression analysis. McGowan finds no relationship between the measure of new colonies created and the Bergesen and Schoenberg coding of the existence of a war. McGowan tested for a simultaneous correlation – examining the correlation between war and expansion within each single year. There are two problems with this finding. The hypothesis that wars and colonial expansion should occur in the same year sounds faulty to me. I would not expect expansion by core powers in peripheralizing areas to occur simultaneously with war among core powers. Bergesen and Schoenberg seem to suggest that these variables are correlated within larger blocks of time with a time lag between them. My guess is that the making of war with other core powers does not leave resources free for extensive adventures in the periphery. We know that some colonies change hands during or just after a core war, but these cases should be deducted from a measure of system expansion (see note 1).

The three different factors theorized to be behind system expansion are:

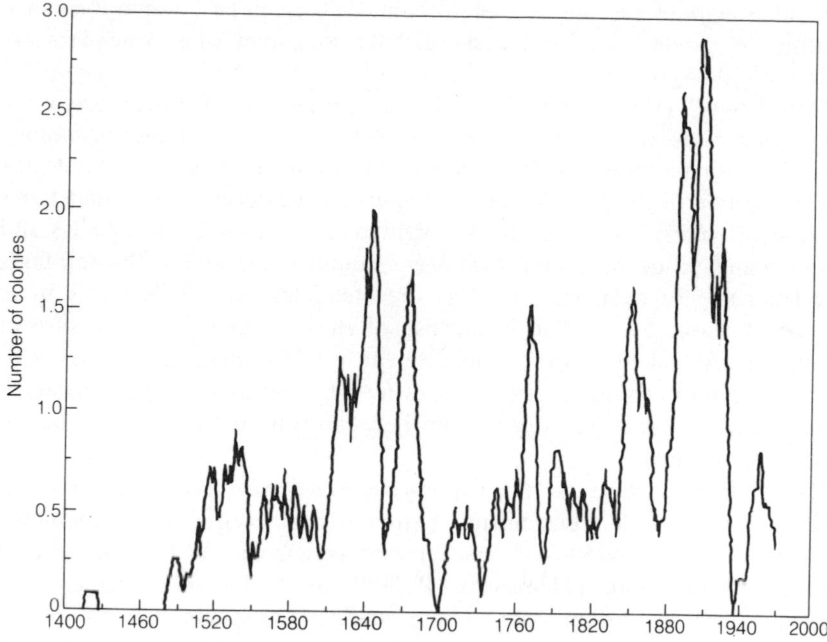

FIGURE 13.4 *An 11-year moving average of the number of colonies established, 1415–1969*
Source: Bergesen and Schoenberg (1980:234)

demand for cheap raw materials; need for new investment opportunities due to the declining rate of profit on investments within the core; and the glut of core markets resulting in the search for new effective demand in the periphery. These three factors are most likely to occur at different points in the Kondratieff cycle. Increased demand and rising prices for raw materials occur during an upswing when production is expanding. The need for new investment opportunities and markets occurs at the peak and during the downswing. In addition Walter Goldfrank (personal communication) points out that during downturns there are pressures for new areas of settlement for the unemployed, thus pushing toward expansion at the frontiers.

McGowan's finding of no simultaneous relationship between the creation of new colonies and the presence/absence of core war may be due to the contradictory operation of the above factors, or it may be due to the crude measure of core war used by Bergesen and Schoenberg. Goldstein's (1988) findings are based on the *severity* of core wars, the number of persons killed. This measure shows the intensity of core conflict as well as its presence/absence. My guess is that the *simultaneous* time series correlation between core war severity and the expansion of colonial empires will be shown to be negative or zero because of the trade-offs in the costs of core war and colonial expansion. I predict, however, a significant association when time lags are analyzed.[3]

Terry Boswell (1989) has performed a time series regression analysis of the relationship between colonialism, warfare, the K-wave, and the hegemonic sequence. Using a measure of war *intensity* the annual number of battle deaths as a proportion of the total European population (different from Goldstein's measure of *severity* which is the unweighted number of battle deaths) and Bergesen and Schoenberg's measure of net cumulative colonies, Boswell finds no relationship between wars among core states and colonialism. My main reservation about this finding is the use of the net cumulative measure of colonialism. As stated above, combining the establishment of colonies with their termination confuses two very different processes. Future research should examine the lagged relationship between warfare and the number of colonies established.

Boswell finds support for the hypotheses in Chase-Dunn and Rubinson (1977) regarding the relationship between colonialism, the hegemonic sequence and K-waves. K-wave upswings are associated with less colonialism; downturns with more colonialism. Periods of "hegemonic victory" are associated with less colonialism. These findings are encouraging but they suffer from the same defects mentioned above: the net cumulative number of colonies was used and the "measure" of hegemony is a set of dummy variables based on the dates asserted by Hopkins and Wallerstein (1979).

It is important to remember Goldstein's (1988:176) argument that sequential "cycle time" rather than strictly stationary periodicity is the appropriate form of analysis for many social phenomena. We would not expect, for example, a constant lag of exactly x number of years to characterize the relations among world-system variables in each period. A test for lagged relationships should allow for this by utilizing at least five-year blocks of time. The methodological problems associated with time series analyses of world-system processes are considered in chapter 15.

Resistance in the Periphery

Regarding the notion of resistance from the periphery we should examine another figure produced by Bergesen and Schoenberg (1980:235) of the number of colonies terminated. Remember that resistance takes many forms – including labor slowdowns, flight to refuge regions, demonstrations, strikes, banditry, tax evasion, protectionism, import substitution, expropriation, armed rebellion which is quashed, and successful rebellions which expel the colonial power, such as occurred in the US, Haiti, and the Spanish colonies of Latin America in the late eighteenth and early nineteenth centuries. The conditions for resistance are always present in the periphery, so why should we expect peripheral resistance to cluster in time across many very different peripheral situations? Andre Gunder Frank (1972) has argued that resistance in the periphery clusters during core wars and high levels of core competition because the level of control by core powers is diminished. Also it may be easier for peripheral countries to play core powers off against one another in such periods.

Another factor which may produce the clustering of successful peripheral resistance in time is related to the hegemonic sequence. A rising hegemon often supports the liberation of the colonies of other core powers. This situation produces the spectacle of a policy of "liberation" which supports anti-colonial movements in other colonial empires while simultaneously extending its own (in the name of free trade) by force. Robinson and Gallagher (1953) described this aspect of British policy in the first half of the nineteenth century as the "imperialism of free trade." A milder, but functionally equivalent, version was United States anti-colonialism after World War II.

Observing figure 13.5 we see that the termination of colonies does cluster over time, with the biggest peaks being the decolonization of the Americas in the late eighteenth and early nineteenth centuries, and the decolonization of most of the rest of the African and Asian periphery after World War II.

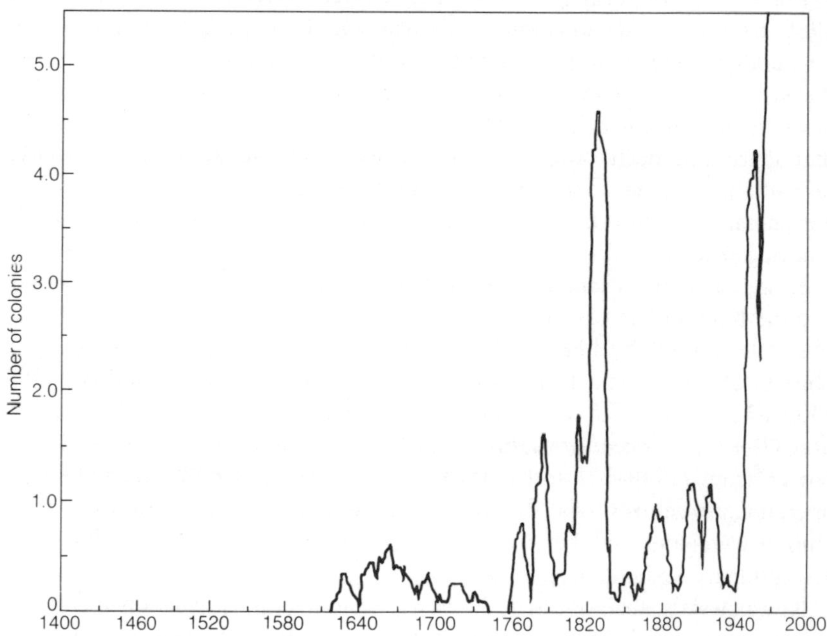

FIGURE 13.5 *An 11-year moving average of the number of colonies terminated, 1415–1969*
Source: Bergesen and Schoenberg (1980:235)

While the British fought hard to retain the thirteen colonies which became the United States (and these new states were aided by a contending core power, France) it was not much later that these same British aided the national liberation movements of Latin America against Spain, thus contributing to the first big wave of decolonization. After World War II it was the United States, the new hegemonic core power, which, again in the name of free trade, supported the dismantling of the empires of other core powers. The Dutch hegemony did not produce such an upsurge, perhaps because, though the Dutch too espoused a liberal international order, no one thought to apply this idea to the pagans and Moslems of the East Indies. Rather a policy of "armed trade" prevailed in which Portuguese colonies were either taken by force or burned to the ground lest they compete with nearby Dutch establishments. Much of this action occurred in areas which, according to Wallerstein (1974), were still external arenas outside the boundaries of the European world-economy. Plunder and pillage have become somewhat less frequently employed by core powers over the centuries and this may partly account for the rising success of peripheral resistance movements in obtaining formal state sovereignty.

A time series analysis of peripheral resistance has been carried out by David Kowalewski (1987) who has coded the existence and success of revolutionary movements in 34 peripheral and semiperipheral countries between 1821 and 1985. Kowalewski demonstrates the existence of an upward trend over time in revolutionary activity in the periphery, and this is shown to be independent of the secular increase in the amount of coverage of peripheral events in the news media from which activities are coded. Kowalewski's results also show that there has been no accompanying trend in the amount of success of revolutionary movements over the same time period. He surmises that peripheral revolutionaries are "making more revolution now but perhaps enjoying it less."

Kowalewski also examines propositions which link the hegemonic sequence and the Kondratieff wave to peripheral resistance with his data on revolutions. His indicator of the hegemonic sequence is a series of periods designating phases of the world-leadership cycle as defined by Modelski (1978). Modelski's periodization into phases of global power (1822–48), delegitimation (1849–73), deconcentration (1874–1913), global war (1914–45), global power again (1946–73) and delegitimation (1973-) is both conceptually and operationally controversial. In any case Kowalewski does not find any striking empirical relationship between these periods and changes in the level of revolutionary activity or success.

Kowalewski's analysis does, however, demonstrate a relationship between revolutionary activity and the Kondratieff wave. Revolutionary activity is much more likely to occur during three upswings of the Kondratieff wave than during four downswings. Revolutionary success was not found to be regularly related to the phases of the Kondratieff wave. Further research needs to be done using better measures of resistance and better measures of world-system cycles before we can know about the causalities involved, but the surmise that periphery-wide waves of resistance exist and are related to larger world-system processes is supported by Kowalewski's findings.

Protectionism and the Colonial Regulation of Trade

Another set of related hypotheses about cycles in core/periphery relations refer to the political regulation of trade through colonial monopolies and protectionism. We know that Johan DeWitt, the seventeenth-century stadholder of Amsterdam, wrote pamphlets about the universal benefits of international free trade; and Hugo Grotius, the Dutch legal philosopher, formulated the doctrine of the free use of the seas (which became the basis for the international law of the sea) during the Dutch hegemony. At this same period the English were becoming more nationalistic, expelling Jewish merchants and attempting to protect their woolen textile industry against cheap Dutch imports.

Later, during a period in which competitive advantage begun to turn in favor of the British, Adam Smith developed a theory of market-regulated exchange in which the general welfare would be maximized by the abolition of state interference in economic transactions. Somewhat later, during the industrial boom based on cotton textile production, Cobden and Bright campaigned for British and international reduction of tariffs. And the Americans followed suit. After remaining protectionist during nearly its whole period of upward mobility in the world-system, the US finally became the advocate of free trade after World War II, establishing the GATT agreements.

The above narrative indicates that hegemonic core powers like free trade, while those with less market power most often favor protection. About this there is little disagreement. Stephen Krasner (1976) has added that smaller core powers that have small home markets and are dependent on imports also favor free trade, although Dieter Senghaas (1985:23) points out that only Switzerland and the Netherlands have maintained a continuous free trade policy. It has likewise been noticed that peripheral capitalists, who are exporting goods to the core and importing from the core, also favor free trade, although here the matter of colonial monopoly sometimes cuts a different way. English sugar planters in the Caribbean were often unable to beat the prices of competing operations in Brazil or on the less soil-depleted Caribbean islands. Thus they lobbied for colonial quotas and price supports. US cotton planters exporting to England were, on the other hand, staunch defenders of free trade.

Again we see that different groups have different interests, and the particular way in which each is inserted into the complex mosaic which is the world-system is going to weigh heavily on the decision to support protectionism or free trade.

Stephen Krasner (1976) examined three indicators of openness versus closure in the world-system: protectionist taxation by states; the ratio of the average size of the national domestic market to foreign trade; and the degree of concentration of trade within regional areas or colonial empires. On the basis of these three features he concluded that the structure of trade and political regulation of trade has alternated between periods of relative openness and periods of relative closure. Examining the nineteenth and twentieth centuries, he finds five periods (Krasner, 1976:330):

> Period I (1820–1879): Increasing openness – tariffs are generally lowered; trade proportions increase. Data are not available for trade patterns. However, it is important to note that this is not a universal pattern. The United States is largely unaffected: its tariff levels remain high (and are in fact increased during the early 1860s) and American trade proportions remain almost constant.[4]
>
> Period II (1879–1900): Modest closure – tariffs are increased; trade proportions decline modestly for most states. Data are not available for trade patterns.
>
> Period III (1900–1913): Greater openness – tariff levels remain generally unchanged; trade proportions increase for all major trading states except the United States. Trading patterns become less regional in three out of the four cases for which data are available.
>
> Period IV (1918–1939): Closure – tariff levels are increased in the 1920's and again in the 1930's; trade proportions decline. Trade becomes more regionally encapsulated.
>
> Period V (1945-*c.*1970): Great openness – tariffs are lowered; trade proportions increase, particularly after 1960. Regional concentration decreased after 1960. However, these developments are limited to non-communist areas of the world.

To this we may add a sixth period following 1970 in which tariffs are again rising.

As mentioned above, a more recent study by Tim McKeown (1983) disputes Krasner's argument that the decline of protectionism among core states is due to the action of the hegemonic state. McKeown shows that the British state did not aggressively pursue a policy to induce other core powers to lower their tariffs. Nevertheless the hegemons adopt free trade earlier and keep it longer than competing core states. Suzanne Frederick's (1987) critique of Krasner and the other theorists of "hegemonic stability" argues that free trade breaks out during a period of instability following the beginning of the hegemon's decline. Certainly the motives of the hegemon and the competing powers differ, and perhaps we should pay more attention to the timing, location, and degree of changes in protectionism than Krasner has done. But Frederick's conclusion about the "instability of free trade" is wholly dependent on her use of Modelski's dating of the power (hegemonic) sequence, and thus suffers from the same defect as studies described above.

The idea of a cycle of the core/periphery exchange structure from bilateral to multilateral exchange would predict a shift back toward a more bilateral pattern of trade in the recent period since 1970. This should show up in rising levels of export partner concentration (the percentage of exports going to a single other nation). Table 13.2 shows evidence to the contrary, however. Except for the OPEC nations, every category of countries experienced a decline in export partner concentration between 1970 and 1980, indicating that the international trade matrix is continuing to become more multilateral in this period.

TABLE 13.2 *Recent trends in export partner concentration, 1970–1980*

Type of country	*Number of countries*	*1970 (%)*	*1980 (%)*
Industrial	18	24.2	24.1
Centrally planned	6	33.6	29.0
OPEC	6	33.4	37.3
NICs	8	28.4	25.8
Middle income	25	31.0	28.7
Low income	20	37.6	30.9
All countries	83	31.1	28.6

Source: Müller (1988)

It may be that the increase in OPEC partner concentration is due to heightened levels of competition among core powers for access to oil exacerbated by the OPEC oil cartel. This probably encourages a more bilateral politically determined structure of exchange in the world oil market.

While some of Krasner's periods correspond with well known phases of the Kondratieff, others do not; for example the long period between 1820 and 1879. It is, of course, possible that variations of smaller amplitude occurred within the long period in the middle of the nineteenth century, but the current crude level of measurement is inadequate to detect them. A more quantitative approach to the measurement of the average height of protectionist barriers is desirable, and also feasible.

Core/Periphery Cycles in the Terms of Trade

Raul Prebisch's (1949) important work on the unequal returns to gains in productivity in the core and periphery emphasized the long-term deterioration of the terms of trade for peripheral exports. However, Prebisch's claim that the terms of trade for peripheral exports always decline has been disproven. Michael Barratt-Brown (1974) first presented evidence showing cyclical variations in the terms of trade between core and periphery, and this has recently been further supported by data analyzed by Paul Bairoch. Bairoch (1986:205–8) finds that "between the 1870s and the 1926–29 period the terms of trade for primary products relative to manufactured goods improved by some 10–25 percent." This is contrary to the results of the League of Nations study by Folke Hilgerdt which Prebisch and, much later, Rostow (1978:98) used as evidence of changes in the terms of trade. Bairoch argues that the main problem with the League of Nations study is that it employed only British data on import and export prices and the import prices include a large component of transport costs, which were falling throughout the period. Bairoch also notes that export prices of British manufactures were rising more rapidly during this period than those of other competing core powers (due to falling productivity in Britain), which also biases the terms of trade figures when only British prices are used. Bairoch goes on to observe:

> The fact that the terms of trade, or in more precise and "technical" terms the net barter terms of trade of less developed countries have improved, does not mean that this is necessarily a positive development. It would have been so if this had been accompanied by a rise in wages and in other incomes as has happened in the developed countries. While the real wages of primary-goods producers in the Third World remained stagnant between the 1870's and the 1920's the real wages of the producers of manufactured goods in the developed world increased by some 100–160 percent in the same period. This implies that in 1926–29 an average Third World worker could buy with his average wage 10–25 percent more manufactured goods than his grandparents could around 1875, while an average worker in the developed world could buy with his average wage 80–130 percent more primary goods originating from the Third World than had been possible for his grandparents. In more technical terms, this means that the factorial terms of trade for primary goods from the Third World declined. (1986:206)

Bairoch presents a table (1986:207; table 13.6) which shows that the net barter terms of trade of the peripheral countries improved from 1938 to 1950–54 and then deteriorated until 1960–64, then improved until 1970 and then deteriorated again until 1983 when the data series ends. Excluding the major oil exporting countries, the terms of trade of the peripheral countries tend to vary inversely with those of the core countries until 1970. After that the terms of trade of both core and peripheral countries worsen together and inversely with those of the oil exporters.

Bairoch notes the paradox that the post-World War II worsening of the peripheral terms of trade coincides with the decolonization and political independence of many of the peripheral countries. He attributes this to a number of causes: the slowdown in demand and increase in supply of many primary products; the development of core-produced synthetic substitutes; tariffs on the importation of some tropical goods; and

> technological progress that has reduced the input coefficients of raw materials in manufacturing industry and, last but not least, what is called the Singer–Prebisch thesis. This thesis suggests that due to weaker organization, the unequal relationship between the developed and the underdeveloped worlds leads to a situation where, in the case of primary products, the gains in productivity are translated into a decline in prices, while in the case of manufacturers, those gains are translated into higher salaries and profits. The irony is that, to a certain extent, independence could mean a freer hand for big purchasing companies to press for lower prices since, in such a case, the local social situation has no effect on the developed country. (1986:207)

Bairoch also mentions the possibility that part of the terms of trade deterioration since the 1950s could have been due to productivity increases in tropical agriculture which were greater than the increases in the productivity of manufactured goods.

While evidence of cyclical variations in the net barter terms of trade is convincing, the variations noted do not seem to correspond in any simple way with other world-system cycles. The improvement noted in the late nineteenth century occurs during the upswings and downswings of Kondratieffs and during the generally declining phase of British hegemony, while the variations noted after World War II occur during the golden age of US hegemony and the beginning of its decline.

Hopkins and Wallerstein (1979:496) outline a more complex model which posits a set of shifts in the demand for core (high wage) and peripheral (low wage) products over a pair of K-waves. The hypothesized changes in core/periphery terms of trade as applied to the two twentieth-century K-waves do not correspond well with the changes found by Bairoch.

What is still at issue is the matter of the factorial terms of trade, which takes into account changes in wage differentials. Data are not presently adequate for the detection of cycles. But according to Bairoch the factorial terms of trade worsened during the period around the turn of the century at the same time as the net factor terms improved. It would appear that this worsening probably continued after World War II when the net factor terms declined.

This is further indication of a secular trend in the direction of an increasing relative gap in the purchasing power of core and peripheral workers; both groups are increasing their purchasing power, but at different rates.

Cycles of Capital Exports to the Periphery

Capital exports and colonization are very different kinds of expansion toward the periphery, yet the model presented above hypothesizes that both of these are related to the hegemonic sequences and the K-wave. Recent work by Ulrich Pfister and Christian Suter (Suter, 1987; Suter and Pfister, 1989; Pfister and Suter, 1987) focuses on the cyclical features of the international financial system which links the core and periphery. Pfister and Suter (1987) posit a theory which links the Kondratieff wave to capital exports from the core, capital imports by peripheral countries, and international financial crises which are triggered by defaults in the periphery. Suter (1987) also hypothesizes that international financial crises will be more severe during multicentric periods of the hegemonic sequence because no single hegemonic financial center is able to perform the role of "lender of last resort." He examines data on core capital exports, peripheral imports of capital, and financial crises to determine the cyclical nature of these and their relationship to Kuznets cycles, Kondratieff cycles, and the hegemonic sequence.

Summarizing the theoretical argument made by Pfister and Suter (1987), Suter (1987:6) writes:

> . . .capital flows into the periphery occur in later stages of the long wave when markets of the core are saturated and profit rates begin to decline due to the exhausted innovative potential. Since returns on equity investment are low, capital tends to flow into the more profitable financial assets. This rising supply of international liquidity meets a corresponding demand from peripheral countries, which have not been fully integrated yet into the development process of the longwave. Structural constraints, however, such as short-falls in export earnings, low returns on external capital, and consumptive uses of external resources due to legitimatory pressures on governments, cause low income effects of imported capital. This means that the profits from investments financed by external resources do not match debt service obligations linked with these capital flows. Thus, peripheral borrowers tend to incur large debts towards the end of a long wave. As a consquence, the international financial system is over-extended and increasingly prone to disruption and crisis.

Suter notes that the above theory, along with the long wave explanations of Mandel (1980) and Mensch (1978), predicts a clustering of international financial flows from the core to the periphery towards the end of a Kondratieff upswing and during the beginning of the downswing phase. In contrast,

Rostow's (1978) theory of Kondratieffs as driven by changes in the terms of trade between raw materials and manufactured goods predicts that capital imports of sovereign borrowers occur during the upswing of the Kondratieff price cycle.

Suter and Pfister's (1986) findings about cycles of capital exports from the core are based on general surveys of the issuance of government-backed bonds. They conclude that there are seven boom periods of capital exports since the beginning of the nineteenth century (Suter and Pfister, 1986: table 1). These occur in the early 1820s, the late 1830s, the 1860s and early 1870s, the 1880s, the decade before World War I, the 1920s, and the 1970s.[5]

Suter (1987) also presents two case studies of cycles of capital imports, one for Peru and one for the United States. Peru illustrates the prototypical model of dependent underdevelopment in which Kondratieff-related periods of externally financed investment booms in extractive exports failed to stimulate much long-run economic growth and were followed by economic crisis and default. The US is, of course, a different story. It also imported capital cyclically and the individual state governments defaulted on foreign loans, but the overall outcome was much different. The US succeeded in establishing autocentric accumulation and a dynamic of capital intensive growth which was oriented toward production for the domestic market, thus moving into the expanding core of the world-economy. Suter and Pfister (1986) closely examine four other cases: Liberia, Argentina, Turkey, and Spain.

Suter argues that the patterns of capital exports and capital imports that he observes can be explained by understanding different periods as phases of the expansion process of the capitalist world-system. The first half of the nineteenth century does not reveal cyclical patterns of international finance because, he argues, the mechanisms of international finance produced by industrialization are as yet insufficiently developed.[6]

During the second half of the nineteenth century Suter finds both Kuznets and Kondratieff waves of development affecting international financial cycles. He interprets this as involving two different processes. The Kuznets cycle – a 15 to 25-year business cycle – allegedly operated only within the sphere of the growing "Atlantic economy" (an inner circle of recent settlement in which population migrations, housebuilding, and railroad building booms are important). Brinley Thomas's (1954) analysis of the inversely related British and US Kuznets cycles was the original work which set off a tradition of research on inversely related economic cycles. While Rostow (1978) declared that the Kuznets cycle has no general validity, being a process which is revealed only under special circumstances, Suter disagrees. He argues that the Kuznets cycle existed within the expanding inner circle of core capitalist growth, and he claims that evidence of it can be seen not only in the late nineteenth century but also in the interwar period. In the postwar period only the Kondratieff wave is evident in international financial cycles. Amin (1974) and others have argued that the shorter cycles have been dampened by the countercyclical Keynesian economic policies employed by states, but that the longer cycle remains because it flows from an international dynamic not controllable by any state.

Cycles of Financial Crisis

Suter also studies debt crises, defaults, and international loan reschedulings. His Chart 6 (Suter, 1987:21) graphs the number of countries in default, the number of occurrences of default from 1815 to 1950, and the number of loan reschedulings from 1950 to 1984. This graph reveals that debt crises are highly correlated with Kondratieff waves, with high default levels occurring during downswing periods, as the theoretical approach taken by Pfister and Suter predicts. The most interesting finding, however, is the combination of the analysis of the cycles of debt crises with a regional specification of the countries experiencing the financial difficulties (Suter, 1987:22, table 2). This shows that the areas accounting for the major financial crises shifted from period to period while the cycle of debt crises varied regularly with the Kondratieff wave of the world economy. In the crisis period from 1825 to 1840 the areas most affected were nine US states, Portugal, Colombia, Venezuela, Ecuador, Mexico, Spain, Brazil, and Greece. Suter points out that not only do the regions involved vary, but the particular combination of factors which contributed to the debt crises varied. In the 1820s the decolonizing Latin American countries employed their external financing to make anti-imperial war on Spain, an investment which apparently did not result in big financial returns for the core financiers whose money was used. A similar use was made of external financing by Greeks rebelling against the Ottoman Empire. Suter categorizes these as "consumption expenditures," but our knowledge of the hegemonic sequence and strategic political–military competition suggests that there may have been long-term political paybacks to these "investments."

In the debt crisis period from 1875 to 1882 the major defaulting countries were Turkey, Egypt, Peru, Mexico, eleven Southern US states, Tunisia, Uruguay, Costa Rica, Honduras, Venezuela, and Colombia. Some of these were the same countries which defaulted before, but a number of others were new. In the period from 1932 to 1939 the defaultors were Germany, Chile, Brazil, Cuba, Peru, Bolivia, Uruguay, Colombia, Yugoslavia, Greece, Mexico, Bulgaria, and Panama. The presence of Germany shows that even core states can get caught in the debt trap. And in the period of reschedulings during 1982 and 1983 the countries involved were Brazil, Mexico, Venezuela, Argentina, Chile, Poland, Peru, Yugoslavia, Ecuador, Turkey, and Romania. The earlier discussion of clusterings in time despite variations across space is demonstrated by these findings, which indicate that strong world-system-level processes are operating to produce overall core/periphery patterns even though the particular circumstances of peripheral countries vary somewhat independently in determining the experience of each area. The contention that debt crises occur only in countries which have attracted core capital for the first time (Ford, 1968) or which are weakly integrated into the world economy is contradicted by the existence of many countries which repeat the debt crisis cycle.

Suter also hypothesizes that international financial crises will be more severe during a period of multicentricity in the hegemonic sequence, and this is borne out by the numbers for the 1930s compared to earlier crises and more recent ones. Pfister and Suter (1987) have also argued that the ability of the contemporary international financial system to avoid (or postpone) collapse is due to the increased ability of international financial institutions to co-ordinate debt rescheduling. Suter contends that the greater integration of international organizations such as the IMF frees the international financial system to some extent from dependence on a hegemonic core power to perform the role of supplying world money as the "lender of last resort." He also points out that in earlier crises upwardly mobile semiperipheral countries were often able to weather financial crises without collapsing. Some of the current countries having debt problems (e.g. Spain, South Korea, and Algeria) are seen as able to service their debts and avoid collapse, while for others the situation is much more grim.

CONCLUSIONS

What can we conclude about cycles in core/periphery relations? Of course more work needs to be done, as suggested several times above. We still have much to do at the level of discovering the temporal relations among variables. Measurement of variables needs more work in order to specify cyclical variations. It is much easier to determine overall trends. The existing research confirms that there are indeed cyclical variations but we are still uncertain about the true relations in time among many of these features. The core/periphery trade network, including trade partner concentration, tariff barriers, and colonial trade monopolies is found to vary from period to period, and is related in a general way (but not simply) to the hegemonic sequence. The waves of decolonization, one form of resistance from the periphery, occur during the upswing and peak of the hegemonic sequence when the hegemon supports the break-up of the colonial empires of the other core states. The Kondratieff wave is less tightly related to the hegemonic sequence than we have earlier supposed. Waves of colonization are likely to be related to the Kondratieff/core war severity cycle, but we don't know the exact timing of the relationship. Flows of capital from the core to the periphery are related to the

Kondratieff wave, occurring approximately at the peak of an upswing, and international financial crises which are triggered by defaults in the periphery occur during Kondratieff downswings. As mentioned in note 5, visual comparison of the graphs of waves of capital exports with the waves of colonial expansion suggests that these two types of expansion are not simply related to one another in time.

Evaluation of the causal model presented in figure 13.2 is impossible at this point. Our review of the few studies which have tried to examine core/periphery cycles does, however, suggest some changes. Different sorts of expansion (capital exports versus colonialism) may have somewhat different causes, as might the three indicators of core/periphery trade structure used by Krasner. Protectionism, trade partner concentration, and the average ratio of domestic production to foreign trade probably have somewhat different causes. And "core conflict" must be differentiated to distinguish between economic protectionism and warfare.

It is premature to produce new causal models before we have done additional data-gathering and made more progress on the temporal relations among variables. A summary of the main conclusions reached in part III on the core/periphery hierarchy is contained on pages 9–10 of the Introduction. We now turn to a consideration of the metatheoretical assumptions and empirical methods used in world-system research.

PART IV

Metatheory and Research Methods

The shift to a world-system frame of reference necessarily raises questions of epistemology and the philosophy of science. Is there a stance *vis-à-vis* these problems which is most appropriate for understanding world-systems? Are certain methodologies ruled out? What difficulties do we encounter as we attempt to build theories about world-systems and to subject those theories to evidence, and how can these be overcome?

Only a few authors have directly addressed these questions in the terms just used, but there is, of course, a wider literature which is relevant. Most of the controversies which have rocked social science since its beginnings about how we should scientifically study human societies are germane, and so are the particular twists and turns, attacks and defenses, which have been so evident in recent years.

Simply because there is now only one world-system the method of historical interpretation has seemed preferable to most world-system scholars. In the following chapters I will argue that the comparative method as it has developed within modern empirical social research provides a valuable set of tools for world-system studies, notwithstanding certain problems which emerge when we utilize these tools. I will discuss the claims of authors who have disputed the value of particular kinds of comparison, e.g. quantitative crossnational studies, and will describe solutions to the problems encountered when we use comparative methods to study a single world-system.

There is now only one world-system. Its spatial scale is grand and variations within it are striking. Thus many world-system studies have focused on the particular qualities of periods or places, and have employed the method of historical interpretation. While these studies are valuable additions to our knowledge and rich sources of hypotheses about the world-system, their theoretical contributions can only be evaluated by the use of comparative research designs.

Of course the very systemness of the now-global world-system is itself a problem, and a research question. My project, only begun in this book, is to formulate and test models of the modern world-system which can explain its past and predict its future, and hopefully be of use in transforming it into a more humane set of social relations. This project assumes that the world-system is fairly systemic. You can not model something which is so ephemeral that its structure and dynamic nature change very rapidly or are infinitely complex.

Chapter 14 on theory construction discusses the nature of world-system theory and criticisms of the structural approach. It describes a continuum of positions ranging from ideographic historicism to completely ahistorical nomothetic theory, and it argues against the tide of recent attacks on structuralism. The ontological status of the world-system is compared with that of other units of analysis in the social sciences. It is pointed out that, contrary to the common assumption, levels of abstraction are not necessarily related to the spatial scale of units of analysis. Three types of world-system models are described and the problems of concept formation, dialectical modeling, and the implications of structural theories for political action are discussed.

Chapter 15, on methods, confronts the claim that we need a new method of research in order to study world-systems. It discusses the logic of comparative method, case studies, and quantitative analysis. It describes Galton's problem – the problem of the independence of cases – and its solution, the taking account of non-independence, including contextual and relational variables, within the theoretical model. Then problems of applying the generalized logic of time series analysis to the whole world-system are confronted. Cross-national, transnational and multilevel research designs are considered, as are the prospects for comparing large numbers of historical world-systems.

14

Theory Construction

Recent attacks upon structuralism and formal theorizing in the social sciences have occurred within the context of a global ideological shift toward the right. The renewal of nineteenth-century glorifications of the free market and entrepreneurial profits by neoconservatives has been surprising, but even more curious is the left's drift to the center. This has occurred in many forms – the emphasis on modernizing the state sector and increasing its productivity, the shift toward markets and profit incentives in the "socialist" states, and Eurocommunist support for nationalism, state capitalism, and austerity. We know that academia and world politics are not separate islands, and so it is tempting to assert a connection between the renewed emphasis on methodological individualism and the shift away from analyses of structural and institutional forces in both political ideology and social science.

Exactly what this connection is I cannot say. The *Zeitgeist* seems to affect us all, and all of our activities. I am not arguing that all those who have attacked Marxist structuralism are tools of the capitalists. Rather I want to make the case that the building of a formal structural theory of capitalist accumulation remains an important goal for social science and a potentially valuable contribution to the creation of a more humane, egalitarian, and balanced world society, and one that is less likely to send our collective experiment with life up in smoke.

In my view the structuralism of Louis Althusser and his students has been attacked on the wrong grounds. The effort to formulate a structural theory of capitalist develoment, now understood at the world-system level, is a necessary effort if we are to collectively get control of this headless horseman, this driverless (or multidrivered) behemoth which is almost certainly hurtling us all toward the precipice.

A DEFENSE OF THEORY

E. P. Thompson (1978) has made perhaps the most influential attack on Althusserian structuralist theory in his essay "The poverty of theory." Thompson argues that men and women are more than simply occupants of structural positions, merely agents of social forces. They are historical actors who actively negotiate and struggle to create their own lives and to change (or maintain) existing social institutions. A structuralist theory is condemned because it implies a mechanical view of human beings hopelessly caught and scuttled along by social forces beyond their control. This debilitates purposive action and promotes fatalism. Structural theories are also themselves ideological weapons by which power is legitimated, and this power is used to oppress and exploit people. Stalinism and the Third International are suggested as a pertinent example.

As a substitute for structuralism Thompson puts forth his own method of historical analysis which emphasizes the authorship of culture by individuals and classes engaging in struggles to survive and create a better world. The historical contingency of outcomes is emphasized, as are the elements of consciousness and intentional organization.

Thompson has been joined by a large number of other academic Marxists who have made similar arguments with respect to particular subject areas, or in general philosophical and methodological terms. The critique of Marxist structuralism has succeeded in mobilizing a broad rejection in favor of historicist, voluntarist, particularistic (area or local) studies. The growing popularity of the deconstructionist critique, which demolishes all theories as textual tools of political power, is also quite evident.[1]

Here I will formulate my own critique of Althusserian structuralism, and I will argue for a renewed effort to build a formal theory of the deep structure of capitalism, rather than a rejection of all theories.

THE HISTORICIST/STRUCTURALIST CONTINUUM

First I want to pose the existence of a continuum between two extreme metatheoretical positions in the philosophy of social science and locate various intermediate positions on that continuum. The end points are what have been called nomothetic versus ideographic analysis. There is a long history of contention within all the social science disciplines between these two very different stances. Indeed many of the disciplines exhibit a somewhat cyclical pattern of variation in terms of the popularity of approaches along this continuum (e.g. Harris, 1968). Nomothetic analysis attempts to formulate general laws which explain the regularities, patterns, and forms of change exhibited by a phenomenon. In social science the most completely nomothetic formulations assert that a single ahistorical model can account for all human social systems, large or small, primitive, ancient, or modern. Talcott Parsons and his followers represent this position, contending that the idea of social structure (composed of normatively defined statuses and relations) and a list of systemic necessities can be usefully applied to two-person dyads, small groups, organizations, national societies, and global systems.

Ideographic analysis, the other end of the continuum, focuses on what is unique about a person, a time period, or a locale. Rather than asking what cases have in common, it stresses their differences. It paints in rich detail, endeavoring to evince the mentality, both cognitive and affective, of a historical setting. This is what I am calling historicism.[2] While this effort constitutes a valid and valuable exercise in the humanities, many of its proponents assert that a more generalizing approach imposes a false philosophy of physical science on human beings. Beings which can alter their own behavior intelligently and in ways difficult to predict are not billiard balls, it is contended. Social scientists respond that even "thick description" implicitly makes comparisons and utilizes generalizations in order to make its narrative statements intelligible.[3]

Perry Anderson (1980) has formulated a valuable response to E. P. Thompson's attack on structuralist theory which rescues much of what is valuable in the Althusserian apparatus while acknowledging the dialectical nature of structural determination and voluntaristic action. Anthony Giddens (1979) has addressed this issue in great detail and his work is perhaps the most systematic effort to resolve the problem, but one quickly tires of the discussion of structure, agency, and action at a purely abstract level. I am not agreeing with the historicists that every theory or piece of research must contain people, places, and events, as Charles Tilly (1984) has argued, but the absence of a specified context behind Giddens's discussion leaves one wondering. The discussion of structures, agency, power, ideology, and social change at such a completely abstract and general level sounds like so much talk. But perhaps I am only revealing my own predilection for a stance near the middle of the continuum.

In between the extreme poles of total generalization and pure description are an infinite number of possible combinations of the two, not only with the quantitative mix varying, but also with the scope and nature of content assigned in different ways. Many sociologists have argued that "grand theory" is vacuous (e.g. C. Wright Mills, 1959). On the other hand, "theories of the middle range" applied to particular contexts are alleged to be more scientifically valid and socially useful (Merton, 1957).

Fernando Henrique Cardoso and Enzo Faletto (1979) introduce their important study of dependency in Latin America with a description of their "historical–structural" method, which emphasizes the differences among several qualitative types of dependency situations and the possibilities for maneuver within the structural constraints which emanate from the core (see also Bennett and Sharpe, 1985:9–13).

Immanuel Wallerstein has characterized his focal unit of analysis as "historical systems," a term which neatly captures the dialectical antinomy between ideographic and nomothetic analyses. Wallerstein's approach emphasizes the interaction between the historicity of socio-economic systems and their deep structural or essential elements. In this he is similar to Marx. Marx criticized the ahistorical generalizations of classical political economy which ignored the unique qualities of different modes of production. Assumptions about timeless human nature, he pointed out, obscure the social origins of institutions and the qualitative transformations which occur in the development of human societies. Rather than attempting to model all socioeconomic systems, Marx focused on capitalism, an historical mode of production with its own unique logic of development and contradictory tendencies. But whereas Marx attempted to formulate his deep structural model explicitly in the volumes of *Capital*, Wallerstein's remarks about theory and his somewhat casual approach to theoretical specification reveal a semiphenomenological attitude. The statement of editorial policy in the Braudel Center's journal, *Review*, refers to "the transitory (hueristic) nature of theories." Wallerstein's penchant for narrative first and theoretical discussion second, and his ambivalent and contradictory record regarding the definition of his own concepts, place him further toward the historicist end of the continuum than Marx or Althusser.

Althusser and his followers have been criticized for excessive structuralism and the allegedly associated sins listed in the discussion of E. P. Thompson above. But I do not think these are the main problems with Althusser's approach. A structural theory of the tendential laws of capitalism, rather than implying a deterministic universe in which political action is necessarily futile, is rather a guide to the weak links and openings for positive socialist politics, or it ought to be. There is no contradiction here because *no one* claims that all social action is determined by structural forces. A Marxist structural theory, as Engels (1935) long ago pointed out, is an effort to say how historical forces are moving and to indicate what is possible for "scientific socialism" within that context. Both structural theories and historical accounts can be used to legitimate political power. A good (or true) theory can be used for bad ends, but this possibility is not an argument for ripping down all theories.

Althusser and Balibar's approach (Balibar, 1970) is valuable precisely because they make the distinction between:

1 the mode of production – an abstract level of analysis which specifies essential structural tendencies of a socio-economic system; and
2 the level of the social formation – a concrete and directly observable

level of historical events and social institutions which may contain more than one mode of production as well as more purely conjunctural features which combine to determine historical events.

The distinction between the deep structure and the conjunctural level of historical events is contained within the overall analysis. Althusser and his students are more explicit about the content of the deep structural level, and they put more emphasis on its causal importance than does Wallerstein or other scholars who are closer to the historicist end of the continuum.

Of course it is not only a matter of the relative emphasis of structure and conjuncture, but also the substantive content of the distinction. Among the structures, Parsons makes norms and values the master variables. Exactly how one understands the distinction between "base" and "superstructure" (or between essence and epiphenomena) is of great importance to the substantive content of a theory. In chapter 1 I have proposed a reformulation of Marx's model of capitalist accumulation which not only changes the framework of analysis to the level of world-systems, but also argues that certain elements such as state-formation, nation-building, and class formation (which Marx consigned to the conjunctural) should instead be incorporated into the model of deep structure. Here I am not defending those substantive theoretical decisions, but rather the prior decision to continue the project to produce a structural theory.

My own criticism of Althusser et al. focuses, not on the structuralist project but on the content of the theorization (see chapter 1), and also on the failure of the Althusserians to concern themselves with the confrontation between theoretical formulation and empirical research. The philosophy of praxis employed by the Althusserians defines the confrontation with the empirical world in terms of political activity. I do not agree that political practice is a substitute for systematic comparative research designed to distinguish among contending theoretical formulations. Rejecting systematic comparative research as a bourgeois method, the Althusserians became mired in a scholastic world of textual interpretation, rationalistic deductive analysis, and political debate. Many of those Marxists who were concerned with the real world of ongoing social movements outside of the immediate context of French political debates turned away from structuralism. Thus Manuel Castells, himself an early proponent of Althusserian structuralism, embraced historicism in the form of a kind of populist romanticism (see Molotch, 1984), throwing out theory with the bath.

My defense of comparative empirical analysis is contained in the following chapter. Here I only want to point out that deductive reasoning, the logical exposition and critique of theoretical concepts and propositions, is only half of the process of scientific theory production. The other half is inductive empirical research. The central tendency of American sociology has been the opposite error – research without theory. As Arthur Stinchcombe (1968) and many others have pointed out, research can only distinguish between theories which predict different things, and so it is important to formulate contending theories in ways which make it clear what they do and do not imply about the empirical world.[4] Admittedly this demanding ideal of how theory construction ought to proceed is rarely followed, and I have not been able to completely follow it in this book. Nevertheless, archaic as it may seem, it is one of the main justifications I offer for my theoretical effort, and for the review of comparative research results.

ONTOLOGY

In many discussions with students and colleagues in sociology I have discovered the curious assumption of a connection between spatial scale and the level of abstraction. Many seem to assume that the world-system is abstract, whereas an individual person is concrete. I have also observed this error in the published works of distinguished social scientists (e.g. Tilly, 1984:14). But on reflection everyone will admit that there is no necessary connection between size and abstraction. The sun is not more abstract than the earth. I am not more abstract than an ant. The world-system is not directly observable to the eye, and this may be part of the reason why some people think of it as more abstract than smaller levels of analysis. But neither is the earth visible as a whole to most eyes. And yet we would all agree that it, and many other things such as atoms and the solar system, are concrete entities. The psychology of visual perception has established that we employ ideas even in our perception of the immediately visible. But this does not mean that everything is equally abstract. Though I need the concept "chair" to see the chair, I and most philosophers of knowledge believe that a chair is more concrete than is (say) beauty.

In social science most of us believe that individuals really exist and that they are more concrete than classes or nations. Since Lukács we have been cautioned to beware the reification of society.[5] But John W. Meyer, a consummate structuralist, has pointed out that we more often reify the individual. As we all know from our undergraduate courses, the self is socially constructed and biological individuals are conceptualized very differently in different kinds of societies. But let us assume that individuals exist. It does not follow that larger levels of analysis are less concrete. At the most concrete level the world-system is composed of all (or nearly all) of the people on earth, and the material interconnections (direct and indirect) among them. It is large, but it is not abstract, or not more abstract than other, smaller, objects of social science analysis.

But scale does affect the patterns which are observable. When we use a telescope we see very different things from when we use the naked eye or a microscope, even when these are pointed at the same "reality." There is little point in arguing about which are the real concrete patterns or objects. Rather, if we are writing history we may choose to focus on one or another scale of analysis for its own sake, as we choose between different aesthetic styles. But if we are making science we will wish to understand the causal processes by which patterns change, and we will ask which level of analysis accounts for more variation in a designated outcome variable (explanandum). This last effort may require the study of different levels of analysis simultaneously, a matter that is discussed in the next chapter.

MODELS OF THE WORLD-SYSTEM

World modeling is an enterprise which has proceeded largely unconnected with the world-system perspective. Here we will comment on the possible relations between these two projects and designate three types of models which are part of the effort to construct a theory of world-systems.

World modeling is a data-gathering and simulations effort by different groups of scholars. Much of this work is valuable because it focuses on the world economy as a whole as the unit of analysis and it uses empirical data to forecast trends. The theoretical models used to created the simulations have varied greatly from project to project, but none of the main projects has utilized the kind of theory developed in this book, a theory which uses Marx's accumulation model of capitalist development as its starting point. I would concur with Patrick McGowan (1980) that, despite the very different paradigms employed by world modelers and the world-system perspective, these two projects can be useful to one another.

Levels of Specification

I would like to distinguish between three levels at which we may specify models of the modern world-system. The first can be called a descriptive model. This type of model specifies the relationships in time between the several cycles and trends which are features of the world-system that vary over time. Such a model is implied by the discussion of cycles and trends in chapter 2 and several authors have presented such temporal models (e.g. Chase-Dunn, 1978:170; Hopkins and Wallerstein, 1979:496–7). This sort of model does not specify causal relations among variable features. Rather it simply predicts regular temporal relations among different variables. This descriptive level of analysis is rarely ever presented without some discussion of causal relations. It is a valuable theoretical effort in its own right to make explicit hypotheses about temporal regularities because it facilitates the posing of empirical questions.

The second type of model is a specification of the causal relations among variables which are features of the whole world-system or features of subunits, such as zones, nation states, etc. An example of such a model is given in figure 13.2 and a series of similar examples are contained in McGowan's (1985) critique of Bergesen and Schoenberg's (1980) study of cycles of colonialism. Procedures for testing these causal models are discussed in the following chapter. Their value is that they make explicit our arguments about what causes what, and therefore they can be helpful in evaluating different theoretical arguments about processes of the world-system.

A third type of theoretical specification is one which formulates a theory of the deep structure or the main engine which drives the world-system. Marx's theory of the capitalist mode of production is such a model. It posits the existence of structural tendencies which can account for the long-run dynamics of growth and reproduction of a socio-economic system. The specification of such a deep structural model may be formalized in a number of different ways. Part of Marx's model has been formalized as an axiomatic theory of logically related statements by Nowak (1971). Morishima (1973) has mathematically specified major aspects of Marx's accumulation model. Models of the deep structure need not be completely formalized, but formalization makes assumptions clearer and makes it easier to see the empirical implications of a set of central theoretical statements.

It should be pointed out that the language of deep structure versus surface-level appearances does not require the nominalist philosophy of Hegelian idealism. We need not assume that there is "really" an unobservable essence beneath the complexities of empirical appearances. The model of the deep structure is like a map. It is a simplification of the territory that helps us get where we want to go, to explain and predict as much as possible. It is desirable that the map be as simple as it can be, while still remaining helpful. Here again we find the continuum between historicism and completely ahistorical theory. Historicism copies the territory in rich detail, without an attempt to simplify. On the other hand, the map of completely general ahistorical theory is so simple that only the most analytic features are drawn, e.g. the grid of longitude and latitude. These features will provide a rough guide for all locations, but will not provide sufficient information to be helpful for most particular purposes.[6] Thus it is not so much a question of the real existence of the deep structure but rather the usefulness of the model for explanation, prediction, and action. And in this sense there are varying degrees of truthfulness rather than an absolute truth.

Concept Formation

Cardoso (1977) argues that concepts should not be rigidly defined and/or converted into one-dimensional variables, because the social reality being studied is a dynamic, contradictory reality which is oversimplified by such precision. This objection may be partly based on Marx's notion that theoretical concepts in the social sciences should be reflective of the relational and contradictory character of social processes themselves (Marx, 1973). I think that this is an important methodological idea, but it should not prevent us from making tentative definitions clear in order to see how they may be useful in explaining empirical reality. Operationalizing a concept does not permanently commit us to either the definition or the particular indicator we employ to measure it. Cardoso is right to point out that we should be aware of the assumptions behind converting a concept like dependency into a one-dimensional variable. Indeed, the evidence of crossnational research confirms that dependency is a multidimensional phenomenon (see chapter 10).

Much of the concern about the implicitly static and mechanistic nature of formal causal models (e.g. Bach, 1977) seems to be the result of a misunderstanding of the logic of causal analysis. All non-experimental research is an attempt to infer underlying causal processes from data over which we have little control. The type of variables used (qualitative, metric, linear or curvilinear, multidimensional or not) and the logic and nature of the causal relations that are implied in a particular model are up to the theoretical imagination of the researcher. It is true that the most commonly tested models assume one-way causation and linear relations among variables, but these assumptions are by no means necessary to causal modeling.

Dialectics and Contradiction

Cardoso (1977) and Bach (1977) argue that conventional causal imagery should not be applied to dependency and world-system processes because these processes are dialectical and contradictory. Presumably these authors are making a claim about objective reality; if we can be clear about what is meant by a dialectical process, there is no inherent reason why a dialectical model cannot be specified and tested.

Many students of social structure prefer to use dialectics as an heuristic aid to thinking about processes of social change. As such, the general notions of contradiction, opposition, and qualitative transformation can be quite useful for interpreting complex historical situations, and this heuristic aid is not at all incompatible with causal propositions of a more conventional kind. When we assert that there is a negative causal relationship between, for example, dependence on foreign investment and economic growth (Bornschier and Chase-Dunn, 1985), we do not deny the interactive and reactive nature of the relationships between transnational corporations, peripheral states, and peripheral workers. What we are asserting is that on the whole, over many cases, in the long run, *ceteris paribus*, the more dependent a country is on foreign capital the slower it is likely to develop economically. The possibility that there may be exceptions, or that some countries may be able to successfully combine foreign investment with a certain kind of growth, does not disprove the general contention. Propositions of this kind can easily be combined with a dialectical heuristic.

More problematic is the specification of formal dialectical propositions within a model. If we contend that a particular process or relationship is dialectical it is possible to formally specify the meaning of this assertion. Although it is unpalatable to many dialecticians, we can translate the notion of contradiction into conventional causal logic. Thus contradiction may be understood as:

> causal vectors that affect a dependent variable in opposite ways;
> variables that affect one another (reciprocal causation); or
> a variable that negatively affects itself over time (negative feedback).

It is true that most causal models in social research employ only fairly simple assumptions about feedback, reciprocal causation and interaction, but much more complex forms of causation have been successfully modeled with fairly standard mathematical tools.

Most serious dialecticians are not satisfied with such a simple translation of the central notions of dialects (contradiction, opposition, and qualitative transformation) into conventional causal logic, however. They argue that Aristotelian logic precludes the simultaneous existence of opposites, so a new logic and mathematics is required. Work has begun to create a formalized dialectical logic and mathematics (Rescher, 1977; Alker, 1982). This type of work may eventually allow us to construct dialectical models that clearly specify the meaning of opposition, contradiction, synthesis, and qualitative transformation in ways that make them empirically disconfirmable. This line of work was suggested by Erik Wright (1978: chapter 1). He elaborated a number of "modes of determination" which are particularly appropriate to the task of modeling the causal structures of Marxian theory.

CRITICAL THEORY, DETERMINISM, AND POLITICAL PRACTICE

Structuralist theory, formal modeling, and quantitative comparative studies have been attacked by those who argue that dependency and world-system studies should expose and condemn the structures of domination. Critical theory and deconstructionism want to expose positive social science as bourgeois ideology, and the argument is made that both the philosophy of knowledge and the comparative methodology used in normal social science are actually class-based mystifications. Cardoso (1977) contends that quantitative comparative research is necessarily uncritical because it must wear the mantle of "value-free" objective science.

My general defense of quantitative comparative methods is contained in the next chapter. Here I want to argue for the political value of a renewed effort in the realm of structural theory. If we already had an adequate theory of capitalist accumulation and sufficient understanding of the dynamics of world-system processes and the nature of the transformation of modes of production, then we could go on to particular applications of this knowledge in social struggles. But the current "crisis of Marxism" reveals that certain basic problems about the nature of capitalism and socialism have not yet been resolved. That is why it is politically sensible to exert effort toward the reformulation of a positive theory of capitalist accumulation. If we could simply accept Marx's model and apply it to the world of the twentieth century then we would not need to produce a new (or revised) theory. A structural theory, however, is more than a call to action. It is a model of how the socio-economic system actually works, its dynamics of growth and competition, and the inherent contradictions which produce pressures for transformation.

Bach (1977) and Cardoso (1977) argue that the construction of formal models implies a deterministic view of development which ignores the voluntary efforts of individuals and classes to resist and to alter the structures that are exploiting and underdeveloping them. On the contrary, models in social science are most usually probabilistic rather than deterministic, thus to allow for the complexity and indeterminacy of human behavior. Knowledge of the likelihood of a social outcome given certain conditions is a potential contributor to human freedom. We do not become more determined by understanding the laws of nature or the tendencies of social systems. On the contrary, we become freer. For example, models of dependency that show the size and nature of average effects on a national economy caused by an increase (or decrease) in dependence on foreign investment can be useful in helping policy-makers in peripheral countries avoid the negative consequences of exploitation by transnational corporations.

There is also the question of the uses of causal models and quantitative research for informing political practice. There are many political organizations and movements that might make good use of the results of comparative research on world-system processes. But just as policy-makers and planners cannot apply models mechanically to every situation, so in politics (especially in politics) practice is more an art than a science because of the complex and conjunctural nature of the task. This means that, as in medicine, the results of research must be used by informed and artful practitioners.

As I see it the main use of a structural theory of the capitalist world-economy is its potential to help us distinguish social changes and political forces which reproduce capitalism from those which contribute to its transformation, and to identify "weak links" where political efforts at transformation can bear the most fruit. If the twentieth century is the beginning of a period of transition to a socialist world-system, but the extant "socialist" states are functional parts of the capitalist world-economy (Chase-Dunn, ed., 1982b), we need a clearly specified theory of capitalism to help us distinguish newly emerging forms which contribute to the transformation of the system from those which reproduce, further expand and deepen it. And our new theory should also have implications for the question of agency in the building of socialism.

15

Research Methods

Many of the long-standing methodological feuds within the social sciences have been extended to the question of the correct way to study world-systems. The continuum of metatheoretical stances discussed in the last chapter generally corresponds with a set of preferences regarding methodology. I say generally because some theorists disapprove of empirical research in any form, while some "raw empiricists" disdain theory. But among those who are willing to risk contact with the messy empirical world there is a vast gap between proponents of the case study and proponents of systematic comparative analysis. As with metatheory, there are many positions in between. Some researchers differentiate among qualitative types. Some combine case studies with quantitative analysis of a large number of cases (e.g. Paige, 1975).

Charles Ragin and David Zaret (1983) contrast Weber's individualizing approach with Durkheim's generalizing approach. Weber constructed ideal types in order to analyze the differences between the Orient and the Occident. Durkheim analyzed large numbers of cases in order to verify a general model which was intended to apply to all cases. Ragin and Zaret convincingly argue that both strategies are valuable depending upon the goals of the study. And they make a valiant effort to demonstrate the complementarity of these strategies. Adherents of these methodological stances need not always engage in a confrontation in which the historians and area specialists assert that it was *different* in Barcelona in 1934, while the world-system theorists retort that it was just one more instance of struggle on the terrain of the world-system.

Either of these strategies (individualizing or generalizing) can be usefully applied to the world-system, depending on what we are trying to accomplish. A purely historicist approach would focus on the unique conjunctural qualities of the world-system during a particular period. Since there is only one world-system, the case study seems most appropriate. If it is believed that structural models which seek to tease out fundamental dynamics are inappropriate and misleading (a claim which reduces to the assertion that the reality is either so very complex or so rapidly changing that its structure cannot be accurately specified) then only a history is possible. A history may be useful, however, even when a more structural model is supposed. Structural models do not account for everything. Conjunctural events still need to be chronicled. The mentalities, the struggles of individuals and classes, need to be described and interpreted.

On the other hand, the same single case can also be studied structurally. It is not true that a case study precludes a structural analysis. It is possible to formulate models of the structural processes operating in a single case and to test those models using a generalized version of the logic of time series analysis. Time series analysis measures changes in variables over time and enables us to test models of the causal relations among these variables. The problems which this approach encounters when we try to apply it to the world-system are considered below. Here I simply want to make the point that having only one case does not limit us to historical or qualitative methods.

CROSSNATIONAL STUDIES

Contrary to what has been argued by some authors (e.g. Bach, 1980), the study of other levels of analysis can be quite relevant to world-system theory. Though I will devote much space below to examining how we can study the world-system as a whole, this does not imply that studies of other units of analysis such as individuals, organizations, classes, states, zones, etc. are irrelevant for our understanding of the world-system. Indeed, our conception of the world-system as a holistic structure includes these levels. It is not merely the largest layer of long-distance interaction. It includes all the short-range links as well. This is reflected in our conceptualization of the world economy as the whole which is composed of all the national economies along with the international and transnational economic structures and networks of exchange. Indeed some world-system processes *must* be studied by examining smaller units of analysis such as nation states or transnational firms. For example, studies of the effects of location in the core/periphery hierarchy on national economic development must use countries as the unit of analysis, and this is surely a research problem which emanates from world-system theory. The analysis of the world-system has implications for processes which operate at many levels, not just at the level of the world-system as a whole.[1]

GALTON'S PROBLEM

The comparison of cases is a useful and meaningful form of research for evaluating propositions which are implied by world-system theory. The strategy of comparative analysis does not emanate, as some have implied, solely from the practice of survey research in sociology. Non-experimental research designs have a long history in the natural sciences, as well as in economics. The fact that sociologists learned the logic of comparison through the technique of survey analysis is largely a historical accident, although this legacy does affect some of our practices (e.g. methodological individualism) and our vocabulary. Similarly the use of probabilistic models has been affected by the logic of sampling. We still talk of "sample size" when we mean the number of cases we are analyzing. But the logic of probability has many useful applications beyond the sampling problem.

We can draw valid inferences from comparing a number of cases only when those cases can be treated as independent instances of the process under study. This is one of the basic tenets of comparative logic (Zelditch, 1971). We cannot increase our number of cases meaningfully by including the same case twice because this is not an independent instance. This problem was first highlighted in social science by Sir Francis Galton's critique of the comparative method proposed by Edward Tylor. Tylor had proposed that social structural and cultural processes could be studied by comparing correlations of attributes across cultures. Galton pointed out that some of the resulting correlations would stem from cultural diffusion rather than from the functional interdependence of institutions. Raoul Naroll (1968) suggested that this problem could be solved by comparing cases in which cultural diffusion could not have occurred. This is one way of "controlling out" the effects of a variable, in this case diffusion. A more general solution is to measure non-independence and to include the hypothesized sources of non-independence in the model, thus controlling for them. This is done in a number of different ways.

A piece on the methods of studying national societies written by Terence Hopkins and Immanuel Wallerstein (1967) (and since disavowed by them) suggested a set of distinctions which are helpful here. Hopkins and Wallerstein contended that national societies develop due to causes which are internal, relational, and contextual. Internal causes are variable characteristics of the national society itself. Relational causes are those variables which impinge on a national society due to its relations with other national societies, for example the dependence of a national economy on foreign investment. Contextual variables emanate from characteristics of the world situation as a whole, for example the level of world industrialization. Once we have conceptualized the sources of non-independence among a set of cases and operationalized these we can use the method of quantitative comparative analysis.[2] It is not necessary to find cases which are completely unconnected with each other.

CORRECT METHODS

My stance is somewhat eclectic on the question of correct methods. I think that both historical interpretive studies and quantitative comparative studies can be useful approaches to the world-system. Historical studies are useful because some things really are conjunctural and impossible to analyze structurally, and also because they often generate hypotheses and conceptualizations which stimulate the formulation of structural theories. Also, once we have successfully established one or more structural theories, case studies which take a closer look at a process on the ground can be helpful in telling us exactly how structural forces operate. These cases or instances are best selected after comparative analysis has already shown the outlines of the structural process. We can investigate the mechanisms which link causal variables by studying "typical" cases, and we can examine contingencies by looking at deviant cases.

Contrary to the liberal spirit of the above, some world-system militants contend that the correct study of the world-system requires a new methodology, or at least precludes the usefulness of some methods, especially quantitative comparative analysis. Terence Hopkins (1978) and Robert Bach (1980) argue that we should completely rethink our methodological and epistemological assumptions when we take the world-system as the object of study. They call for the development of a new method more appropriate for understanding the nature of the modern world-system. The reasoning behind their concerns needs to be examined in an atmosphere which is clear of the smoke of the sterile debate between historicists and structuralists or between the adepts of quantitative versus qualitative analysis. These old "ethnic" boundaries often motivate intense debates, but they rarely produce new knowledge.

Robert Bach (1980) organizes his argument about the desirability of a new method around two ideas: the notion of the "singular process," and the idea of a "spatio-temporal whole." The world-system is said to be characterized by a set of singular processes, which are features of the whole system and cannot be understood by analyzing sub-parts or smaller units. This claim is part of the stance of theoretical holism, which holds that the logic of the socio-economic system – the capitalist mode of production – is a feature of the whole system, and that all causal and developmental logics within an empirical world-system must be aspects of this logic of the whole. This matter has been discussed at the theoretical level in chapter 1. It basically rules out the possibility that the dominant mode of production is articulated with other modes, and it equates the logical boundaries of a mode of production with the spatial boundaries of a world-system. Bach seeks to extend this theoretical holism to a methodological holism. His argument implies that *only* study of the world-system as a whole is relevant for understanding the world-system.

THE AGGREGATION PROBLEM

One reason Bach may be worried about subunit comparisons is the aggregation problem. This problem is analyzed generally by Michael Hannan (1971). It is the inferential error which corresponds to the opposite of the ecological fallacy. The ecological fallacy occurs when an association between two variables at the level of a set of larger units of analysis (e.g. census tracts) is used as evidence in support of an assertion about an analogous relationship at a smaller unit of analysis (e.g. households, individuals). For example, it may be observed that there is a correlation between the average level of education and the average income of households when we compare census tracts, but this is not evidence for this association at the level of households. It is not impossible that poor Ph.D.s and rich high school dropouts live in the same neighborhoods. Conversely, evidence of an association at the level of a smaller unit is not evidence of the analogous association at a larger level. This is the aggregation problem which is mentioned in chapter 11 in the context of the discussion of crossnational research and its implications for questions about the mechanisms which reproduce the core/periphery hierarchy.

The aggregation problem does *not* imply, however, that it is meaningless to aggregate characteristics of subunits in order to construct a measure of a feature of a larger unit. The world economic product can be usefully estimated by summing the GNPs of all countries.

SUBUNIT COMPARISONS

Neither does the aggregation problem imply that crossnational or other subunit comparisons are irrelevant for world-system theory. The rise and decline of hegemons, the effects of international power–dependence relations on national development, the effects of location in the core/periphery hierarchy on class formation and class struggles – these are all world-system processes which can be usefully studied by comparing national societies to one another. It is simply not the case that world-system theory only has implications for processes which operate at the level of the whole system.

Much of the reason for rejecting crossnational comparisons of large numbers of countries apparently stems from misunderstandings about the assumptions behind such research. Critics have contended that crossnational quantitative analysis implies that all nation states are the same, or that national development is a static, mechanistic, deterministic process (e.g. Cardoso, 1977; Palma, 1978; Bach, 1980). Quantitative analysis of a large number of cases does not imply any of these things, as clearly explained by Richard Rubinson (1977a). Thus, though there are "singular processes" which operate at the level of the whole world-system, and it is true that analysis of smaller units cannot directly test propositions about these (the aggregation problem), world-system theory also has implications for processes which operate within and upon smaller units such as nation states and transnational firms. These can usefully be studied by systematically comparing cases, and by taking non-independence into account in the theoretical model and the empirical research design.

SPACE AND TIME

The second concept which Robert Bach uses in his argument in favor of a new methodology for world-system scholarship is the idea of the "spatio-temporal whole" (Bach, 1980). He claims that the capitalist world-system has a feature which makes it difficult to apply the standard tools of comparative research. It is alleged that the processes which operate at the level of the whole system are not only singular, but that they are processes in which *time and space are integral features* rather than simply dimensions on which instances are arrayed. This is a fascinating contention, and one that will surely stimulate much interest among social geographers, who are always looking for new and theoretically interesting ways of conceptualizing space (e.g. N. Smith, 1984). But what does Bach really mean? He says that time and space are integral features of world-system processes. Time and space are features of all social processes in the sense that they enter into the determination of outcomes. Bach is somewhat vague as to how this claimed special feature of the world-system differs from social processes operating at smaller levels. Possibly he means that the *social meaning* of time and space is an important feature of the cultural and economic structures of capitalism. This is undoubtedly true, but I fail to see how this supports Bach's claim that conventional comparative methods are inappropriate for world-system studies.

Certainly there are special problems relating to the temporal and spatial dimensions which come up when we try to study the whole world-system. Many of these are discussed below. The unreflective application of any methodology, including historical interpretation, is unwise. But I am not convinced by Bach's argument that we should throw crossnational analysis or survey research, or formal comparative method in general, out of our tool box before we approach the world-system.

WORLD-SYSTEM CHARACTERISTICS

In proposing the formal comparative study of variable characteristics and processes of the world-system as a whole I am asserting, at the minimum, that such a system exists and can be studied in its own right. The stronger claim that this larger system has great causal importance for the development of smaller institutions and entities can only be subjected to empirical research once world-system processes have been specified and operationalized. The focus of this section is on the problems of studying the relationship between different variable characteristics of the whole system. This is distinct from the problem of studying the contextual effects of world-system characteristics on national development or the relational effects of a nation's position in the larger system on its own development. For now I am focusing on the causal relations between different characteristics of the whole world-system.

There is only one world-system now, but historically there have been many and a social scientist may make systematic comparisons across these cases in order to bring evidence to bear on a hypothesis. Wallerstein does this effectively with his comparison between the emerging European world-economy and the Chinese world-empire in the sixteenth century (1974:52–63). This approach is discussed in the last section of this chapter. Another strategy, the one to be considered here, is to employ methods which enable the comparison of a single system to itself over time. We can use the generalized logic of time series analysis to test propositions about relationships between system-wide characteristics which vary over time. Time series analysis is a statistical technique for testing causal models in which *time points are the units of comparison* (Hibbs, 1974). Thus it compares a system to itself over time in order to examine the relationships among variable characteristics. This requires that theoretically relevant variables have been conceptualized and operationalized, and that comensurable data are available over a long enough time period for processes of interest to operate.

Operationalization and Measurement

The idea of employing time series analysis to study the world-system raises a number of critical empirical questions. What are the spatial boundaries of the system and how have they changed over time? Can data gathered on nation states be used to study world-system processes? Can variables be measured over long enough periods to make valid inferences possible? Does the logic of causal analysis apply to world-system events in a straightforward way? Are long-run processes amenable to comparative research and proposition-testing? Complete answers to these questions depend on the particular proposition being investigated, but I will give examples and suggest possible approaches.

Spatio-temporal Mapping

Any effort to apply the general logic of time series analysis to the world-system as a whole must be able to specify the spatial boundaries of the system. In order to measure characteristics which vary over time we must know which areas to include and which to exclude. For example, my study of changes in the rank–size distribution of world cities (Chase-Dunn, 1985a) required decisions about which cities to include in the European-centered world-economy at various time points. I employed the rough "spatio-temporal mapping" produced by the Braudel Center scholars (Fernand Braudel Center, n.d.), but this is itself a tentative and preliminary specification.

The problem of the spatial boundaries of a world-system is both theoretical and operational. It is necessary to have a clear theoretical conceptualization of spatial boundaries before we can make headway on the measurement problem. But it would be disingenuous to imply that these two problems are completely separated in practice. A theoretical definition which is completely impossible to operationalize is useless. Thus we must use our knowledge of potentially available information in conjunction with the construction of a theoretical definition.

I argued in chapter 1 for a separation between the notions of logical and spatial boundaries. The deep structural logic of a system can change without changes in its spatial boundaries and vice versa. Thus system logic ought not to be used to draw spatial boundaries between world-systems. This separation makes it possible for there to be more than one mode of production within an existing world-system. This simplifies the problem of spatial boundaries to one of establishing some (specified) form of connectedness. It is not necessary to decide which deep structural logic is operating in any instance in order to determine the spatial boundaries of a system.

The theoretical specification of spatial boundaries is still contentious however, even after we have separated it from the problem of the mode of production. There are contending definitions, and most scholars agree that spatial boundaries are "fuzzy." Different aspects of a world-system (e.g. political–military and economic) may have somewhat different spatial extents. For example, a region may have been formally incorporated as a colony of a core power, but not yet linked into the world economic network, or vice versa. Fuzziness is also related to time. Immanuel Wallerstein contends that the process of incorporation operates over at least a 50-year period within which it is difficult to say whether or not a particular region is in or out. This implies that mapping which employs shorter intervals is necessarily somewhat arbitrary. Thomas Hall (1986) has argued that incorporation should be conceptualized as a continuum of types. This approach introduces an additional source of "fuzziness."

Wallerstein's simplest definition of the spatial boundaries of a world-system focuses on links in an interdependent network of the exchange of "fundamental commodities," by which he means food and other necessities of everyday life. He excludes the exchange of "preciosities" (luxuries) which are alleged not to have important consequences for the exchanging parties or their societies. Charles Tilly (1984:62) argues that the spatial boundaries of a world-system should be understood generally in terms of coherence and interdependence. He correctly points out that allowing any connection at all to constitute grounds for inclusion results in most areas of the globe having been parts of a single "system" for millenia, a usage employed by Lenski and Lenski (1982). The notion that everything is somehow connected to everything else, while undoubtedly true, is not very useful to a science of human society.

Tilly proposes a "rule of thumb for connectedness" based (not surprisingly) on political control. He suggests that the boundaries of a world-system can be drawn as follows:

> the actions of powerholders in one region of a network rapidly (say within a year) and visibly (say in changes actually reported by nearby observers) affect the welfare of at least a significant minority (say a tenth) of the population in another region of the network. (1984:62)

Both Wallerstein's and Tilly's definitions have conceptual and operational problems. Tilly's is more precise, but the precision is admittedly arbitrary. Nevertheless, to operationalize we are often forced to make such arbitrary dichotomies, and it is useful to recognize them as such because we may want to alter them later when other empirical problems become more evident.

Tilly's definition does not specify the boundaries of the "network," and it seems to imply a system which has a single center. Both the modern and many ancient world-systems were (and are) multicentric and thus require that we conceptualize indirect as well as direct economic and political connections.

A third definition of interconnection based on interactive political–military conflict is suggested by David Wilkinson (1987). Wilkinson proposes that polities which are engaged in sustained political–military competition with one another should be considered parts of the same "world-system/civilization."

Wallerstein's effort to rule out the exchange of preciosities is problematic when we look at primitive and ancient world-systems, and even the early modern world-system, as convincingly argued by Jane Schneider (1977). Prestige goods have played an important political role in most precapitalist world-systems, and indeed it has been argued that intersocietal prestige economies have constituted the most important element in some premodern world-systems (e.g. Blanton and Feinman, 1984). Also as Schneider points out, bullion was used as a means for hiring mercenaries in both modern and ancient world-systems, and this is hardly a matter which can be considered epiphenomenal to the reproduction of power structures. The point here is that fundamental goods networks constitute one network level because of the cost of transport, while the range of preciosities is much greater, but these latter must be taken into account in any theory which seeks to explain social change.

Perhaps we need to define sub- and super-world-systems based on this distinction. If so the sixteenth-century European world-economy was a subsystem within a larger multicentric Eurasian super-world-system. This kind of specification of boundaries complicates things to some extent, but it allows us to continue with the analysis of world-systems without consigning clearly important transactions to the basket of epiphenomena.

These theoretical issues notwithstanding, I want to move on to some of the measurement problems. Assume we have a clear theoretical definition of spatial boundaries. I already mentioned the problem of fuzziness. This is an instance of the problem of measurement error, and we have developed a set of tools for dealing with this. If measurement error is randomly distributed it will not distort the outcome of studies of associations among variables. If it is systematically biased it may affect such outcomes, and is a bigger problem. In the context of world-system boundaries it is likely that we have *better information* and *more information* the closer we get to the core and the more recent is the time period we are studying. These systematic measurement errors should be kept in mind whenever we seek to test any particular proposition.

Another point may be obvious, but is not always appreciated. I learned this from my experience with crossnational research. The spatial and temporal scale of research changes the significance of measurement error. In connection with the topic at hand, error associated with the spatial boundary of a world-system may be extremely important if one is trying to explain what happened in a particular city but much less consequential if one is trying to measure the level of a world-system characteristic such as the world city-size distribution. In other words, whether Constantinople is in or out is quite important if you are studying Constantinople, but less important if you are studying the whole world-system.

Validity and Reliability

As mentioned above, problems of operationalizing variables differ greatly depending on the era being studied. For earlier periods we must usually rely on partial information and extrapolate to the system as a whole. Thus Braudel and Spooner (1967) estimate the growing integration of sixteenth-century Europe by comparing trends in food prices in those European cities for which price series are available. For later periods more complete information across the system is available, and it is in an increasingly comparable form.

The operationalization of abstract variables over long periods of time often requires the use of different indicators in different periods. Thus, for instance, the timing of the Dutch hegemony in economic competitive advantage might be measured in terms of the extent to which Dutch products and services replaced those of competitors in the sixteenth and seventeenth centuries. The particular leading sectors which were important in this period are, of course, very different from the ones which indicated the relative competitive advantage of the British economy in the late eighteenth and nineteenth centuries, and those which were important for the US hegemony of the twentieth century (see Thompson, 1986 and chapter 9 above). Thus the validity of these measures of the concentration of competitive advantage in the core is dependent on the accuracy of judgments about which are the leading edge industries over long periods of time.

Limitations of Aggregating Data on Nation States

The very structure of data-gathering institutions may distort the available information in systematic ways which create problems of inference (Wallerstein, 1983b). For example, many of the most comparable data series are measures of characteristics of nation states. This institutional fact, which derives from the importance of the nation states as tax-gatherers and controllers of flows, makes the study of certain world-system processes difficult. For example, Frederic Lane (1966:496–504) and Jane Jacobs (1984) argue that cities are the most important unit of analysis for the study of economic growth. Samir Amin (1980) contends that classes and class interactions at the world level are important determinants of state structures and economic development. If these claims are true, data which are aggregated from information on nation states may misrepresent the operation of world-system processes. Table 12.3 estimates characteristics of the whole system by aggregating nation state data. It shows trends in the concentration of world resources from 1960 to 1980. This table has interesting implications for the study of the gap between core and peripheral countries, but it does not tell us what changes may have occurred in the distribution of resources among cities of the world or social classes. If the table had been aggregated from city data or class data the results might have been very different.

Transformation of Nation State Data

It is possible, however, to transform data based on nation states to make them more suitable for world-system research. For example, if we want to know the distribution of world monetary income among households we can use GNP data (national income) plus information from studies of intranational income distribution among households to produce an estimate of the world distribution of income among households. This has been done in the research reported by Bourguignon, et al. (1983), discussed in chapter 12.

Similarly we can estimate the distribution of income among social classes in the world by using occupational wage data from the International Labour Organization. Studies of social class using occupational characteristics (e.g. Wright, 1976) could be matched to the occupational categories used by the ILO. By this method we could produce an estimate of world income distribution among social classes.

Detailed examination of national accounts, census information, and the use of special studies to estimate parameters across the system can certainly provide theoretically relevant measures which do not depend on the nation state as the unit of analysis. The existence of Gross National Product data mean that, at some point in the data-gathering process, there must be information (or at least estimates) on the monetized transactions completed by individuals, households, firms, sectors, and the state. This information can be aggregated on other than a national basis if it can first be obtained in enough detail across the system. Much of this detailed information, however, is not available for other than the most recent periods, and thus the study of long-run processes must use less complete information. Although this reduces the level of certainty we can have in results, these important processes should not be ignored for this reason.

The use of nation state data should not be dismissed as a tool for studying the world-system.[3] For some theoretical purposes nation states *are the relevant unit of analysis* and the aggregation of national data, or the study of "international" patterns of interaction, may shed light on hypotheses about the world-system. For example, the causal model proposed in chapter 13 hypothesizes that changes in the relative distribution of productive advantage among core states affect the pattern of exchange and control between core states and peripheral areas. Although for both of these variables it is not the states themselves that are the only actors, the fact that actors are located within or associated with particular states or colonial areas is of direct theoretical importance. And thus data which are organized by nation state are appropriate to testing the proposition.

Combination of Data from Different Countries in the Same Indicator

The example given above of the attempt to measure the relative distribution of competitive advantage among core states involves the combination of data from different countries in the same indicator. The problems of working with historical trade data from a single nation are many (e.g. Schlote, 1952:3–40) but they are complicated immensely when one tries to combine such data from different countries. For example, I have estimated one aspect of Britain's hegemony over the US by determining the degree of penetration of British cotton manufactures into the clothing market of the United States from 1800 to 1900. This involved the construction of a ratio of the value (or quantity) of

British cotton manufactures imported into the US to the value (or quantity) of all textiles consumed in the US (Chase-Dunn, 1980: 215). Data for the numerator of this ratio are found in British sources while data for the denominator are from US sources. Different commodity categories and different units of quantity and value are used in the two sources. This requires careful attention to the appropriateness of combining different categories.

Another way in which data from different countries are combined is in the production of the measures produced by network analysis. These measures have been discussed in the section on measurement of world-system position in chapter 10. The use of international trade matrices can be a valuable way of studying the shape of the world-system and how it changes over time (e.g. Smith and White, 1986). And this kind of measure has also been used to study the world-system causes of national development. This is accomplished by using the location of each country within a block produced by the network analysis as an attribute of that country in crossnational analysis (e.g. Snyder and Kick, 1979; Nemeth and Smith, 1985). Recall also the contention that these network measures are superior because they are more "relational" than other measures, and my demur in note 5 to chapter 10.

Non-continuous Data Series

Another difficulty in attempting to construct data series over long periods of time is that the methods of data-gathering and conventions of presentation often change radically over time. This creates non-continuous series which may place in jeopardy the task of determining the timing of a downturn or upturn in a fluctuation. For instance, in the above example we want to know when British textiles began to penetrate the US market, and when US domestic production began to push out British textiles. The timing of these two changes in the direction of trends is crucial to our understanding of the British hegemony and its interaction with US development. Non-continuous series make such a determination difficult. And, in addition, decisions about what to compare, which commodity categories, rates of exchange, prices, etc. to use in computing the ratio, affect our estimates of the timing of these trend reversals. Such decisions must be made carefully. An excellent study which reflects insightfully on these difficulties is Modelski and Thompson's (1988) examination of world sea power.

The Width of a Time Point: Measurement Error in Time

Here is another question about the applicability of conventional causal logic to world-system research. One of the basic canons of causal analysis holds that a change in variable A causes a change in variable B if and only if the associated change in variable A precedes the change in variable B in time. The future cannot cause the past. In practice we often use historical events such as wars, regime changes, economic crises, etc. as indicators of underlying structural changes. The problem is that these events are often not direct simultaneous indicators of the underlying structural changes which we wish them to measure, and thus the apparent time sequence of indicators (events) may not reflect the true causality between variables.

The exact timing of, say, the outbreak of a revolution or war may be determined by factors which are conjunctural or only loosely related to underlying world-system processes. And yet the propensity for warfare or revolution to occur within a certain broad period may indeed be connected with underlying structural processes. If we are using an event as an indicator of a structural variable the exact timing of the event (e.g. the day and month) may represent mainly measurement error, while the fact that the event occurred within a broader (e.g. ten-year) period may be the relevant fact for our purposes of measurement.

Another way to think about this is that, when we are considering very long-run structural processes, the relevant width of a time point may be very wide. That is, the events which indicate changes in underlying variables may be "simultaneous" even when they are years apart in historical time. Andre Gunder Frank (1978:20) asserts that *simultaneity* of events disparate in space, while not proof of a causal relationship, is an important clue for world-system analysis. My point is that simultaneity should be defined broadly enough to allow for measurement errors due to lags between underlying structural changes and the "events" we use to indicate them.[4] And also the fact that event (A) occurs a few months or years later than event (B) should not be taken as proof that (A) (or rather the variable which it indicates) could not have caused (B). Their sequencing in historical time may not reflect the direction of true structural causality.

Few Instances of Long-run Processes

Another difficulty which time series analysis of world-system data must confront is the problem of few instances. If one is studying a very long-run process, e.g. the K-wave, there have been only eleven of these cycles since the beginning of the Europe-centered world-system. This means that a test of any theory about the causes of these cycles will be necessarily somewhat inconclusive because of the small number of "cases" (instances). This is the intersection between what is historically unique and what is scientifically proveable. The degrees of freedom rapidly run out as the complexity of the explanation exceeds the number of independent instances we can study. This does not mean we should abandon the general logic of time series analysis, but rather that we must be willing to accept low levels of certainty. An example is provided by Goldstein's (1988) study of core wars and K-waves. He finds that his model is supported in ten out of the eleven instances. This is very unlikely to have occurred by chance, but only a few more contrary cases would have cast doubt on his model as a general explanation. With few cases it is easy to disprove hypotheses, but hard to prove them.

Sequencing and "Cycle Time"

Joshua Goldstein (1988:chapter 8), in his discussion of methods problems encountered when studying variable characteristics of the world-system, describes an approach to social cycles which I find very helpful. Goldstein points out that social cycles are rarely perfectly periodic, unlike some of the cycles which occur in physical processes. Thus attempts to decompose long economic cycles into their components which use Fourier or spectral analysis (e.g. Adelman, 1965) are misleading because they assume that social cycles should closely approximate sine waves. Goldstein proposes instead the notion of "cycle time" in which social cycles are allowed to have variable periods. It is generally recognized that the Kondratieff wave varies in length from peak to peak from about 40 to about 60 years. Goldstein argues that we should rely more on the sequencing of events and trend reversals rather than their exact spacing along the time dimension. This is a valuable suggestion, although we should be somewhat careful about its application. We have already mentioned above a related concern about the relationship between events and underlying structural variables: the width of a time point. That discussion put into question the complete reliance on temporal priority as an indicator of the direction of causation.

Another problem is the extent of periodic cycle variation which is allowable. If our data indicated, for example, that K-waves varied in their period from (say) 20 to 80 years we would probably reconsider the value of a "cyclical" model. Robert Philip Weber (1987) has explained analytic differences between three kinds of "cycles." Weak cycles do not have "fairly constant" periodicity and are termed fluctuations. Moderate cycles have "fairly constant" periodicity, and strong cycles have, in addition, regular amplitude and symmetry. What constitutes "fairly constant" in world-system research will need to be determined in practice. K-waves and war severity waves are moderate cycles. The hegemonic sequence is probably a fluctuation with peak curves being about the same length and troughs of very different lengths.

OTHER RESEARCH DESIGNS

Above we have discussed problems associated with studying relationships among variable characteristics of the world-system as a whole. This is but one of several possible research designs which have been or could be used to study world-system processes. The following discussion compares six other broad types of non-experimental research designs. It proposes the application of two new approaches: designs for testing multilevel models, and cross-world-system comparisons.

The six types of research design are:

1 time series studies of single countries;
2 crossnational studies;
3 event histories;
4 a design which examines the effects of world-system contextual variables on national development;
5 multilevel models, and two research designs for testing them; and
6 cross-world-system studies.

Each of these categories is actually a broad collection of possible approaches in terms of the way in which the temporal and spatial aspects of comparison are utilized to study causal processes.

First, though, let us consider the problem of the choice of a unit of analysis. This is a research decision which ought to be determined by theoretical considerations. Ideally we would choose units in which independent and comparable instances of the process of theoretical interest are operating. But often, and especially in world-system studies, different units of analysis affect one another and completely independent instances are difficult to find. Above we have outlined the solution to Galton's problem – the inclusion of hypothesized non-independence into the theoretical model and into the comparative analysis. But the yardstick of relative independence is still useful in the selection of a unit of analysis. Other considerations also affect the choice of a unit of analysis such as the availability of comparable data and the existence of policy instruments which make it possible to employ research findings in political practice. These last considerations ought not to overwhelm theoretical considerations, however. If availability of hard data or "policy relevance" were primary considerations we would never study the world-system as a whole.

If the dependent variable is a characteristic of countries, such as national economic growth, then the best choice of unit of analysis is the country. It would be possible to make inferences about national growth on the basis of a study of firms, regions, or cities but such inferences would be subject to assumptions which could introduce errors. Traditionally, quantitative comparative research has required a rectangular data set in which the "cases" dimension contains instances of a single focal unit of analysis. Having chosen a focal unit of analysis we may use information on other units, or on the focal unit's relationship to other units or larger systems, but all these must be transformed into attributes of the focal unit. These transformations also involve assumptions which may be fraught with error, and thus we seek below to develop a multilevel research design in which the same model can contain data on different units of analysis. But first let us review more typical research designs in which there is a single unit of analysis.

Time Series Studies of Single Countries

Time series analysis is a method of testing causal hypotheses using data collected over time (Hibbs, 1974). Thus, if we believe that dependency retards economic growth, we can measure changes over time in the level of dependency and economic growth for a single country and test the hypothesis. In this method time points are the unit of analysis. Certain practical limitations to this design are suggested by the results of crossnational research. First, multiple regression analysis, which is a useful technique for estimating causal relations among variables, requires at least 30 datum-points for estimates to be stable. The time lapse between points must be a function of the time over which meaningful change in the variables of interest takes place. Most of the variables of interest to dependency theory or world-system analysis are structural characteristics of large social units, and these change only slowly. This means that, for example, yearly time points are not usually sufficiently independent instances of the process under study. Five- or ten-year intervals between measurements may be necessary, and 30 five-year intervals span a period of 150 years. For most variables it will be difficult to accurately measure variation over such a long time period because of the deficiencies of available data.

This practical limitation makes most studies of a single country impractical for purposes of formal hypothesis testing. However, such a design may be useful for studying variables which change meaningfully over shorter periods, or for determining the particularities of the country under consideration. The modeling of world-system processes as they occur in a single country allows one to build in conditions which may be specific to each country (e.g. Duvall and Freeman, 1981). Such models should presumably assuage some of the more historicist critics of quantitative studies, such as Cardoso (1977).

Crossnational Designs

Seven different crossnational designs are employed in the 17 studies on the effects of international economic dependence reviewed by Bornschier et al. (1978). These designs all combine data from different countries, and they differ chiefly in the way in which the time dimension is employed. They all use measures of dependency which characterize a country's relational position in the larger world-economy, that is *vis-à-vis* other countries. The designs which employ measures of change over time are superior to those that don't because of the reciprocal causal relations between economic growth and international economic dependence, and because of the time-lagged nature of dependence effects.

Rather than rehashing the description and evaluation of these designs (which is contained in Bornschier et al., 1978) I will focus on a design which is particularly useful for world-system studies. It is called "pooled cross-sections," but more properly might be termed pooled panel analysis (Hannan and Young, 1977). This design employs data on countries measured at several time points and uses both countries and time points as the unit of comparison (country-times). It throws together in one analysis the cross-sections (or panels) from different periods of time. This design is particularly appropriate for studying structural variables which change slowly, such as the city-size distribution of a country (Chase-Dunn, 1979). The number of datum-points is increased considerably, thus overcoming one of the limitations of other crossnational research designs: a rather small number of cases. There are only about 150 countries in 1970. If we study periods before the post-World War II decolonization period the number of sovereign countries decreases considerably.

If a process of theoretical interest changes only slowly a short time lag contains mostly measurement error. Pooled panel analysis allows the use of more widely-spaced measurement points and the specification of longer time lags, because the number of "cases" is increased when "country-times" are analyzed.

One possible problem with pooled panel analysis is its assumption that the structure of causation remains constant across different time periods. The cycles and trends of the larger world-system may alter the structure of causal processes operating at the national level. Volker Bornschier (1985: table 1) has found that the causal structure of national economic growth which was shown to have operated during the post-World War II K-wave upswing changed dramatically in the period of downswing from 1976 to 1981. These changes may themselves be periodic (cyclical), as when the relationship between economic nationalism and national growth alters according to whether the larger system is economically expanding or stagnating, or transformational in the sense that the structure of causation is altered in a completely new way.

Event History Analysis

Of those research designs which analyze more than one point in time, most use regular intervals of time for the measurement of variables. Thus crossnational panel designs usually measure variables every so many years, at regular intervals. Event histories record the actual exact time of the occurrence of events and use this additional temporal information about timing and sequencing in testing causal models (Allison, 1984; Tuma and

Hannan, 1984). The most obvious usage of this approach is for the analysis of categorical variables in which the timing of changes between discrete states can be determined exactly, but Tuma and Hannan (1984) have extended the use of event history analysis to continuous variables as well.

Hannan and Carroll (1981) have used event history analysis to reanalyze a crossnational panel study of the causes of changes in the formal political structures of regimes (Thomas et al., 1979). The study analyzes different national-level and international relational causes of changes in the level of regime centralization (see chapter 6). Their findings differ from those of the earlier study and, since their analysis employs more information about timing and sequencing, they conclude that event history analysis is a superior method for macro-comparative studies.

It is difficult to argue against the use of more complete information, but the reanalysis by Hannan and Carroll suggests a number of cautions. Above we have discussed the problem of the width of a time point. If it is true that largely conjunctural features determine the exact timing of events, or rather alter (randomly perhaps) the length of the lag between a significant change in a structural variable and the event we use to indicate this structural variable, then the use of "exact" time and sequencing may introduce noise rather than new information.

Also the use of a more complicated research design may run into additional problems of data availability. Hannan and Carroll were forced to drop one of the two indicators of world-system position used in the prior study for this reason. Investment dependence is not available over the whole time period they study, and is not available in yearly estimates. Thus they dropped this measure from the analysis. They found that the other measure of world-system position, export partner concentration, did not operate as a cause of changes in regime form, contrary to the panel analysis findings of Thomas et al. (1979). This bolstered the conclusion presented by Tuma and Hannan (1984:321) that the world-system interpretation has been disconfirmed by the event history analysis.

This raises the question of the costs and benefits of the development of more and more sophisticated methods. Most new methods increase the resource costs and narrow the feasible scope of research. The gains in better inferences must be weighed against these increased costs and constraints. When the choice of methods determines which research problems will be studied the tail is wagging the dog. This is one reason why social scientists with an appreciation of theory are wary of the rapid revolutionizing of methodological techniques. Event history analysis may indeed turn out to be a better way to study world-system processes, but further efforts to compare it with older methods should be more chary about conclusions which are based on less information, rather than more.

World-system Effects on National Societies

Most of the crossnational world-system studies which have been done examine the effects of a country's position within a hierarchical world structure. Hopkins and Wallerstein (1967) distinguish between these *relational characteristics* (attributes of countries due to their position in a larger structure) and contextual characteristics of the world-system as a whole. They point out that, for example, as the level of world industrialization increases it may become harder for any nation to industrialize. John Boli (1980: table 5.4) employs an ingenious method for testing such propositions. He is concerned with the way in which changes in the concentration of world economic power affect the dominance of states over their own populations. He measures the percentage of world trade controlled by the largest trading nation at seven decennial time points and then estimates the effect of this world-contextual variable on the national characteristic (state dominance) by combining the two variables in a single analysis. While countries remain the focal unit of analysis, each country receives the score of the world variable at each of the seven time points, and the seven temporal cross-sections are pooled. This research design could fruitfully be employed to test other hypotheses about the effects of changes in world-system characteristics on national development.

Multilevel Analyses

We can imagine theoretical models in which different kinds of units are simultaneously included (Teune, 1979). We implicitly include many levels of analysis when we make a model of a single unit. For example, when we study countries or firms we imagine that the behavior of and interaction among individuals or classes are systematically related to the model, but we don't usually specify these relationships. In the discussion of contextual effects above I gave an example of how Boli (1980) tests the hypothesis that change in one level causes change in another. But a more complete understanding of social reality would specify the interaction between many different levels of overlapping units, some hierarchically nested, some intersecting the boundaries of others.

Multilevel research designs will enable us to answer questions about the relative size of interlevel effects. The "internal–external" debate has often wrongly assumed that world-system theory only addresses processes which operate at the international level, whereas the world-system is holistically conceived as containing international, national, and intranational processes. In other words all these things are "internal" to the world-system. But we may nevertheless want to ask about the relative importance of international-level versus national-level processes in determining certain outcomes. Does the position of a country in the larger world-system or, alternatively, the nature of its national class structure have greater consequences for national development? Such a comparison would have to be specified more exactly, but this is the kind of question which might be answered by research designs which can test multilevel models.

Imagine, for example, a theoretical model in which there are two focal units of analysis, such as cities and countries. Attributes of other units (firms, classes, the world-system) are hypothesized to affect both cities and countries in a single model. This model can be represented by figure 15.1.

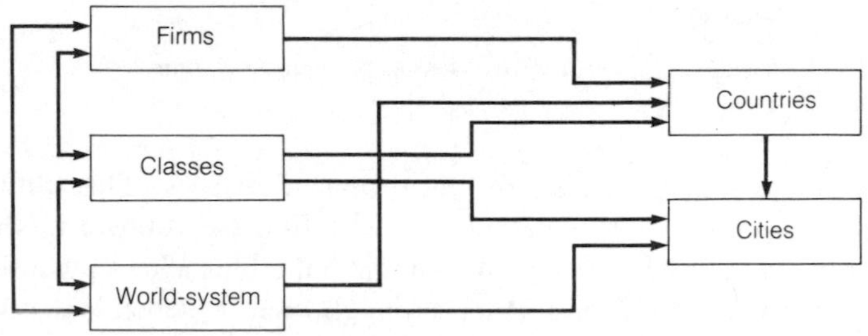

FIGURE 15.1 *Recursive multilevel model*

Figure 15.1 only shows the units of analysis in this multilevel model. Any real theory would analyze attributes or variable characteristics of these units. Now let us consider what types of research design could be used to estimate such a model and how data-sets could be organized to allow this estimation. The most common way in which such models are estimated is the use of, in this case, two different data matrices. In the first data-set (matrix A) the case base will be countries because the dependent variable is an attribute of countries and all other units will be variables which will implicitly be treated as attributes of nation states. In the second data-set (matrix B) the case base will be cities, and likewise all the variables will be implicitly treated as attributes of cities. These two matrices may both contain the same information but this information will have to be reorganized in order to estimate both equations.

Single matrix multilevel time series There is, however, a research design which will permit the estimation of both equations from a single data matrix. This design can be described as *time series analysis with data on different units*. It potentially can allow any of the units which are included in the model to be analyzed as the dependent variable, and thus multilevel models can be estimated from a single data matrix. A matrix of this type is illustrated in figure 15.2.

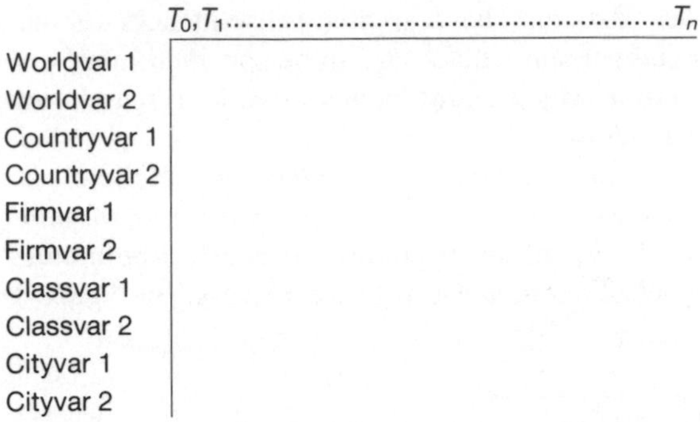

$T_0, T_1 \ldots\ldots T_n$

Worldvar 1
Worldvar 2
Countryvar 1
Countryvar 2
Firmvar 1
Firmvar 2
Classvar 1
Classvar 2
Cityvar 1
Cityvar 2

FIGURE 15.2 *Single matrix format for multilevel time series*

In this design time points are the focal unit of analysis. This differs from pooled cross-sections or the method used by Boli (see above) in that time points are not combined with any other single unit. This allows great flexibility in the choice of dependent variable, although once a dependent variable is chosen all independent variables will be implicitly treated as attributes of the unit of the dependent variable.

What are the assumptions behind such a design? When we do simple crossnational analysis (one time point, many countries) we are assuming that the countries are instances in which the process we want to study operate. Commonly we think of the differences among countries as variation over space because countries are territorially organized units and do not occupy the same space. But this is simply a convenience. Countries are not completely *independent* instances, and so we build their non-independence into our models in the form of relational or contextual variables which we treat as attributes of the countries. The point here is that spatial separation does not in itself tell us about relations (or non-relations) among countries (Naroll, 1968).

If there is a hypothesized relationship between countries which affects the dependent variable of interest we must include it in the model, and if we do not include a variable we are assuming that it is unrelated to the other independent variables and can safely be relegated to the error term. In the time series designs discussed above, the convenient dimension on which we hang observations of instances is temporal rather than spatial, and like variation over space, variation over time may or may not reveal independent instances (e.g. auto-correlation). Non-independence must be included in the model, and the failure to include it will result in misspecification and errors of inference.

The advantage of using time rather than space for multilevel analysis is that it is a dimension which is common to all units regardless of their spatial organization, and thus we can include units which are parts of other units, or those which overlap others, as long as we specify their causal relations correctly in our model. Most discussions of multilevel analysis focus on units which are hierarchically nested (e.g. Hannan and Young, 1976) but this is not a necessary condition for the design proposed here.

This design also allows for a great deal of flexibility in grouping units, so we can easily test alternative methods of aggregating. Hypothetically such a design could include information on all units of analysis and on each of the individual cases at all levels. These data could be aggregated in many different ways or be used in disaggregated form. The limitations and tradeoffs involved with the use of this single matrix multilevel design are examined by Chase-Dunn et al. (1982). They also explain how to use panel analysis to solve identification problems in multilevel designs which examine different data matrices for each unit of analysis.

My hope is that the above discussion will encourage further consideration of the methods for testing multilevel models. We may be able to resolve some of the confusion and disagreement about the importance of larger and smaller levels of analysis for determining outcomes if we include these together in the same models.

Cross-world-system Studies

Despite my contention that time series analysis of the modern world-system can be used in the process of world-system theory construction, it could be argued that a theory of the deep structure cannot be tested by studying only one world-system. Indeed it might be the case that if we want to understand what is structurally distinctive about the contemporary world-system we need to compare it to systems which are really different. In any case, we may be able to gain understanding of the processes by which modes of production become transformed by studying earlier instances of transformation and comparing them to the contemporary situation.

Was the rise and fall of world-empires directly related to the transformation of modes of production or was that relationship a more complicated one? How do the concepts which we have developed for studying the capitalist world-economy help us (or hinder us) when we begin to analyze really different world-systems? Is it true that there have been many world-empires but few (or mostly short-lived) world-economies? How many distinct world-systems have there been in the history of human social development? What is a useful typology for classifying world-systems so that we can understand how they are systematically different and how they are the same?

I have begun to work on some of these questions (Chase-Dunn, 1986) and so have other scholars (e.g. Ekholm and Friedman, 1982; Blanton and Feinman, 1984; Mathien and McGuire, eds, 1986; Kohl, 1987; Rowlands et al., eds, 1987). But here I would like to discuss the feasibility of a cross-world-system research design, one that would use world-systems as the unit of analysis and enable us to test causal propositions about world-system processes by comparing large numbers of world-systems.

This idea brings a number of problems immediately to mind. Many of the difficulties we encounter when we do crossnational comparisons are encountered again, only most of them are worse. Are world-systems sufficiently comparable to be considered a unit of formal comparative analysis? What about the independence of units (Galton's problem)? Problems of data availability and comparability are certainly stupendous. Is it possible to obtain a representative sample of historical world-systems?

Obviously a lot of conceptual and theoretical work would need to precede any serious attempt to construct a data-set composed of world-systems. The spatial boundary problems discussed above would have to be resolved, or at least clarified sufficiently so that contending specifications could be compared. Contending theoretical approaches would have to be clearly specified so that we could direct our attention and resources productively. The idea of the core/periphery hierarchy would have to be reconceptualized in a way that facilitates cross-world-system comparisons without evacuating its theoretical content. Do relevant data-sets already exist? Rein Taagepera (1978) has organized a data-set which contains the territorial size and temporal duration data of more than 100 historical empires from 3000 BC to the present. There may be other such data-sets.

There are two main macrocomparative research traditions which should be examined for suggestions about how to resolve these problems. Crossnational research is obvious. The other is the Human Relations Area File (HRAF), a massive effort by anthropologists to create a comparative data-set for the analysis of cultures (Murdock, 1957). The HRAF uses societies rather than world-systems as the unit of analysis and most of the variable characteristics coded are not relevant to the theoretical questions asked by the world-system perspective. Douglas White and Michael Burton (1987) are engaged in an effort to add world-system variables to the Standard Cross Cultural Sample, a representative subset of the societies contained in the HRAF. This promises to be a valuable contribution to comparative world-system research and it has the advantage of building on a huge amount of previous work. But, while this approach can potentially answer questions about the effect of world-system variables on societal development, it cannot be used to study dependent variables which are characteristics of world-systems themselves. I suspect that the big questions regarding the transformations of modes of production can only be answered by using world-systems themselves as the unit of analysis.

I am not an advocate of large science for its own sake. A project which studied large numbers of world-systems might easily consume the entire National Science Foundation budget for the social sciences. Assertions about the potential value of such a project should be critiqued, and preliminary studies should be conducted to explore the value of a strategy which compares world-systems. My guess, however, is that intersocietal systems have long been the units in which the most important historical and developmental processes have operated, and thus studies based on these units will be found to provide a better understanding of social change.

The main conclusions of part IV on metatheory and methods are summarized on pages 10 to 12 of the Introduction. Now we turn to a consideration of some major unresolved problems suggested by the foregoing structural approach to the modern world-system.

16

Implications

This last chapter reflects on some unresolved problems, and then discusses implications for new scholarly work and for political practice. We will take another look at the main conclusions reached and examine the links and voids between them.

Despite the somewhat *ex cathedra* tone of the theoretical conclusions presented in this book, they are certainly not the last word. Problems and gaps remain within my own formulation, and the process of systematically comparing my theory with contending theories has not really begun. The intended road of formal theory construction and empirical research which evaluates contending theories has been recommended, but only a few steps down that road have been taken. My own theory is insufficiently formalized to allow certainty about the empirical propositions which may be deduced from it. And, since we have only recently extended our frame of reference to whole world-systems, the relevant phenomena have been observed and theorized about for only a short time. I expect that other contending world-system theories will emerge from the several theoretical perspectives which can be seen entering the fray.

In order to compare theories we must be able to deduce contrary empirical propositions from them. The real test of a theory is its power in explanation and prediction. I am sure, for example, that my theory and the power cycle theory of Modelski and Thompson imply some of the same propositions and some that are contrary, but at the current level of formalization it is difficult to precisely specify these. Once they are specified, empirical research may go beyond its current role in examining single propositions and partial causal structures to become more directly relevant to the theory construction project.

Of course theories do not win or lose because of "crucial experiments." Thomas Kuhn's (1962) depiction of paradigm revolutions contends that an accepted "normal science" paradigm only falls when its failures to account for anomalies accumulate to some tipping point where a new, more powerful, formulation is proposed and triumphs. But this scenario is only a possible future for social science. We have not yet reached sufficient consensus to constitute a normal science paradigm. Rather we live in a world of multiparadigm clashes in which empirical research does not have much affect on the commitment of scientists to one or another body of axioms. This is true partly because social science is young, and partly because it is more political than are the physical and biological sciences.

The project of theory construction and empirical research I am advocating for world-system analysis cannot be naive about these things, but neither do they vitiate the effort. Someday social science will come of age, perhaps in a world in which class struggles are less intense. Theorizing the world-system can help bring such a world about, and may contribute to the maturity of social science within that future world.

SPATIAL AND LOGICAL BOUNDARIES

Even within the metaparadigm in which I am working, historical materialism, there are several unresolved problems with my formulation. I argue that Wallerstein's totality assumption, which contends that each world-system has only one mode of production, creates insoluble problems for understanding contradictions between modes of production and their transformation. Thus I distinguish between the spatial boundaries of world-systems and the logical boundaries of modes of production. But if it is not true that the mode of production is a feature of the world-system as a whole (as Wallerstein contends), what is the unit which should be characterized as having one or another mode of production? Is it the firm, the household, the nation state, the core/periphery hierarchy, or what? I agree with Wallerstein that exploitation and domination are multilevel phenomena which cannot be adequately understood by looking only at the "point of production." Many Marxists (e.g. Dobb, 1963; Brenner, 1977) have argued that the logic of a mode of production is determined by the interaction between a direct producer and his/her immediate overseer. I have no quarrel with the spate of recent studies which examine control structures within the work place, but I agree with Wallerstein that we ought not to treat these relations as the kernel (monad) of the capitalist mode of production. But if the kernel is neither the world-system as a whole nor the firm, where is it?

Another related problem is this. If a world-system can have more than one mode of production within it, how can we understand the spatial boundaries between modes? More specifically: if, as I argue, the capitalist mode of production includes both core and peripheral capitalism, where are the other modes of production with which capitalism is articulated? Am I suggesting that there are locations beyond the periphery, but within the world-system, which can be understood as the domain of non-capitalist modes?

These problems assume that modes of production are easily located in space or identified with particular entities. It would be conceptually neat to be able to do so, and such a specification would undoubtedly have important political implications. But the best solution is, I think, another approach. The notion of a mode of production is an analytic idea about the logic of social relations, the systematic way in which the needs of people are met through social organization and institutions, and the structures of power which control production and distribution. As such there is no single most appropriate unit of analysis which distinguishes between different logics. Similarly, spatial delineations can only correspond roughly to differences in the logic of production and reproduction. Thus elements of other modes of production can, in principle, be anywhere within a world-system which is dominated by the capitalist mode of production.

The logic of socialism – democratic and collective rationality – can exist partially within the so-called "socialist" states, while at the same time these also contain elements of capitalism and elements of the tributary modes and while they remain parts of the larger capitalist world-system. Likewise the logic of socialism may exist to some extent within workers' organizations in capitalist countries, and indeed, within some capitalist organizations. Ernest Mandel (1970) has suggested that street lights (free and publicly provided) are an instance of socialist logic within the capitalist mode of production.[1] Some aspects of the tributary mode of production are certainly present in the extant socialist states,[2] and this is also the case within capitalist states to the extent that some policies are motivated by the fiscal needs of the state. We have also seen that, though the most successful core states employ a largely profit-oriented approach to international competition, there are other contending states which choose a path of conquest which is much closer to the tributary mode. Thus elements of both competitive commodity production and political–military domination are present in the capitalist world-economy.

What makes it a capitalist world-system is the relative importance of commercialization, market competition, and capitalist accumulation compared to earlier tributary world-systems. Also, various elements of the kin-based (normative) mode of production continue to operate within households in which subsistence production for use and distribution according to normatively regulated expectations operates. This kind of income-pooling is not only a characteristic of households, however. Such normatively regulated logics can also be seen in larger solidarities such as ethnic groups and nations in which mutual aid, altruism, and non-market-mediated interactions certainly occur. To point out that these instances of non-capitalist relations are articulated with and dependent upon the capitalist mode of production is simply to reiterate that this world-system is dominated by the logic of capitalist accumulation. These non-capitalist relations are undoubtedly differentially distributed, but it would be folly to try to specify a single unit of analysis or a particular spatial location for them.

The above does not constitute back-pedalling on my reformulation of the nature of capitalism. I still maintain that the interstate system and the core/periphery hierarchy are constitutional parts of the capitalist mode of production because they are necessary to its reproduction. Remember Foster-Carter's (1978) distinction between articulation and contradiction discussed in chapter 1. Some activities which themselves display the logic of a non-capitalist mode of production are at the same time firmly articulated with, dependent upon, and functional for capitalism. Others are in conflict with capitalism and are potential threats to its continued dominance. My redrawing of the logical boundaries of capitalism must needs take account of this distinction, although it is a difficult one to make in many instances.

CONSTANTS, CYCLES AND TRENDS

In chapter 2 I presented a schema of world-system cycles and trends which is in the nature of a set of hypothesized features of the world-system as a whole. These features were produced by eye balling the history of the modern world-system. They are based on induction, but on the roughest kind of induction. One obvious empirical job which needs to be done is to investigate the reality of these hypothesized cycles and trends. Some of the work has already been done, and it is reported in other chapters, but chapter 13 revealed that much more work is needed.

The other problem is more theoretical. What is the relationship between the specification of the nature of capitalism in chapter 1, which was mostly adduced from prior theorizing and theoretical disputes, and the roughly inductive schema hypothesized in chapter 2? Ideally we would be able to specify the links between the deep structure – called "system constants" in chapter 2 – and the patterns which are hypothesized to be observable features of the world-system as a whole.

Some of this has been done. For example, chapter 9 discusses the causation of the rise and fall of hegemonic core powers, a world-system fluctuation. But most of the linkages between the system constants and the system cycles and trends are unexamined, a void which demands further attention.

This is the main disjuncture in the book's argument. The relations among the various structures hypothesized to compose the capitalist mode of production have been addressed in detail. Part II examines the interdependencies between the interstate system and capitalist accumulation, and part III analyzes the links between the interstate system, core capitalism, and the core/periphery hierarchy. Chapter 13 proposes a causal model of the relationships among several world-system variables.

CORENESS AND PERIPHERALITY

Certainly the last word on the analytic definition of the core/periphery hierarchy has not been said. I have already received a critique from Giovanni Arrighi, who contends that my use of relative capital intensity is theoretically and empirically flawed. It is easy to recommend more research on coreness and peripherality, but this analytic question is also heavily linked to theoretical desiderata, and these should be given consideration. How does the proposed definition fit with the rest of the theory? how easy is it to operationalize? and how heavy a causal determinant of other outcomes can it be shown to be? These are complicated matters but ones which ought not to be ignored, or resolved by eclecticism or raw empiricism – at least if we are serious about world-system theory.

On the other hand, below I will recommend a purely empirical approach to measuring world-system position. This is not seen as the complete arbiter over the analytic problem, but it may well have important implications for theory as well as measurement.

RESEARCH LACUNAE

I am sure that there have been important studies which my survey has omitted. So much good comparative work is coming out that any attempt to be complete is soon obsolete, and I undoubtedly have overlooked studies which ought to have been included. My apologies to authors and readers.

To my mind the most gaping empirical hole is the need for a quantitative comparative study of the world-system position of nation states and colonial areas in the nineteenth and twentieth centuries. As explained in chapter 10, I don't believe it makes sense to spend a lot of effort trying to locate the empirical boundaries between the core, peripheral, and semiperipheral zones, although studies of the whole core/periphery hierarchy would be useful in answering questions about trends in inequality and other changes in structure. In order to do comparative studies of the causes and effects of world-system position we need measures which can at least rank countries, and more metric measures would be useful for both crossnational and whole hierarchy studies. Because so many countries are in the periphery we especially need data which will allow us to measure *differences among peripheral countries*. Once this job is done we will be able to answer questions about upward and downward mobility, changes in mobility rates over time,[3] and the causes and consequences of world-system position.

Part of the above study ought to focus on differences among core powers and the hegemonic sequence, as Thompson's (1986) pathbreaking study of leading sectors of core production (reviewed in chapter 9) has done. We need a more exact understanding of the timing of the concentration and dispersion of both economic and political–military capacities in the hegemonic sequence. It would be ideal if the proposed study could benefit from a theoretically deduced analytic definition of coreness and peripherality, but realistically that problem is not likely to be resolved to everyone's satisfaction soon. So I propose a more eclectic empirical approach which uses the dimensions suggested by several different theoretical traditions and compares them. This means studying military and economic forms of power and their interaction.

Within these broad categories there are many subdimensions. Naval and air force power with a global reach has been studied for "great powers" by Modelski and Thompson (1988). More conventional forces need to be added and the comparison of semiperipheral and peripheral militaries needs to be included. For national economic power we want to include measures of overall economic productivity such as GNP per capita, but also different forms of international economic power/dependence such as investment dependence, the several forms of trade dependence, aid and debt dependence, among others. Dependency here also implies the other side of the coin. Some countries are relatively dominant with regard to these dimensions. Many of the measurement problems discussed in chapter 15 will be encountered in this study. It will take a fairly substantial amount of resources to overcome these and to produce a series of parallel indicators which decay as we go back in time and toward the periphery. My guess is that we will be able to do a fair job back into the middle of the nineteenth century.

In addition, chapters 5 through 13 and chapter 15 raise many problems which could stand further comparative research. Rather than my detailing these here, the interested scholar is encouraged to examine these chapters. But one particularly important problem is the transformation of modes of production. I take the liberty of discussing this below despite only a piecemeal understanding of the processes of the transformation of systemic logic. The best way to understand the transformation of systemic logic is to study this process as it has actually occurred in earlier world-systems. This is why it is important to undertake a comparative study of world-systems and modes of production, a proposal outlined in the last part of chapter 15.

POLITICAL IMPLICATIONS

What are the political implications of the above? First I must qualify everything that follows because of the still tentative formulation of my theory and the remaining gaps in the corpus of systematic world-system research. At this point the following implications are no more than hints about directions for political practice. I am justified in appending this discussion because of some of the frightening conclusions about warfare which world-system theory implies, and because of the absurdity of material deprivation in an age when the technological problems for providing basic needs are obviously solved.

A central question for any strategy of transformation is the question of agency. Who are the actors who will most vigorously and effectively resist capitalism and construct socialism? Where is the most favorable terrain, the weak link where concerted action could bear the most fruit? Samir Amin (1980a) contends that the agents of socialism are most heavily concentrated in the periphery. It is there that the capitalist world-system is most oppressive, and thus peripheral workers and peasants, the vast majority of the world proletariat, have the most to win and the least to lose.

On the other hand Marx and many contemporary Marxists have argued that socialism will be most effectively built by the action of core proletarians. Since core areas have already attained a high level of technological development, the establishment of socialized production and distribution should be easiest in the core. And organized core workers have had the longest experience with industrial capitalism and the most opportunity to create socialist social relations.

I will contend that both the "workerist" and the "Third Worldist" positions have important elements of truth, but there is another alternative which is suggested by my structural theory of the world-system: the semiperiphery as the weak link.

Core workers may have experience and opportunity, but some of them lack motivation because they have benefited from a non-confrontational relationship with core capital. The existence of this labor aristocracy divides the working class in the core and, in combination with a large middle strata, undermines political challenges to capitalism. Also the "long experience" in which business unionism and social democracy have been the outcome of a series of struggles between radical workers and the labor aristocracy has created a residue of trade union practices, party structures, legal and governmental institutions, and ideological heritages which act as barriers to new socialist challenges. Nevertheless it is true that even small victories in the core (e.g. further expansion of the welfare state, opposition to imperial policies, etc.) have important effects on peripheral and semiperipheral areas because of demonstration effects and the power of core states.

Another reason to emphasize the importance of even small gains for socialism in the core is suggested by an analysis of how capitalism came to be a dominant mode of production. Commercialization, markets, money, and even the production of commodities by wage labor existed in many of the precapitalist world-systems. Both Roman and Chinese world-empires were highly commercialized, but the tributary mode of production maintained domination over the developmental dynamics of both of these empires in part because bourgeois forces never obtained autonomous state power within core areas. On the other hand there were "capitalist" states in semiperipheral areas, autonomous city states such as Dilmun, Tyre, Sidon, Carthage, and Venice which produced and traded commodities in the interstices of the world-empires. It was the coming to state power of bourgeois groups *within core states* which was the qualitative leap which distinguished the Europe-centered world-economy from earlier world-systems.[4] This implies that core areas are indeed crucial for the institutionalization of a mode of production in a world-system.

The main problem with "Third Worldism" is not motivation, but opportunity. Socialist movements which take state power in the periphery are soon beset by powerful external forces which either overthrow them or force them to abandon most of their socialist program. Anti-systemic movements in the periphery are most usually anti-imperialist class alliances which succeed in establishing at least the trappings of national sovereignty, but not socialism. The low level of the development of the productive forces also makes it harder to establish socialist forms of accumulation, although this is not impossible in principle. It is simply harder to share power and wealth when there is very little of either.

SEMIPERIPHERAL SOCIALISM

These things are less true of the semiperiphery. Here we have both motivation and opportunity. Semiperipheral areas, especially those in which the territorial state is large, have sufficient resources to be able to stave off core attempts at overthrow and to provide some protection to socialist institutions if the political conditions for their emergence should arise. Semiperipheral regions experience more militant class-based socialist revolutions and movements because of their intermediate position in the core/periphery hierarchy. While core exploitation of the periphery creates and sustains alliances among classes in both the core and the periphery, in the semiperiphery an intermediate world-system position undermines class alliances and provides a fruitful terrain for strong challenges to capitalism. Semiperipheral revolutions and movements are not always socialist in character, as we have seen in Iran. But when socialist intentions are present there are greater possibilities for real transformation than in the core or the periphery. Thus the semiperiphery is the weak link in the capitalist world-system. It is the terrain upon which the strongest efforts and biggest successes to establish socialism have been made, and this is likely to be true of the future as well.

On the other hand, the results of the efforts so far, while they have undoubtedly been important experiments with the logic of socialism, have left much to be desired. The tendency for authoritarian regimes to emerge in the so-called socialist states betrays the notion of a freely constituted association of direct producers. And the imperial control of Eastern Europe by the Russians is an insult to the idea of proletarian internationalism. Democracy within and between nations is a constituent element of the logic of socialism, although admittedly not an unproblematic one. I have argued at length elsewhere (Chase-Dunn, ed, 1982b) that the existing socialist states have failed to institutionalize a self-reproducing socialist mode of production because of the strong threats and opportunities emanating from the larger capitalist world-system. The conflictual interstate system and the direct threats from capitalist core states encourage militarism, authoritarianism, and "defensive" imperialism. The existence of a dynamic and competitive world market encourages corruption, consumerism, and political opportunism by the "new class" of technocrats and bureaucrats who can bolster their own positions by either competing with the capitalist core or mediating the importation of sophisticated technology.

But it does not follow that efforts to build socialism in the semiperiphery will always be so constrained and thwarted. The revolutions in the Soviet Union and the People's Republic of China have increased our collective knowledge about how to build socialism despite their only partial successes and their obvious failures. Their existence widens the space available for other experiments with socialism.

It is important for all of us who want to build a more humane and peaceful world-system to understand the lessons of socialist movements in the semiperiphery, and the potential for future, more successful, revolutions there. But for me and most of my audience political action in the semiperiphery is not an option. As a citizen of a core state I have opportunities and responsibilities which I would be remiss to give up in an effort to directly engage in political action elsewhere. Of course I can and should support such action from where I am, and perhaps with important effects. But my largest opportunity for progressive political impact is within my own nation and upon my own state. Though this fact is itself a structural constraint of the contemporary world-system, it is a structural fact which I would be naive to ignore.

UNITED STATES SOCIALISM?

So what does my theory imply about socialist political practice in the United States in the last decade of the twentieth century? This is a declining hegemonic core state. The processes of rapid growth and imperial success which have long undermined socialist politics in the US are less salient now, and so there should be new openings for building socialism. On the other hand, if the United Kingdom is a relevant comparison, the remnants of hegemony do not pass quickly. It is very unlikely that the United States will experience a socialist revolution in which a working-class party seizes state power and rapidly socializes the major means of production. A revolutionary situation requires a weak and divided state, a weak and divided ruling class, and a strong and well-organized socialist party. All these conditions are lacking and are not likely to emerge soon.

Revolution, however, is not the only road to socialism. John Stephens (1980) has shown that important steps toward democratic socialism can be achieved by the route of political class struggle within capitalist core states. In the US the return of the liberals to presidential power in a context in which the old liberal ideology has been exhausted may be fertile ground for the struggle for a national industrial policy and economic democracy (see Carnoy and Shearer, 1980). While these reforms will not in themselves constitute a socialist mode of production, we should not underestimate their potential contribution to social justice in the US and abroad.

Some critics of the world-system perspective have argued that emphasis on the structural importance of global relations leads to political do-nothingism while we wait for socialism to emerge at the world level. The world-system perspective does indeed encourage us to examine global-level constraints (and opportunities), and to allocate our political energies in ways which will be most productive when these structural constraints are taken into account. We are also urged to expend resources on transorganizational, transnational, and international socialist relations, but it does not follow that building socialism at the local or national level is futile.

I have argued elsewhere that a simple domino theory of the transformation to socialism is misleading and inadequate. Suppose that all firms or all nation states adopt socialist relations internally but continue to relate to one another through competitive commodity production and political–military conflict. Such a hypothetical world-system would still be dominated by the logic of capitalism, and that logic would be likely to repenetrate the "socialist" firms and states. This cautionary tale advises us to invest political resources in the construction of multilevel (transorganizational, transnational, and international) socialist relations lest we simply repeat the process of driving capitalism to once again perform an end run by operating on a yet larger scale.

A SOCIALIST WORLD SYSTEM

These considerations lead us to a discussion of socialist relations at the level of the whole world-system. The emergence of democratic collective rationality (socialism) at the world-system level is likely to be a slow process. What might such a world-system look like and how might it emerge? It is obvious that such a system will require some kind of a democratically-controlled world federation which can effectively adjudicate disputes among nation-states and eliminate warfare. This is a bare minimum. There are many other problems which badly need to be coordinated at the global level such as ecological difficulties and a more balanced pattern of economic development. But a socialist world government should not monolithically centralize everything. The Soviet style command economy is a poor model even for a nation-state. Socialist markets can be used to regulate the production and distribution of many goods and services, and planning and regulation of many activities can be decentralized. A socialist world-system ought to be culturally pluralistic, and some optimal level of multilevel decentralization (as proposed by Galtung, 1980) is compatible with a constitutionally limited federal world state which regulates those functions which need to be co-ordinated at the global level.

How might such a world state come into existence? The process of the growth of international organizations which has been going on for at least 150 years will eventually result in a world state if we are not blown up first. Even international capitalists have some uses for global regulation, as is attested by the International Monetary Fund and the World Bank. These capitalists do not want the massive economic and political upheavals which accompany collapse of the world monetary system, and so they support efforts to regulate "ruinous" competition and beggar-my-neighborism. Some of these same capitalists also fear nuclear holocaust, and so they may support a strengthened global government which can effectively adjudicate conflicts among nation states.

Of course capitalists know as well as others that effective adjudication means the establishment of a monopoly of legitimate violence. The process of state formation has a long history, and the king's army needs to be bigger than any combination of private armies which might be brought against him. This prospect is a frightening spectre to many, but especially to international capitalists who either consciously or unconsciously realize that such a level of centralization of military power would mean the end of the interstate system. Nevertheless I think we can expect some support for further world-state-formation from capitalists and their political allies, and furthermore it is likely that such an emergent world state would be under the domination of capitalists, at least for a while.

While the idea of a world state may be a frightening spectre to some, I am optimistic about it for several reasons. First, a world state is probably the most direct and stable way to prevent nuclear holocaust, a desideratum which must be at the top of everyone's list. Secondly, the creation of a global state which can peacefully adjudicate disputes among nations will transform the existing interstate system. As I argued in part II, the interstate system is the political structure which stands behind the manueverability of capital and its ability to escape organized workers and other social constraints on profitable accumulation. While a world state may at first be dominated by capitalists, the very existence of such a state will provide a single focus for struggles to socially regulate investment decisions and to create a more balanced, egalitarian, and ecologically sound form of production and distribution.

Is this a pipe dream? Are not other outcomes possible, such as fascism, continued capitalism, or nuclear annihilation? Of course other outcomes are possible. My structuralism is not inevitabilist unilinear evolution. A computer malfunction, completely conjunctural, unrelated to any systemic process of social change, could kill all life on our planet at any minute. One of the first political tasks is to dismantle this balance of terror. World fascism is also a possible outcome of a grave economic and political crisis. But fascism in the past has been a desperate effort by capitalists and their political allies to maintain power in the face of a strong challenge from the left. Capitalism does not now face a deep crisis or a strong socialist challenge at the world-system level. Even a collapse of the current international financial system is not likely to lead to a concerted challenge from the Left in most countries.

It seems more likely that capitalism will muddle through, responding to challenges piecemeal, expanding international and transnational organizations cyclically as it has done for centuries, until the world political system is relatively centralized. The rise and decline of hegemonic core states will either end, or will slow down as the world bourgeoisie becomes more politically and economically integrated. The gap between the core and the periphery will begin to diminish, reducing the dampening effect of the core/periphery hierarchy on class struggles. As efforts to protect the livelihood of workers, the environment, and human rights become increasingly oriented toward the emerging world state they will become more and more organized around internationalism, and the logic of socialism will eventually gain the upper hand.

Socialism is not the utopian end of history. It is simply the next progressive step, as was capitalism. Socialism is not inevitable or perfect, and neither is it immutable. But it is certainly preferable to the current system of violent conflict, uneven development, and exploitation.

Glossary of World-System Terms

Colonial empire an empire in which one of the core states within an interstate system exercises formal political domination over territories abroad. Distinguished from "world-empire" (see below) in which a single state apparatus exercises formal domination over the whole core of a world-system.

Commodity chain a tree-like sequence of production processes and exchanges by which a product for final consumption is produced. These linkages of raw materials, labor, the sustenance of labor, intermediate processing, final processing, transport, and final consumption materially connect most of the people within the contemporary world-system. See chapter 10.

Core a region or "zone" in which most of the production activity is core production (see below). The core comprises a group of states which are not necessarily contiguous with one another in space. See chapter 10.

Core/Periphery hierarchy a spatially differentiated continuum of socially structured inequality based on the concentration of different kinds of economic production in different areas. In the contemporary world-system this corresponds fairly well with the hierarchy of "developed" and "less-developed" countries. See chapter 10.

Core production the production of core commodities using relatively (*vis-à-vis* the whole current world-system) capital intensive technology and relatively skilled and highly paid labor. See chapters 1 and 10.

Empire formation the transformation of an interstate system into a world-empire.

External arena a region outside the spatial boundaries of a world-system with which there is a trade in preciosities.

Fundamental goods basic goods such as food and raw materials that compose the everyday life material consumption of the masses of people. Distinguished from "preciosities." See below and chapter 15.

Hegemon the most powerful state in an interstate system. In the capitalist world-economy this includes both economic power (comparative advantage in the production of core commodities) and military power. See chapter 9.

Hegemonic core a relatively unequal distribution of power among core states such that one state has a rather large share of both economic and military power. Contrasted with "multicentric core" (see below). See chapters 9 and 13.

Hegemonic sequence a process in which the core of a world-economy oscillates between a hegemonic and a multicentric distribution of economic and military power among core states. This corresponds to the rise and fall of hegemons. See chapters 9 and 13.

Interstate system a system of unequally powerful and competing states in which none of the states is powerful enough to dominate the whole system. See "world-empire" below and chapters 7 and 8.

K-wave the Kondratieff long business cycle in which production, investment, and prices oscillate between growth and stagnation phases within an approximately 40- to 60-year period.

Logical boundaries major disjunctures between the logics of modes of production.

Modes of production the deep structural logics of socio-economic systems. Major modes are normative (kin-based), tributary, capitalist, and socialist.

Multicentric core a relatively equal distribution of economic and military power among core states. See chapters 9 and 13.

Peripheral production the production of peripheral commodities using technology which is relatively low in capital intensity and labor which is paid low wages and is usually politically coerced compared to labor in core areas. See chapters 1 and 10.

Peripheralization the processes by which regions are incorporated into the world-system and become located in a peripheral position in the core/periphery hierarchy.

Periphery those regions in which periphery production is predominant.

Preciosities luxury goods which have high value due to scarcity in areas into which they are imported, but much lower value at their point of origin. Distinguished from "fundamental goods" (see above). See chapter 7, note 8 and chapter 15, "Spatio-temporal mapping."

Semiperiphery those regions which contain either a relatively balanced mix of core and peripheral production, or in which production is predominantly at intermediate levels of capital intensity and labor remuneration. See chapter 10.

World-economy a type of world-system in which the territorial network of economic exchange is politically structured as an interstate system.

World economy the total sum of economic relationships contained in a world-system, including intranational, transnational, and international production and exchange.

World-empire a type of world-system in which the territorial economic network is largely contained within a single state apparatus.

World-system a whole social system (not necessarily global) composed of cultural, normative, economic, political, and military relations which is bounded by a territorial network of regularized exchange of material goods. Regarding the problem of spatial boundaries of world-systems, see chapter 15, "Spatio-temporal mapping."

Notes

Introduction

1 See the frontispiece statement on editorial policy in the Braudel Center journal, *Review*. It refers to the "transitory (heuristic) nature of theories." The practice of using loosely defined concepts to interpret world history has proven fruitful, but some critics have said that the world-system perspective is heavy with concepts, but light on theory. It should be noted that the Braudel Center scholars have produced a collection of more analytic essays (see Hopkins and Wallerstein (eds.), 1982).

2 For a preliminary overview of the development of stateless, ancient, and modern world-systems see Chase-Dunn (1986).

PART I THE WHOLE SYSTEM

1 The deconstructionists correctly argue that all structural theories and claims to universalistic science are themselves acts of power. For them it follows that all such theories should be attacked and destroyed, and that historicist description is the only possible non-elitist form of explanation. While it is true that structuralist theories have been used badly – to justify exploitation and oppression – these theories are not themselves a major cause of exploitation and oppression; nor would evil cease if all ideology were historicist. A truer and more universal understanding of the causes of exploitation and oppression can be of use to those who would like to eliminate them.

2 Wolf's analysis falters when he arrives at modern capitalism, which he analyzes in orthodox Marxist terms. He fails to take account of the systemic links between capitalist accumulation, the interstate system, and the core/periphery hierarchy.

3 Taxed small commodity producers (yeomen, artisans, etc.) and wage laborers are also to be found within many societies dominated by the tributary mode of production.

Chapter 1 The Deep Structure: Real Capitalism

1 It is questionable as to whether or not classical European feudalism ought to be considered a mode of production in its own right. It may be more fruitfully understood as an instance of the decentralized phase of a cycle of centralization (empire) and decentralization (feudalism) which had been spiraling along for millennia during the

development and expansion of tributary modes of production (see Ekholm and Friedman, 1982; Mann, 1986: chapter 5).

2 The problem of dialectically qualitative transformation of one such system into another is difficult to model, but here we may get some help from the mathematics of catastrophe theory (see Renfrew, 1984). The few formal or mathematical specifications of Marx's model of capitalist accumulation (Nowak, 1971; Morishima, 1973) have not approached the problem of system transformation.

3 Max Weber's theoretical approach is less systemic than that of Marx but he does present a notion of the theoretical essence of capitalism which solves, in a way different from that I am proposing, the problem of the relationship between capitalism and the state. Weber's notion of capitalism focuses on "formal rationality" rather than commodity production. Formal rationality is the concern for the efficiency of means rather than a direct focus on ends. Quantitative calculation and rational decision-making are the important thing, while non-capitalist rationality ("substantive rationality") focuses on the delineation of ideals. For Weber formal rationality, especially in the form of rational capital accounting, is the essential core of capitalism. Markets and wage labor are only important contextual conditions for the development of profit-oriented industry which employs rational capital accounting. The state is brought in as an important contextual variable, but also more directly as a bearer of formal rationality itself. Rational–legal authority and bureaucratic administration are additional forms taken by formal rationality, although the connection between rational–legal authority and the notion of formal rationality as concern for *efficient* means is somewhat strained. Extremely rationalized legal systems are not necessarily more efficient than common-law or judge-based systems. Weber argues that rational–legal law and courts facilitate rational economic activity by making legal and state action more predictable than other forms of authority. It is arguable that it is the actual content of contract, property, and market law which facilitates capitalism, rather than the systematization of law.

Weber's focus on formal rationality biases the evaluation of capitalism by asserting that its essence is efficiency. Profit-making is alleged to be a neutral goal, not a substantive value, and to be only an indicator of efficient economic action. This has served as an important source of ideological mystification within sociological theory (especially for Parsons) because of the uncritical linkage between individualized rationality and efficiency. It is often assumed that individual action is the only kind which can be rational, while collective orientations are identified with "traditional" societies or with modern irrationality as evidenced by affective involvement with collective solidarities (nationalism, social movements, so-called "collective behavior" – mobs, riots, revolutions, etc.). Thus capitalism and individualism are rational while socialism and collective orientations focus on vague ideals such as justice and equality which are necessarily affective and irrational. This formulation receives support from economists who prove with elegant mathematical theories that maximizing the collective welfare is impossible.

Certainly capitalism has been the motive force for the development of planning and calculation techniques, as indeed of almost all other technologies, but this does not prevent socialists from adopting these, especially linear programming, for the purposes of arriving at a more just mode of production. There is no technical reason why socialist planning cannot maximize both individual and collective outputs efficiently in terms of resource scarcities and tradeoffs. The experiments with such techniques in socialist states have, to date, all but ignored democratic inputs into such planning, although recent reform movements have raised this issue. Whether democracy will simply mean more markets and profit incentives (a move toward capitalism) or new forms of democratic control over collective planning remains to be seen.

4 This definition of the core/periphery hierarchy is similar to Kautsky's discussion of commodity circuits between urban and rural areas within a regional division of labor (see Lipton, 1977:115–21; also Banaji, 1980). Alternative conceptualizations of core and periphery are considered in chapter 10.

5 Jeffrey Paige (1975:13) correctly understands the peripheral smallholder as "a worker in an agricultural system controlled by urban financial interests." Paige approvingly quotes Marx's description of the nineteenth-century French peasantry as applicable to peripheral smallholders producing agricultural exports: "The small-holding of the peasant is now only the pretext that allows the capitalist to draw profits, interest and rent from the soil, while leaving it to the tiller of the soil himself to see how he can extract his wages."

6 The problem of world-system boundaries and modes of production is further considered in my comparison of stateless, ancient and modern world-systems (Chase-Dunn, 1986). Also, there is a discussion of competing definitions of world-system boundaries in chapter 15.

Chapter 2 Constants, Cycles, and Trends

1 Certain methodological problems associated with the analysis of cycles are discussed in chapter 15.

2 The hegemonic sequence has been shown to correspond to changes in the population size hierarchy of the world city system (Chase-Dunn, 1985a).

3 These "precapitalist" forms of production, which are articulated with capitalist commodity production, have often been analyzed in terms of the way in which they subsidize the lifetime cost of reproducing the work force. It is certainly true that such forms have been allowed to exist, or have been actively created, by the policies of colonial powers seeking to sustain a low wage labor force. On the other hand, the struggles of peripheral workers to maintain some independence of capitalist commodity production has also been an important cause of the continued existence of these forms. Excellent studies of the processes of reproduction and breakdown of these forms of production in peripheral areas are those by Kahn (1980), Murray (1980), Warman (1980), Meillassoux (1981), and Rodney (1981).

Chapter 3 Stages of Capitalism or World-system Cycles?

1 In the preface to the first German edition of volume 1 of *Capital* Marx writes: "The country that is more developed industrially only shows, to the less developed, the image of its own future" (Marx, 1967a:8–9).

2 This was first argued by Rosa Luxemburg (1968) and has been elaborated by Mandel (1975) and Amin (1975). Mandel insists that primitive accumulation is a separate process from capitalist production itself, while Amin and Frank (1979a) see "primary accumulation" as a characteristic of peripheral capitalism.

Chapter 4 The World-system since 1945: What has Changed?

1 David Gordon (1980) has developed an admirable conceptual structure for a theory of stages, breaking hypothetical qualitatively different stages into general phases based on a Marxian theory of capitalist accumulation. Unfortunately he does not designate the particular stages to which his scheme applies.

2 Recall the discussion of the terms "transnational" and "international" on p. 52 in chapter 2.

3 Chirot has revised this assessment in the new edition of his text on the world-system (Chirot, 1986). He now admits that some areas of the "Third World" remain peripheral.
4 Although the larger semiperipheral countries have also promoted industrial exports, and these have grown rapidly, they constitute only a small proportion of industrial output in these countries. Gereffi and Evans (1981:51) show that exports as a percentage of total sales by transnational manufacturing firms has indeed risen in both Mexico and Brazil, but in 1972 it was still only 5.1 percent in Mexico and 3.5 percent in Brazil. The Korean case is analyzed from a world-system perspective in Chase-Dunn (1987).
5 Saskia Sassen-Koob (1985) has also explored the effects of international immigration on the structure of New York's economy. A very similar shift occurred in London in the 1880s as Irish immigrants to the East End provided the workers for a swollen informal sector. This earlier "peripheralization of the core," which occurred during the decline of England's hegemony in industrial production, is studied in fascinating detail by Gareth Stedman Jones (1971).

Chapter 5 World Culture, Normative Integration, and Community

1 Normative integration does not preclude exploitation, oppression, or institutionalized inequality. Much recent anthropological work on stateless societies stresses contradictory interests based on gender and age-based stratification. Nevertheless most still argue that the magnitude of inequality based on normative integration not backed up by coercive institutions is limited.
2 Polanyi's use of the term "redistribution" was somewhat unfortunate, implying as it does a kind of functional pooling and redistribution of resources. Polanyi apparently adopted the term from the analysis of semistratified chiefdoms. Most recent analysts, especially those interested in distinguishing modes of production, emphasize the coercive nature of states, the use of threats, conquest, and politically organized exploitation in those societies which are characterized by the "tributary modes of production."
3 My friend and colleague Katherine Verdery, an anthropologist, strongly argues against the presuppositions of a Parsonsian notion of normative systems based on consensus about values and internalized norms, even as a *bête noire* in the discussion of world culture. Anthropologists have been moving toward a notion of culture as negotiations around the interpretation of symbols, and this modifies the picture of those societies which I have characterized as integrated primarily by normative consensus. I would agree that consensus is never complete and unproblematic, and neither do individuals smoothly carry out the role prescriptions to which they have been socialized. The process of consensus-formation is always problematic, but the primacy of normative negotiations as a producer of social order varies across societies and groups. The degree of consensus and the centrality of normative integration are variables, and it makes sense to inquire in any particular case what role they play in determining the dynamics of a system.
4 Subunit solidarities and the collective values which they exhibit sometimes contradict the individualistic logic of capitalism and provide a basis for anti-systemic movements. But, as noted in previous chapters, these challenges have so far only given impetus to the expansion of the spatial scale of capitalist firms and markets.
5 The relationship between nationalism and the state in peripheral areas only becomes complementary following decolonization, and even then there may be nationalist challenges to particular regimes which are perceived as dominated by a core power.

6 Efforts to apply Gramsci's notion of ideological hegemony to the world-system (e.g. R. Cox, 1983; Gill and Law, 1986) have had to ignore the fact of the relatively low level of cultural consensus at the global level, which reduces the importance of ideological domination. Albert Bergesen's effort to apply Durkheimian ideas of moral boundary maintenance to the world-system (Bergesen, ed., 1980: chapter 1) foundered on this same problem. Like Parsons and Durkheim, the Gramscian notion of ideological hegemony assumes that cultural integration is central to the maintenance of social order.

PART II STATES AND THE INTERSTATE SYSTEM

Chapter 6 States and Capitalism

1 While some extreme materialists may view ideology and politics as completely epiphenomenal, I agree with those who stress their importance. Politics, like the medical arts, is more an applied than a pure science. It utilizes general theory as a guide to action in conjunctural situations in which the particularities may matter as much as the general conditions.

2 The lists of countries in each category are given on pp. xix–xxi of World Bank, *World Tables*, volume 2 (1983). A more complete breakdown of central government finances, beginning for most countries in 1975, is given in the second series of tables in volume 1 of the *World Tables*. These show current revenues from different sources as well as expenditures on various categories such as public enterprise, defense, education, health, social security and welfare, and housing and community services. A comparative study of the differing capacities of states in these various types of activities should be able to put these data to good use.

3 Evans and Stephens (1988) do not use the vocabulary of core and periphery; rather they prefer to discuss early and late industrializers. Nevertheless their synthesis of Moore's approach and the "class power" approach developed recently by social democratic Marxists to explain the emergence of welfare state structures is an important contribution to understanding core/periphery differences in regime form.

4 The two apparent exceptions are state socialism and the Islamic revival. The theory of the dictatorship of the proletariat is, in principle, a further extension of democratization of political power. It was originally understood by Marx as a transitional period on the way toward the "withering away of the state." Actual authoritarian socialist states, on the other hand, are justified as necessary means for defending against internal and/or external threats. The idea of socialism constitutes a further extension of democracy into the realm of the economy. Islamic fundamentalism is a major exception to legitimation from below, but it may be understood as a reactive movement against commodification (as is socialism) which utilizes a traditional hierarchical ideology. Many types of religious fundamentalism emerge periodically within the development of capitalism as displaced or threatened groups try to protect themselves from unwanted changes. Islamic fundamentalism is this sort of movement, but it receives an extra dose of energy because it corresponds to peripheral opposition to core domination and also is a reactive civilizational response to European cultural domination.

5 The Chilean regime of Pinochet is portrayed by Portes and Kincaid (1985) as the exception to the rule, being based on a personal and patriarchal type of authority rather than on the more bureaucratic form of authoritarianism found in the other Southern Cone countries.

Chapter 7 Geopolitics and Capitalism: One Logic or Two?

1 Marxist theory has usually disdained the seemingly artificial distinctions between economics and politics which have become enshrined in the academic disciplines. Marx asserted a holism of the underlying processes operating within a mode of production. But the use of a deterministic logic to justify alleged necessity by Stalinist ideologues added fuel to the revolt against "economism" which had begun with Luxemburg, Gramsci, and Lukács. Poulantzas (1973) took this theoretical tendency to its most extreme point within Marxism. Claudia von Braunmühl (1978) and the other German "state derivation" theorists have reintegrated the new theories of the state by utilizing Marx's basic theoretical concepts to account for the operation of capitalist states. Von Braunmühl has done the most interesting work at the conceptual level to integrate the role of the larger *interstate system* and the operation of the world market within a framework of basic Marxist concepts.

2 Stephen Krasner notes the similarities between the structural Marxist "relative autonomy" theory and his own statecentric "realist" approach to international political economy (Krasner, 1978:32).

3 The reader is also reminded of another matter of usage. The glossary distinguishes between "world-economy," a type of world-system in which the spatial economic network is overlain by a multicentric and competitive interstate system, and "world economy" (unhyphenated) a reference to the structure of global economic production and exchange. A world-economy is a whole socio-economic system, while a world economy is only one aspect of such a system, the territorial network of material production and exchange. It should also be noted that the term "world economy" includes both international and intranational economic production and exchange.

4 Thanks to Guenther Roth for pointing out the connection between Weber's idea and the work of von Ranke. The quotation from *General Economic History* was brought to my attention by Volker Bornschier (1987).

5 See chapter 9 for a comparison of this view of the interaction of class struggle and economic growth with Mancur Olson's theory as specified in his *The Rise and Decline of Nations* (1982).

6 On the prior origins of the European interstate system Zolberg (1981) is ambiguous. At one point he argues that the formation of the European world-economy contributed to the crystallization of the interstate system, while at other points he refers to the prior existence of states and the logic of military expansion. Fernand Braudel (1984:324) contends that the European balance of power mechanism operated from the thirteenth century on.

7 Skocpol is inconsistent on the issue of the autonomy of the interstate system. In her text quoted above she seems to assert that the interstate system and the logic of geopolitical domination are substantially autonomous from the capital accumulation process, but in a footnote (1979:299) she approvingly quotes Otto Hintze: "the affairs of the state and of capitalism are inextricably interrelated . . . these are only two sides, or aspects, of one and the same historical development."

8 The exchange of "unequals" involves exchanging goods which have little value to their producers but great value to their consumers. Ernest Mandel (quoted in Frank, 1979a) refers to the exchange of "unequals" which occurs before social systems interact substantially enough such that their divisions of labor come to be sufficiently integrated to produce what Marx (1967a) referred to as "abstract labor" – the equivalence of qualitatively different types of labor in terms of a single system of value. Of course the formation of abstract labor and the equivalence of labor values is a slow process which is never complete, even within an integrated commodity economy. But in a single

interactive commodity economy there is a tendency toward the exchange of equal values which subjects the division of labor itself to periodic reorganizations which reflect changes in the average socially necessary labor time needed to produce a product. The exchange of unequals tends to become the exchange of labor value equivalents as merchant capital "acts as a solvent on precapitalist relations of production." Wallerstein's (1979a) distinction between preciosities and fundamental goods is similar in some ways to the idea of the exchange of unequals. Preciosities are defined as luxury goods which have high value in one area (due to scarcity) but much lower value in their area of origin. Wallerstein uses this idea to argue that exchange of fundamental goods (bulk foods and raw materials) bound world-system territorial trade networks, while the exchange of preciosities (such as the long-distance luxury trade between Europe and China) is relatively unimportant for the dynamics of development within separate world-systems. But the exchange of unequals may involve either luxuries or bulk goods such as food. The key point is that the amounts of labor time embodied in the goods exchanged are unequal because the goods are not regularly exposed to the price-equilibrating effects of an integrated market. This is not to be confused with "unequal exchange" (Emmanuel, 1972), which occurs *within* an integrated commodity economy due to differences in wage levels or the productivity of technology (see chapter 11).

9 The businessmen of Amsterdam not only invested in the British East India Company (in competition with the Dutch East India Company) but actually sold arms to the British during the Anglo-Dutch wars. A similar lack of patriotism was made evident by the successful suit which the General Motors Corporation brought against the United States Air Force for destruction of property by the bombing of GM plants *in Germany* during World War II.

10 Modelski's explanation of the rise of hegemonic core powers in terms of a "desire to create a global order . . . an expression of the will to power, the urge to control and to dominate, to imprint a pattern on events" (1978: 224) also seems an unlikely candidate for explaining much of the variance. He does not clearly explain why this desire emerges in 1500 or how it is differentially distributed across time and space to explain the rise and fall of hegemonic core powers. Modelski's (1982) more recent work acknowledges, in principle, the interdependence of political and economic processes, but his account continues to emphasize a "great power" theory of history which ignores the division of labor between the core and the periphery, as well as the specifically capitalist nature of central institutions in the modern world-system (see chapter 8).

Chapter 8 Warfare and World-Systems

1 Most precapitalist world-empires allowed less "private" autonomy of the ownership of land from the state than was the case in the Roman world. Thus the law of private property and contract among individuals was highly developed in Rome.

2 To say this is not to argue that market efficiency is just. Collective rationality and justice requires a social structure which subjects major investment decisions to a calculus of social needs in which market efficiency is only one desideratum.

3 Some precapitalist interstate systems were composed exclusively of city states while others were composed of mixes of city states and empire states. Thus the Greek city states were part of a larger interstate system in which the Persian Empire was the dominant core. The later Greek empires were parts of a larger world-system in which empire states were competing with one another. The idea of a world-empire in which a single state monopolizes the *entire* network of material exchange is actually somewhat of a rarity, but there have been many systems in which an empire state was the

predominant core of a world-system, and these should be considered world-empires. The important variable is the degree of political centralization within a world-system.

4 Indeed Ekholm and Friedman (1982) have argued that the modern world-system is not fundamentally different from earlier core/periphery systems in which political power was the main determinant of system expansion and contraction. In a very general sense they are right. The 500-year expansion of the modern world-economy may be only its formative period moving toward world-state-formation and a more centralized political integration. But the particular dynamics of this historical system based on capitalist institutions (as outlined above), and our concern for humanizing the social processes which appear to be beyond our collective control, make close attention to the particularities of our system desirable.

Chapter 9 The Rise and Decline of Hegemonic Core Powers

1 Anderson (1974a) depicts the relocation of the capital of the empire in Constantinople and the split between the Eastern and Western Empires as part of the devolution of the Roman Empire rather than as a process of hegemonic fall and rise which revitalized the mode of production. Although Anderson may be guilty of "orientalism" at other points in his analysis I think the basic thrust of his contentions about the Byzantine Empire are correct. It was less a case of a new upwardly mobile hegemonic power than of a contracting survival of the earlier Roman Empire.

2 In an insightful and witty discussion of the origins and methodology of Wallerstein's world-system perspective, Walter Goldfrank points to what he calls the "Goldilocks Principle" which is frequently found in Wallerstein's explanations – "not too cold, not too hot, but just right." Of relevance here is the point summarized by Goldfrank (1979a:46: "to the general correlation of state strength with core production, he [Wallerstein] adds the nuances that hegemonic core states need less active state machineries than their rivals, and that advancing semiperipheral states take a more active economic role than any."

3 Andre Gunder Frank (1979a) points out that a relatively equal distribution of income, with a large home market for consumption goods, is a necessary, but certainly not a sufficient, condition for upward mobility in the world-economy.

4 Frederic Lane (1979:15–19) shows that the Portuguese entry into the spice trade did not ever employ the lowering of prices to drive competitors from the market. The blockade of the movement of spices through the Red Sea and the Persian Gulf would have allowed the Portuguese to sell spices more cheaply than the Venetians, who continued to pay protection costs to the Soldan of Egypt. But the Portuguese blockade instead caused pepper prices to rise, even in Lisbon, and even when the Venetians again began meeting a large proportion of the demand. This illustrates the exclusive commitment of the Portuguese to the precapitalist economic strategy of administered monopoly prices, and partly explains their failure to develop core production. The Portuguese relied exclusively on this form of profit-taking, even to the extent of not utilizing a price-lowering strategy when it would have led to greater returns. In this they inflexibly followed the tribute-gathering logic of precapitalist systems.

5 While London and New York were the largest cities in the modern world-system during the periods of their national hegemony, Amsterdam was never higher than fourth among core cities in terms of population size (Chase-Dunn, 1985a).

6 This is not a mystery because, as inheritors of the Western science of development, we know most about the English "birthplace of modernization." Thus even students of the world-system tend to generalize from it, even though the overall perpective commands us to treat it no differently than the others.

7 A more detailed analysis of the upward mobility of the United States in the nineteenth century which focuses on tariff policy is contained in Chase-Dunn (1980).

8 A similar set of figures with a slightly different comparison base is shown in table 12.3. This shows the US percentage of world GNP as 32.1 percent in 1960, 28.5 percent in 1970 and 26.9 percent in 1980.

9 Choucri and North's (1975) study of the processes which led up to World War I contains an interesting second chapter which compares the "national capabilities" of the "major powers" during the period from 1870 to 1915. Graphs depict the populations, iron and steel production, national income (total and per capita), foreign trade, marine tonnage, and colonial area for Britain, France, Germany, Italy, Russia, and Austria–Hungary. The United States is not included because it allegedly was irrelevant to the onset of the Great War.

10 The figures in table 9.1 should be interpreted as rough indicators only. The main point is that total GNP includes a factor due to population size, while GNP per capita is much closer to what we mean by a developed national economy. The use of GNP figures for the nineteenth century is especially hazardous because of differences in national accounting procedures and the problem of currency exchange rates. Even post-World War II national accounting figures have required major adjustments to take into account differences in purchasing power of currencies across national boundaries (see Kravis et al., 1982). Nevertheless the figures in table 9.1 undoubtedly give a closer estimate of the relative core status of the great powers than the original table presented by Kugler and Organski, which was based on total GNP unweighted by population.

11 A similar explanation is suggested for the high GDP per capita figure for Australia in 1870 (see Maddison, 1982: table 1.4) and the high GNP per capita figures of oil exporters in recent decades (see chapter 10).

12 A measure which is highly correlated with the proportion of national product in agriculture, is the proportion of the labor force employed in agriculture. Maddison (1982: table 2.2) shows that the Dutch economy was much more industrialized in 1700 than was the economy of the United Kingdom on the basis of the percentage of the work force in agriculture services and industry. But by 1890 the United Kingdom had pulled far ahead of the Netherlands (see table 9.3).

TABLE 9.3

	Netherlands %	UK %
1700		
Agriculture	40	60
Industry	33	15
Services	27	25
1890		
Agriculture	33	16
Industry	31	44
Services	36	40

Source: Excerpted from Maddison (1982:35, table 2.2).

PART III ZONES OF THE WORLD-SYSTEM

10 Core and Periphery

1 Of course this discussion of nested hierarchies has only considered those structures which are easily conceived in spatial terms. The actual nested hierarchy also contains features which are spatially organized in even more complicated ways, such as classes and political organizations.

2 Another form of intermediate activity should also be noted because it has consequences which are somewhat similar to those of the types of semiperipherality defined above. Certain political and/or economic entrepreneurs mediate core/periphery relations. The New England merchant capitalists involved in the "triangle trades" in the eighteenth century, and the New York bankers who financed the transportation and sale of cotton from the US South to the English Midlands in the nineteenth century perhaps ought to be called semiperipheral capitalists. And the notion of a subimperial power suggests that a state may perform the role of a subaltern for a core power within a particular region of the periphery. These forms of intermediation certainly have consequences for the actors which differentiate them from both core and peripheral others. I will not propose that these instances of mediation between core and periphery constitute part of the definition of semiperipherality, but we ought to keep them in mind when we are studying particular semiperipheries.

3 This notion may also prove important for understanding the rise of semiperipheral marcher states in the process of ancient empire-formation (see Mann, 1986: chapter 5; Chase-Dunn, 1988).

4 See Fernand Braudel's (1984:299) discussion of national wealth, national income, and methods of estimating per capita national income for the seventeenth and eighteenth centuries. There are, of course, large problems of comparability of GNP figures across countries. See note 10 to chapter 9.

5 All researchers agree that the core/periphery hierarchy is relational in the sense that it involves relations of power and dependence among entities. The advocates of network analysis argue that their measures are truly relational and structural, while other less complex measures are merely attributional, being based on attributes of units rather than relations among units. My own position is that there is no hard and fast division between attributes of an entity and relations between entities. Sometimes, as with symbolic interactionism, the identity of a unit is a major constituent element of that unit's interaction with other units. A variable characteristic of a unit may in fact be an indicator of that unit's relationship with other units, as with investment dependence of nation states which is measured by the amount of foreign-owned equity capital within a country. But even attributes which seem to be wholly "internal" such as GNP per capita may be useful indicators of relations among units or position in a larger system when they are used in comparative analysis.

6 Mintz (1974) produced an early anthropological analysis of local/world-system links. Other anthropologists who have done this kind of work are Ekholm and Friedman (1980), Kahn (1980), Warman (1980), Verdery (1983), Fox (1985), and Trouillot (1988). Historians and sociologists have also done similar studies. I already mentioned Hall (1986, 1988). Others are Murray (1980), Rodney (1981), and So (1986).

7 Bairoch shows the following figures for Europe and the population of European colonies. Russia is included in the figures for Europe.

TABLE 10.1 *Comparison of population of Europe and its colonies, 1700–1913*

Year	*Population (millions)* *Europe*[a]	*European colonies*	*Colonies compared to Europe (%)*
1700	140	16	11
1750	160	22	14
1800	207	120	58
1830	242	240	100
1860	294	270; 680[b]	92;252
1900	414	490; 960[b]	118;232
1913	481	530;1030[b]	110;214

[a]Includes Russia
[b]The first figure excludes China, the second includes it
Source: Bairoch (1986:197)

8 O'Brien later discusses the Baltic trade when considering the flows of bullion into Europe, but he does not distinguish between peripheralized Poland on the one hand and Russia, which Wallerstein (1974: chapter 6) argues was an external arena until it became incorporated into a semiperipheral position within the European world-economy in the eighteenth century. Wallerstein (1983b) has published a response to O'Brien's article which, in addition to my criticisms, points out the deficiences of economic statistics which fail to estimate the inputs of non-wage labor.

9 Wallerstein argues that plunder is undertaken in external arenas, while incorporation into the periphery involves a shift to production of peripheral commodities using coerced labor. When we begin to compare the processes of peripheralization that operate in different world-systems we may want to understand plunder as one important form of peripheral exploitation rather than simply a prelude to unequal exchange. Plunder tends to destroy the plundered society, while peripheral exploitation underdevelops it. Nevertheless there have been fairly long-lasting core/periphery hierarchies based exclusively on plunder (e.g. Kelly, 1985).

11 Reproduction of the Core/Periphery Hierarchy

1 Charles Lipson's fascinating study of the changing international regime which supports foreign-held private property and investment in peripheral countries reveals that the degree to which foreign investment depends directly on military power has declined, and that the growing ideology of sovereign national development has decreased the extent to which core states can guarantee the property rights of core investors in the periphery (Lipson, 1985).

2 Chase-Dunn (1981) analyzes the case of the United States from a similar perspective.

3 The exception to this has been the OPEC oil cartel, but the difficulties of keeping this cartel together and the failure of attempts to create cartels for other raw materials and agricultural products support the above generalization.

4 The number of developing countries for which data were available for the described estimates was 33 for GNP per capita and 26 for electrical energy consumption per

capita. With such small numbers estimates can be heavily influenced by one or two cases.

Chapter 12 Recent Trends

1 William Dixon's (1985) study of trends in commodity concentration (the tendency for a country's exports to be concentrated in one or a few main commodities) and partner concentration (the tendency for exports to be sent to one other country) concludes that there has been little or no change in the distribution of these forms of trade dependence between 1955 and 1975. But Dixon's (1985:182) tables show that the mean levels of these variables decline for both semiperipheral and peripheral groups of countries, confirming the trends cited above in Bornschier and Chase-Dunn (1985:52). Dixon's conclusion that there is no change is based on his decomposition of the components of change into "structural" change and "positional" change, but he does not explain how the technique he uses for decomposition separates out these two components of change (Dixon, 1985:179).
2 Similar upward trends in debt dependence for the period between 1970 and 1982 are shown for several types of debt in peripheral countries of Africa, Asia, and the Americas in Sell and Kunitz (1986–7: table 2).
3 Interpolation is required between the country closest to 20 percent of the world's population and the next country listed in order to estimate the proportion of world GNP controlled by exactly 20 percent of the world's population in countries highest on GNP per capita. This table follows the method of an earlier table which examined changes in the distribution of world resources from 1950 to 1970 (Meyer, et al., 1975: table 2). Though it is calculated in a similar way, the sources used and the cases included are different, and thus the proportions at any point in time vary to some extent. These tables are intended to show change over time. The exact size of proportion estimates are influenced by the particular countries included. Because data availability differs across sources the proportions will differ, but changes over time should still indicate trends in world-system inequality. In this regard table 12.3 and the earlier version presented by Meyer et al. (1975) lead to similar conclusions.
4 A study by Breedlove and Nolan (1988) study reveals a trend toward increasing inequality in the global distribution of GNP per capita among 120 countries. Breedlove and Nolan compute Gini coefficients for five-year intervals between 1960 and 1980, and while the average GNP per capita increased for the core, the semiperiphery, and the periphery over this time period, the amount of relative inequality among all the countries indicated by the Gini coefficient increased as well.
5 There are a few surprises, such as the inclusion of Japan in the middle group rather than in the top quintile. Japan's lack of domestic energy supplies has encouraged a relatively more frugal use of energy in industrial production. Its rapid growth in this period contributed to the world-level redistribution.

13 World-system Fluctuations

1 Bergesen and Schoenberg sensibly do not include reorganizations of existing colonies as instances of expansion. Thus they exclude 22 new Spanish governors sent to head "intendencias" during the decentralization of the Spanish empire in the late seventeenth and eighteenth centuries. I would also want to exclude instances in which European colonial powers acquired colonies from one another, either by force or through treaty. As table 13.1 shows, there were 61 cases of this kind in Henige's data, and they were unevenly distributed over time, peaking in the eighteenth century. These

TABLE 13.1 *Colonial governors sent, 1415–1969*

Century	*Expansion*	*Traded or taken*	*Divided or consolidated*	*Totals*
15th	6	0	0	6
16th	49	1	1	50
17th	76	11	5	91
18th	47	25	17	89
19th	100	11	2	113
20th	53	13	0	66
Totals	331	61	24	415

Source: Henige (1970)

are probably more an indicator of contention among core powers than an indicator of territorial expansion of the world-system.

My examination of the Henige data also suggests interesting differences between core powers in the timing of their colonial expansion. Despite Bergesen and Schoenberg's insistence that we look only at characteristics of the whole world-system, figure 13.3 shows colonies established by each core power by centuries. Countries with few colonies, such as Sweden, Denmark, Russia, Italy, Japan, and the United States, have not been included.

Figure 13.3 shows what all students of colonialism know – the first wave was the work of Spain and Portugal with the Dutch, British, and French joining in later, and the

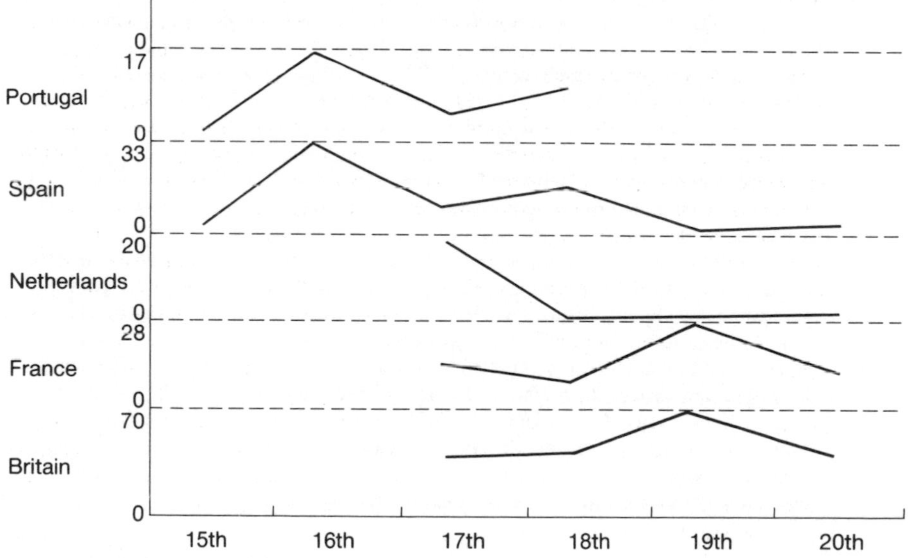

FIGURE 13.3 *New colonies established by separate core states*

second wave was almost entirely the job of the French and the British, both of whom weighed in heavily in the nineteenth century. The older core powers joined in for the second wave, as did several new core powers and upwardly mobile semiperipheral countries, but they were all minor partners compared to the British and the French. In terms of totals the British account for the greatest portion of colonialism with a total of 172 for the whole time period covered by Henige. The French and the Spanish are far behind with 65 and 59, followed by Portugal (38), Netherlands (23), the United States (8), Germany (7), Italy (5), Japan (5), Denmark (3), Belgium (2), Sweden (2), and Russia (1).

2 Pat McGowan (1985:488) notes that Europe also had an earlier wave of colonial expansion "beginning with the Crusades of the twelfth century, that established the Crusader states in the Holy Land and that culminated in the commercial empires of Venice and Genoa in the Levant in the fourteenth and fifteenth centuries, including the colonies of Crete, Cyprus, and many Black Sea ports."

3 McGowan (1985: table 4) does find a positive relationship between the cumulative net number of colonies and Bergesen and Schoenberg's measure of war, but I do not accord this finding much importance because both the measure of colonialism, which includes both cumulative colonies and colonial terminations, and the measure of war have serious problems, as discussed above.

4 Actually the United States joined in the free trade movement between 1846 and 1860, lowering tariff barriers during a period in which Southern control of the federal state and the presidency was at its zenith. The election of Lincoln brought in a new coalition which supported renewed protectionism, and also provoked the secession of South Carolina (Chase-Dunn, 1980).

5 It should be noted that visual inspection indicates that this periodization of the expansion of capital exports is not closely related to the cycles of the number of new colonies established as revealed in figure 13.4 above. The 1860s/1870s boom of capital exports appears during a trough of colonial expansion, while the pre- and post-World War I periods of capital export growth occur on the downswing of a colonial expansion wave which had peaked in about 1890. Thus, the two types of expansion are apparently neither in phase nor inversely related.

6 The conception of cycles of world-system development described in chapter 3 would, of course, contradict this claim in many ways. First, the industrial revolution which began in England in the eighteenth century was the most extensive (up to that time) of a number of previous "revolutions" in which rapid technological development, the increase in capital intensity in both manufacturing and agriculture, and the emergence of new lead "industrial" sectors, had occurred. The earlier industrial revolutions were undoubtedly of less magnitude as well as harder to measure, but economic history strongly supports their existence. This perspective does not, however, provide an explanation for Suter's finding that international financial flows do not reveal cyclical characteristics in the first half of the nineteenth century. Suter himself observes that international financial centers in earlier centuries moved geographically with changes in the hegemonic leader from the centrality of the Medici in Florence through the Fuggers to Antwerp, Amsterdam, London, and New York (see also Braudel, 1984). While the capital exports of Britain and France do not seem to correspond to Kondratieff waves in the first half of the nineteenth century, Suter finds that a debt crisis does correspond to the Kondratieff in that period.

PART IV METATHEORY AND RESEARCH METHODS

Chapter 14 Theory Construction

1 Among Marxist social scientists in the United States there are not many who continue to take an explicitly structuralist approach. A notable exception is Erik Wright (1985) and the circle of "analytic Marxists."

2 Karl Popper (1972) uses the term historicism in a nearly opposite way, and his usage has become popular. For Popper historicism meant teleological causation and unilinear evolution, qualities which he identified with Marxist theory. Structuralist theory need not be functionalist or teleological, and neither must it embrace a simple version of deterministic unilinear evolution.

3 Charles Tilly's (1984:81) valuable discussion of different strategies of comparison adds a second dimension. In addition to the continuum I have discussed, which he terms individualizing versus universalizing comparison of instances of a phenomenon, Tilly proposes that scholarly approaches differ also in terms of their usage of differentiated forms of a phenomenon. Some analysts propose only a single form, whereas others conceptualize multiple forms. This second dimension enables Tilly to crossclassify comparative strategies in a way which yields, in addition to individualizing and universalizing approaches, encompassing and variation-finding types. Encompassing comparisons analyze different levels of analysis simultaneously e.g. the world-system and national states. Variation-finding studies examine how variables are systematically but differently interconnected in different cases.

4 I have long expected that the shift to the world-system level of analysis (as a frame of reference and as a focal unit of analysis in its own right) would eventually lead to the application of modernization theory and the Parsonian approach to the world-system. This has occurred in the work of George M. Thomas et al. (1987) and Roland Robertson (Robertson and Lechner, 1985). The only book to explicitly contrast different theoretical approaches to the world-system is William R. Thompson's (1983) *Contending Approaches to World-system Analysis*.

5 Charles Tilly's (1984) quite sensible plea for the grounding of comparative studies in a relatively concrete setting even though the foci of analysis are "big structures, large processes, and huge comparisons," makes the case that the concept of "society" has been particularly abused as an abstraction by social theorists. While I am sympathetic with his effort, Tilly's main difficulty with the term "society" is that it is hard to bound a concrete society in time and space. Thus "German society" is a messy idea when we try to say when, where, and which people are included within it. But I am not convinced that this proves that the idea of society is a bad idea. My reservations stem from my own somewhat limited exposure to German society, which despite its complex nature and messy boundaries, is more than simply a mythical national identification. The concept "civilization" is similarly problematic, but this is not reason enough to dispense with it, at least until a substitute specification which captures the complexities of the idea has been developed.

6 Karl Marx describes his own metatheoretical approach in the *Grundrisse*:

> Thus, if I were to begin with the population, this would be a chaotic conception [*Vorstellung*] of the whole, and I would then, by means of further determination, move analytically towards ever more simple concepts [*Begriff*], from the imagined concrete towards ever thinner abstractions until I had arrived at the simplest determinations. From there the journey would have to be retraced until I had

finally arrived at the population again, but this time not as a chaotic conception of a whole, but as a rich totality of many determinations and relations. (Marx, 1973:100)

Chapter 15 Research Methods

1 This same point is made with regard to other levels of analysis in Morris Zelditch, Jr's essay, "Can you study an army in the laboratory?" (Zelditch, 1969).

2 As in any experimental or non-experimental research design there may be things going on that we don't know about, that are not included in our model, and these may account for the relationships we find. A critic who suggests this, however, is generally required to be more specific, to outline the source of the hypothesized spuriousness. If the critics' claim is plausible it is incumbent on the researcher to include the new variable in his model and to test for its effects on the relationships.

3 The need for an omnibus crossnational data bank has been the topic of discussion at recent meetings of the International Studies Association and the American Political Science Association. Professors Dina Zinnes and Richard Merritt of the University of Illinois at Champaign-Urbana have formed a multidisciplinary committee on "Data Development for International Research" and this group has obtained support from the National Science Foundation for the improvement and integration of crossnational data, including that which is relevant for international political economy.

4 A related point is made by Doran and Parsons (1980:959) in their discussion of the measurement of the timing of a "critical period" in the cycle of relative power among core states.

Chapter 16 Implications

1 One implication of the focus on logical boundaries already discussed in my book on socialist states (Chase-Dunn, 1982b), is that we cannot be so sanguine about the definition of socialism as Marx and Engels were. Reacting to the detailed blueprints of the utopian socialists, they were happy to leave the specification of the contents of socialism up to the worker's movement. In light of the history of efforts to establish socialism since then, it is obvious that things are more problematic. We want to be able to say more definitely which political initiatives represent progress toward socialism, and which do not. It is not a simple matter of intention, or reading the formal program or constitution. Use of the word socialism does not guarantee its content – for example, national socialism. I have only defined socialism very broadly as *democratic collective rationality*. This definition raises many theoretical and empirical questions about the actual content of socialist programs, institutions, and political initiatives. This difficult problem is heavy with social and political philosophy, and beyond the intended bounds of this book, which has focused on the nature of capitalism. The two problems are not unrelated in reality, as the question of logical boundaries implies, but I feel that to go further toward a more elaborate and concrete specification of the content of the socialist mode of production would take us into a problem which should be the topic of another work.

2 We need not agree with Wittfogel's (1957) thesis of "oriental despotism" in order to see elements of the tributary mode of production in the contemporary socialist states. To the extent that a technocratic and bureaucratic class uses state power to extract surplus product from direct producers we have a version of the tributary mode. Samir Amin (1980a) terms these societies "statist." None of this is to deny, however, that they

also contain significant elements of the logic of socialism in the laws which forbid private ownership of large-scale means of production, welfare, and employment guarantees, and in some cases important forms of economic democracy.

3 An extremely crude effort to do this using seat-of-the-pants coding of world-system position was presented in Chase-Dunn (1983).

4 This occurred first in the medieval cities of feudal Europe, spurring the emergence of nation states in which kings were dependent for financial support on urban capital. Later the bourgeois Dutch and English revolutions brought capitalists to autonomous control over nation states within a core region, this for the first time in history.

Bibliography

Adelman, Irma 1965: "Long cycles – fact or fiction?" *American Economic Review* 55, 3: 444–63.

Alavi, Hamza 1972: "The state in post-colonial societies: Pakistan and Bangla-Desh." *New Left Review* 74, 59–81.

Alker, H. 1982: "Logic, dialectics, politics: some recent controversies." In H. R. Alker (ed.), *Dialectical Logics for the Political Sciences*, Poznan Studies in the Philosophy of the Sciences and the Humanities, Amsterdam: Kodopi, vol. 7.

Allison, Paul D. 1984: *Event History Analysis: regression for longitudinal event data*. Beverly Hills, Ca.: Sage.

Althusser, Louis and Etienne Balibar 1970: *Reading Capital*. Trans. Ben Brewster. London: New Left Books.

Amin, Samir 1974: *Accumulation on a World Scale*. New York: Monthly Review Press. 2 vols.

—— 1975: *Unequal Development*. New York: Monthly Review Press.

—— 1977: *Imperialism and Unequal Exchange*. New York: Monthly Review Press.

—— 1980a: *Class and Nation, Historically and in the Current Crisis*. New York: Monthly Review Press.

—— 1980b: "The class structure of the contemporary imperialist system." *Monthly Review*, 31(8), 9–26.

Anderson, Perry 1974a: *Passages from Antiquity to Feudalism*. London: New Left Books.

—— 1974b: *Lineages of the Absolutist State*. London: New Left Books.

—— 1980: *Arguments within English Marxism*. London: New Left Books.

Arrighi, Giovanni 1978: *The Geometry of Imperialism*. London: New Left Books.

—— 1982: "A crisis of hegemony." In Samir Amin, Giovanni Arrighi, Andre Gunder Frank and Immanuel Wallerstein, *Dynamics of Global Crisis*, New York: Monthly Review Press, 55–108.

Arrighi, Giovanni (ed.) 1985: *Semiperipheral Development: the politics of southern Europe in the twentieth century*. Beverly Hills, Ca.: Sage.

Arrighi, Giovanni and Jessica Drangel 1986: "Stratification of the world-economy: an explanation of the semiperipheral zone." *Review*, 10(1), 9–74.

Ashley, Richard K. 1984: "The poverty of neo-realism." *International Organization*, 38(2), 225–6.

Bach, Robert L. 1977: "Methods of analysis in the study of the world-economy." *American Sociological Review*, 42(5), 811–14.

—— 1980: "On the holism of a world-systems perspective." In Terence K. Hopkins and Immanuel Wallerstein (eds), *Processes of the World-System*, Beverly Hills, Ca.: Sage, 289–310.

Bairoch, Paul 1975: *The Economic Development of the Third World Since 1900*. Berkeley: University of California Press.

—— 1976: "Europe's gross national product: 1800–1975." *Journal of European Economic History*, 5, 273–340.

—— 1986: "Historical roots of economic underdevelopment: myths and realities." In Wolfgang J. Mommsen and Jurgen Osterhammel (eds), *Imperialism After Empire: continuities and discontinuities*, London: Allen and Unwin, 191–216.

Bairoch, P. and J. M. Limbor 1968: "Changes in the industrial distribution of the world labour force, by region, 1800–1960." *International Labour Review*, 98(4), 311–36.

Balibar, Etienne 1970: "The basic concepts of historical materialism." In Louis Althusser and Etienne Balibar, *Reading Capital*. New York: Random House, 199–308.

Banaji, Jarius 1980: "Summary of selected parts of Kautsky's 'The Agrarian Question.'" In Harold Wolpe (ed.), *The Articulation of Modes of Production*, London: Routledge and Kegan Paul, 45–92.

Banks, Arthur S. 1971: *Cross-polity Time Series Data*. Cambridge, Mass.: MIT Press.

Baran, Paul and Paul Sweezy 1966: *Monopoly Capitalism*. New York: Monthly Review Press.

Barbour, Violet 1963: *Capitalism in Amsterdam in the 17th Century*. Ann Arbor: University of Michigan Press.

Barker, Colin 1978: "The state as capital." *International Socialism* 2(1), 16–42.

Barr, Kenneth 1979: "Long waves: A selective annotated bibliography." *Review* 2(4), 675–718.

—— 1981: "On the capitalist enterprise." *Review of Radical Political Economics* 12(4), 60–70.

Barrat-Brown, Michael 1974: *The Economics of Imperialism*. London: Penguin.

Bellah, Robert N., Richard Madsen, William M. Sullivan, Ann Swidler, and Steven M. Tipton 1986: *Habits of the Heart: individualism and commitment in American Life*. New York: Harper and Row.

Bennett, Douglas C. and Kenneth E. Sharpe 1985: *Transnational Corporations Versus the State: the political economy of the Mexican auto industry*. Princeton, NJ: Princeton University Press.

Benton, Ted 1984: *The Rise and Fall of Structural Marxism*. New York: St Martin's Press.

Bergesen, Albert 1980: "From utilitarianism to globology: the shift from the individual to the world as a whole as the primordial unit of analysis." In Albert Bergesen (ed.), *Studies of the Modern World-System*. New York: Academic Press, 1–12.

—— 1981: "Long economic cycles and the size of industrial enterprise." In Richard Rubinson (ed.), *Dynamics of World Development*, Beverly Hills, Ca.: Sage, 179–91.

—— 1983: "The class structure of the world-system." In W. R. Thompson (ed.), *Contending Approaches to World System Analysis*. Beverly Hills, Ca: Sage, 43–54.

—— 1985a: "Cycles of war in the reproduction of the world economy." In Paul M. Johnson and William R. Thompson (eds), *Rhythms in Politics and Economics*. New York: Praeger, 313–31.

—— 1985b: "How to model the cyclical dynamics of the world-system." *Review* 8(4), 501–12.

Bergesen, Albert (ed.) 1980: *Studies of the Modern World-System*. New York: Academic Press.

Bergesen, Albert and Ronald Schoenberg 1980: "Long waves of colonial expansion and contraction, 1415–1969." In Albert J. Bergesen (ed.), *Studies of the Modern World-System*, New York: Academic Press, 231–78.

Bergesen, Albert and Chintamani Sahoo 1985: "Evidence of the decline of American hegemony in world production." *Review*, 8(4), 595–611.

Bergesen, Albert, Roberto M. Fernandez, and Chintamani Sahoo 1987: "America and the changing structure of hegemonic production." In Terry Boswell and Albert Bergesen (eds), *America's Changing Role in the World System*, New York: Praeger, 157–76.

Berry, Albert, Francois Bourguignon, and Christian Morrison 1983: "The level of world inequality: how much can one say?" *Review of Income and Wealth*, 29, 217–41.

Biersteker, Thomas J. 1978: *Distortion or Development?: contending perspectives on the multinational corporation*. Cambridge, Mass.: MIT Press.

Blanton, Richard and Gary Feinman 1984: "The mesoamerican world-system." *American Anthropologist*, 86(3), 673–82.

Blau, P. M. 1964: *Exchange and Power in Social Life*. New York: Wiley.

Block, Fred 1977: *The Origins of International Economic Disorder: a study of United States international monetary policy from World War II to the present*. Berkeley: University of California Press.

—— 1978: "Marxist theories of the state in world systems analysis." In Barbara H. Kaplan (ed.), *Social Change in the Capitalist World Economy*, Beverly Hills, Ca.: Sage, 27–38.

Boli, John 1979: "The ideology of expanding state authority in national constitutions, 1870–1970," in Meyer and Hannan (eds) 222–37.

—— 1980: "Global integration and the universal increase of state dominance, 1870–1970." In A. Bergesen (ed.), *Studies of the Modern World System* New York: Academic Press, 77–109.

Bollen, Kenneth 1983: "World-system position, dependency and democracy: the cross-national evidence." *American Sociological Review*, 48, 468–79.

Bornschier, Volker 1976: *Wachstum, Konzentration und Multinationalisierung von Industrieunternehmen*. Frauenfeld und Stuttgart: Verlag Huber.

—— 1980: *Multinationale Konzerne, Wirtschaftspolitik und nationale Entwicklung im Weltsystem*. Frankfurt and New York: Campus Verlag.

—— 1983: "Dependent reproduction in the world system: a study on the incidence of 'dependency reversal.'" In Charles F. Doran, George Modelski and Cal Clark (eds), *North/South Relations: studies of dependency reversal*, New York: Praeger, 97–116.

—— 1985: "World social structure in the long economic wave." Paper presented at the annual meeting of the International Studies Association, March 5–9.

—— 1987: "The business of violence and legitimacy." A paper presented at annual meeting of the International Studies Association, Washington, DC, April 15.

Chapter 14 in V. Bornschier, *Westliche Gesellschaft im Wandel*. Frankfurt and New York: Campus Verlag, 1988.

Bornschier, Volker and Thanh-huyen Ballmer-Cao 1979: "Income inequality: A crossnational study of the relationships between MNC penetration, dimensions of the power structure and income distribution." *American Sociological Review*, 44(3), 487–506.

Bornschier, Volker and Christopher Chase-Dunn 1985: *Transnational Corporations and Underdevelopment*. New York: Praeger.

Bornschier, Volker and Otto Hartlieb 1981: "Weltmarktabhängigkeit und Entwicklung: Übersicht über die Evidenzen und Reanalyse." *Bulletin of the Sociological Institute*, 39 (October), University of Zurich.

Bornschier, Volker and Peter Heintz (eds) 1979: *Compendium of Data for World-Systems Analysis*. Sociological Institute, University of Zurich.

Bornschier, Volker and Jean-Pierre Hoby 1981: "Economic policy and multi-national corporations in development: the measurable impacts in cross-national perspective." *Social Problems*, 28(4), 363–77.

Bornschier, Volker, C. Chase-Dunn, and R. Rubinson 1978: "Cross-national evidence of the effects of foreign investment and aid on economic growth and inequality: A survey of findings and a reanalysis." *American Journal of Sociology*, 84(3), 651–83.

Borrego, John 1982: "Metanational capitalist accumulation and the reintegration of socialist states." In C. Chase-Dunn (ed.), *Socialist States in the World-System*. Beverly Hills, Ca.: Sage, 114–47.

Boswell, Terry 1989: "Colonial empires and the capitalist world-system: a time-series analysis of colonization, 1650–1960." American Sociological Review 54, 2: 180–97.

Bourguignon, F., A. Berry and C. Morrison 1983: "The world distribution of incomes between 1950 and 1977." *Economic Journal*, 93, 331–50.

Bousquet, Nicole 1980: "From hegemony to competition: cycles of the core?" In Terence K. Hopkins and Immanuel Wallerstein (eds), *Processes of the World-System*, Beverly Hills, Ca.: Sage, 46–83.

Braudel, Fernand 1972: *The Mediterranean and the Mediterranean World in the Age of Philip II*. New York: Harper and Row, 2 vols.

—— 1975: *Capitalism and Material Life: 1400–1800*. New York: Harper and Row.

—— 1977: *Afterthoughts on Material Civilization and Capitalism*. Baltimore, Md.: Johns Hopkins University Press.

—— 1984:*The Perspective of the World*. Vol. 3 of *Civilization and Capitalism*. Trans. Sian Reynolds. New York: Harper and Row.

Braudel, F. P. and F. Spooner 1967: "Prices in Europe from 1450 to 1750." In E. E. Rich (ed.), *The Economy of Expanding Europe in the Sixteenth and Seventeenth Centuries*, vol. 4, *Cambridge Economic History of Europe*, 378–486, Cambridge: Cambridge University Press.

Braverman, H. 1974: *Labor and Monopoly Capital*. New York: Monthly Review Press.

Breedlove, William L. and Patrick D. Nolan 1988: "International stratification and inequality 1960–1980." International Journal of Contemporary Sociology 25, 3–4: 105–23.

Brenner, Robert L. 1977: "The origins of capitalist development: a critique of neo-Smithian Marxism." *New Left Review* 104, 25–92.

Brunt, P. A. 1971: *Social Conflicts in the Roman Republic*. New York: Norton.

Bukharin, Nicolai 1973 [1915]: *Imperialism and World Economy*. New York: Monthly Review Press.

Bunker, Stephen 1983: "Center-local struggles for bureaucratic control in Bugisu, Uganda." *American Ethnologist* 10(4), 749–69.

—— 1984: "Modes of extraction, unequal exchange, and the under-development of an extreme periphery: the Brazilian Amazon, 1600–1980." *American Journal of Sociology* 89(5), 1017–64 (March).

—— 1985: *Underdeveloping the Amazon: extraction, unequal exchange and the failure of the modern state*. Urbana: University of Illinois Press.

Burawoy, Michael 1979: *Manufacturing Consent*. Chicago: University of Chicago Press.

Burke, Peter 1974: *Venice and Amsterdam: a study of 17th century elites*. London: Temple Smith.

Cain, P. J. and A. G. Hopkins 1986: "Gentlemanly capitalism and British expansion overseas I: The old colonial system, 1688–1850." *Economic History Review*, 2nd Ser., 39(4), 501–25.

Cameron, David R. 1978: "The expansion of the public economy: A comparative analysis." *American Political Science Review*, 72(4), 1243–61.

Caporaso, James 1981: "Industrialization in the periphery: the evolving global division of labor." In W. Ladd Hollist and James Rosenau (eds), *World System Structure: continuity and change*, Beverly Hills, Ca.: Sage, 140–71.

Cardoso, Fernando Henrique 1973: "Associated-dependent development: theoretical and practical implications." In Alfred Stepan (ed.), *Authoritarian Brazil*, New Haven, Conn.: Yale University Press.

—— 1977: "The consumption of dependency theory in the United States." *Latin American Research Review*, 12(3), 7–24.

Cardoso, Fernando Henrique and Enzo Faletto 1979 [1971]: *Dependency and Development in Latin America*. Berkeley: University of California Press.

Carnoy, Martin and Derek Shearer 1980: *Economic Democracy: the challenge of the 1980s*. White Plains, NY: M. E. Sharpe.

Chase-Dunn, Christopher 1975: "The effects of international economic dependence on development and inequality: a cross-national study." *American Sociological Review* 40, 720–38 (December).

—— 1976: "Toward a formal comparative study of the world-system." A working paper and transcribed talk delivered at the Fernand Braudel Center, December 8. Published as a working paper of Seminar II: Historical Geography of Social and Economic Structures of the Modern World-System, Braudel Center, SUNY-Binghamton.

—— 1978: "Core-periphery relations: the effects of core competition." In Barbara H. Kaplan (ed.), *Social Change in the Capitalist World Economy*, Beverly Hills, Ca.: Sage, 154–76.

—— 1979: "Comparative research on world-system characteristics." *International Studies Quarterly*, 23(4), 601–23.

—— 1980: "The development of core capitalism in the antebellum United States: tariff politics and class struggle in an upwardly mobile semi-periphery." In A. Bergesen (ed.), *Studies of the Modern World-System*, New York: Academic Press, 189–230.

—— 1981: "Interstate system and capitalist world-economy: one logic or two?"

International Studies Quarterly 25(1), 19–42.

—— 1982a: "The uses of formal comparative research on dependency theory and the world-system perspective." In Harry Makler, Albert Martinelli and Neil Smelser (eds), *The New International Economy*, London: Sage Publications, 117–40.

—— 1983: "Inequality, structural mobility and dependency reversal in the capitalist world-economy." In Charles F. Doran, George Modelski, and Cal Clark (eds), *North/South Relations: studies of dependency reversal*, New York: Praeger, 73–95.

—— 1984: "Levels of urban primacy in zones of the world-system since 1800." Paper presented at the annual meeting of the American Sociological Association, San Antonio, Texas, August 27.

—— 1985a: "The system of world cities: A.D. 800–1975." In M. Timberlake (ed.) *Urbanization in the World Economy*, New York: Academic Press, 269–92.

—— 1985b: "The coming of urban primacy in Latin America." *Comparative Urban Research* 11(1–2), 14–31.

—— 1986: "Types of world-systems." A paper presented at the annual meeting of the International Studies Association, Anaheim, Ca., March 26.

—— 1987: "The Korean trajectory in the world-system." In Kyong-dong Kim (ed.), *Dependency Issues in Korean Development*, Seoul: Seoul National University Press, 270–304.

—— 1988: "Comparing world-systems: toward a theory of semiperipheral development." *Comparative Civilizations Review* (Fall).

Chase-Dunn, Christopher (ed.) 1982b: *Socialist States in the World-System*. Beverly Hills, Ca.: Sage.

Chase-Dunn, Christopher, Aaron Pallas, and Jeffrey Kentor 1982: "Old and new research designs for studying the world-system: a research note." *Comparative Political Studies* 15, (3):341–56.

Chase-Dunn, Christopher and Richard Rubinson 1977: "Toward a structural perspective on the world-system." *Politics and Society*, 7(4), 453–76.

—— 1979: "Cycles, trends and new departures in world-system development." In John W. Meyer and Michael T. Hannan (eds), *National Development in the World-System*, Chicago: University of Chicago Press, 276–96.

Chatterjee, Partha 1975: *Arms, Alliances and Stability*. New York: John Wiley.

Chaudhuri, K. N. 1985: *Trade and Civilisation in The Indian Ocean*. Cambridge: Cambridge University Press.

Chirot, Daniel 1977: *Social Change in the Twentieth Century*. New York: Harcourt Brace Jovanovich.

—- 1986: *Social Change in the Modern Era*. New York: Harcourt Brace Jovanovich.

Choucri, Nazli and Robert C. North 1975: *Nations in Conflict: national growth and international violence*. San Francisco, Ca.: Freeman.

Clapham, J. H. 1966: *Economic Development of France and Germany*. Cambridge: Cambridge University Press.

Coale, Ansley J. 1974: "The history of the human population." *Scientific American*, September, 15–28.

Collier, David (ed.) 1979: *The New Authoritarianism in Latin America*. Princeton NJ: Princeton University Press.

Collins, Randall 1986: *Weberian Sociological Theory*. Cambridge: Cambridge University Press.

Cox, Oliver 1959: *The Foundations of Capitalism*. New York: Philosophical Library.

Cox, Robert W. 1983: "Gramsci, hegemony and international relations: an essay in method." *Millenium: Journal of International Studies*, (122), 162–75.

Crosby, Alfred W. 1972: *The Columbian Exchange: biological and cultural consequences of 1492*. Westport, Conn.: Greenwood Press.

Crouzet, François 1982: *The Victorian Economy*. New York: Columbia University Press.

Curtin, Phillip 1984: *Cross-cultural Trade in World History*. Cambridge: Cambridge University Press.

Davis, Ralph 1973: *The Rise of the Atlantic Economies*. Ithaca, NY: Cornell University Press.

Dehio, Ludwig 1962: *The Precarious Balance*. New York: Vintage.

de Janvry, Alain 1981: *The Agrarian Question and Reformism in Latin America*. Baltimore, Md.: Johns Hopkins University Press.

de Janvry, Alain and Frank Kramer 1979: "The limits of unequal exchange." *Review of Radical Political Economics*, 11(4), 3–15.

Deyo, Frederic C. 1981: *Dependent Development and Industrial Order: an Asian case study*. New York: Praeger.

Dixon, Marlene 1982: "Dual power: the rise of the transnational corporation and the nation-state." *Contemporary Marxism* 5, 129–46.

Dixon, William J. 1985: "Change and persistence in the world system: an analysis of global trade concentration, 1955–1975." *International Studies Quarterly*, 29(2), 171–90.

Dobb, Maurice 1963 [1947]: *Studies in the Development of Capitalism*. New York: International Publishers.

Domhoff, G. William 1978: *The Powers That Be: processes of ruling class domination in America*. New York: Vintage.

Doran, Charles F. 1971: *The Politics of Assimilation: hegemony and its aftermath*. Baltimore, Md.: Johns Hopkins University Press.

Doran, Charles F. and Wes Parsons 1980: "War and the cycle of relative power." *American Political Science Review*, 74, 947–65.

Doran, Charles, George Modelski and Cal Clark (eds) 1983: *North/South Relations: studies of dependency reversal*. New York: Praeger.

Dos Santos, Teotonio 1963: "El nuevo caracter de le dependencia." Santiago: *Cuadernos de Estudios Socio-economicos* (10), Centro de Estudios Socio-economicos, Universidad de Chile.

Durkheim, Emile 1964 (1893): *The Division of Labor in Society*. New York: Free Press.

Duvall, Raymond D. and John R. Freeman 1981: "The state and dependent capitalism." *International Studies Quarterly*, 25(1), 99–118.

Eckstein, Susan 1983: "Cuba and the capitalist world economy." In C. Chase-Dunn (ed.), *Socialist States in the World System*, Beverly Hills, Ca.: Sage, 203–18.

Edwards, Richard 1979: *Contested Terrain: the transformation of the workplace in the twentieth century*. New York: Basic Books.

Ekholm, Kasja and Jonathan Friedman 1980: "Toward a global anthropology." In L. Blusse, H. L. Wesseling and G. D. Winius (eds), *History and Under-development*, Leyden: Center for the History of European Expansion, Leyden University, 61–76.

—— 1982: "'Capital' imperialism and exploitation in ancient world-systems." *Review*, 6(1), 87–110.

Emmanuel, A. 1972: *Unequal Exchange: a study of the imperialism of trade*. New York: Monthly Review Press.

Engels, Frederick 1935 [1878]: *Socialism: utopian and scientific*. New York: International Publishers.

—— 1972 [1884]: *The Origin of the Family, Private Property and the State*. New York: International Publishers.

Evans, Peter 1979: *Dependent Development: the alliance of multinational, state and local capital in Brazil*. Princeton, NJ: Princeton University Press.

—— 1985: "Transnational linkages and the economic role of the state: an analysis of developing and industrialized nations in the post-World War II period." In Peter Evans, Dietrich Rueschemeyer, and Theda Skocpol (eds) *Bringing the State Back In*, Cambridge, Cambridge University Press, 192–226.

—— 1986: "State, capital and the transformation of dependence: the Brazilian computer case." *World Development*, 14(7), 791–808.

Evans, Peter and Michael Timberlake 1980: "Dependence, inequality and growth in less developed countries." *American Sociological Review*, 45, 531–52.

Evans, Peter, Dietrich Rueschemeyer, and Theda Skocpol (eds) 1985: *Bringing the State Back In*. Cambridge: Cambridge University Press.

Evans, Peter, Dietrich Rueschemeyer, and Evelyne Huber Stephens (eds) 1985: *States versus markets in the world-system*. Beverly Hills, Ca.: Sage.

Evans, Peter and John Stephens 1988: "Development and the world economy." In Neil J. Smelser (ed), *Handbook of Sociology*. Newbury Park, Ca.: Sage.

Falk, Richard 1982: "Contending approaches to world order." In Richard Falk, Samuel S. Kim, and Saul H. Mendlovitz (eds), *Toward a Just World Order*, Vol. 1., Boulder, Co.: Westview Press, 146–74.

Feagin, Joe R. 1985: "The global context of metropolitan growth: Houston and the oil industry." *American Journal of Sociology*, 90(6), 1204–29.

Fernand Braudel Center n.d.: "Spatio-temporal map of the world-economy." Unpublished manuscript, SUNY-Binghamton.

Ferris, Wayne H. 1973: *The Power Capability of Nation-States: international conflict and war*. Lexington, Mass.: D. C. Heath.

Fiala, Robert 1983: "Inequality and the service sector in less developed countries: a reanalysis." *American Sociological Review* 48:421–28.

Fieldhouse, D. K. 1966: *The Colonial Empires from the Eighteenth Century*. New York: Dell.

Finley, M. I. 1973: *The Ancient Economy*. Berkeley: University of California Press.

Firebaugh, Glenn 1985: "Core-periphery patterns in urbanization." In Michael Timberlake (ed) *Urbanization in World-Economy*, New York: Academic Press, 293–304.

Firebaugh, Glenn and Bradley P. Bullock 1986: "Level of processing of exports: new estimates for 73 less-developed countries in 1970 and 1980." *International Studies Quarterly* 30(3), 333–50.

Fischer, Fritz 1967: *Germany's Aims in the First World War*. New York: Norton.

Flannery, Kent V. 1982: "The golden marshalltown: a parable for the archeology of the 1980s." *American Anthropologist*, 84(2).

Flora, Peter 1983: *State, Economy and Society in Western Europe, 1815–1975*, Vol. 1, *The Growth of Mass Democracies and Welfare States*. Chicago: St James Press.

Ford, Alec George 1968: "Overseas lending and international fluctuations: 1879–1914." In A. R. Hall (ed.), *The Export of Capital from Britain 1870–1914*, London: Methuen, 84–102.

Forsythe, Dall W. 1977: *Taxation and Political Change in the Young Nation, 1781–1833*. New York: Columbia University Press.

Foster-Carter, Aidan 1978: "The modes of production controversy." *New Left Review*, 107, 47–78.

Fox, Richard G. 1985: *Lions of the Punjab: culture in the making*. Berkeley: University of California Press.

—— 1987: "Gandhian socialism and Hindu nationalism: cultural domination in the world-system." *Journal of Commonwealth and Comparative Politics*, 9, 233–47.

Fox-Genovese, Elizabeth and Eugene D. Genovese 1983: *Fruits of Merchant Capital: slavery and bourgeois property in the rise and expansion of capitalism*. New York: Oxford University Press.

Frank, Andre Gunder 1969: *Latin America: Underdevelopment or revolution?* New York: Monthly Review Press.

—— 1978: *World Accumulation, 1492–1789*. New York: Monthly Review Press.

—— 1979a: *Dependent Accumulation and Underdevelopment*. New York: Monthly Review Press.

—— 1979b: *Mexican Agriculture 1521–1630: transformation of the mode of production*. Cambridge: Cambridge University Press.

—— 1980: "Long live transideological enterprise!" In A. G. Frank, *Crisis: In the World Economy*. New York: Holmes and Meier, 178–262.

—— 1981: *Crisis: In the Third World*. New York: Holmes and Meier.

Frederick, Suzanne Y. 1987: "The instability of free trade." In George Modelski (ed.), *Exploring Long Cycles*. Boulder, Co.: Lynne Rienner, 186–217.

Friedmann, Harriet 1978: "World market, state and family farm: social bases of household production in an era of wage labor." *Comparative Studies in Society and History*, 20(4), 545–86.

Fröbel, Folker, Jürgen Heinrichs, and Otto Kreye 1980: *The New International Division of Labor*. Cambridge: Cambridge University Press.

Galtung, Johan 1971: "A structural theory of imperialism." *Journal of Peace Research*, 8(2), 81–117.

—— 1980: *The True Worlds: a transnational perspective*. New York: The Free Press.

—— 1981: "Western civilization: anatomy and pathology." *Alternatives*, 7, 145–69.

Galtung, Johan, Tore Heiestad and Erik Rudeng 1980: "On the decline and fall of empires: The Roman Empire and Western imperialism compared." *Review*, 4(1), 91–154.

Genovese, Eugene D. 1971: *The World the Slaveholders Made*. New York: Vintage.

—— 974: *Roll, Jordan Roll*. New York: Pantheon.

Gereffi, Gary 1983: *The Pharmaceutical Industry and Dependency in the Third World*. Princeton,: NJ Princeton University Press.

Gereffi, Gary and Peter Evans 1981: "Transnational corporations, dependent development and state policy in the semiperiphery: a comparison of Brazil and Mexico." *Latin American Research Review*, 16(3), 31–64.

Gershenkron, Alexander 1962: *Economic Backwardness in Historical Perspective*. Cambridge, Mass.: Harvard University Press.

Gibson, Bill 1980: "Unequal exchange: theoretical and empirical findings." *Review of Radical Political Economics*, 12(3), 15–35.

Giddens, Anthony 1979: *Central Problems in Social Theory: action, structure and contradiction in social analysis*. Berkeley: University of California Press.

Gill, Stephen and David Law 1986: *The Global Political Economy*. Brighton: Wheatsheaf.

Gilpin, Robert 1975: *U.S. Power and the Multinational Corporation*. New York: Basic Books.

—— 1981: *War and Change in World Politics*. Cambridge: Cambridge University Press.

Goldfrank, Walter 1977: "Who rules the world? class formation at the international level." *Quarterly Journal of Ideology*, 1(2), 32–7.

—— 1978: "Fascism and world-economy." In Barbara H. Kaplan (ed.), *Social Change in the Capitalist World Economy*. Beverly Hills, Ca.: Sage, 75–120.

—— 1979a: "Paradigm regained: The rules of Wallerstein's world-system method." A paper presented at conference on Methods of Historical Social Analysis, Cambridge, Mass., October 18–20.

—— 1981: "Silk and steel: Japan and Italy between the wars." In Richard Tomasson (ed.), *Comparative Social Research*, Vol. 4, Greenwich, Conn.: Jai Press.

—— 1983: "The limits of an analogy: Hegemonic decline in Great Britain and the United States." In Albert Bergesen (ed.), *Crises and the World-System*, Beverly Hills, Ca. Sage, 143–54.

Goldfrank, Walter (ed.) 1979b: *The World-System of Capitalism: past and present*. Beverly Hills, Ca.: Sage.

Goldstein, Joshua S. 1985: "Kondratieff waves and war cycles," *International Studies Quarterly* 29(4), 411–44.

—— 1988: *Long Cycles: prosperity and war in modern age*. New Haven, Conn.: Yale University Press.

Gordon, David M. 1980: "Stages of accumulation and long economic cycles." In Terence K. Hopkins and Immanuel Wallerstein (eds), *Processes of the World-System*, Beverly Hills, Ca.: Sage, 9–45.

Gramsci, Antonio 1971 (1935): *Selections from the Prison Notebooks*. New York: International Publishers.

Griffin, Keith B. 1969: *Underdevelopment in Spanish America*. London: Allen and Unwin.

Habermas, Jürgen 1970: *Toward a Rational Society*. Boston: Beacon.

Hale, Charles A. 1968: *Mexican Liberalism in the Age of Mora, 1821–1853*. New Haven, Conn.: Yale University Press.

Hall, Thomas D. 1986: "Incorporation in the world-system: toward a critique." *American Sociological Review*, 51(3), 390–402.

—— 1989: *Social Change in the Southwest, 1350–1880*. Lawrence, KS: University Press of Kansas.

Hamilton, Nora 1982: *The Limits of State Autonomy: post-revolutionary Mexico*. Princeton, NJ.: Princeton University Press.

Hannan, Michael T. 1971: "Problems of aggregation." In H. M. Blalock (ed.), *Causal Models in the Social Sciences*, Chicago: Aldine.

Hannan, Michael T. and Alice A. Young 1976: "On certain similarities in the estimation of multi-wave panels and multi-level cross sections." Technical Report

16, Consortium on Methodology for Aggregating Data in Educational Research, Vasquez Associates, Milwaukee.

—— 1977: "Estimation in panel models: results on pooling cross sections and time-series." In David R. Heise (ed.), *Sociological Methodology*, San Francisco: Jossey-Bass.

Hannan, Michael T. and Glenn R. Carroll 1981: "Dynamics of formal political structure: an event history analysis." *American Sociological Review*, 46, 19–35.

Harris, Marvin 1968: *The Rise of Anthropological Theory*. New York: Harper and Row.

Hart, Jeffrey A. 1980: "The policy of the U.S. toward the NIEO." Paper prepared for the fifth annual Hendricks Symposium, "U.S. International Economic Policy in an Age of Scarcities," University of Nebraska-Lincoln, April 10–11.

Hartman, John and Pamela B. Walters 1985: "Dependence, military assistance and development: a cross-national study." *Politics and Society* 14, 431–58.

Harvey, David 1982: *The Limits to Capital*. Chicago: University of Chicago Press.

Hawley, Amos 1981: *Urban Society: an ecological approach*, 2nd edition. New York: Wiley.

Hawley, James P. 1983: "Interests, state foreign economic policy, and the world-system: the case of the U.S. capital control programs, 1961–1974." In Pat McGowan and Charles W. Kegley (eds), *Foreign Policy and the Modern World-System*, Beverly Hills, Ca.: Sage, 223–54.

Hechter, Michael 1975: *Internal Colonialism: the Celtic fringe in British national development 1536–1966*. Berkeley: University of California Press.

Heintz, Peter with the collaboration of S. Heintz 1973: *The Future of Development*. Berne: Huber.

Henderson, W. D. 1965: *Britain and Industrial Europe: studies in British influence on the industrial revolution in Western Europe, 1750–1870*. London: Leicester University Press.

Henige, David P. 1970: *Colonial Governors from the 15th Century to the Present*. Madison: University of Wisconsin Press.

Herrera, Amilcar O., Hugo D. Scolnik, Graciela Chichilnisky, Gilberto C. Gallopin, Jorge E. Hardoy, Diana Mosrovich, Enrique Oteiza, Gilda L. de Romero Brest, Carlos E. Suarez, and Luis Talavera 1976: *Catastrophe or New Society?: a Latin American world model*. Ottawa: International Development Research.

Hibbs, Douglas A., Jr. 1974: "Problems of statistical estimation and causal inference in time-series regression models." In Herbert Costner (ed.), *Sociological Methodology 1973–74*, San Francisco: Jossey-Bass.

Hilferding, Rudolf 1981 [1923]: *Finance Capital: a study of the latest phase of capitalist development*. London: Routledge and Kegan Paul.

Hilton, Rodney (ed.) 1976: *The Transition from Feudalism to Capitalism*. London: New Left Books.

Hindess, Barry and Paul Q. Hirst 1975: *Pre-Capitalist Modes of Production*. London: Routledge and Kegan Paul.

Hinsley, F. H. 1967: *Power and the Pursuit of Peace*. London: Cambridge University Press.

Hirschman, Albert O. 1963: *The Strategy of Economic Development*. New Haven: Yale University Press.

—— 1980 [1945]: *National Power and the Structure of Foreign Trade*. Berkeley: University of California Press.

Hobsbawm, E. J. 1959: *Primitive Rebels*. New York: Norton.

—— 1968: *Industry and Empire*. Baltimore, Md.: Penguin.

Hopkins, Keith 1978a: "Economic growth and towns in classical antiquity." In Philip Abrams and E. A. Wrigley (eds), *Towns in Societies*, Cambridge: Cambridge University Press.

—— 1978b: *Conquerors and Slaves*. Cambridge: Cambridge University Press.

Hopkins, Terence K. 1978: "World-system analysis: methodological issues." In Barbara H. Kaplan (ed.), *Social Change in the Capitalist World Economy*, Beverly Hills, Ca.: Sage Publications, 199–218.

—— 1979: "The study of the capitalist world-economy: some introductory considerations." In Walter Goldfrank (ed.), *The World-System of Capitalism: Past and Present*, Beverly Hills, Ca.: Sage Publications, 21–52.

Hopkins, Terence K. and Immanuel Wallerstein 1967: "The comparative study of national societies." *Social Science Information*, 6(5) 25–8. Reprinted in Amatai Etzioni and Fredric L. Dubow (eds), *Comparative Perspectives: Theories and Methods*, Boston: Little, Brown, 1970, 183–204.

—— 1977: "Patterns of development in the modern world-system." *Review* 1(2), 111–46. Reprinted in T. K. Hopkins and I. Wallerstein (eds), *World-Systems Analysis: Theory and Methodology*, Beverly Hills, Ca.: Sage, 1982, 41–82.

—— 1979: "Cyclical rhythms and secular trends of the capitalist world-economy." *Review* 2(4), 483–500. Reprinted in T. K. Hopkins and I. Wallerstein (eds), *World-Systems Analysis: Theory and Methodology* Beverly Hills, Ca.: Sage, 1982, 104–20.

—— 1986: "Commodity chains in the world-economy prior to 1800." *Review* 10(1), 157–70.

Hopkins, Terence K. and Immanuel Wallerstein (eds) 1982: *World-Systems Analysis: Theory and Methodology*. Beverly Hills, Ca.: Sage.

Hyden, Goran 1980: *Beyond Ujamaa in Tanzania: underdevelopment and an uncaptured peasantry*. Berkeley: University of California Press.

Hymer, Stephen 1979: *The Multinational Corporation: a radical approach*. Cambridge: Cambridge University Press.

Inkeles, Alex 1975: "The emerging social structure of the world." *World Politics*, 27(4), 467–95.

Jacobs, Jane 1984: *Cities and the Wealth of Nations*. New York: Random House.

Jenkins, Rhys 1984: "Divisions over the international division of labor." *Capital and Class*, 22, 28–57.

Johnson, Dale L. (ed.) 1985: *Middle Classes in Dependent Countries*. Beverly Hills, Ca.: Sage.

Jones, Gareth Stedman (1971): *Outcaste London: a study in the relationship between classes in Victorian society*. Oxford: Clarendon Press.

Kahn, Joel S. 1980: *Minangkabau Social Formations: Indonesian peasants and the world-economy*. New York: Cambridge University Press.

Kaldor, Mary 1978: *The Disintegrating West*. New York: Hill and Wang.

Kay, Geoffrey 1975: *Development and Underdevelopment: a Marxist analysis*. London: St Martin's Press.

Kelly, Raymond C. 1985: *The Nuer Conquest: the structure and development of an expansionist system*. Ann Arbor: University of Michigan Press.

Kentor, Jeffrey 1981: "Structural determinants of peripheral urbanization: the effects of international dependence." *American Sociological Review*, 46, 201–11.

Keohane, Robert and Joseph S. Nye 1977: *Power and Interdependence.* Boston: Little, Brown.

Keyfitz, Nathan 1978: "Understanding world models." In Karl F. Schuessler (ed.), *Sociological Methodology 1978.* San Francisco: Jossey-Bass.

Kick, Edward L. 1980: "World-system properties and mass political conflict within nations: theoretical framework." *Journal of Political and Military Sociology*, 8, 175–90.

King, Anthony D. 1984: *The Bungalow: the production of a global culture.* London: Routledge and Kegan Paul.

Kohl, Philip 1987: "The use and abuse of world systems theory: the case of the 'pristine' West Asian state." In *Archeological Advances in Method and Theory*, 11, New York: Academic Press, 1–35.

Kondratieff, N. D. 1979 (1926): "The long waves in economic life." *Review* 2(4), 519–62.

Kowalewski, David 1987: "Peripheral revolutions in world-system perspective 1821–1985." A paper presented at the annual meeting of the International Studies Association, Washington, DC, April.

Krasner, Stephen D. 1976: "State power and the structure of international trade." *World Politics*, 28(3), 317–47.

—— 1978: *Defending the National Interest: raw materials investments and U.S. foreign policy.* Princeton, NJ: Princeton University Press.

—— 1985: *Structural Conflict: the Third World against global liberalism.* Berkeley: University of California Press.

Kravis, Irving B., Alan Heston, and Robert Summers 1982: *World Product and Income: international comparisons of real gross product.* Baltimore, Md: Johns Hopkins University Press.

Kriedte, Peter, Hans Medick, and Jürgen Schlumbohm 1981: *Industrialization Before Industrialization: rural industry in the genesis of capitalism.* Trans. Beate Schempp. Cambridge: Cambridge University Press.

Kugler, Jacek and A. F. K. Organski 1986: "The end of hegemony: says who?" Paper prepared for the annual meeting of the International Studies Association, Anaheim, Ca. March.

Kuhn, Thomas S. 1962: *The Structure of Scientific Revolutions.* Chicago: University of Chicago Press.

Kukreja, Sunil and James D. Miley 1988: "The relationship between world system position and the division of labor: a cross-national analysis." *Sociological Spectrum* 8:49–66.

Kuznets, Simon 1971: *Economic Growth of Nations: total output and production structure.* Cambridge: Harvard University Press.

LaClau, Ernesto 1977: *Politics and Ideology in Marxist Theory.* London: New Left Books.

Landes, David 1968: *The Unbound Prometheus.* Cambridge: Cambridge University Press.

Lane, Frederic C. 1966: "Units of economic growth historically considered." In *Venice and History: The Collected Papers of Frederic C. Lane*, Baltimore, Md.: Johns Hopkins University Press, 496–504.

—— 1973: *Venice: a maritime republic.* Baltimore, Md.: Johns Hopkins University Press.

—— 1979: *Profits from Power: readings in protection rent and violence-controlling enterprises*. Albany: State University of New York Press.

Lange, Peter 1985: "Semiperiphery and core in the European context: reflections on the postwar Italian experience." In G. Arrighi (ed.), *Semiperipheral Development*, Beverly Hills, Ca.: Sage, 179–214.

Läpple, Dieter 1985: "Internationalization of capital and the regional problem." In John Walton (ed.), *Capital and Labour in the Urbanized World*, London: Sage, 43–75.

Lattimore, Owen 1940: *Inner Asian Frontiers of China*. New York: American Geographical Society.

—— 1962: *Studies in Frontier History: collected papers 1928–1958*. London: Oxford University Press.

Lee, Su-Hoon 1988: *State-building in the Contemporary Third World*. Ph.D. dissertation, Boulder, CO: Westview Press.

Lenin, V. I. 1965 [1916]: *Imperialism: the highest stage of capitalism*. Peking: Foreign Languages Publishing House.

Lenski, Gerhard and Jean Lenski 1982: *Human Societies*. New York: McGraw-Hill. 4th edition.

Lenski, Gerhard and Patric Nolan 1984: "Trajectories of development: a test of ecological-evolutionary theory." *Social Forces*, 63(1), 1–23.

Levy, Jack S. 1983: *War in the Modern Great Power System, 1495–1975*. Lexington: University Press of Kentucky.

—— 1985: "Theories of general war." *World Politics*, 27(3), 344–74.

Lipset, Seymour M. 1977: "Why no socialism in the United States?" In S. Bialer and S. Sluzar (eds), *Sources of Contemporary Radicalism*, Boulder, Co.: Westview Press, 31–149.

—— 1981: "Industrial proleteriat in comparative perspective." In J. Triska and C. Gati (eds), *Blue Collar Workers in Eastern Europe*. London: Allen and Unwin, 1–28.

Lipson, Charles 1985: *Standing Guard: protecting foreign capital in the nineteenth and twentieth centuries*. Berkeley: University of California Press.

Lipton, Michael 1977: *Why Poor People Stay Poor: urban bias in world development*. Cambridge, Mass.: Harvard University Press.

London, Bruce and Bruce Williams 1988: "Multinational corporate penetration, protest and basic needs provision in non-core nations: a cross-national analysis." *Social Forces* 63(3), 16–32.

Lunday, James E. 1980: "State formation in the United States, 1837–1860: effects of world market position on political change and mobilization for war in the Northern states." Ph.D., Department of Sociology, Johns Hopkins University.

Luxemburg, Rosa 1968 (1913): *The Accumulation of Capital*. New York: Monthly Review Press.

McGowan, Pat 1980: "A political-economy of the world-system perspective on global modeling." Paper prepared for the conference on Large-Scale Global Modeling, Berlin Science Center, West Berlin, July 14–17.

—— 1985: "Pitfalls and promises in the quantitative study of the world-system: a reanalysis of Bergesen's 'long waves' of colonialism." *Review* 8(4), 477–500.

McKeown, Timothy J. 1983: "Hegemonic stability theory and 19th century tariff levels in Europe." *International Organization* 37, 1:73–91.

McNeill, William H. 1963: *The Rise of the West*. Chicago: University of Chicago Press.

—— 1964: *Europe's Steppe Frontier, 1500–1800*. Chicago: University of Chicago Press.

—— 1982: *The Pursuit of Power: technology, armed force and society since a.d. 1000*. Chicago: University of Chicago Press.

Maddison, Angus 1982: *Phases of Capitalist Development*. New York: Oxford University Press.

Malinowski, Bronislaw 1961 [1921]: *Argonauts of the Western Pacific*. New York: Dutton.

Mandel, Ernest 1970: *An Introduction to Marxist Economic Theory*. New York: Pathfinder Press.

—— 1975: *Late Capitalism*. London: New Left Books.

—— 1978: *The Second Slump*. London: New Left Books.

—— 1980: *Long Waves of Capitalist Development: the Marxist interpretation*. London: Cambridge University Press.

Mann, Michael 1986: *The Sources of Social Power: a history of power from the beginning to a.d. 1760*. Cambridge: Cambridge University Press.

Mao Zedong 1967 [1937]: "On contradiction." In *Selected Works*, Vol. 1, Peking: Foreign Languages Publishing House.

Marini, Ruy Mauro 1972: "Brazilian sub-imperialism." *Monthly Review*, 23(9), 14–24.

Marshall, T. H. 1965: *Class, Citizenship and Social Development*. New York: Anchor Books, Doubleday and Co.

Marx, Karl 1967a [1867]: *Capital*, Vol. I. New York: International Publishers.

—— 1967b [1894]: *Capital*, Vol. III. New York: International Publishers.

—— 1976 [1867]: *Capital*, Vol. I. Harmondsworth, Middlesex: Penguin.

—— 1973 [1857–58]: *Grundrisse: foundations of the critique of political economy*. New York: Random House.

—— 1978 [1852]: *The Eighteenth Brumaire of Louis Bonaparte*. Peking: Foreign Languages Press.

Mathien, Frances J. and Randall H. McGuire (eds) 1986: *Ripples in the Chichimec Sea: new considerations of southwestern-mesoamerican interactions*. Carbondale: Southern Illinois University Press.

Meillassoux, Claude 1981: *Maidens, Meal, and Money: capitalism and the domestic economy*. Cambridge: Cambridge University Press.

Mensch, Gerhard 1978: *Stalemate in Technology*. Cambridge, Mass., Ballinger.

Merton, Robert K. 1957: *Social Theory and Social Structure*. Glencoe, Ill.: The Free Press.

Meyer, David R. 1986: "The world system of cities: relations between international financial metropolises and South American cities." *Social Forces*, 64(3), 553–81.

Meyer, John W. 1987: "The world polity and the authority of the nation-state." In George M. Thomas, John W. Meyer, Francisco O. Ramirez, and John Boli, *Institutional Structure: constituting state, society, and the individual*, Beverly Hills, Ca.: Sage, 41–70.

Meyer, John W. and Michael T. Hannan (eds) 1979: *National Development and the World System: educational, economic and political change, 1950–1970*. Chicago: University of Chicago Press.

Meyer, John W., John Boli-Bennett, and Christopher Chase-Dunn 1975: "Convergence and divergence in development." *Annual Review of Sociology*, 5(1), 223–46.

Meyer, William 1987: "Testing theories of cultural imperialism: international media and domestic impact." *International Interactions*, 13(4), 353–74.

Michalet, Charles-Albert 1976: *Le Capitalisme Mondial*. Paris: Presses Universitaires de France.

Milkman, Ruth 1979: "Contradictions of semi-peripheral development: The South African case." In Walter L. Goldfrank (ed.), *The World-system of Capitalism: past and present*, Beverly Hills, Ca.: Sage, 261–84.

Mills, C. Wright 1959: *The Sociological Imagination*. New York: Grove Press.

Mintz, Sidney W. 1974: *Caribbean Transformations*. Baltimore, Md.: Johns Hopkins University Press.

—— 1977: "The so-called world system: local initiative and local response." *Dialectical Anthropology*, 2, 253–70.

—— 1978: "Was the plantation slave a proletarian?" *Review*, 2(1), 81–98.

—— 1985: *Sweetness and Power: the place of sugar in modern history*. New York: Viking.

Mitchell, Brian R. 1975: *European Historical Statistics 1750–1970*. New York: Columbia University Press.

—— 1982: *International Historical Statistics: Africa and Asia*. New York: New York University Press.

Modelski, George 1964: "Kautilya: foreign policy and international system in the ancient Hindu world." *American Political Science Review*, 58(3), 549–60.

—— 1978: "The long cycle of global politics and the nation-state." *Comparative Studies in Society and History*, 20(2), 214–35.

—— 1982: "Long cycles and the strategy of United States international economic policy." In William P. Avery and David P. Rapkin (eds), *America in a Changing World Political Economy*, New York: Longman, 97–118.

Modelski, George and Thompson, W. R. 1987: "Testing cobweb models of the long cycle of world leadership." In G. Modelski (ed.), *Exploring Long Cycles*, Boulder, Co.: Lynne Rienner.

—— 1988: *Sea Power in Global Politics, 1494–1943*. Seattle: University of Washington Press.

Molotch, Harvey 1984: "*Romantic Marxism: Love is (still) not enough*." A review of Manuel Castells, *The City and the Grassroots. Contemporary Sociology*, 13(2).

Moon, Bruce E. 1983: "The foreign policy of the dependent capitalist state." *International Studies Quarterly* 27, 3:315–40.

Moore, Barrington 1966: *The Social Origins of Dictatorship and Democracy*. Boston: Beacon Press.

Morganthau, Hans 1952: *Politics Among Nations*. New York: Alfred A. Knopf.

Morishima, Michio 1973: *Marx's Economics: a dual theory of value and growth*. Cambridge: Cambridge University Press.

Morrison, Donald G. et al. 1972: *Black Africa: a comparative handbook*. New York: Free Press.

Mouzelis, Nicos 1986: *Politics in the SemiPeriphery: early parliamentarism and late industrialization in the Balkans and Latin America*. New York: St Martin's Press.

Müller, Georg 1988: *Comparative World Data: a statistical handbook for social science*. Baltimore, Md.: Johns Hopkins University Press.

Murdock, George P. 1957: "World ethnographic sample." *American Anthropologist*, 59, 664–87.

Murphy, Craig 1984: *The Emergence of the NIEO Ideology*. Boulder, Co.: Westview Press.

Murray, Martin 1980: *The Development of Capitalism in Colonial Indochina (1870–1940)*,

Berkeley: University of California Press.
Myrdal, Gunnar 1957: *Economic Theory and Underdeveloped Regions*. New York: Harper and Row.
Naroll, Raoul 1968: "Some thoughts on comparative method in cultural anthropology." In Hubert M. Blalock, Jr and Ann B. Blalock (eds), *Methodology in Social Research*, New York: McGraw-Hill, 236–77.
Nemeth, Roger and David A. Smith 1985: "International trade and world-system structure: a multiple network analysis." *Review*, 8(3).
Neuman, Stephanie G. 1984: "International stratification and third world military industries." *International Organization* 38, 1:167–97.
Nolan, Patrick D. 1984: "Status in the world economy and national structure and development." In Gerhard Lenski (ed.), *Current Issues and Research in Macrosociology, International Studies in Sociology and Social Anthropology*, Vol. 37, Leiden: E. J. Brill, 109–20.
—— 1988: "World system status, techno-economic heritage, and fertility." *Sociological Focus* 21, 1:9–33.
Nolan, Patrick and Gerhard Lenski 1985: "Technoeconomic heritage, patterns of development, and the advantage of backwardness." *Social Forces*, 64(2), 341–58.
Nowak, Leszek 1971: "Problems of explanation in Marx's *Capital*." *Quality and Quantity*, 2, 311–37.
O'Brien, Patrick 1982: "European economic development: the contribution of the periphery." *The Economic History Review*, 35(1), 1–18.
O'Conner, James 1973: *The Fiscal Crisis of the State*. New York: St Martin's Press.
O'Donnell, Guillermo 1978: "Reflections on the patterns of change in the bureaucratic-authoritarian state." *Latin American Research Review*, 13, 3–38.
—— 1979: "Tensions in the bureaucratic-authoritarian state and the question of democracy." In David Collier (ed.), *The New Authoritarianism in Latin America*, Princeton, NJ: Princeton University Press, 285–318.
Ollman, B. 1976: *Alienation: Marx's Conception of Man in Capitalist Society*. 2nd edition. New York: Cambridge University Press.
Olson, Mancur 1982: *The Rise and Decline of Nations*. New Haven,: Yale University Press.
Organization for Economic Cooperation and Development (OECD) 1969–1974: *Geographical Distribution of Financial Flows to Developing Countries*. Paris: OECD.
—— 1982: *External Debt of Developing Countries*. Paris: OECD.
Organski, A. F. K. 1968: *World Politics*. New York: Alfred A. Knopf.
Organski, A. F. K. and Jacek Kugler 1980: *The War Ledger*. Chicago: University of Chicago Press.
Paige, Jeffery M. 1975: *Agrarian Revolution: social movements and export agriculture in the underdeveloped world*. New York: Macmillan.
Palloix, Christian 1979: "The self-expansion of capital on a world scale." *Review of Radical Political Economics*, 9, 1–28.
Palma, Gabriel 1978: "Dependency: a formal theory of underdevelopment or a methodology for the analysis of concrete situations of underdevelopment?" *World Development* 6, 7/8, 881–924.
Parry, J. H. 1966: *The Establishment of European Hegemony 1415–1715*. New York: Harper and Row.

Parsons, Talcott 1961: "Order and community in the international system." In James N. Rosenau (ed.), *International Politics and Foreign Policy*. New York: Free Press, 120–9.

—— 1966: *Societies: Evolutionary and Comparative Perspective*. Englewood Cliffs, NJ: Prentice-Hall.

—— 1971: *The System of Modern Societies*. Englewood Cliffs, NJ: Prentice-Hall.

Petras, James, with A. E. Havens, M. H. Morley, and P. DeWitt 1981: *Class, State and Power in the Third World*. Montclair, NJ: Allanheld, Osmun.

Pfister, Ulrich 1984: "Debt and development: a cross-sectional study of the relationships between external debt and economic growth in developing countries." Sociological Institute, University of Zürich.

Pfister, Ulrich and Christian Suter 1987: "International financial relations as part of the world system." *International Studies Quarterly*, 31(3), 239–72.

Phelps-Brown, E. H. and S. J. Handfield-Jones 1952: "The climacteric of the 1890s." Oxford Economic Papers, New Series, 4(3).

Phelps-Brown, E. H. and S. V. Hopkins 1955: "Seven centuries of building wages." *Economica*, August, 195–206.

Polanyi, Karl 1944: *The Great Transformation*. Boston: Beacon.

—— 1957: "The economy as instituted process." In Karl Polanyi, Conrade M. Arensberg, and Harry W. Pearson (eds), *Trade and Market in the Early Empires*, Chicago: Regnery, 243–69.

—— 1977: *The Livelihood of Man*. Ed. Harry W. Pearson. New York: Academic Press.

Polanyi, Karl, Conrad M. Arensberg, and Harry W. Pearson (eds) 1957: *Trade and Market in the Early Empires*. Chicago: Regnery.

Popper, Karl 1972: *The Poverty of Historicism*. London: Routledge and Kegan Paul.

Portes, Alejandro 1981: "The informal sector: definition, controversy, and relation to national development." *Review*, 7(1), 151–74.

Portes, Alejandro and Robert Bach 1985: *Latin Journey: Cuban and Mexican Immigrants in the United States*. Berkeley: University of California Press.

Portes, Alejandro and A. Douglas Kincaid 1985: "The crisis of authoritarianism: state and civil society in Argentina, Chile and Uruguay." *Research in Political Sociology*, 1, 49–77.

Portes, Alejandro and John Walton 1981: *Labor, Class, and the International System*. New York: Academic Press.

Poulantzas, Nicos 1973: *Political Power and Social Classes*. London: New Left Books.

—— 1975: *Classes in Contemporary Capitalism*. London: New Left Books.

Prebisch, Raul 1949: *The Economic Development of Latin America and its Principal Problems*. CEPAL (E/CN. 12/89/Rev. 1). Reprinted in *Economic Bulletin for Latin America*, 7 (1), 1962.

Ragin, Charles C. and David Zaret 1983: "Theory and method in comparative research: two strategies." *Social Forces*, 61(3), 731–54.

Ragin, Charles and York Bradshaw 1986: "International economic dependence and human misery, 1938–1980: a global perspective." Presented at the annual meeting of the International Studies Association, Anaheim, Ca.

Ramirez, Francisco O. and Richard Rubinson 1979: "Creating members: the political incorporation and expansion of public education." In John W. Meyer and Michael T. Hannan (eds), *National Development and the World System: Educational, Economic and Political Change, 1950–1970*, Chicago: University of Chicago Press, 72–84.

Ray, James Lee and J. David Singer 1973: "Measuring the concentration of power in the international system." *Sociological Methods and Research*, 1(4), 403–37.

Renfrew, Colin 1984: "Systems collapse as social transformation." In C. Renfrew, *Approaches to Social Archeology*. Cambridge, Mass.: Harvard University Press, 366–89.

Rescher, Nicholas 1977: *Dialectics: a controversy-oriented approach to the theory of knowledge*. Albany, NY: SUNY Press.

Riley, James C. 1980: *International Government Finance and the Amsterdam Capital Market 1740–1815*. Cambridge: Cambridge University Press.

Robertson, Roland and Frank Lechner 1985: "Modernization, globalization and the problem of culture in world-systems theory." *Theory, Culture and Society*, 2(3), 103–17.

Robinson, R. and J. Gallagher 1953: "The imperialism of free trade." *Economic History Review*, 6(1), 1–14.

Rodney, Walter 1981: *A History of the Guyanese Working People, 1881–1905*. Baltimore,: Md. Johns Hopkins University Press.

Rose, Stephen J. 1986: *The American Profile Poster*. New York: Pantheon.

Ross, Robert J. S. and Kent Trachte 1983: "Global cities and global classes: the peripheralization of labor in New York City." *Review* 6(3), 393–431.

—— Forthcoming: *Global Capitalism: The New Leviathan*. Albany: State University of New York Press.

Rostow, W. W. 1978: *The World Economy: history and prospect*. Austin: University of Texas Press.

Rowlands, Michael, Mogens Larsen, and Kristian Kristiansen (eds) 1987: *Centre and Periphery in the Ancient World*. Cambridge: Cambridge University Press.

Rubinson, Richard 1976: "The world-economy and the distribution of income within states: a cross-national study." *American Sociological Review*, 41, 638–59.

—— 1977a: "Reply to Bach and Irwin." *American Sociological Review*, 42(5), 817–21.

—— 1977b: "Dependence, government revenue, economic growth, 1955–1970." *Studies in Comparative International Development*, 12, 3–28.

—— 1978: "Political transformation in Germany and the United States." In Barbara H. Kaplan (ed.), *Social Change in the Capitalist World Economy*, Beverly Hills, Ca.: Sage, 39–74.

Rubinson, Richard and Deborah Holtzman 1981: "Comparative dependence and economic development." *International Journal of Comparative Sociology*, 22(1–2), 86–101.

Rueschemeyer, Dietrich and Peter B. Evans 1985: "The state and economic transformation: toward an analysis of the conditions underlying effective intervention." In Peter B. Evans, Dietrich Rueschemeyer, and Theda Skocpol (eds), *Bringing the State Back In*. Cambridge: Cambridge University Press, 44–77.

Rupert, Mark E. and David P. Rapkin 1985: "The erosion of U.S. leadership capabilities." In Paul M. Johnson and William R. Thompson (eds), *Rhythms in Politics and Economics*, New York: Praeger, 155–80.

Sahlins, Marshall 1972: *Stone Age Economics*. New York: Aldine.

Sapir, Edward 1949: *Selected Writings in Language, Culture and Personality*, Ed. David Mandelbaum Berkeley: University of California Press.

Sassen-Koob, Saskia 1985: "Capital mobility and labor migration: their expression in core cities." In Michael Timberlake (ed.), *Urbanization in the World-Economy*, New York: Academic Press, 231–68.

Schiller, Herbert I. 1969: *Mass Communications and the American Empire*. New York: A. M. Kelley.

Schlote, Werner 1952 [1938]: *British Overseas Trade from 1700 to the 1930s*. Trans. W. O. Henderson and W. H. Chaloner. Oxford: Basil Blackwell.

Schneider, Jane 1977: "Was there a pre-capitalist world-system?" *Peasant Studies*, 6(1), 20–9.

Schumpeter, Joseph 1939: *Business Cycles*. Vol. 1. New York: McGraw-Hill.

—— 1955 [1919]: "The sociology of imperialism." In *Imperialism and Social Classes*. New York: Meridian Books.

Seers, Dudley 1983: *The Political Economy of Nationalism*. New York: Oxford University Press.

Sell, Ralph R. and Stephen J. Kunitz 1986–7: "The debt crisis and the end of an era in mortality decline." *Studies in Comparative International Development*, 21(4), 3–30.

Semyonov, Moshe and Noah Lewin-Epstein 1986: "Economic development, investment dependence, and the rise of services in less developed nations." *Social Forces*, 64(3), 582–98.

Senghaas, Dieter 1985: *The European Experience: a historical critique of development theory*. Dover, NH: Berg Publishers.

Shils, Edward A. and Morris Janowitz 1948: "Cohesion and disintegration in the Wehrmacht in World War II." *Public Opinion Quarterly*, 12, 280–315.

Singer, J. David 1979: *The Correlates of War: I: Research Origins and Rationale*. New York: Free Press.

Singer, J. David, Stuart Bremer, and John Stuckey 1979: "Capability distribution, uncertainty and major power war, 1820–1965." In J. David Singer (ed.), *The Correlates of War: Research Origins and Rationale*. New York: Free Press, 265–98.

Singer, J. David and Melvin Small 1966: "The composition and status ordering of the international system: 1815–1940." *World Politics*, 28, 236–82.

Sklar, Holly (ed.) 1980: *Trilateralism: The Trilateral Commission and Elite Planning for World Management*. Boston: South End Press.

Skocpol, Theda 1977: "Wallerstein's world capitalist system: a theoretical and historical critique." *American Journal of Sociology*, 82(5), 1075–90.

—— 1979: *States and Social Revolutions*. Cambridge: Cambridge University Press.

—— 1985: "Bringing the state back in: strategies of analysis in current research." In Peter Evans et al. (eds), *Bringing the State Back In*. Cambridge: Cambridge University Press, 3–43.

Small, Melvin and J. David Singer 1973: "The diplomatic importance of states, 1816–1970: an extension and refinement of the indicator." *World Politics*, 25, 577–99.

Smelser, Neil 1959: "A comparative view of exchange systems." *Economic Development and Cultural Change*, 7, 173–82.

Smith, David A. and Douglas R. White 1986: "A dynamic analysis of international trade and world-system structure: 1965–1980." A paper presented at the annual meeting of The International Studies Association, Anaheim, Ca. March.

Smith, Joan, Immanuel Wallerstein, and Hans-Dieter Evers 1984: *Households and the*

World-Economy. Beverly Hills, Ca.: Sage.

Smith, Neil 1984: *Uneven Development: nature, capital and the production of space*. Oxford: Basil Blackwell.

Snyder, David and Edward L. Kick 1979: "Structural position in the world-system and economic growth, 1955–1970: a multiple network analysis of transnational interactions." *American Journal of Sociology*, 84(5), 1096–126.

So, Alvin Y. 1986: *The South China Silk District: local historical transformation and world-system theory*, Albany: State University of New York Press.

Sokolovsky, Joan 1983: "China and the struggle to withdraw from the world system." In C. Chase-Dunn (ed.), *Socialist States in the World-system*, Beverly Hills, Ca: Sage, 157–80.

—— 1985: "Logic, space and time: the boundaries of the capitalist world-economy." In Michael Timberlake (ed.), *Urbanization in the World-economy*, New York: Academic Press, 41–52.

Stepan, Alfred 1978: *The State and Society: Peru in comparative perspective*. Princeton, NJ: Princeton University Press.

Stephens, John 1980: *The Transition from Capitalism to Socialism*. Atlantic Highlands, NJ: Humanities Press.

—— 1987: "Democratic transition and breakdown in Europe, 1870–1939: a test of the Moore thesis." Working Paper 101, Kellog Institute, University of Notre Dame.

Stevenson, Robert L. and Donald L. Shaw 1984: *Foreign News and the New World Information Order*. Ames: University of Iowa Press.

Stinchcombe, Arthur L. 1968: *Constructing Social Theories*. New York: Harcourt, Brace and World.

—— 1978: *Theoretical Methods in Social History*. New York: Academic Press.

—— 1983: *Economic Sociology*. New York: Academic Press.

Strange, Susan 1986: *Casino Capitalism*. Oxford and New York: Basil Blackwell.

Strange, Susan and Robert Tooze (eds) 1981: *The International Politics of Surplus Capacity: competition for market shares in the world recession*. London: George Allen and Unwin.

Sunkel, Osvaldo 1973: "Transnational capitalism and national disintegration in Latin America." *Social and Economic Studies*, 22(1), 132–76.

Suter, Christian 1987: "Long waves in core-periphery relationships within the international financial system: debt-default cycles of sovereign borrowers." *Review*, 10(3).

Suter, Christian and Ulrich Pfister 1989: "Global debt waves and the role of political regimes," in W. P. Avery and D. P. Rapkin (eds), *Markets, Politics and Change in the Global Political Economy*. International Political Economy Yearbook, Vol. IV. Boulder, CO: Lynne Reinner.

Sweezy, Paul 1976 [1950]: "A critique." In Rodney Hilton (ed.), *The Transition from Feudalism to Capitalism*, London: New Left Books, 35–56.

Sylvan, David, Duncan Snidal, Bruce M. Russett, Steven Jackson, and Raymond Duvall 1983: "The peripheral economies: penetration and economic distortion, 1970–1975." In William R. Thompson (ed.), *Contending Approaches to World System Analysis*, Beverly Hills, Ca.: Sage, 79–114.

Szymanski, Albert 1971: *The Dependence of South America on the United States*. Ph.D. Dissertation, Department of Sociology, Columbia University.

—— 1973: "Military spending and economic stagnation." *American Journal of Sociology*, 79(1).

—— 1975: "Dependence, exploitation and development." *Journal of Military and Political Sociology*, 1, 15–29.

—— 1981: *The Logic of Imperialism*. New York: Praeger.

—— 1983a: *Class Structure: a critical perspective*. New York: Praeger.

—— 1983b: "The socialist world system." In C. Chase-Dunn (ed.), *Socialist States in the World-system*, Beverly Hills, Ca.: Sage, 57–84.

Taagepera, Rein 1978: "Size and duration of empires: systematics of size." *Social Science Research*, 7, 108–27.

Tardanico, Richard 1978: "A structural perspective on state power in the capitalist world-system." A paper prepared for the annual meeting of the American Sociological Association, San Francisco.

—— 1982: "Revolutionary state-making in the periphery: Mexico, 1924–1928." *Comparative Studies in Society and History*, 23(2).

Taylor, Charles L. and M. C. Hudson 1972: *World Handbook of Political and Social Indicators*. New Haven, Conn.: Yale University Press.

Taylor, John G. 1979: *From Modernization to Modes of Production: a critique of the sociologies of development and underdevelopment*. London: Macmillan.

Teune, Henry 1979: "Cross-level analysis: a case of social inference." *Quality and Quantity*, 13, 527–37.

Thomas, Brinley 1954: *Migration and Economic Growth: A Study of Great Britain and the Atlantic Economy*. Cambridge: Cambridge University Press.

Thomas, Clive Y. 1984: *The Rise of the Authoritarian State in Peripheral Societies*. New York: Monthly Review Press.

Thomas, George M., Francisco O. Ramirez, John W. Meyer, and Jeanne Gobalet 1979: "Maintaining national boundaries in the world system: the rise of centralist regimes." In John W. Meyer and Michael T. Hannan, *National Development and the World System*, Chicago: University of Chicago Press, 187–206.

Thomas, George M., John W. Meyer, Francisco O. Ramirez, and John Boli 1987: *Institutional Structure: Constituting State, Society, and the Individual*. Beverly Hills, Ca.: Sage.

Thompson, E. P. 1978: *The Poverty of Theory and Other Essays*. New York: Monthly Review.

Thompson, William R. 1983a: "Succession crises in the global political system: a test of the transition model." In Albert Bergesen (ed.), *Crises in the World-System*, Beverly Hills, Ca.: Sage, 93–116.

—— 1983b: "Cycles, capabilities and war: an ecumenical view." In W. R. Thompson (ed.), *Contending Approaches to World-System Analysis*, Beverly Hills, Ca.: Sage, 141–63.

—— 1983c: "Uneven growth, systemic challenges, and global wars." *International Studies Quarterly*, 27(3), 341–55.

—— 1986: "Leading sectors, systemic leadership and global war." Paper presented at the annual meeting of the American Political Science Association, Washington, DC, August 28. Forthcoming in W. R. Thompson, *On Global War: Historical Structural Approaches to World Politics*. Columbia: University of South Carolina Press.

Thompson, William R. (ed.) 1983: *Contending Approaches to World-System Analysis*.

Beverly Hills, Ca.: Sage.

Thompson, William R. and Karen A. Rasler 1988: "War and systemic capability reconcentration." *Journal of Conflict Resolution*, 32.

Thompson, W. R. and L. G. Zuk 1982: "War, inflation and the Kondratieff long wave." *Journal of Conflict Resolution*, 26(4), 621–44.

Tilly, Charles 1984: *Big Structures, Large Processes, Huge Comparisons*. New York: Russell Sage.

—— 1985: "War making and state making as organized crime." In Peter Evans, Dietrich Rueschemeyer and Skocpol (eds), *Bringing the State Back In*, Cambridge: Cambridge University Press, 169–91.

Timberlake, Michael (ed.) 1985: *Urbanization in the World-Economy*. New York: Academic Press.

Timberlake, Michael and Kirk R. Williams 1984: "Dependence, political exclusion, and government repression: some cross-national evidence." *American Sociological Review*, 49, 141–6.

Timberlake, Michael and James Lunday 1985: "Labor force structure in the zones of the world-economy, 1950–1970." In Michael Timberlake (ed.), *Urbanization in the World-Economy*, New York, Academic Press 325–50.

Toynbee, Arnold 1967: "Anarchy by treaty, 1648–1967." In Fred L. Israel (ed.), *Major Peace Treaties of Modern History*, New York: McGraw-Hill, xiii–xxix.

Trimberger, Ellen Kay 1978: *Revolution from Above: military bureaucrats and development in Japan, Turkey, Egypt and Peru*. New Brunswick, NJ: Transaction Books.

Trotsky, Leon 1932: *The History of the Russian Revolution*. Vol. 1. New York: Simon and Schuster.

Trouillot, Michel-Rolph 1988: *Peasants and Capital: Domenica in the World Economy*. Baltimore, Md.: Johns Hopkins University Press.

Tuma, Nancy B. and Michael T. Hannan 1984: *Social Dynamics: Models and Methods*. New York: Academic Press.

Van Duijn, J. J. 1983: *The Long Wave in Economic Life*. London: Allen and Unwin.

Vanneman, Reeve 1979: "Strategies for the Southasian semi-periphery: cashews and crankshafts." Presented at the annual meeting of the Association for Asian Studies, Los Angeles.

Väyrynen, Raimo, 1988: "Economic fluctuations, military expenditures and warfare in international relations." A paper presented at the 12th Annual Conference on the Political Economy of the World-System, Emory University, Atlanta, March 24.

Verdery, Katherine 1983: *Transylvanian Villagers: three centuries of economic, political and ethnic change*. Berkeley: University of California Press.

Vernon, Raymond 1966: "International investment and international trade in the product cycle." *Quarterly Journal of Economics*, 80, 190–207.

—— 1971: *Sovereignty at Bay*. New York: Basic Books.

Vilar, Pierre 1976: *A History of Gold and Money*. Trans. Judith White. Atlantic Highlands, NJ: Humanities Press.

von Braunmühl, C. 1978: "On the analysis of the bourgeois nation state within the world market context." In J. Holloway and S. Piccioto (eds), *State and Capital: A Marxist Debate*, Austin: University of Texas Press, 160–77.

von Ranke, Leopold 1887 [1824]: *Histories of the Latin and Teuton Nations: 1495–1514*. Trans. Philip Ashworth. London: George Bell and Sons.

von Werlhof, Claudia 1984: "The proletariat is dead; long live the house-wife?" In Joan Smith et al., *Households and the World-Economy*, Beverly Hills, Ca.: Sage, 131–50.

Walker, Richard Louis 1953: *The Multi-state System of Ancient China*. Hamden, Conn.: Shoe String Press.

Wallerstein, Immanuel 1974: *The Modern World-system I: capitalist agriculture and the origins of the European world-economy in the sixteenth century*. New York: Academic Press.

—— 1979a: *The Capitalist World-Economy*. Cambridge: Cambridge University Press.

—— 1979b: "Kondratieff up or Kondratieff down?" *Review*, 2(4), 663–74.

—— 1979c: "The Ottoman empire and the capitalist world-economy: some questions for research." *Review*, 2(3), 389–400.

—— 1980a: *The Modern World-System II: mercantilism and the consolidation of the European world-economy, 1600–1750*. New York: Academic Press.

—— 1980b: "'The withering away of the states.'" *International Journal of the Sociology of Law*, 8, 369–78.

—— 1983a: *Historical Capitalism*. London: Verso.

—— 1983b: "A comment on O'Brien." *Economic History Review*, 36(4), 580–3.

—— 1984a: "The three instances of hegemony in the history of the capitalist world-economy." In Gerhard Lenski (ed.), *Current Issues and Research in Macrosociology, International Studies in Sociology and Social Anthropology*, vol. 37, Leiden: E. J. Brill, 100–8.

—— 1984b: *The Politics of the World-Economy: the states, the movements and the civilizations*. Cambridge: Cambridge University Press.

—— 1986: "The incorporation of the Indian subcontinent into the capitalist world-economy." *Economic and Political Weekly*, 21(4), 28–39.

Walton, John 1981: "The internationalization of capital and class structures in the advanced countries: The United States case." In Alejandro Portes and John Walton, *Labor, Class and the International System*, New York: Academic Press, chapter 5.

—— 1985: "The third 'new' international division of labor." In J. Walton (ed.), *Capital and Labor in the Urbanized World*, London: Sage, 3–16.

Waltz, Kenneth N. 1979: *Theory of International Politics*. Reading, Mass.: Addison-Wesley.

Ward, Kathryn B. 1984: *Women in the World-System: its impact on status and fertility*. New York: Praeger.

Ward, Michael Don and Harold Guetzkow 1979: "Toward integrated global models: from economic engineering to social science modeling." *Journal of Policy Model*, 1(3), 445–64.

Warman, Arturo 1980: *We Come to Object: the peasants of Morelos and the national state*. Baltimore, Md.: Johns Hopkins University Press.

Warren, Bill 1980: *Imperialism: Pioneer of Capitalism*. London: New Left Books.

Weber, Max 1978 [1922]: *Economy and Society*. 2 vols. Eds Guenther Roth and Claus Wittich Berkeley: University of California Press.

—— 1981 [1927]: *General Economic History*. New Brunswick, NJ: Transaction.

Weber, Robert Philip 1981: "Society and economy in the Western world system." *Social Forces* 59, 4:1130–48.

—— 1987: "Cycles of the third kind." *European Journal of Political Research* 15:145–53.

White, Douglas R. and Michael L. Burton 1987: "World-systems and ethnological theory." Research proposal funded by the National Science Foundation.

Whorf, Benjamin Lee 1956: *Language, Thought and Reality*. New York: John Wiley.

Wilkinson, David 1987: "Central civilization." *Comparative Civilizations Review*, 17, 31–59.

Williams, Kristen M. 1985: "Is 'unequal exchange' a mechanism for perpetuating inequality in the modern world system?" *Studies in Comparative International Development*, 20(3), 47–73.

Willoughby, John 1986: *Capitalist Imperialism, Crisis and the State*. London: Harwood Academic Press.

Wilson, C. H. 1957: *Profit and Power: A Study of England and the Dutch Wars*. London: Longman.

Winckler, E. A. 1979: "China's world-system: social theory and political practice in the 1970's." In W. A. Goldfrank (ed.), *The World-System of Capitalism: past and present*, Beverly Hills, Ca.: Sage, 53–72.

Wittfogel, Karl 1957: *Oriental Despotism: A Comparative Study of Total Power*. New Haven, Conn.: Yale University Press.

Wolf, Eric 1982: *Europe and the People Without History*. Berkeley: University of California Press.

Wolfe, Alan 1980: "Capitalism shows its face: giving up on democracy." In Holly Sklar (ed.), *Trilateralism: the trilateral commission and elite planning for world management*, Boston: South End Press, 295–307.

Wolpe, Harold (ed.) 1980: *The Articulation of Modes of Production: essays from economy and society*. London: Routledge and Kegan Paul.

Wood, Robert E. 1980: "Foreign aid and the capitalist state in underdeveloped countries." *Politics and Society*, 10(1), 1–34.

—— 1986: *From Marshall Plan to Debt Crisis: foreign aid and development choices in the world economy*. Berkeley: University of California Press.

Woodruff, William 1967: *Impact of Western Man: a study of Europe's role in the world economy 1750–1960*. New York: St Martin's Press.

World Bank (IBRD) 1983: *World Tables, 3rd edition*. Vol. 1, Economic Data, vol. 2, Social Data.

Wright, Erik O. 1976: "Class boundaries in advanced capitalist societies." *New Left Review*, 98, 3–41.

—— 1978: *Class, Crisis and the State*. London: New Left Books.

—— 1985: *Classes*. London: Verso.

Wright, Erik O. and Bill Martin 1987: "The transformation of the American class structure, 1960–1980." *American Journal of Sociology*, 93(1), 1–29.

Wuthnow, Robert 1980: "The world-economy and the institutionalization of science in seventeenth-century Europe," and "World order and religious movements." In Albert Bergesen (ed.), *Studies of the Modern World-System*, New York: Academic Press, 25–76.

Zaretsky, Eli 1976: *Capitalism, the Family and Personal Life*. New York: Harper and Row.

Zeitlin, Maurice 1984: *The Civil Wars in Chile (or the bourgeois revolutions that never were)*. Princeton: Princeton, NJ: University Press.

Zelditch, Morris, Jr. 1969: "Can you study an army in the laboratory?" In A. Etzioni

(ed.), 2nd edition. *Complex Organizations: a sociological reader*, 528–39.
—— 1971: "Intelligible Comparisons." In Ivan Vallier (ed.), *Comparative Methods in Sociology*, Berkeley: University of California Press, 267–308.
Zinn, Howard 1980: *A People's History of the United States*. New York: Harper and Row.
Zolberg, A. R. 1981: "Origins of the modern world system: a missing link." *World Politics*, 23(2), 253–81.

Index